T0202926

Lecture Notes of the Institute for Computer Sciences, Social Informatics and Telecommunications Engineering 438

More information about this series at https://link.springer.com/bookseries/8197

Xiaolin Jiang (Ed.)

Machine Learning and Intelligent Communications

6th EAI International Conference, MLICOM 2021
Virtual Event, November 2021
Proceedings

 Springer

Editor
Xiaolin Jiang
Jinhua Advanced Research Institute
Jinhua, China

ISSN 1867-8211   ISSN 1867-822X (electronic)
Lecture Notes of the Institute for Computer Sciences, Social Informatics
and Telecommunications Engineering
ISBN 978-3-031-04408-3   ISBN 978-3-031-04409-0 (eBook)
https://doi.org/10.1007/978-3-031-04409-0

This Springer imprint is published by the registered company Springer Nature Switzerland AG
The registered company address is: Gewerbestrasse 11, 6330 Cham, Switzerland

Preface

We are delighted to introduce the proceedings of the sixth edition of the European Alliance for Innovation (EAI) International Conference on Machine Learning and Intelligent Communications (MLICOM 2021). This conference brought together researchers, developers, and practitioners around the world who are leveraging and developing machine learning and intelligent communications.

The technical program of MLICOM 2021 consisted of 28 full papers in oral presentation sessions in the main conference tracks. The conference tracks were as follows: Track 1 - Internet of Vehicles Communication Systems; Track 2 - Applications of Neural Networks and Deep Learning; Track 3 - Intelligent Massive MIMO Communications; Track 4 - Intelligent Positioning and Navigation Systems; Track 5 - Intelligent Space and Terrestrial Integrated Networks; Track 6 - Machine Learning Algorithms and Intelligent Networks; and Track 7 - Image Information Processing.

Coordination with the steering chairs, Imrich Chlamtac, Xin Liu, and Xin-Lin Huang was essential for the success of the conference. We sincerely appreciate their constant support and guidance. It was also a great pleasure to work with such an excellent organizing committee team who worked hard in organizing and supporting the conference. We are grateful to the Technical Program Committee, who completed the peer-review process for the technical papers and helped to put together a high-quality technical program. We are also grateful to the conference managers, Karolina Marcinova and Rupali Tiwari, for their support and to all the authors who submitted their papers to the MLICOM 2021 conference and workshops.

We strongly believe that the MLICOM conference provides a good forum for all researchers, developers, and practitioners to discuss all science and technology aspects that are relevant to machine learning and intelligent communications. We also expect that future MLICOM conferences will be as successful and stimulating as this year's, as indicated by the contributions presented in this volume.

Xiaolin Jiang
Guo Tieliang
Zhao Fujun
Ren Mingyuan

Organization

Steering Committee

Imrich Chlamtac   University of Trento, Italy
Xin Liu   Dalian University of Technology, China
Xin-Lin Huang   Tongji University, China

Organizing Committee

General Chair

Xiaolin Jiang   Jinhua Advanced Research Institute, China

General Co-chairs

Zhang Wenxiang   Wuzhou University, China
Zhao Jinxian   Heilongjiang University of Science and Technology, China

Technical Program Committee Chairs

Guo Tieliang   Wuzhou University, China
Zhao Fujun   Heilongjiang University of Science and Technology, China
Ren Mingyuan   Jinhua Advanced Research Institute, China

Sponsorship and Exhibit Chairs

Li Zhijun   Wuzhou University, China
Wang Jin   Wuzhou University, China

Local Chairs

Han Tian   Jinhua Advanced Research Institute, China
Dong Changchun   Jinhua Advanced Research Institute, China
Qingjiang Yang   Heilongjiang University of Science and Technology, China

Workshops Chairs

Mo Zhiyi	Wuzhou University, China
Guo Hui	Wuzhou University, China
Li Zhijun	Wuzhou University, China
Wang Jin	Wuzhou University, China
Zhao Fujun	Heilongjiang University of Science and Technology, China
Han Tian	Jinhua Advanced Research Institute, China
Yu Guanghua	Heihe University, China

Publicity and Social Media Chairs

Han Tian	Jinhua Advanced Research Institute, China
Dong Changchun	Jinhua Advanced Research Institute, China
Qingjiang Yang	Heilongjiang University of Science and Technology, China

Publications Chairs

Bao Peng	Shenzhen Institute of Information Technology, China
Chunying Fang	Heilongjiang University of Science and Technology, China
Gong Ping	Wuzhou University, China

Web Chairs

Dong Changchun	Jinhua Advanced Research Institute, China
Liu Fugang	Heilongjiang University of Science and Technology, China

Posters and PhD Track Chairs

Mo Zhiyi	Wuzhou University, China
Guo Hui	Wuzhou University, China
Yu Guanghua	Heihe University, China

Technical Program Committee

Fugang Liu	Jinhua Advanced Research Institute, China
Changchun Dong	Jinhua Advanced Research Institute, China
Huanyu Zhou	Wuzhou University, China
Mingyuan Ren	Jinhua Advanced Research Institute, China
Xiaolin Jiang	Jinhua Advanced Research Institute, China
Tian Han	Jinhua Advanced Research Institute, China
Yang Feng	Jinhua Advanced Research Institute, China
Yixue Yao	Jinhua Advanced Research Institute, China

Contents

Deep Learning Network for Frequency Offset Cancellation in OFDM Communication System

Qingyang Guan and Shuang Wu[✉]

College of Engineering, Xi'an International University, Xi'an 710077, China
wooshuang@126.com

Abstract. A deep learning network for OFDM system is proposed to eliminate the CFO (carrier frequency offset) interference in OFDM system. The CFO greatly reduces the BER performance for the communication system. The frequency offset interference introduced needs to be eliminated before signal demodulation. Therefore, we propose the method to eliminate weights by establishing a deep learning network, and then form the optimization elimination weight matrix through iteration. Among them, the hidden layer and weights are trained and fine-tuned in the forward direction to cancel the interference introduced by CFO. Compared with MMSE and LS algorithm, the proposed deep learning network greatly improves the bit error rate performance. The simulation has proved that the proposed deep learning network algorithm has BER performance in OFDM systems.

Keywords: Deep learning network · Carrier frequency offset · BER

1 Introduction

For multi-user detection of OFDM links communication systems, signal interference is not only due to the frequency selective fading of the multipath channel, but greater interference induced by the carrier frequency offset. When the number of subcarriers in the system is determined, the frequency offset range is larger, and the interference of multi-user access is more serious. Therefore, the access interference introduced by the difference of multi-user CFO is the key to the detection of the uplink user of the low-orbit broadband satellite communication system.

For this kind of problem, many documents have studied the problem of OFDM (Orthogonal Frequency Division Multiple Access) multi-user access interference cancellation. Early literature used traditional single-user detection algorithms to resist multi-user interference. Literature [1] proposed a multi-user interference cancellation algorithm based on the Least Square (LS) criterion and based on the Minimum Mean Square Error (Minimum Mean Square Error, MMSE) criterion of multi-user interference cancellation algorithm, but the algorithm needs to obtain more prior knowledge, and the cancellation accuracy is not high. Literature [2] proposes an iterative way to eliminate

X. Jiang (Ed.): MLICOM 2021, LNICST 438, pp. 1–8, 2022.
https://doi.org/10.1007/978-3-031-04409-0_1

multi-user access interference, but the algorithm needs to eliminate sub-carrier interference one by one, and the complexity of the algorithm is relatively high. Choi proposed a time-domain multi-user carrier frequency offset compensation algorithm [3], but the accuracy is poor. Pun proposed the iterative detection algorithm [4], which requires larger number of matrix operations after each iteration operation, which is relatively complex. Literature [5] proposed a SIC algorithm to eliminate multi-user access interference. On this basis, the literature [6] proposes to sort the sub-carriers according to the order to improve the elimination accuracy of the SIC algorithm to a certain extent. Literature [7] sorts the sub-carriers according to power, and literature [8] sorts the sub-carriers according to the Signal Interference and Noise Ratio (SINR). Although the ordering of sub-carriers improves the accuracy of SIC algorithm elimination to a certain extent, the elimination of sub-carrier interference increases the signal processing delay of the SIC algorithm, and also affects the achievability of the SIC algorithm, and the SIC algorithm is affected by the initial value of each user's frequency offset estimation. The degree of influence is greater.

Literature [9] analyzes the frequency offset interference of OFDM. Literature [10] uses virtual sub-carriers to eliminate carrier frequency offset interference. This algorithm uses odd-numbered carriers to transmit complete OFDM symbols, and all even-numbered carriers are virtual carriers. Literature [11] uses the Expectation Maximum (EM) algorithm to iterate to eliminate frequency offset interference, and gives the frequency offset elimination range, and also analyzes the characteristics of the frequency domain interference matrix introduced by frequency offset interference. Some documents use Carrier Frequency Offset (CFO) estimation to eliminate frequency offset interference. For CFO estimation, literature [12–14] uses cyclic prefix for CFO estimation, and improves CFO estimation performance by increasing the length of cyclic prefix, but increasing the cyclic prefix length will reduce the system bandwidth utilization. Literature [15] adopts a decision-oriented blind estimation algorithm of carrier frequency offset, which uses the phase of the demodulated signal to estimate the frequency offset. Literature [16] adopts the maximum likelihood criterion (Maximum Likelihood, ML) criterion for joint estimation of carrier frequency offset and channel, but the complexity is relatively high. Literature [17] modifies the cost function to reduce the complexity, but the range of frequency offset estimation is limited. Literature [18] applies phase-locked loop technology (PLL, Phase Locked Loop) to CFO tracking of OFDM system, but the algorithm has a slower convergence speed and a limited tracking range of carrier frequency offset. In order to be suitable for time-varying multipath channels, literature [19] uses training sequences for joint estimation of CFO and channel, but the accuracy is affected by the length and number of training sequences. Many algorithms cannot be directly applied to OFDM communication systems due to the complexity of engineering, or the length of the training sequence is too long, or the convergence speed is slow.

2 System Model

2.1 Signal Processing Model

The following analyzes the performance of OFDM under Doppler frequency shift. Define $x(n)$ is the time-domain signal at the transmitter; $h(n, l)$ is the L-path channel impulse response, and the time-domain signal $r(n)$ at the receiver is,

$$y(n) = \sum_{l=0}^{L-1} x(n)h(n, l) \tag{1}$$

α is the relative FO interference factor, and N is the number of OFDM carriers. After relative motion produces interference, the received signal is expressed as

$$r(n) = \sum_{l=0}^{L-1} x(n)h(n, l)e^{j2\pi n\alpha/N} \tag{2}$$

Perform N-point FFT on the received signal with frequency offset, and after parallel-to-serial conversion, the frequency domain signal $R(k)$ is obtained, which can be expressed as

$$R(k) = X(k)H(k)P(0) + \sum_{\substack{i=0 \\ i\neq k}}^{N-1} X(l)H(l)P(i - k) \tag{3}$$

Among them, $H(k)$ is the frequency domain response of the channel, and $P(k)$ is the frequency domain interference introduced by the frequency offset, which can be expressed by a matrix as

$$P = \begin{bmatrix} p(0) & \cdots & p(N-1) \\ p(N-1) & \ddots & p(N-2) \\ \vdots & p(0) & \vdots \\ p(1) & \cdots & p(0) \end{bmatrix} \tag{4}$$

Equation (4) can obtain the interference matrix P, which is a Toeplitz matrix. The element can be expressed as

$$p(k) = p(k + N) \tag{5}$$

where, $(\cdot)^{-1}$ is the inverse of the matrix, and $(\cdot)^H$ is the conjugate transpose of the matrix. It can be expressed as

$$P^{-1} = P^H \tag{6}$$

The elements of a matrix can be written in recursive form

$$p(k) = \Gamma \cdot p(k - 1) = \Gamma^2 \cdot p(k - 2) = \cdots = \Gamma^i \cdot p(0) \tag{7}$$

The first term of Eq. (7) represents the non-carrier interference part.

$$P(i - k) = \frac{\sin(\pi(i + \alpha - k)}{N \sin(\frac{\pi}{N}(i + \alpha - k))} \cdot \exp(j\pi(\frac{N - 1}{N})(i + \alpha - k)) \tag{8}$$

The formula (8) also shows that due to the influence of frequency offset, which can be expressed as

$$|\alpha_{k,i}|^2 = \frac{\sin^2(\pi[(i - k) + \alpha])}{N^2 \cdot \sin^2(\pi[(i - k) + \alpha]/N)} \tag{9}$$

3   System Model

3.1   Signal Processing Model

The optimization goal is the minimum mean square (MSE) between the received signal and the desired output signal. The equation means that the optimized cost function exhibits a strong nonlinear behavior. Therefore, it is difficult to solve this problem with linear methods and maximum likelihood algorithms.

Therefore, a non-linear weight solution method based on deep learning network is proposed to solve the non-linear problem. The OFDM communication system is seriously affected. Figure 1 shows a typical for signal processing flow. Both the transmitter and the receiver know the training symbols, and they are also considered reference symbols. The deep learning network can iteratively converge through training symbols, and the trained network has the optimal weight and can be used for frequency offset cancellation.

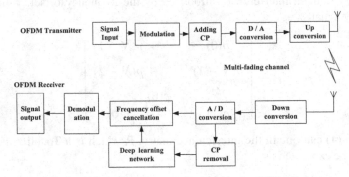

Fig. 1. Signal processing block diagram in OFDM link

3.2   Deep Learning Network Establishment for Carrier Frequency Offset Cancellation

Define the objective function can be expressed as,

$$J(n) = \sum_{n=1}^{N} \|\phi(n) - r(n)\|^2 + \tau^n \cdot \|w(n)\|^2 \tag{10}$$

where, τ is exponential weighting factor. $w(n)$ represents the deep learning network weight. $r(n)$ represents the output for the deep learning network

Define,

$$J(n) = \sum_{n=1}^{N} \left\| \phi(n) - w^*(n) \cdot r(n) \right\|^2 + \tau^n \cdot \|w(n)\|^2 \tag{11}$$

Optimization,

$$w^* = \underset{w \in C^{nxk}}{\arg \min} J(n) \tag{12}$$

$e(n)$ is defined as error.

We obtain,

$$e(n) = \phi(n) - w^*(n)r(n) \tag{13}$$

The gradient vector is,

$$\frac{\partial J(n)}{\partial w(n)} = 0 \tag{14}$$

Further, we could obtain,

$$w(n) = \left[\sum_{n=1}^{N} \phi(n)\phi^*(n) + \lambda^n I \right]^{-1} \cdot \left[\sum_{n=1}^{N} \phi(n)\phi^*(n) \right] \tag{15}$$

Define,

$$\Lambda(n) = \sum_{n=1}^{N} \phi(n)\phi^*(n) + \lambda^n I \tag{16}$$

Further,

$$\Lambda(n) = \left[\sum_{n=1}^{N-1} \phi(n)\phi^*(n) + \lambda^{n-1} I \right] + \phi(n)\phi^*(n) \tag{17}$$

$$\Lambda(n) = \lambda \Lambda(n-1) + \phi(n)\phi^*(n) \tag{18}$$

We could also obtain,

$$w(n) = w(n-1) + \Lambda^{-1}(n-1)\phi(n)e^*(n-1) \tag{19}$$

3.3 Proof of Validity

Substituting $e^{j2\pi\xi n/N}$ into (5), we finally get,

$$e(n) = \phi(n) - r(n) = \phi(n) - \phi(n) \cdot e^{j2\pi\alpha n/N} \cdot w(n) = \phi(n) \cdot \left[1 - e^{j2\pi\alpha n/N} \cdot w^*(n)\right] \tag{20}$$

Updating $w(n)$, we could obtain that D is also a constant value.
We obtain as,

$$w(n) = w(n-1) + e^*(n) \cdot \phi(n) = w(n) + D \cdot \left[e^{j2\pi n\alpha/N} - w(n)\right] \tag{21}$$

$$w(n) = (1 - D)^n \cdot w(0) + D \cdot (1 - D)^{n-1} \cdot \sum_{n=1}^{N-1} (1 - D)^{-n} \cdot e^{j2\pi n\alpha/N}, n > 0 \tag{22}$$

Taking the limit, we could obtain,

$$w_\infty = \lim_{n \to \infty} w(n) = \frac{D}{e^{j2\pi\alpha/N} - (1 - D)} e^{j2\pi n\alpha/N} \tag{23}$$

After mathematical operation,

$$r(n) = w_\infty^* \cdot w(n) = \frac{D}{e^{-j2\pi\alpha/N} - (1-D)} e^{-j2\pi n\alpha/N} \cdot x(n) \cdot e^{j2\pi n\alpha/N} = \frac{D}{e^{-j2\pi\xi/N} - (1-D)} \cdot \phi(n) \tag{24}$$

From Eq. (24), we can obtain that the output can be compensated with weights of deep learning network.

4 Experimental Classification Results and Analysis

Assuming that the required signal transmission bit rate of the OFDM link of the system is 40 Mbit/s. At this time, the maximum relative carrier frequency deviation is 0.35. Using BPSK modulation, each sub-carrier in each OFDM symbol can transmit 1 bits, and $240/1 = 240$ sub-carriers are required to meet the transmission rate requirements. 4 more zero-padded sub-carriers can be added to facilitate the implementation of 256-point FFT/IFFT. α_{max} is the maximum Normalized frequency offset, which is defined as the ratio between frequency offset and bandwidth.

We simulate the relationship between BER and SNR through frequency offset cancellation performance. The relationship between the bit error rate (BER) and the average SNR is shown in Fig. 2 and Fig. 3, respectively. The results of the iterative algorithm and the compensation method proposed in the no frequency offset, no cancellation, MMSE algorithm, LS algorithm are given. By investigating these numbers, it can be clearly shown that no cancellation will be affected by ICI and has a high error background. The MMSE algorithm performs well because ICI and MUI can be deleted. The performance of the deep learning network algorithm is better than that of the MMSE algorithm because it can significantly reduce the impact of noise enhancement.

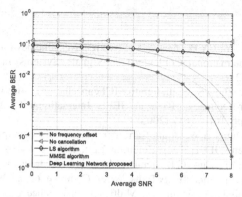

Fig. 2. BER curves under different average SNR, $\alpha_{max} = 0.05$

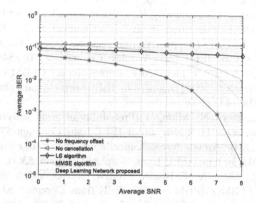

Fig. 3. BER curves under different SNR, $\alpha_{max} = 0.35$

5 Conclusion

A deep learning network for OFDM system is proposed to eliminate the carrier frequency offset interference of OFDM system. The carrier frequency offset greatly reduces the bit error rate performance of the communication system. The frequency offset interference introduced by the carrier needs to be eliminated before signal demodulation. First, we establish frequency offset cancellation weights through a deep learning network. Therefore, we propose a way to eliminate weights by establishing a deep learning network, and form a system optimization elimination weight matrix through iteration. Secondly, we use positive fine-tuning to train the hidden layer and weights. It has been proved that in the same training sequence, the frequency offset-assisted deep learning network model has higher performance on communication error rate.

Acknowledgment. This work was supported by the Scientific Research Initiation Funds for the Doctoral Program of Xi'an International University (Grant No. XAIU2019002), Regional Innovation Capability Guidance Project (Grant No. 2021QFY01-08) and the General Project of science and Technology Department of Shaanxi Province (Grant No. 2020JM-638).

References

1. Cao, Z.R., Tureli, U., Yao, Y.D.: Analysis of two receiver schemes for interleaved OFDMA uplink. In: IEEE International Conference on Signals, Systems and Computers, vol. 2, pp. 1818–1821 (2002)
2. Huang, M., Chen, X., Zhou, S., et al.: Iterative ICI cancellation algorithm for uplink OFDMA system with carrier-frequency offset. In: IEEE International Conference on Vehicular Technology, vol. 3, pp. 1613–1617 (2005)
3. Choi, J.H., Lee, C., Jung, H.W., et al.: Carrier frequency offset compensation for uplink of OFDM-FDMA systems. IEEE Trans. Commun. Lett. 4(12), 414–416 (2000)
4. Pun, M.O., Morelli, M., Kuo, C.J.: Iterative detection and frequency synchronization for OFDMA uplink transmissions. IEEE Trans. Wirel. Commun. 6(2), 629–639 (2007)
5. Fantacci, R., Marabissi, D., Papini, S.: Multiuser interference cancellation receivers for OFDMA uplink communications with carrier frequency offset. In: IEEE International Conference on Globecom 2004, vol. 5, pp. 2808–2812 (2004)
6. Trajkovic, V.D., Rapajic, P.B., Kennedy, R.A.: Adaptive ordering for imperfect successive decision feedback multiuser detection. IEEE Trans. Commun. 56(2), 173–176 (2008)
7. Tevfik, Y., Huseyin, A.: Carrier frequency offset compensation with successive cancellation in uplink OFDMA systems. IEEE Trans. Wireless Commun. 6(10), 3546–3551 (2007)
8. Hou, S.W., Ko, C.: Intercarrier interference suppression for OFDMA uplink in time and frequency selective rayleigh fading channels. In: IEEE International Conference on Vehicular Technology, pp. 1438–1442 (2008)
9. Weeraddana, P., Rajatheva, N., Minn, H.: Probability of error analysis of BPSK OFDM systems with random residual frequency offset. IEEE Trans. Commun. 57(1), 106–116 (2005)
10. Huang, D., Letaief, K.B.: An interference cancellation scheme for carrier frequency offsets correction in OFDMA systems. IEEE Trans. Wireless Commun. 53(7), 1155–1165 (2005)
11. Yong, S., Xiong, Z., Wang, X.: EM-based iterative receiver design with carrier-frequency offset estimation for MIMO OFDM systems. IEEE Trans. Commun. 53(4), 581–586 (2005)
12. Lashkarian, N., Kiaei, S.: Class of cyclic-based estimators for frequency-offset estimation of OFDM systems. IEEE Trans. Commun. 48(12), 2139–2149 (2000)
13. Krongold, B.S.: Analysis of cyclic-prefix correlation statistics and their use in OFDM timing and frequency synchronization. In: IEEE International Conference on Signals, Systems and Computers, pp. 1466–1470 (2005)
14. Stoica, P., Soderstrom, T.: Statistical analysis of MUSIC and subspace rotation estimates of sinusoidal frequencies. IEEE Trans. Signal Process. 39(8), 1836–1847 (1991)
15. Visser, M.A., Zong, P.P., Bar-Ness, Y.: A novel method for blind frequency offset correction in an OFDM system. In: IEEE International Conference on Personal, Indoor and Mobile Radio Communications, vol. 2, pp. 816–820 (1998)
16. Chiavaccini, E., Vitetta, G.M.: Maximum-likelihood frequency recovery for OFDM signals transmitted over multipath fading channels. IEEE Trans. Commun. 52(2), 244–251 (2004)
17. MerliFZ, V.: Blind feedforward frequency estimation for OFDM signals transmitted over multipath fading channels. IEEE Trans. Wireless Commun. 6(6), 2055–2059 (2007)
18. Kuang, L.L., Ni, Z.Y., Lu, J.H., et al.: A time-frequency decision-feedback loop for carrier frequency offset tracking in OFDM systems. IEEE Trans. Wireless Commun. 4(2), 367–373 (2005)
19. Ylioinas, J., Juntti, M.: EM based iterative receiver for joint decoding and channel parameter estimation in space-frequency turbo coded OFDM. In: IEEE International Conference on Personal, Indoor and Mobile Radio Communications, pp. 1–5 (2006)

Research on the Rising Phenomenons in the Bit Error Rate Performances of LT-Based UEP Codes

Qingyang Guan and Shuang Wu[✉]

College of Engineering, Xi'an International University, Xi'an 710070, China
gqy_gqy@163.com, wooshuang@126.com

Abstract. The LT-based UEP codes have attracted much attentions in the past decades, because which codes can be used to overcome the issue that some different parts of data have different reliability requirements. But all the existing LT-based UEP codes provide UEP properties at the cost of lower transmission efficiency. In this paper, we focus on the phenomenon that the BER curves of such code would not monotonically decreases as UEP property grows. By quantized the BER of RUEP codes, and compared through two manners to illustrate the BER performances of such code, a useful design principle is given to avoid too lower transmission efficiency and too higher encoding and decoding complexity.

Keywords: LT codes · Unequal error protection · Waterfall region · Error floor · BER

1 Introduction

Rateless codes is a type of capacity-approaching error-correcting codes in which the code rate are dynamically. The most well known rateless code such as LT codes [1], Raptor codes [2] and Spinal codes [3]. Luby Transform (LT) codes is the first class of rateless codes which designed to transmit data on binary erasure channel (BEC), and the encoding and decoding complexities of LT codes are both equal to $O(k \log k)$.

Rateless codes with the unequal error protection (UEP) property have attracted much attentions in the past decade, and many classes of rateless codes which can provide UEP properties have been invented [4–7]. But nearly all of these codes are LT-based, and all these codes provide UEP properties at the price of lower transmission efficiency. For this reason, we will figure out and analyze how to avoid to lower transmission efficiency by transmitting data using the LT-based UEP codes.

© ICST Institute for Computer Sciences, Social Informatics and Telecommunications Engineering 2022
Published by Springer Nature Switzerland AG 2022. All Rights Reserved
X. Jiang (Ed.): MLICOM 2021, LNICST 438, pp. 9–16, 2022.
https://doi.org/10.1007/978-3-031-04409-0_2

As the codes proposed by Rahnavard *et al.* is most famous class of LT-based UEP code [5], and the authors have provided a useful quantized expression by using and-or tree technique [8]. Then we focus on this class of code. By compared the performances between BER versus overhead and BER versus UEP weight two manners, a useful design principle have been proposed.

The organize of this paper is as follows. Section 2 briefly review two classes of well known LT-based UEP codes, and the BER versus overhead of these codes are compared. Then the quantization analysis on RUEP codes is given in Sect. 3, and the phenomenon some BER curves are not monotonically is also been illustrated. In Sect. 4, we reveal the reason of the aforementioned phenomenon, and provide a disign principle to design the LT-based UEP codes proposed by [5]. And the concluding remarks of this paper is drawn in Sect. 5.

2   Related Work

As the LT-based UEP codes have attracted the attentions of much researchers, many classes coding schemes have been invented. All the existing LT-based UEP codes can be divided into two categories. The one is the LT-based UEP codes with only one encoder in each code. For the other one, there are several sub encoders in each LT-based UEP code.

The most well-known class of LT-based UEP codes is proposed by Rahnavard, *et al.* [5], which belongs to the first category. To distinguish with the other LT-based UEP codes, the codes in [5] are named as Rahnavard UEP (RUEP) codes in this paper. In a given RUEP code, the input bits can be divided into different blocks, by allocated the different selecting probabilities for input bits in different blocks, the input bits can be decoded to provide various BER performances. It is worth to given the definition of UEP weight of RUEP codes. Assuming there are $\alpha_1 k, \alpha_2 k, \ldots, \alpha_i k, \ldots$ input bits in the blocks $b_1, b_2, \ldots, b_i, \ldots$, and the selecting probabilities of the blocks are $q_1, q_2, \ldots, q_i, \ldots$, where $\sum_i \alpha_i = 1$ and $\sum_i q_i = 1$, then the UEP weight of input bits in ith block is given by $K_i = \frac{q_i}{\alpha_i}$. And a higher weight would leading to a better BER performance of the input bits in the related block.

The most well known LT-based UEP codes in the second category is Expanding Window Fountain (EWF) codes [6]. Different with the LT-based UEP codes in first category, there are several encoders existed in each EWF code. In a EWF code, the input bits also been divided into blocks $b_1, b_2, \ldots, b_i, \ldots$, and the input bits in block b_i are same as which of the RUEP codes. The UEP wight of EWF codes are not given in [6], instead of the selecting probabilities ρ_i of each window w_i. By allocates a sub encoder for each window w_i, the input bits in first i windows are selected randomly to generate output bits. As the input bits in a fronter window have been selected in more windows than which of the later blocks, the input bits in fronter blocks can provide better BER performances than which of the later blocks, and the differences BER performances of different blocks can be determined by adjusted the corresponding selecting probabilities.

To illustrate the BER performances of the aforementioned two classed of LT-based UEP codes, we compared the RUEP and EWF codes with two blocks, in

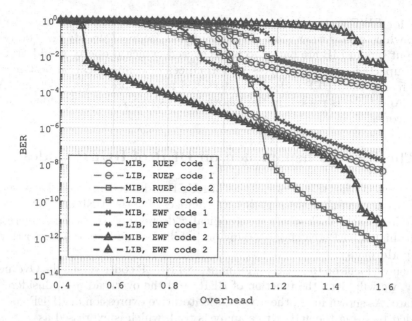

Fig. 1. The BER performances of RUEP and EWF codes.

which there are $0.1k$ and $0.9k$ input symbols in the first and second block, respectively. As there are only two blocks in each code, then the block in which the input symbol can provide better BER performances are dubbed More Important Block (MIB), and the other one is named as Less Important Block (LIB).

The coding parameters of RUEP and EWF codes in Fig. 1 are given as follows. The encoders in both RUEP and EWF codes share the same output degree distribution given by [2], which is given following.

$$\Omega(x) = 0.007969x^1 + 0.493570x^2 + 0.166220x^3 + 0.072646x^4 \qquad (1)$$
$$+0.082558x^5 + 0.056058x^8 + 0.037229x^9 + 0.055590x^{19}$$
$$+0.025023x^{64} + 0.003137x^{66}.$$

For RUEP codes, the UEP weights are $K_{MIB,1} = 2$ and $K_{MIB,2} = 3$, respectively. And the selecting probabilities of MIBs of EWF codes are $\rho_{MIB,1} = 0.1$ and $\rho_{MIB,2} = 0.2$. By observed on Fig. 1, for both the RUEP and EWF codes, the MIBs can provide better BER performances than their pair LIBs. And one can find that for RUEP codes, the UEP property (the gap between the BER curves) of a pair MIB and LIB blocks would as larger as a higher UEP weight adopted. For EWF codes, the UEP property would increases with selecting probability of MIB block growth.

As for EWF codes, the Unequal Recovery Time (URT) properties are too larger, which means when most of the input bits are have already been decoded, the input bits in LIB are barely to be recovered, which property would dramatically impacted on the timeliness performances of communication systems, for which reason the RUEP codes have attracted much more attentions than EWF codes. And for this reason, in the follows of this paper, we would focus on the RUEP codes.

3   The Rising Phenomenon on BER of RUEP Codes

In this section, the BER performances of RUEP codes is concerned. By observed in Fig. 1, one can find that the BER performances of both RUEP and EWF codes, the BER of each block would monotonically decreasing as overhead increases, and the higher UEP weight or selecting probability would leading a better (lower) BER performance.

Then we focus on the BER performances of RUEP codes versus the Overhead. Firstly, we will given the function of BER, and the overhead γ is considered as a variate. As shown in [5], the asymptotic iterative expression of RUEP codes is provided by using the and or tree analysis tool, which is expressed as

$$y_{l,i} = \lambda_i \left(1 - \sum_d \omega_d \left(\sum_i q_i (1 - y_{l-1,i})\right)^{d-1}\right), \tag{2}$$

where $\lambda(x) = \frac{\Lambda'(x)}{\Lambda'(1)}$ and $\omega(x) = \frac{\Omega'(x)}{\Omega'(1)}$, and $\Lambda(x)$ is the input degree distribution of input bits. It is worth to noting that when l is enough large, $y_{l,i}$ would tends to the BER of the given RUEP code.

Let $P_{released}$ denote the probability that an arbitrary selected output bits can be decoded to recover a input bits, then which probability can be expressed by

$$P_{released} = \sum_d \omega_d \left(\sum_i q_i (1 - y_{l-1,i})\right)^{d-1}, \tag{3}$$

and the BER probability is given by

$$P_{BER} = \lambda_i (1 - P_{released}). \tag{4}$$

As shown in [5], when $k \to \infty$, $\lambda_i(x)$ can be computed by

$$\lambda_i(x) = \frac{\Lambda_i'(x)}{\Lambda_i'(1)} = \frac{(\bar{d}_i \gamma) e^{\bar{d}_i \gamma(x-1)}}{(\bar{d}_i \gamma) e^{\bar{d}_i \gamma(x-1)} \mid_{x=1}} = e^{\bar{d}_i \gamma(x-1)}, \tag{5}$$

where $\bar{d}_i$ is the average of input bits in b_i, and which is

$$\bar{d}_i = \frac{\gamma k q_i \Omega'(1)}{\alpha_i k} = \frac{\gamma q_i \Omega'(1)}{\alpha_i}. \tag{6}$$

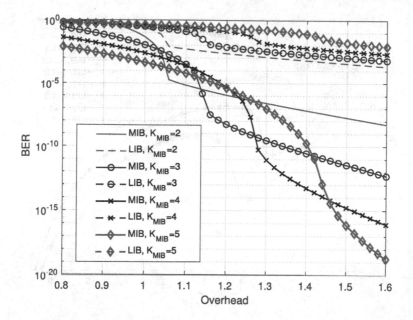

Fig. 2. The BER performances of RUEP codes versus overheads.

Then Eq. (4) can be rewritten as

$$P_{BER} = \exp\left\{ \frac{\gamma^2 q_i \Omega'(1)}{\alpha_i} (-P_{released}) \right\}, \tag{7}$$

as there is only one variate γ in the right part of Eq. (7), then the BER is a function of γ, and BER is monotonicity decreases as γ increases. By observed on Fig. 2, it is can be found that the BER performances of each blocks is goes better with overhead grows, whatever the UEP weight is adopted.

By given a fixed overhead γ, and let the q_i is a variate, then we can arbitrary say that BER is also monotonicity decreases as q_i increases. But by consider on the existed LT-based UEP codes, which is a paradox, actually in all the existing LT-based UEP codes, when UEP weight grows, the BER performances are not monotonicity decreases. By focus on RUEP codes, which phenomenon can be illustrated by observed on Fig. 3.

In Fig. 3, the overheads are set as constants, and the UEP weights are considered as variates. Then it is easily to see that the BER curves are not monotonously, and in some region, the BER performance would turned to goes worse as UEP weight K_{MIB} grows.

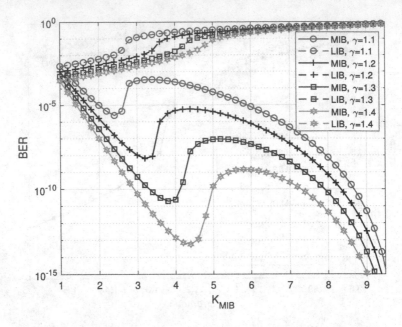

Fig. 3. The BER performances of RUEP codes versus UEP weight.

4   Discussion on Rising Phenomenon on BER Performances of RUEP Codes

To find out the reason about the phenomenon in which the BER performances rises as K_{MIB} increases, we given the compare in Fig. 4 and Fig. 5. By setting three pair of points $a1$, $a2$ and $a3$ both in these two figure, one can easily find that the points which are figure outed are strictly same. By observed at the points of $a1$, as which points in Fig. 4 belongs to the error floor region, which points belongs to the region in which the BER of MIB are monotonicity decreases, and for the points of $a3$, as the point are belongs to the waterfall region, then its comparison points in Fig. 5 belongs to the region in which the BER of MIB are rising.

The comparison results in Fig. 4 and Fig. 5 illustrated that the beginning points of waterfall and error floor regions would as larger as UEP weight K_{MIB} bigger, and the higher UEP properties would leading to lower transmission efficiencies.

As the higher UEP property would leading to lower transmission efficiency, and the larger overhead will leading to higher encoding and decoding complexities, which means for practice, the RUEP codes should be carefully designed. As in waterfall region the BER performances went better much quickly than which of the error floor region, an appropriated RUEP code should satisfies that the required BER performances just emerged near by the point between the waterfall and error floor regions.

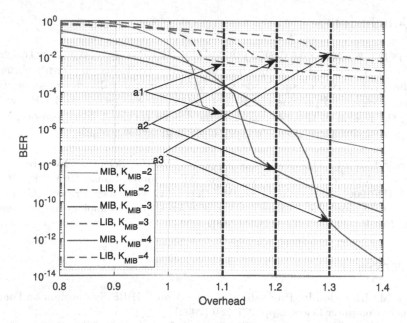

Fig. 4. The compared BER performances of RUEP codes versus overhead.

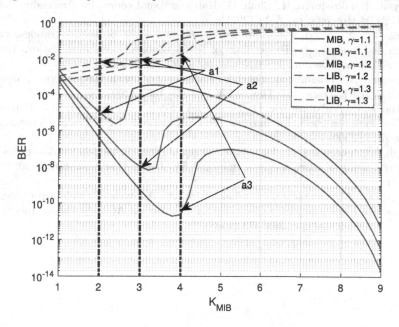

Fig. 5. The compared BER performances of RUEP codes versus UEP weight.

5 Conclusion

In this paper, we propose a design principle for RUEP code to avoid low transmission efficiency and higher computing complexity. By focus on the phenomenon that the BER curves of such code would not monotonically decreases as UEP property grows, and provide the BER function of overhead γ and UEP weight K_{MIB}, the reason of this phenomenon have been revealed. Furthermore, based on the revealed reason, the design principle is given as a result.

Acknowledgment. This work was supported by the Scientific Research Initiation Funds for the Doctoral Program of Xi'an International University (Grant No. XAIU2019002), Regional Innovation Capability Guidance Project (Grant No. 2021QFY01-08) and the General Project of science and Technology Department of Shaanxi Province (Grant No. 2020JM-638).

References

1. Luby, M.: LT codes. In: Proceedings of 43rd Annual IEEE Symposium on Foundations of Computer Science, pp. 271–280 (2002)
2. Shokrollahi, A.: Raptor codes. IEEE Trans. Inf. Theory **52**, 2551–2567 (2006)
3. Perry, J., Balakrishnan, H., Shah, D.: Rateless spinal codes. In: Proceedings of the IEEE ACM HotNets, pp. 6–11 (2011)
4. Rahnavard, N., Fekri, F.: Finite-length unequal error protection rateless codes: design and analysis. In: Proceedings of IEEE Global Telecommunications Conference, St. Louis, Missouri, USA, vol. 3, pp. 1353–1357 (2005)
5. Rahnavard, N., Vellambi, B., Fekri, F.: Rateless codes with unequal error protection property. IEEE Trans. Inf. Theory **53**(4), 1521–1532 (2007)
6. Sejdinovic, D., Vukobratovic, D., Doufexi, A., Senk, V., Piechocki, R.J.: Expanding window fountain codes for unequal error protection. IEEE Trans. Commun. **57**, 2510–2516 (2009)
7. Talari, A., Rahnavard, N.: Distributed unequal error protection rateless codes over erasure channels: a two-source scenario. IEEE Trans. Commun. **60**(8), 2084–2090 (2012)
8. Luby, M.G., Mitzenmacher, M., Shokrallahi, A.: Analysis of random processes via and-or tree evaluation. In: Proceedings of 9th Annual ACM-SIAM Symposium on Discrete Algorithms, pp. 364–373 (1998)

Ensemble Classification Technique for Cultural Heritage Image

Sathit Prasomphan[✉]

Department of Computer and Information Science, Faculty of Applied Science, King Mongkut's University of Technology North Bangkok, 1518 Pracharat 1 Road, Wongsawang, Bangsue, Bangkok 10800, Thailand
sathit.p@sci.kmutnb.ac.th

Abstract. This research aims to propose an ensemble classification technique for cultural heritage image. In the case of Thai architecture, the cultural heritage content was extracted. The key contribution of this study was the creation of an ensemble classification technique for recovering information from a cultural heritage images in order to convey a story inside it. Through the learning of machine learning and image processing, the cultural heritage of Thai archaeological site architecture was generated, including the story of the archaeological site. The significant information contained inside the cultural heritage image was extracted and presented to those who are interested in its contents. The appearance of the form within an image can be used to differentiate image qualities such as era, architecture, and style. The classification result of the ensemble classification technique is used to examine the experimental findings of cultural heritage content retrieval. Photographs of Thai archaeological site architecture from world heritage provinces in Thailand were categorized in this investigation, for example, images from Phra Nakhon Si Ayutta province, Sukhothai province, and Bangkok, which represent the Ayutthaya, Sukhothai, and Rattanakosin eras in sequential sequence. On average, the proposed ensemble classification technique does have an accuracy of 80.83%.

Keywords: Cultural heritage · Content retrieval · Ensemble classification technique · Machine learning · Image processing

1 Introduction

Cultural heritage is mainly composed of both tangible and intangible cultural heritage. Paintings, sculptures, monuments, and archaeological sites also meet the definition of tangible cultural heritage. Performing arts, rural dancing, and folklore are among the categories of intangible cultural heritage. Both Thai and foreign tourists are traveling to the temple to experience its historical tradition. These ten target industries, which can be grouped into two categories, have the potential to drive the country's economic growth engine and increase competitiveness. The first group is the extension of the previous five industries, consisting of modern automotive industry, smart electronics industry, tourism

X. Jiang (Ed.): MLICOM 2021, LNICST 438, pp. 17–27, 2022.
https://doi.org/10.1007/978-3-031-04409-0_3

industry, agriculture, and biotechnology, and food for the future. The second group is adding five future industries, which is a new industry that Thailand has competitive potential, and there are interested investors consisting of: industrial robotics, aviation and logistics industry, biochemical industry, digital industry, comprehensive medical industry. The tourist business is another one of these target areas that will have an impact on the country's income. In addition, for the younger generation to learn, a tourism sector in the locations where cultural heritage transpired will be required. Buildings, monuments, and locations with historical value, aesthetics, archeology, or anthropology are referred to as cultural heritage. Architecture, sculpture, art, or natural archeology, such as caves or important places that may be human-made or because of natural are all examples of cultural heritage. The history of each country shows the ancestors greatness of those times through ancient monuments or antiquities. Knowing the history of cultural heritage or archaeological sites will effect on the pound of long history in that place for the new generation in the country. In this research, we aim to develop an effective cultural heritage content retrieval that enables the retrieval of stories that appear in those cultural heritages for the knowledge of future generation's interests. We realized that creating a cultural heritage information management system with ensemble classification technique, especially for Thai architecture by showing interesting information within images to present to interested people would be benefit. The development consists of generating stories from the cultural heritage images. We used the appearance of the shape for showing characteristics of the archaeological site and link to the era of the ancient monuments architecture that was created, including explaining the story of the archaeological site through machine learning and image processing. This research is a study and development of knowledge, which relies on specific data sets within Thailand. We organize the rest of each section as follows. Theory of cultural heritage in case of architecture and research on automatic sentence retrieval from pictures is introduced in Sect. 2. The ensemble classification technique for cultural heritage image algorithm for retrieving information from the cultural heritage images is detailed in Sect. 3. In Sect. 4, the results and discussions are explained. After that, we conclude the paper in Sect. 5.

2   Related Work

2.1   Cultural Heritage

One of the tangible cultural heritage in Thailand that is well known to people inside the country and the foreigner is the pagoda or Stupa. The main purpose for building the stupa or pagoda is to collect the symbol of religion. Several shapes or architecture of the stupa occurs and related to the era of that building. We can divide the main architecture of pagoda into three categories, which are Sukhothai architecture, Ayutthaya architecture, and Rattanakosin architecture. In Sukhothai architecture can be divided in to these styles: the bell-shaped style, the Prang style, etc. In Ayutthaya architecture, the Prang style is frequently occurred. Finally, in Rattanakosin, architecture can be classified into these categories: the square wooden pagoda style, the Prang style, etc. The cultural heritage of each architecture can be shown in Figs. 1, 2 and 3.

Fig. 1. Examples of cultural heritage in Sukhothai architecture: the lotus blossom style, the bell-shaped style, the Prang style, and the Chomhar style [1, 12].

2.2   Research on Automatic Sentence Retrieval from Pictures

In this section, we briefly explain the related research on automatic sentence retrieval from the picture. Uday et al. [2] developed a prototype that would allow them to access Indian Digital Heritage Space (IHDS) monument data. Using transfer-learning techniques, they presented image classification and query-based retrieval of image labels. Authors in [3, 5, 6] proposed the recurrent neural network-based algorithm for generating an automatic sentences from pictures. An algorithm for generating natural language descriptions of image regions was described by Karpathy and Li [3]. Farhadi et al. [4] designed a new approach for calculating a score that connects an image to a text. To attach a descriptive sentence to a given image, the value utilized the score relating an image. They suggested a framework for simulating the link between image, mean, and sentence space. The DT-RNN model, proposed by Socher et al. [7], is a recursive neural network-based method for determining the relationship between an image and texts. The DT-RNN present systematic phrases into a vector space for image retrieval using dependency trees. Content-based image retrieval, which is focused on color, texture, or shapes, is another way for searching a large image library. However, using low-level image features and high-level image semantic has an influence on the algorithms' performance. In [8] used color histograms to image index. The weight distribution of the

Fig. 2. Example of cultural heritage in Ayutthaya architecture [1, 12].

Fig. 3. Examples of cultural heritage in Rattanakosin architecture [1, 12].

Gaussian was used in the experiments. In [9] used image retrieval algorithm with color histogram using vector modeling to converting the image into a histogram and store it in the database. To retrieve the image from database, the image histogram search was performed by comparing the histogram between images and histogram of the image in the database using the similarity in the vector model. To measure the similarity between searching image and reference image, the similarity value was used, which the similarity score closest to 1 means these two images are similar. In [10] presented the research by converting RGB color features into color features based on the HSV model, after that the searching image feature are used to compare with the reference feature image in the database. A digital amulet retrieval using the nearest neighbor method by Facktong [11]. In this research, gray surface matrix analysis was performed using a gray matrix. From the above research, several issues were difficult to perform that effect to the accuracy of algorithms, and the current problem is how to add the caption of image which has its ability as same as the aspect of human ability. According to these several issues, in this research, we proposed an algorithm for retrieving contents in the images. A cultural heritage content retrieval by ensemble classification technique was introduced. The cultural heritage content in case of Thai's architecture was retrieved. In this research, the main contribution was to develop a classification algorithm for retrieving information from a cultural heritage image for telling the story inside that image.

3 Ensemble Classification Technique for Cultural Heritage Image

To perform the process of ensemble classification technique for cultural heritage image, the following algorithms were executed.

ALGORITHM: Ensemble classification technique for cultural heritage image

1. Image input: Collect the image of Thai cultural heritage to learn more about it. The database contains the training Thai cultural heritage image, which will be compared to the input image.
2. Pre-processing: To improve the image quality, convert the RGB Thai cultural heritage image to grayscale and apply the image improvement algorithm.
3. Edge detection: The next process is analyzing the edges that pass through or near the point of interest. It is measured by comparing the intensity of the closest data points or finding the line, which surrounds the object inside the image. We used laplacian method to find the edge of image.
4. Feature extraction: to retrieve the identity of each image to be a vector for using in the training and testing processes, feature extraction was used. In this step, we used convolution neural network algorithm for the process to get key points inside image.
5. Training image with convolution neural network.
6. Using ensemble classification technique to classify the category of input image.
7. Matching the most similar image between the input image and the reference image in the database.
8. Generating cultural heritage descriptions.

End

3.1 Ensemble Classifier

Ensemble classifier is a model that combines numerous classifiers to solve the same problem by making a final judgment based on the results of all classifiers. Vote ensemble uses the same training data with multiple classifiers, bootstrap aggregating (Bagging) uses random training data and constructs a single ensemble model, and random forest is similar to bagging technique but instead of using random data, it randomly selects attribute from dataset and uses several decision trees as classifiers in the ensemble model. The vote ensemble with base classifiers was chosen in this study because it has a low computing complexity and a diverse theoretical basis. By combining the combined model with a weighted majority vote, the suggested model intends to eliminate bias and redundancy. If the ensemble's classifiers do not produce the same classification result, it is appropriate to try to give the more capable classifiers greater power in the final choice. We called this step is weighted majority vote. The formula for weighted majority vote is shown in Eq. 1.

$$y = argmax_i \sum_{j=1}^{m} w_j p_{ij} \tag{1}$$

The T classifiers are class-conditionally independent with accuracies $p_1 \ldots p_T$. The optimal weights for the weighted majority-voting rule can be shown in Eq. 2.

$$w_t = p_t/(1 - p_t) \tag{2}$$

So when referring to the above formula:

y is the weighted average predicted probability of class membership.
p_{ij} is the probability for individual i for class membership of class according to classifier/prediction model j.
w_j is the weight for prediction model j's prediction.

3.2 Convolution Neural Network

The convolution neural network was applied for getting the description of cultural heritage. The CNN architecture employed in our study was set up with the following details in the feature extraction step: An input layer, an output layer, and numerous hidden layers make up the convolutional neural network architecture. A set of convolutional layers combine with a multiplication or other dot product to generate the hidden layers of a CNN. The activation function is usually a RELU layer, which is followed by hidden layers such as a pooling layer, fully connected layers, and normalization layer. Back-propagation is frequently used in the final convolution to better weight the product. Within the convolutional layers, the technique concatenated the input and transfers the result to the next layer. Each receptive field-specific convolutional neuron processes data exclusively for that field. To speed up the underlying computation, convolutional networks are composed of local or global pooling layers. By pooling layers and combining the outputs of neuron clusters at one layer into a single neuron at the next layer, the data's dimension were reduced. Local pooling combines small clusters, typically 2×2.

Global pooling acts on the neurons of the convolutional layer. In addition, pooling may compute a max or an average. Max pooling uses the maximum value from each of a cluster of neurons at the prior layer. Fully connected layers connect every neuron in one layer to every neuron in another layer. It is in principle the same as the traditional multi-layer perceptron neural network (MLP). Each neuron in a neural network computes an output value by applying a specific function to the input values coming from the receptive field in the previous layer. A vector of weights and bias determines the function that is applied to the input values. Learning in a neural network progresses by making iterative adjustments to these biases and weights. The last step for getting the description of cultural heritage is the matching process, which is the process for matching the most similar image between the input image and the reference image. In this process, a group of data, which have similar characteristics, were retrieved; several images in the group will be occurred. After that, the process of generating the description after the matching process will be performed. Finally, the algorithm will show and set description to the input image.

4   Results and Discussion

4.1   Dataset Collection and Description

The classification result by using the proposed approach to characterize the architecture of Thai cultural heritage image was performed to verify the experimental findings of cultural heritage content retrieval. We obtained the data from UNESCO heritage places in Bangkok, Sukhothai province, and Phra Nakhon Si Ayutta province, which are UNESCO cultural heritage locations in Thailand. Table 1 shows the total number of images used throughout the study.

Table 1. Number of Cultural heritage architecture in the experiments

Cultural heritage architecture	Number of image
Ayutthaya architecture	1670
Sukhothai architecture	1440
Rattanakosin architecture	1460
All	4570

4.2   Performance Indexed

The use of a confusion matrix to reflect the performance of classification results is one of the most powerful strategies. Each row represents the anticipated class, whereas each column represents the original class. The classification result can be displayed while using this technique. Table 2 shows the experimental results of our proposed approach. Tables 3 and 4 shows the experimental results of test data that were classified to the original cultural heritage image with traditional method. Tables 5, 6 and 7 shows the precision, recall, and F1-score of the proposed algorithms: ensemble classification technique, KNN algorithm, neural network, and SIFT with Euclidean distance algorithm.

4.3 Comparing Algorithms

The following algorithm were used for comparing the performance of the proposed algorithms: ensemble classification technique, KNN algorithm, neural network, and SIFT with Euclidean distance algorithm. We compare the efficiency of generating descriptions, which used only the classification results.

Table 2. Confusion matrix of the proposed algorithm by using ensemble classification technique.

Predicted class (architecture)	True class (architecture)		
	Ayutthaya	Sukhothai	Rattanakosin
Ayutthaya	1250	260	160
Sukhothai	105	1320	15
Rattanakosin	217	93	1150

Table 3. Confusion matrix of the KNN algorithm

Predicted class (architecture)	True class (architecture)		
	Ayutthaya	Sukhothai	Rattanakosin
Ayutthaya	987	408	275
Sukhothai	225	1052	163
Rattanakosin	307	101	1052

Table 4. Confusion matrix of neural network and SIFT with Euclidean distance algorithm

Predicted class (architecture)	True class (architecture)		
	Ayutthaya	Sukhothai	Rattanakosin
Ayutthaya	1025	385	260
Sukhothai	369	962	109
Rattanakosin	350	125	985

Table 5. Precision, Recall, F1-score of the proposed algorithm by using ensemble classification technique.

Class	Precision	Recall	F1-score
Ayutthaya	0.7485	0.7952	0.7711
Sukhothai	0.9167	0.7890	0.8481
Rattanakosin	0.9167	0.8679	0.8916

Table 6. Precision, Recall, F1-score of the KNN algorithm

Class	Precision	Recall	F1-score
Ayutthaya	0.5910	0.6498	0.6190
Sukhothai	0.7306	0.6739	0.7011
Rattanakosin	0.7306	0.7060	0.7180

Table 7. Precision, Recall, F1-score of neural network and SIFT with Euclidean distance algorithm

Class	Precision	Recall	F1-score
Ayutthaya	0.6137	0.5877	0.6004
Sukhothai	0.6680	0.6535	0.6607
Rattanakosin	0.6680	0.7274	0.6965

4.4 Experimental Results

In this study, we demonstrate the retrieval performance of cultural heritage content employing classification results from the proposed method to analyze the architecture of Thai cultural heritage images. The classification accuracy determines the accuracy of our image description generator.

Tables 2, 3 and 4 shows the number of tested data that were classified to the original cultural heritage image. Tables 5, 6 and 7 shows the precision, recall, and F1-score of the proposed algorithms: ensemble classification approach, KNN algorithm, neural network, and SIFT with Euclidean distance algorithm.

The classification accuracies with F1-score were shown in Tables 5, 6 and 7. Table 5 shows the F1-score of the proposed algorithm, which is the ensemble classification technique. It gives the accuracy 0.7711, 0.8481, and 0.8916 in Ayutthaya architecture, Sukhothai architecture, and Rattanakosinera architecture.

Table 6 shows the F1-score of using k-NN algorithms. This algorithm gives the accuracy 0.6190, 0.7011, and 0.7180 in Ayutthaya architecture, Sukhothai architecture, and Rattanakosin architecture.

Table 7 shows the F1-score of using neural network and SIFT with Euclidean distance algorithm. This algorithm gives the accuracy 0.6004, 0.6607, and 0.6965 in Ayutthaya architecture, Sukhothai architecture, and Rattanakosin architecture.

According to the findings of this study's experiments, the proposed algorithm for detecting contents in images can yield an average accuracy around 80–90%. An ensemble classification technique for extracting cultural heritage content was introduced, and it outperformed traditional approaches. In the case of Thai architecture, the cultural heritage content was extracted.

As a result, developing a classification method for collecting information from a cultural heritage image in attempt to explain the story embedded inside that image is desirable to those that are interested in this cultural heritage image.

5   Conclusion

For cultural heritage images, we developed an ensemble classification technique. The information of cultural heritage can be used in the research: case study, Thai architecture. The interesting information contained within the photograph will be recovered and presented to those who are interested. The development entails creating narrative out of photographs. It can identify the era of the historic site through delivering the appearance of the shape as well as the unique character of the site. The architecture was developed using machine learning and image processing to include the story of the archaeological site. In addition, if we can show the complete shape of the past from that remains by analyzing the similarity of the image in the database, the image can tell the story of the past.

References

1. Chareonla, C.: Buddhist Arts of Thailand. Buddha Dharma Education Association Inc. (1981)
2. Kulkarni, U., Meena, S.M., Gurlahosur, S.V., Mudengudi, U.: Classification of cultural heritage sites using transfer learning. In: IEEE Fifth International Conference on Multimedia Big Data (BigMM), 11–13 September 2019, pp. 391–397 (2019)
3. Karpathy, A., Li, F.: Deep visual-semantic alignments for generating image descriptions. In: Proceedings of the 2015 IEEE Conference on Computer Vision and Pattern Recognition, VPR 2015, Boston, MA, USA, 7–12 June 2015, pp. 3128–3137 (2015). https://doi.org/10.1109/CVPR201572989328
4. Farhadi, A., et al.: Every picture tells a story: generating sentences from images. In: Daniilidis, K., Maragos, P., Paragios, N. (eds.) ECCV 2010. LNCS, vol. 6314, pp. 15–29. Springer, Heidelberg (2010). https://doi.org/10.1007/978-3-642-15561-1_2
5. Zaremba, W., Sutskever, I., Vinyals, O.: Recurrent neural network regularization. CoRR arXiv: 14092329 (2014)
6. Lee, O.-J., Jung, J.E.: Sequence clustering-based automated rule generation for adaptive complex event processing. Futur. Gener. Comput. Syst. **66**, 100–1099 (2017)
7. Socher, R., Karpathy, A., Le, Q.V., Manning, C.D., Ng, A.Y.: Grounded compositional semantics for finding and describing images with sentences. Trans. Assoc. Comput. Linguist. **2**(2014), 207–218 (2014)
8. Kulikarnratchai, P., Chitsoput, O.: Image retrieval using color histogram in HSV color sampler. In: 29th Electrical Engineering Symposium (EECON-29), pp. 1029–1032 (2006)

9. Sangswang, A.: Image search by histogram comparison using vector models. In: The 2nd National Conferences Benjamit Academic, 29 May 2012 (2012)

10. Kerdsantier, P., Sodanil, M.: Color retrieval system with color histogram using fuzzy set theory. In: The 6th National Conference on Computing and Information Technology (2010)

11. Facktong, P.: Retrieval of digital amulets by extraction techniques and nearest neighbors. J. Inf. Technol. J. **9**(2) (2013)

12. https://pixabay.com/images/search/sukhothai%20historical%20park/

Power Allocation for Sum Rate Maximization of Uplink Massive MIMO System with Maximum Ratio Combining

Fuyuan Liu[1] , Xiangbin Yu[1,2(✉)] , Hui Wang[1], MingLu Li[1], and Jiawei Bai[1]

[1] College of Electronic and Information Engineering, Nanjing University of Aeronautics
and Astronautics, Nanjing 210016, China
yxb_xwy@hotmail.com

[2] Key Laboratory of Wireless Sensor Network and Communication, Shanghai Institute
of Microsystem and Information Technology, Chinese Academy of Sciences, Shanghai, China

Abstract. This paper investigates the sum rate optimization of uplink massive multiple-input multiple-output (MIMO) system with imperfect channel state information (CSI) and maximum ratio combining (MRC) under the constraints of maximum power and minimum rate, and power allocation (PA) schemes are developed to improve the rate. With the help of concave-convex procedure (CCCP) method, a near-optimal PA scheme is proposed to transform the no-concave maximization problem into a concave one. Considering that both small-scale and large-scale fading information are required in near-optimal PA scheme, which will result in high complexity, a suboptimal PA scheme under the case of large number of receive antennas is presented, which only needs large-scale fading information without real-time estimation and frequent feedback. Moreover, it has the rate close to that of near-optimal scheme but with lower complexity. Simulation results show that the sum rate obtained by the near-optimal PA scheme can match that offered by the benchmark scheme well, and the suboptimal scheme can obtain the rate close to that of near-optimal scheme, especially for large number of receive antennas, which verifies the effectiveness of the proposed schemes.

Keywords: Massive MIMO · Power allocation · Sum rate · Imperfect CSI · Maximum ratio combining

1 Introduction

The use of multiple-input multiple-output (MIMO) systems can improve the system capacity without increasing the bandwidth and antenna transmission power. Especially for massive MIMO systems where the base station (BS) is equipped with a large number of antennas, the improvement of system capacity is more obvious [1–3]. It has been shown that the interference among the users can be eliminated for massive MIMO system. Similarly, irrelevant noise can also be eliminated, and the small-scale fading effects are averaged out [4]. Meanwhile, linear detectors on uplink transmission, such as

X. Jiang (Ed.): MLICOM 2021, LNICST 438, pp. 28–37, 2022.
https://doi.org/10.1007/978-3-031-04409-0_4

maximum ratio combining (MRC) detectors and zero-forcing (ZF) detectors, have near-optimal performance in massive MIMO systems. Due to the above advantages, massive MIMO systems are widely studied for fifth generation mobile communication [5].

As an important performance metric in massive MIMO system, sum rate has been widely studied. Reference [6] derived the lower bounds of achievable uplink rate with Jensen's inequality for the massive MIMO system using three linear detection methods. In [7], a power control scheme is developed to maximize the ergodic rate of massive MIMO system with MRC method. The authors of [11] considered the sum rate max-imization problem for cell-free massive MIMO system with ZF method, which sub-jected to the constraints of transmit power and quality of service requirements, e.g., minimum rate requirements. Furthermore, a downlink sum rate maximization problem for co-located massive MIMO system with perfect channel state information (CSI) was considered in [8]. In [9], a power allocation (PA) scheme with the constraints of training duration and the data signal power was formulated to maximize multicell MIMO system rate with MRC receivers. Motivated by the above-mentioned literature, we consider the uplink sum rate maximization problem of co-located massive MIMO under both max-imum power and minimum rate constraints in this paper. The major contributions are listed as follows:

- With imperfect CSI and MRC method, we formulate a sum rate maximization prob-lem of uplink massive MIMO system under both maximum power and minimum rate constraints. With the help of concave-convex procedure (CCCP) method, a near-optimal PA scheme is developed to solve the optimization problem, which can obtain the almost same sum rate by using CVX software but with lower complexity.
- Considering that both small-scale and large-scale fading information are required in near-optimal PA scheme, a low-complexity suboptimal PA scheme is proposed in terms of the characteristics of massive MIMO system (large BS antenna number). This scheme needs large-scale information only, and thus it has lower complexity since timely estimation and frequent feedback of CSI are avoided. Moreover, it has the rate close to that of near-optimal scheme, especially for large receive antenna.

2   System Model

2.1   Uplink Transmission

Here, an uplink single cell massive MIMO system with BS equipped with N antennas is considered. Meanwhile, K single antenna users are uniformly distributed in the cell. The $N \times 1$ received signal vector at BS is

$$\mathbf{y} = \mathbf{G}\mathbf{P}^{1/2}\mathbf{x} + \mathbf{z},\qquad(1)$$

where $\mathbf{G}$ is a $N \times K$ channel matrix with the channel coefficient $g_{nk} = [\mathbf{G}]_{nk}$ between the n-th antenna of BS and the k-th user; $\mathbf{P} = diag\{p_1, ..., p_K\}$ is a transmission power matrix, whose k-th diagonal element represents the k-th user's transmission power. In addition, $\mathbf{x} = [x_1, x_2, ..., x_K]^T$ represents the signal vector transmitted by the K users; $\mathbf{z} \sim \mathcal{CN}(0, \sigma_z^2\mathbf{I}_N)$ is a $N \times 1$ noise vector, where $\mathcal{CN}(0, \mathbf{R})$ denotes the complex

Gaussian distribution with zero-mean and covariance matrix $\mathbf{R}$. Then, the channel coefficient g_{nk} is defined as

$$g_{nk} = \sqrt{\beta_k} h_{nk} \tag{2}$$

where h_{nk} is zero-mean and unit variance Gaussian random variable representing the small-scale fading and β_k represents large-scale fading. As a result, the channel matrix $\mathbf{G}$ is written as

$$\mathbf{G} = \mathbf{H}\mathbf{D}^{1/2}, \tag{3}$$

where $\mathbf{H}$ is the $N \times K$ fast fading matrix and $\mathbf{D} = diag\{\beta_1, ..., \beta_K\}$ is the $K \times K$ large-scale fading matrix.

2.2 Uplink Training

In practice, the uplink training is used to obtain the CSI. We assume that this paper has the same uplink training process as [8]. The received signal vector is

$$\mathbf{Y}_p = \sqrt{\tau}\mathbf{G}\boldsymbol{\Phi}^T + \mathbf{Z}, \tag{4}$$

where $\boldsymbol{\Phi}$ denotes the pilot sequences matrix, τ is a coefficient related to the length of the pilot sequences and the pilot transmit power and $\mathbf{Z} \sim \mathcal{CN}(0, \sigma_z^2 \mathbf{I}_N)$. After minimum mean-square error (MMSE) estimation at BS, the estimation of channel is shown as

$$\hat{\mathbf{G}} = \left(\mathbf{G} + \frac{1}{\sqrt{\tau}}\mathbf{Z}\boldsymbol{\Phi}^*\right)\left(\frac{\sigma_z^2}{\tau}\mathbf{D}^{-1} + \mathbf{I}_K\right)^{-1}, \tag{5}$$

Let $\mathbf{E} = [\mathbf{e}_1, \cdots, \mathbf{e}_K]$ be the channel estimation error. Then we have

$$\hat{\mathbf{G}} = \mathbf{G} + \mathbf{E}, \tag{6}$$

As we know, $\mathbf{E}$ is independent of $\hat{\mathbf{G}}$ after MMSE estimation. In addition, we assume $\hat{\mathbf{g}}_k$ and $\mathbf{e}_k$ are the k-th column of $\hat{\mathbf{G}}$ and $\mathbf{E}$, respectively. Thus we have $\mathbf{e}_k \sim \mathcal{CN}\left(0, \varepsilon_k^2 \mathbf{I}_N\right)$ and $\hat{\mathbf{g}}_k \sim \mathcal{CN}\left(0, \delta_k^2 \mathbf{I}_N\right)$, where $\varepsilon_k^2 = \sigma_z^2 \beta_k / \left(\tau \beta_k + \sigma_z^2\right)$ and $\delta_k^2 = \tau \beta_k^2 / \left(\tau \beta_k + \sigma_z^2\right)$.

2.3 Achievable Uplink Rate with MRC

According to MRC method, the received signal of k-th user is given by

$$r_k = \hat{\mathbf{g}}_k^H \hat{\mathbf{g}}_k p_k^{1/2} x_k + \hat{\mathbf{g}}_k^H \sum_{i=1, i\neq k}^{K} \hat{\mathbf{g}}_i p_i^{1/2} x_i - \hat{\mathbf{g}}_k^H \sum_{i=1}^{K} \mathbf{e}_i p_i^{1/2} x_i + \hat{\mathbf{g}}_k^H \mathbf{z}, \tag{7}$$

With (7), the k-th user's effective SINR is derived as

$$\rho_k = \frac{p_k \|\hat{\mathbf{g}}_k\|^4}{\sum\limits_{i=1, i\neq k}^{K} p_i \left|\hat{\mathbf{g}}_k^H \hat{\mathbf{g}}_i\right|^2 + \|\hat{\mathbf{g}}_k^H\|^2 \sum\limits_{i=1}^{K} p_i \varepsilon_i^2 + \|\hat{\mathbf{g}}_k^H\|^2 \sigma_z^2}, \tag{8}$$

With the above analysis, we can obtain the k-th user's rate as follows

$$R_k = \log_2 \left(1 + \frac{p_k \|\hat{\mathbf{g}}_k\|^4}{\sum\limits_{i=1, i \neq k}^{K} p_i \left|\hat{\mathbf{g}}_k^H \hat{\mathbf{g}}_i\right|^2 + \|\hat{\mathbf{g}}_k\|^2 \sum\limits_{i=1}^{K} p_i \varepsilon_i^2 + \|\hat{\mathbf{g}}_k\|^2 \sigma_z^2} \right), \tag{9}$$

3 Problem Formulation

In this section, we will introduce two effective PA schemes in term of solving the uplink sum rate maximization problem of massive MIMO. From the above analysis, we have a sum rate maximization problem subject to the constraints of maximum power and minimum rate as follows

$$\max_{\mathbf{P}} \eta_{SE}(\mathbf{p}) = \sum_{k=1}^{K} \log_2 \left(1 + \frac{p_k \|\hat{\mathbf{g}}_k\|^4}{\sum\limits_{i=1, i \neq k}^{K} p_i \left|\hat{\mathbf{g}}_k^H \hat{\mathbf{g}}_i\right|^2 + \|\hat{\mathbf{g}}_k\|^2 \sum\limits_{i=1}^{K} p_i \varepsilon_i^2 + \|\hat{\mathbf{g}}_k\|^2 \sigma_z^2} \right) \tag{10}$$

$$s.t. \, 0 \leq p_k \leq P_{\max}, R_k \geq R_{\min}, \forall k \in \{1, 2, ..., K\},$$

To begin with, we transform the minimum rate constraints $R_k \geq R_{\min}, \forall k \in \{1, 2, ..., K\}$ into

$$p_k \geq \frac{\left(2^{R_{\min}} - 1\right) \left[\sum\limits_{i=1, i \neq k}^{K} p_i \left(\left|\hat{\mathbf{g}}_k^H \hat{\mathbf{g}}_i\right|^2 + \|\hat{\mathbf{g}}_k\|^2 \varepsilon_i^2 \right) + \|\hat{\mathbf{g}}_k\|^2 \sigma_z^2 \right]}{\|\hat{\mathbf{g}}_k\|^4 - \left(2^{R_{\min}} - 1\right) \|\hat{\mathbf{g}}_k\|^2 \varepsilon_k^2} \tag{11}$$

where $\|\hat{\mathbf{g}}_k\|^2 - \left(2^{R_{\min}} - 1\right) \varepsilon_k^2 > 0$ will be satisfied. When $y \neq k$, $R_y \geq R_{\min}$ can be transformed into

$$p_k \leq \frac{p_y \|\hat{\mathbf{g}}_y\|^4 - \left(2^{R_{\min}} - 1\right) \left(\sum\limits_{i=1, i \neq y, i \neq k}^{K} p_i \left|\hat{\mathbf{g}}_y^H \hat{\mathbf{g}}_i\right|^2 + \|\hat{\mathbf{g}}_y\|^2 \sum\limits_{i=1, i \neq k}^{K} p_i \varepsilon_i^2 + \|\hat{\mathbf{g}}_y\|^2 \sigma_z^2 \right)}{\left(2^{R_{\min}} - 1\right) \left(\left|\hat{\mathbf{g}}_y^H \hat{\mathbf{g}}_k\right|^2 + \|\hat{\mathbf{g}}_y\|^2 \varepsilon_k^2 \right)} \tag{12}$$

According to the analysis above, with (11) and (12), we define LB_k and UB_k to be the lower and upper bounds of p_k derived from the rate constraints, respectively. Thus, the maximum power and minimum rate constraints in (10) can be changed into

$$LB_k^{near-op} \leq p_k \leq UB_k^{near-op}, \forall k \in \{1, 2, ..., K\} \tag{13}$$

where $UB_k^{near-op} = \min\left(\{x \,|\, x = UB_k, \forall y \in \{1, 2, ..., K\} \setminus k\}, P_{\max}\right)$ and $LB_k^{near-op} = LB_k$. Next, we will introduce a near-optimal PA algorithm with the help of CCCP method to solve the maximization problem (10). Namely, the transformation of objective function in (10) with CCCP method is derived as

$$f(\mathbf{p}) = \sum_{k=1}^{K} \log_2 \left(\sum_{i=1,i\neq k}^{K} p_i |\hat{\mathbf{g}}_k^H \hat{\mathbf{g}}_i|^2 + \|\hat{\mathbf{g}}_k\|^2 \sum_{i=1}^{K} p_i \varepsilon_i^2 + \|\hat{\mathbf{g}}_k\|^2 \sigma_z^2 + p_k \|\hat{\mathbf{g}}_k\|^4 \right)$$

$$- \sum_{k=1}^{K} \log_2 \left(\sum_{i=1,i\neq k}^{K} p_i |\hat{\mathbf{g}}_k^H \hat{\mathbf{g}}_i|^2 + \|\hat{\mathbf{g}}_k\|^2 \sum_{i=1}^{K} p_i \varepsilon_i^2 + \|\hat{\mathbf{g}}_k\|^2 \sigma_z^2 \right)$$

$$= f_1(\mathbf{p}) - f_2(\mathbf{p})$$

$$(14)$$

Based on the first-order Taylor expansion $f_2(\mathbf{p}) \simeq f_2(\mathbf{p}_0) + (\mathbf{p} - \mathbf{p}_0)^T \nabla f_2(\mathbf{p}_0)$, where the gradient of $f_2(\mathbf{p})$ at initial value $\mathbf{p}_0$ is defined as $\nabla f_2(\mathbf{p}_0)$ and and $\mathbf{p}_0$ is initial value, we transform the objective function (14) into a concave one. Therefore, the maximization problem (10) can be transformed into

$$\max_{\mathbf{P}} \quad J_1 = f_1(\mathbf{p}) - f_2(\mathbf{p}_0) - (\mathbf{p} - \mathbf{p}_0)^T \nabla f_2(\mathbf{p}_0)$$
$$s.t. \quad LB_k^{near-op} \leq p_k \leq UB_k^{near-op}, \forall k \in \{1, 2, ..., K\}$$

$$(15)$$

With the above analysis, CVX software can be used to get the optimal value of sum rate [12]. However, there is a particularly high cost of complexity because of low computational efficiency. Therefore, we use the block-coordinate decent (BCD) method [10] to replace the CVX method. The derivative of J_1 with respect to (w.r.t.) p_k is

$$\frac{\partial J_1}{\partial p_k} = \frac{\|\hat{\mathbf{g}}_k\|^2 \varepsilon_m^2 + \|\hat{\mathbf{g}}_k\|^4}{\ln 2 \left(p_k \|\hat{\mathbf{g}}_k\|^4 + \sum_{i=1,i\neq k}^{K} p_i |\hat{\mathbf{g}}_k^H \hat{\mathbf{g}}_i|^2 + \|\hat{\mathbf{g}}_k\|^2 \sum_{i=1}^{K} p_i \varepsilon_i^2 + \|\hat{\mathbf{g}}_k\|^2 \sigma_z^2 \right)}$$

$$+ \sum_{s=1,s\neq k}^{K} \frac{|\hat{\mathbf{g}}_s^H \hat{\mathbf{g}}_k|^2 + \|\hat{\mathbf{g}}_s\|^2 \varepsilon_k^2}{\ln 2 \left(p_s \|\hat{\mathbf{g}}_s\|^4 + \sum_{i=1,i\neq s}^{K} p_i |\hat{\mathbf{g}}_s^H \hat{\mathbf{g}}_i|^2 + \|\hat{\mathbf{g}}_s\|^2 \sum_{i=1}^{K} p_i \varepsilon_i^2 + \|\hat{\mathbf{g}}_s\|^2 \sigma_z^2 \right)}$$

$$- \frac{\|\hat{\mathbf{g}}_k\|^2 \varepsilon_k^2}{\ln 2 \left(\sum_{i=1,i\neq k}^{K} p_{0,i} |\hat{\mathbf{g}}_m^H \hat{\mathbf{g}}_i|^2 + \|\hat{\mathbf{g}}_k\|^2 \sum_{i=1}^{K} p_{0,i} \varepsilon_i^2 + \|\hat{\mathbf{g}}_k\|^2 \sigma_z^2 \right)}$$

$$- \sum_{s=1,s\neq k}^{K} \frac{|\hat{\mathbf{g}}_s^H \hat{\mathbf{g}}_k|^2 + \|\hat{\mathbf{g}}_s\|^2 \varepsilon_k^2}{\ln 2 \left(\sum_{i=1,i\neq s}^{K} p_{0,i} |\hat{\mathbf{g}}_s^H \hat{\mathbf{g}}_i|^2 + \|\hat{\mathbf{g}}_s\|^2 \sum_{i=1}^{K} p_{0,i} \varepsilon_i^2 + \|\hat{\mathbf{g}}_s\|^2 \sigma_z^2 \right)}$$

$$(16)$$

With (13) and (16), the optimal PA of user k is obtained by

$$p_{near-op,k} = \begin{cases} LB_k^{near-op}, & \frac{\partial J_1}{\partial p_k}\Big|_{p_k=LB_k^{near-op}} \leq 0 \\ UB_k^{near-op}, & \frac{\partial J_1}{\partial p_k}\Big|_{p_k=UB_k^{near-op}} \geq 0 \\ p_{near-op,k}^*, & otherwise \end{cases}$$

$$(17)$$

where $p_{near-op,k}^*$ is the zero point of $\partial J_1 / \partial p_k = 0$ obtained with the bisection method. The proposed sum rate optimization scheme is shown as Algorithm 1.

Algorithm 1. Near-optimal PA Algorithm

1: **Initialize** tolerances $\nu > 0$, iterative index $l = 0$ and initial point $\mathbf{p}_0^{(l)}$
2: **repeat**
3:     $l = l + 1$
4:     **Initialize** tolerances $\eta > 0$, iterative index $\mu = 0$ and iterative point $\mathbf{p}^{(\mu)}$
5:     **repeat**
6:         $\mu = \mu + 1$
7:         Compute $\mathbf{p}^{(\mu)} = \mathbf{p}_{near-op}$ via (17)
8:     **until** $\left\| \mathbf{p}^{(\mu)} - \mathbf{p}^{(\mu-1)} \right\| \leq \eta$
9:     Update $\mathbf{p}_0^{(l)} = \mathbf{p}^{(\mu)}$
10: **until** $\left\| \mathbf{p}_0^{(l)} - \mathbf{p}_0^{(l-1)} \right\| \leq \nu$

Meanwhile, we get the initial value point that satisfies the BCD algorithm by solving a minimum rate maximization problem. Although the near-optimal PA scheme has less complexity compared with the CVX scheme, it is related to small-scale and large-scale fading information, which requires CSI feedback frequently. Therefore, a suboptimal PA scheme only depending on the large-scale fading information is developed. The difference from the near-optimal scheme is that the latter doesn't require frequent CSI feedback, which means the lower complexity of suboptimal scheme.

We consider the case of N is very large for uplink massive MIMO, an approximate expression of the objective function in problem (10) is shows as

$$\tilde{\eta}_{SE} = \sum_{k=1}^{K} \log_2 \left(1 + \frac{N p_k \delta_k^2}{\sum\limits_{i=1}^{K} p_i \varepsilon_i^2 + \sigma_z^2} \right) \tag{18}$$

With the similar CCCP transformation process, we get the approximate sum rate optimization problem as follows

$$\begin{aligned} \max_{\mathbf{P}} \quad & J_2 = g_1(\mathbf{p}) - g_2(\mathbf{p}_0) - (\mathbf{p} - \mathbf{p}_0)^T \nabla g_2(\mathbf{p}_0) \\ s.t. \quad & LB_k^{sub-op} \leq p_k \leq UB_k^{sub-op}, \forall k \in \{1, 2, ..., K\} \end{aligned} \tag{19}$$

Importantly, the approximation is close to the original problem (10) only when N is very large. Therefore, there will be obvious performance gap of sum rate between the two proposed PA schemes when N is not large enough, but similar sum rate for very large N. According to (19), the derivative of J_2 w.r.t. y_k is

$$\begin{aligned} \frac{\partial J_2}{\partial p_k} = & \frac{1}{\ln 2} \frac{N\delta_k^2 + \varepsilon_k^2}{N p_k \delta_k^2 + (\sigma_z^2 + \sum_{i=1}^{K} p_i \varepsilon_i^2)} \\ & + \frac{1}{\ln 2} \sum_{i=1, i \neq k}^{K} \frac{\varepsilon_k^2}{N p_i \delta_i^2 + (\sigma_z^2 + \sum_{m=1}^{K} p_m \varepsilon_m^2)} \\ & - \frac{1}{\ln 2} \frac{K \varepsilon_k^2}{\sigma_z^2 + \sum_{i=1}^{K} p_{0,i} \varepsilon_i^2} \end{aligned} \tag{20}$$

Based on BCD method, the suboptimal PA of the k-th user for the problem (10) is shown as

$$p_{sub-op,k} = \begin{cases} LB_k^{sub-op}, & \left.\frac{\partial J_2}{\partial p_k}\right|_{p_k=LB_k^{sub-op}} \leq 0 \\ UB_k^{sub-op}, & \left.\frac{\partial J_2}{\partial p_k}\right|_{p_k=UB_k^{sub-op}} \geq 0 \\ p_{sub-op,k}^*, otherwise \end{cases}, \tag{21}$$

where $p_{sub-op,k}^*$ is the zero point of $\partial J_2/\partial p_k = 0$ obtained with the bisection method. Similarly, the optimal solution of suboptimal PA scheme can be obtained by Algorithm 1.

4   Simulation Results

In this section, the simulation for the proposed PA schemes of the uplink massive MIMO systems with MRC method and imperfect CSI is provided. In order to verify the accuracy of the two schemes, we use the CVX method as a benchmark. This paper considers the case of circle cellular with a radius of 1000 m and $K = 5$ uniformly distributed users. We assume that the reference distance is $d_h = 100$ m and define $\beta_k = s_k/(d_k/d_h)^v$ as the large-scale fading, where s_k is modeled as log-normal RV with a standard deviation $\sigma = 8$ dB, d_k denotes the distance between the k-th user and the BS and $v = 3.8$ represents the path lose exponent. In the following simulation results, the noise power σ_z^2 is set as -104 dBm.

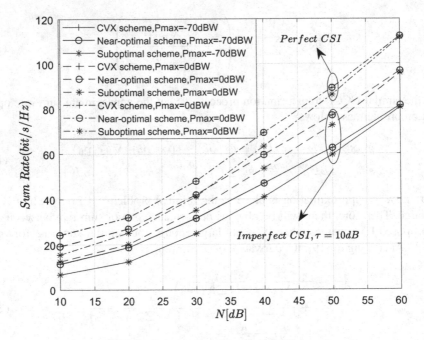

Fig. 1. Sum rate for different τ and $P_{\max}$.

Figure 1 shows the sum rate comparison of the system with different uplink training coefficients τ and maximum power $P_{\max}$ for $R_{\min} = 2$ bit/s/Hz. It can be seen that the sum rate obtained by near-optimal PA scheme always perfectly match that offered by benchmark scheme as N increases. Meanwhile, the sum rate gap between near-optimal scheme and suboptimal scheme gradually decreases as N increases and the two schemes have similar performance of $N = 60$ dB, which is consistent with the analysis in Sect. 3. In addition, the sum rate of $\tau = 10$ dB is lower than that of perfect CSI when $P_{\max} = 0$ dBW. As τ increases, the error variances gradually decreases, which leads to the higher sum rate. As shown in Fig. 1, the sum rate of $P_{\max} = -70$ dBW is lower than that of $P_{\max} = 0$ dBW when $\tau = 10$ dB. The above results verify the feasibility of the two proposed PA schemes.

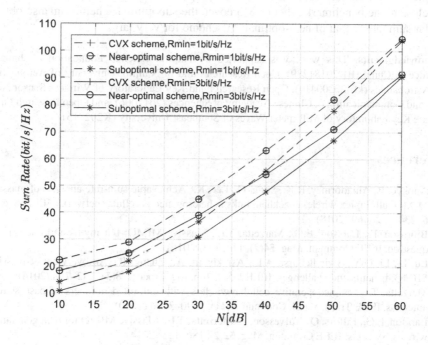

Fig. 2. Sum rate for different $R_{\min}$

Figure 2 presents the sum rate comparison of the system with different rate constraints $R_{\min}$, where $\tau = 10$ dB and $P_{\max} = 0$ dBW. From Fig. 2, the results similar to Fig. 1 is found. Namely, the near-optimal scheme has almost the same rate as the benchmark scheme, and the suboptimal scheme also obtain the rate near to that of near-optimal scheme with the increase of N. Besides, the sum rate under the constraint of $R_{\min} = 3$ bit/s/Hz is lower than that of $R_{\min} = 1$ bit/s/Hz, as expected. This is because when rate constraint is large, the possibility of the system meeting the rate requirement will be greatly decreased. Correspondingly, the system communication will be suspended. As a result, the sum rate will become smaller.

5 Conclusion

We have investigated the sum rate of uplink massive MIMO with MRC and imperfect CSI. Under the constraints of minimum rate and maximum transmit power, we formulate a non-convex maximization problem of sum rate. Then, using the CCCP method, a near-optimal PA scheme is proposed to tackle the problem, and resultant sum rate is almost the same as that offered by the benchmark scheme. Considering that this scheme needs both small-scale and large-scale fading information, a low-complexity suboptimal scheme is developed based on the asymptotic analysis under large N. This suboptimal scheme only requires large-scale information, which avoids frequent feedback and real-time estimation of small-scale information. Thus, the suboptimal scheme has lower complexity. Simulation results show that the proposed schemes are valid, and have the rate close to the benchmark scheme. Moreover, the suboptimal scheme can also obtain similar sum rate to that of near-optimal PA scheme for very large N.

Acknowledgments. This work was supported by Natural Science Foundation of Jiangsu Province in China (BK20181289), Open Research Fund of Nanjing University of Aeronautics and Astronautics (kfjj20200414), Open Research Fund Key Laboratory of Wireless Sensor Network and Communication of Chinese Academy of Sciences (2017006), and Open Research Fund of State Key Laboratory of Millimeter Waves of Southeast University (K202215).

References

1. Anokye, P., Ahiadormey, R.K., Song, C., Lee, K.: Achievable sum-rate analysis of massive MIMO full-duplex wireless backhaul links in heterogeneous cellular networks. IEEE Access **6**, 23456–23469 (2018)
2. Björnson, E., Larsson, E.G., Marzetta, T.L.: Massive MIMO: ten myths and one critical question. IEEE Commun. Mag. **54**(2), 114–123 (2016)
3. Lu, L., Li, G.Y., Swindlehurst, A.L., Ashikhmin, A., Zhang, R.: An overview of massive MIMO: benefits and challenges. IEEE J. Sel. Top. Sig. Process. **8**(5), 742–758 (2014)
4. Marzetta, T.L.: Noncooperative cellular wireless with unlimited numbers of base station antennas. IEEE Trans. Wirel. Commun. **9**(11), 3590–3600 (2010)
5. Larsson, E.G., Edfors, O., Tufvesson, F., Marzetta, T.L.: Massive MIMO for next generation wireless systems. IEEE Commun. Mag. **52**(2), 186–195 (2014)
6. Ngo, H.Q., Larsson, E.G., Marzetta, T.L.: Energy and spectral efficiency of very large multiuser MIMO systems. IEEE Trans. Commun. **61**(4), 1436–1449 (2013)
7. Cheng, H.V., Björnson, E., Larsson, E.G.: Uplink pilot and data power control for single cell massive MIMO systems with MRC. In: IEEE International Symposium on Wireless Communication Systems (ISWCS), pp. 396–400 (2015)
8. Li, M., Wang, T., Wang, S.: Online power allocation for sum rate maximization in TDD massive MIMO systems. In: IEEE Global Communications Conference (GLOBECOM), pp. 1–6 (2019)
9. Sadeghi, M., Yuen, C., Chew, Y.H.: Sum rate maximization for uplink distributed massive MIMO systems with limited backhaul capacity. In: IEEE Globecom Workshops (GC Wkshps), pp. 308–313 (2014)
10. Tseng, P., Yun, S.: Block-coordinate gradient descent method for linearly constrained nonsmooth separable optimization. J. Optim. Theory Appl. **140**, 513–535 (2009). https://doi.org/10.1007/s10957-008-9458-3

11. Bai, X., Zhou, L., Zhou, M., Qiao, X., Zhang, Y., Yang, L.: Sum-rate maximization in cell-free massive MIMO with low-resolution ADCs and ZF receiver. In: IEEE International Conference on Communication Technology (ICCT), pp. 259–263 (2020)
12. Grant, M., Boyd, S.: CVX: MATLAB software for disciplined convex programming, version 2.2, January 2020. http://cvxr.com/cvx

Research on Indoor Passive Location Based on LoRa Fingerprint

Heng Wang[1], Yuzhen Chen[1], Qingheng Zhang[1], Shifan Zhang[1], Haibo Ye[1,3,4(✉)],
and Xuan-Song Li[2,3]

[1] School of Computer Science and Technology, Nanjing University of Aeronautics and
Astronautics, Nanjing, Jiangsu, China
{chenyz,zhangqh,yhb}@nuaa.edu.cn
[2] School of Computer Science and Engineering, Nanjing University of Science and Technology,
Nanjing 210094, China
[3] State Key Laboratory for Novel Software Technology, Nanjing University, Nanjing,
People's Republic of China
[4] MIIT Key Laboratory of Pattern Analysis and Machine Intelligence, Nanjing, China

Abstract. Indoor positioning based on signal fingerprint has always been a hot research topic. But most research requires the object or person to be positioned to carry a positioning device, which is not applicable in some special scenarios. This paper selects LoRa (Long Range) as the research target and proposes an indoor passive positioning system based on LoRa fingerprint. We design and implement the signal sent from the LoRa node devices to the LoRa gateway device and get the RSSI of the nodes, also send it to the proxy server for receiving and processing. In the data processing stage, the difference-limiting filtering algorithm is used to eliminate abnormal data, and the GaussianNB (Gaussian-Naive Bayes) algorithm is used to learn and train the model. Through experiments, the accuracy rates of the two-class and multi-class prediction in the range of 3m are 97.1% and 95.5%, respectively, which verifies the feasibility of applying LoRa signal to indoor passive positioning.

Keywords: LoRa · RSSI · Passive positioning · GaussianNB

1 Introduction

In the past ten years, with the vigorous development of the Internet of Things (IoT) industry, it has also promoted the progress of network and communication technology. Compared with other communication technologies, LPWAN (Low-Power Wide-Area Network) is a technology specifically for IoT application [1]. It transmits information at a lower bit rate, but can transmit longer distance with ultra-low power consumption [2]. At present, common LPWAN technologies include LoRa (Long Range), Sigfox, NWave, etc. Among them, LoRa technology has been widely studied by scholars once it comes out due to its long transmission distance, low power consumption, and high receiving sensitivity [3].

X. Jiang (Ed.): MLICOM 2021, LNICST 438, pp. 38–47, 2022.
https://doi.org/10.1007/978-3-031-04409-0_5

The article [4] uses active positioning to study the propagation model of LoRa signals in an indoor environment, experiments show that LoRa signals can cover most areas of a 6-story reinforced concrete building. Tang *et al.* [5] compares the positioning accuracy of traditional Wi-Fi and LoRa technologies in three different indoor environments (indoor short-distance areas, indoor rectangular wide areas, and indoor rectangular narrow areas). For short-distance indoor areas Wi-Fi and LoRa technology positioning error is about 2–4 m, but in wide and narrow indoor areas, limited by the propagation distance of Wi-Fi signals, the advantages of using LoRa technology for indoor positioning are more obvious. The article [6] proposes a fingerprint algorithm based on LoRa signal, which uses three different difference algorithms to fingerprint the collected data and uses the method of probability theory to estimate the position. Experiments show that the three different algorithms in the outdoor environment are effective and the average positioning accuracy is 28.8 m.

In these studies, the commonly used active positioning method requires the terminal equipment to be placed in a fixed position in advance to receive signals, and the node equipment carried by the positioned object is used to send signals. The terminal equipment receives the signal and calculates the RSSI of the node equipment at this time, then use fingerprint library or propagation distance model to process data and predict location [7]. This method requires the active cooperation of the located object to collect the corresponding data, but in some cases it is not the case. For example, a special area of a large museum or a prison where prohibit people from entering, and illegal intruders do not carry any equipment to be located, but intrusion detection is needed for this area. This paper proposes an indoor passive positioning method based on LoRa technology, the main idea of the method is: LoRa signals are distributed in the indoor space, and the presence or absence of personnel has different effects on the signal, resulting in different changes in the RSSI of different node equipment. Based on this, judge whether there is an intrusion of personnel in a certain area, and further speculate according to the change low of RSSI location information of the intruder.

The structure of this article is as follow. Section 1 gives a brief introduction to the positioning technology, and proposes the experimental plan of this article based on the previous active positioning research. Section 2 introduces the background of LoRa technology and the system built in this paper. Section 3 mainly conducts data preprocessing and model training. Section 4 verifies the feasibility of the scheme through experiments. Finally, it summarizes the work done in this paper and looks forward to the future direction of improvement.

2 Background

This section mainly introduces the composition of LoRa technology and LoRa-based indoor passive positioning system.

2.1 LoRa Technology

In 2013, Semtech released a new data transmission method below 1 GHz-LoRa technology for the industry. LoRa technology mainly includes three layers, from top to bottom are application layer, MAC layer and physical layer [8], as shown in Fig. 1. This technology is deployed in unlicensed frequency bands (i.e. ISM frequency bands). Due to the different use of ISM frequency bands by countries and regions, the allocation of LoRa frequency bands in each region is also different. However, LoRa devices produced by different manufactures can access each other as long as they follow the LoRaWAN protocol (the protocol used by LoRa technology at the MAC layer), so that LoRa node devices and terminal devices can safely communicate in two ways, moreover, this also gives people who use Internet of Things devices greater operation authority [9].

2.2 LoRa-Based Indoor Passive Positioning System

The system mainly includes three parts: LoRa node equipment, LoRa gateway equipment and network server, and its network architecture is shown in Fig. 2.

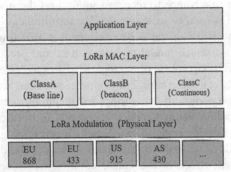

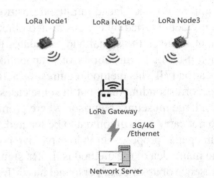

Fig. 1. LoRa technology layer structure

Fig. 2. Indoor passive positioning system architecture

Table 1. Signal frame structure sent by LoRa node device

LoRa node device id: *id1*	Node sending signal frame time: *time1*

Table 2. Signal frame structure sent by LoRa gateway device to network server

Data frame index: *index*	LoRa node device id: *id2*	Gateway sending time: *time2*	LoRa node RSSI: *rssi*

2.2.1 LoRa Node Equipment

The LoRa node device at a fixed location sends an uplink signal frame to the LoRa gateway device [10], the data frame structure is shown in Table 1.

2.2.2 LoRa Gateway Equipment

The LoRa gateway device, which is also fixed at a certain location, analyzes after receiving the uplink signal frame sent by the LoRa node device. Usually, after receiving the signal, the LoRa gateway will also send a downlink signal frame to the LoRa node device, but the frame is only a reply to the node device, and it does not have much meaning. We need to send a data frame containing RSSI information of the LoRa node from the LoRa gateway device to the network server, and the data frame structure is shown in Table 2.

Where *index* is the sequence number of the data frame sent, *id2* is used to distinguish different LoRa node devices, *time2* is the time when the LoRa gateway sends the signal frame to the network server, and *rssi* is the RSSI corresponding to the node.

Standard TCP/IP protocol (such as 3G, 4G, Ethernet) can be used to transmit data from the gateway to the network server. This paper uses the MQTT (Message Queuing Telemetry Transport) protocol, which is a message transmission protocol based on the Publish/Subscribe paradigm and works on the standard TCP/IP protocol suite. It only needs to use very few codes and occupy limited bandwidth to provide instant and reliable data transmission services for remotely connected devices. Because of its low power consumption and less bandwidth, it is widely used in IoT devices.

2.2.3 Network Server

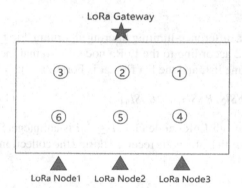

Fig. 3. Experimental site distribution map

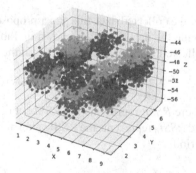

Fig. 4. RSSI distribution map of different LoRa nodes at different locations

This paper uses Apache-Apollo proxy server as the network server in the system. The proxy server is developed from ActiveMQ and can support multiple protocol such as MQTT, STOMP, SSL, etc., so data frames can be sent to the proxy server through the LoRa gateway. When the LoRa gateway uses the MQTT protocol to send data frames, it is necessary to create a unique topic and send all the data to be collected to this topic. On the proxy server side, you can view the publishers and subscribers under the topic, which serves as a message relay station to complete the push of messages from publisher to subscriber. Use Java to write a listener, responsible for receiving messages published under a topic from the proxy server.

3   Data Collection and Processing

3.1   Data Collection

The experiment in this paper is carried out in a rectangular indoor area of 10 m * 8 m. The distribution of LoRa nodes and gateway device is shown in Fig 3. The red five-pointed start is the location of the LoRa gateway, the blue triangle is the location of the 3 LoRa nodes, and the circle mark is the location of the personnel when collecting data. During the experiment, the LoRa gateway device and LoRa node devices were fixed. Data collection is divided into two parts:

1. When there are no people in the experimental area, collect the RSSI of 3 LoRa nodes through the LoRa gateway and proxy server as data set 1, and the data format is Table 2. When a person exits in any circle in Fig. 3, the RSSI of 3 LoRa nodes is collected as data set 2.
2. When there is no person in the experimental area, collect the RSSI of 3 LoRa nodes as data set 3. An experimenter was present at its fixed position for a period of time in the order of the circle in Fig. 3, and collected the RSSI of 3 LoRa nodes as a data set 4. Figure 4 is the RSSI distribution diagram of different LoRa nodes collected in data set 4 (different colors represent different LoRa node devices).

3.2   Data Processing

For the collected data, this paper proposes a difference-limiting filtering algorithm. First, divide the data format as shown in Table 2 according to the LoRa node ID, so that the collected RSSI of the same ID is in the same list, and the list format is Formula (1):

$$RSSI_i = [RSSI_1, RSSI_2, RSSI_3, ..., RSSI_n] \tag{1}$$

where $RSSI_i$ represents the RSSI set of the i-th LoRa node ($1 \leq i \leq 3$, i is an integer), and $RSSI_n$ represents the RSSI value of the n-th LoRa node received during the collection period.

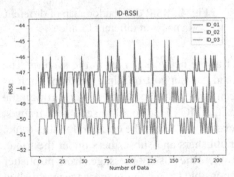 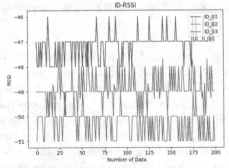

Fig. 5. RSSI value without filtering algorithm   **Fig. 6.** RSSI value after using filtering algorithm

The traditional filtering algorithm, such as the arithmetic average filtering algorithm, which sums the collected n data and divides it by n to obtain the arithmetic average of all data. This method has simple steps, but the sensitivity of processing sudden change data is low, and it is easy to loss some characteristics of data. The limiting filter method is to compare the current data value with the determined last data value. If the difference between the two data values is greater than a certain threshold, the current data is discarded. This method can reduce the data mutation caused by accidental factors to a certain extent, but the result of each time depends on the result determined last time. If the beginning of the data to be processed is abnormal data or there is a small accumulation of errors during data processing, then the result will deviate from the correct result.

This paper proposes to use the difference-limiting filtering algorithm to process the data. The algorithm does not depend on a specific RSSI value, but by calculating the difference $RSSI\Delta$ of two adjacent RSSIs in the data set to determine the current RSSI value processing method. The calculation method of $RSSI\Delta$ is Formula (2):

$$RSSI\,\Delta i = |RSSI_i - RSSI_{i+1}| \tag{2}$$

Then use Formula (3) to average all $RSSI\,\Delta i$:

$$\overline{RSSI\Delta} = (RSSI\Delta_1 + RSSI\Delta_2 + RSSI\Delta_3 + ... + RSSI\Delta_n)/n \tag{3}$$

Compare both $\overline{RSSI\Delta}$ with $RSSI\,\Delta i$, if the difference between the two is less than a certain threshold Δ, then keep the $RSSI_i$. If the difference between the two is greater than the threshold Δ, then the $RSSI_i$ and $RSSI_{i+1}$ will be judged. If the $RSSI_i$ is greater than $RSSI_{i+1}$, then the $RSSI_i - \Delta$ will be regarded as the $RSSI_i$, otherwise the $RSSI_i + \Delta$ will be regarded as the $RSSI_i$. In this way, the collected data can be preprocessed without knowing the real RSSI value of the LoRa node at the current location, which not only can eliminate abnormal data and retain the overall characteristics of the data as much as possible, but also is convenient for subsequent model training. Figures 5 and 6 show the RSSI before and after date processing at a certain collection point.

3.3 Model Training

The data format after processing data sets 1, 2, 3, and 4 is Formula (4):

$$RSSI_i = [RSSI_{i1}, RSSI_{i2}, RSSI_{i3}, ..., RSSI_{i4}] \tag{4}$$

where $RSSI_i$ is the RSSI collection collected by the LoRa gateway device from the i-th LoRa node ($1 \leq i \leq 3$), and $RSSI_{ij}$ is the j-th RSSI collected by the i-th LoRa node device. Continue to process data sets 1 and 2, 3, and the processed data format are:

$$RSSI_m = [[RSSI_{11}, RSSI_{21}, RSSI_{31}], [RSSI_{12}, RSSI_{22}, RSSI_{32}], ..., [RSSI_{in}, RSSI_{jn}, RSSI_{kn}]] \tag{5}$$

where m takes 1 or 2, 3 represents the final data set processed by data set 1 or 2, 3; i, j, $k = 1, 2, 3$ represent the RSSI collected from LoRa nodes 1, 2, 3 respectively; $RSSI_{kn}$ represents the n-th RSSI of the LoRa node with node ID k.

For data set 4, because the continuous positioning problem is more complicated, we divide the area to be positioned into small unit areas to transform the problem into a discrete classification problem. We can obtain multiple RSSI sets as shown in Formula (5), select GaussianNB (Gauss-Naïve Bayes) algorithm to conduct model learning and training on the data set. The GaussianNB algorithm is a classification algorithm based on the Naive Bayes theorem and feature condition assumptions. For a given training data set $X = (x1, x2, x3, ..., xn)$, where $xi = (xi_1, xi_2, ..., xi_n)$, xi_j represents the j-th dimension feature in the i-th training sample, moreover, each sample has its corresponding category $Y = (y1, y2, y3, ..., yn)$. To judge a category of data x to be predicted, from the perspective of probability theory, the problem can be transformed into given x, solve the maximum posterior probability $argmaxP(y_k|x)$, and it can be obtained by Bayes theorem:

$$P(y_k \mid x) = \frac{P(x \mid y_k)P(y_k)}{P(x)} \tag{6}$$

According to the total probability formula, the Formula (6) also can be rewritten as:

$$P(y_k|x) = \frac{P(x \mid y_k)P(y_k)}{\sum_{k=1}^{n} P(x \mid y_k)P(y_k)} \tag{7}$$

Due to the assumption of independence, the characteristics of each dimension are independent of each other, so the conditional probability is:

$$P(x|y_k) = P(x1, x2, ..., xn|y_k) = \prod_{i=1}^{n} P(x_i|y_k) \tag{8}$$

Put Formula (8) into Formula (7) to get:

$$P(y_k|x) = \frac{P(y_k) \prod_{i=1}^{n} P(x_i|y_k)}{\sum_{k=1}^{n} P(y_k) \prod_{i=1}^{n} P(x_i|y_k)} \tag{9}$$

For all y_k, the denominator value in Formula (9) is the same, so $argmaxP(y_k|x)$ can be finally simplified to:

$$argmaxP(y_k x) = argmaxP(y_k) \prod_{i=1}^{n} P(x_i y_k) \tag{10}$$

where $P(y_k)$ is the prior probability, which can be obtained according to the training data set. For continuous variables, even if the Laplace smoothing method is used to process the data, $P(x_i|y_k)$ is still difficult to describe the real situation. The Gaussian model assumes that all dimensional features obey a normal distribution. The density function of the normal distribution is calculated from the sample data, and the posterior probability value is obtained accordingly.

4   Experimental Results

The experimental site is a 10 m * 8 m rectangular indoor area, and the distance between every two adjacent collection points is 3 m. The indoor layout is shown in Fig. 3. Data sets 1 and 2 respectively collect RSSI data of each node device when no one exits and when there is one exits in the room. Its essence is a two-class problem, the purpose is to monitor in real time whether there are people in the area to be located (or personal intrusion). The experiment uses SVM (Support Vector Machine) algorithm and GaussianNB to train the model, and the accuracy of the prediction results is shown in Table 3.

For the judgement of whether there are people indoors, FP and FN are two very important indicators. FP means false positive, which means that when there is no person in the area to be located, it mistakenly thinks that someone exists. FN means false negative, which means that when there is a person in the area to be located, it mistakenly thinks that no one exists. Experimental results show that: although the FN of the SVM algorithm is only 15.7%, its FP reaches 43.5%, that is, there is 43.5% probability that someone will be mistaken for the presence of a person when there is no one, so the result is difficult to apply in practice. However, the FP and FN of the GaussianNB algorithm are relatively low, 1.5% and 4.3%, respectively, which provides the possibility for its practical application.

Data sets 3 and 4 collect the RSSI data of each LoRa node device at each dot in Fig. 3 when there is no person and when there is one person. It can be divided into a

Table 3. Two classification uses SVM and GaussianNB algorithm to predict accuracy

	Unmanned	Manned
SVM	56.5%	84.3%
GaussianNB	98.5%	95.7%

Table 4. Multi-classification uses SVM and GaussianNB algorithm to predict accuracy

	Position0	Position1	Position2	Position3	Position4	Position5	Position6
SVM	53.5%	59%	48.5%	84%	76.5%	70.5%	47%
GaussianNB	98.5%	97.5%	98%	96%	93%	94.5%	91.5%

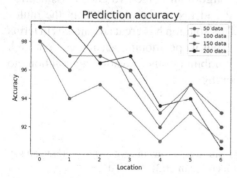

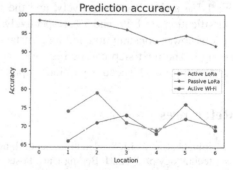

Fig. 7. The prediction accuracy rate of each

Fig. 8. Forecast accuracy of different positioning methods position of different training data set size

multi-classification problem, the purpose is to monitor whether there are people in the area to be in real time, and to further infer where they are in the presence of people. During the experiment, a total of 200 RSSI data were collected in data set 3, 200 RSSI data were collected in each position in data set 4, and the model was trained using SVM algorithm and GaussianNB algorithm. The accuracy of the prediction results is shown in Table 4.

The special position 0 represents the state when no one is present, and the experiment shows: in the case of multiple classifications, the FP value of the SVM algorithm is still very high, and the average probability of correctly predicting each position is only 64.3%, which cannot fully meet the needs of practical applications. The FP value of the GaussianNB algorithm is about 1.5%, and the accuracy of each position prediction is about 95%. We also use 50, 100, 150 and 200 pieces of data for model training on data set 4, and its prediction accuracy is shown in Fig. 7. It can be seen that the difference in the size of the training data set has only a slight difference in the prediction accuracy of each location, and the prediction accuracy at a point closer to the LoRa gateway device is higher than that at a longer distance. And when the person is on the straight line between the LoRa gateway device and the node devices (such as position 2 and 5), the impact on the RSSI of the node is greater, and the prediction accuracy is higher.

We are also using the active positioning method to collect LoRa and Wi-Fi signals at different locations under the same experimental conditions to generate a fingerprint library. Use GaussianNB algorithm to train the model and get the prediction result shown in Fig. 8. Since the active positioning method cannot locate the unmanned state, there is no data at position 0.

5 Conclusion

This paper uses long-distance, low-power LoRa technology to build an indoor passive positioning system based on LoRa signal fingerprints. And collect data in a 10 m * 8 m indoor environment, using difference-limiting filtering algorithm and GaussianNB algorithm to filter the data and model training respectively. Experimental results show that within a range 3 m, the FP and FN of the algorithm in the two-class classification are 1.5% and 4.3%, respectively, and the FP and FN of the algorithm in the multi-classification are 1.5% and 5%, respectively. This solution has great advantages in terms of low power consumption and long distance, but its positioning accuracy is not high enough. The next step can be improved by combining other positioning solutions to further improve the accuracy of indoor positioning.

References

1. Sun, Q., Liu, J., Li, S., et al.: Internet of things: summarize on concepts, architecture and key technology problem. J. Beijing Univ. Posts Telecommun. 3(3), 1–9 (2010)
2. Petajajarvi, J., Mikhaylov, K., Roivainen, A., et al.: On the coverage of LPWANs: range evaluation and channel attenuation model for LoRa technology. In: 2015 14th International Conference on ITS Telecommunications (ITST), pp. 55–59. IEEE (2015)

3. Ayele, E.D., Hakkenberg, C., Meijers, J.P., et al.: Performance analysis of LoRa radio for an indoor IoT applications. In: 2017 International Conference on Internet of Things for the Global Community (IoTGC), pp. 1–8. IEEE (2017)
4. Gregora, L., Vojtech, L., Neruda, M.: Indoor signal propagation of LoRa technology. In: 2016 17th International Conference on Mechatronics-Mechatronika (ME), pp. 1–4. IEEE (2016)
5. Zhouyidan, T., Ningkang, J.: Research on long distance indoor positioning based on LoRra. Comput. Appl. Softw. (4), 28 (2018)
6. Choi, W., Chang, Y.S., Jung, Y., et al.: Low-power LoRa signal-based outdoor positioning using fingerprint algorithm. ISPRS Int. J. Geo Inf. 7(11), 440 (2018)
7. Anjum, M., Khan, M.A., Hassan, S.A., et al.: Analysis of RSSI fingerprinting in LoRa networks. In: 2019 15th International Wireless Communications & Mobile Computing Conference (IWCMC), pp. 1178–1183. IEEE (2019)
8. Sinha, R.S., Wei, Y., Hwang, S.H.: A survey on LPWA technology: LoRa and NB-IoT. ICT Express 3(1), 14–21 (2017)
9. Devalal, S., Karthikeyan, A.: LoRa technology-an overview. In: 2018 Second International Conference on Electronics, Communication and Aerospace Technology (ICECA), pp. 284–290. IEEE (2018)
10. Augustin, A., Yi, J., Clausen, T., et al.: A study of LoRa: Long range & low power networks for the internet of things. Sensors 16(9), 1466 (2016)

Application of Dijkstra Algorithm in Optimal Route Selection Under the Background of TPACK Education Model

Fengling Wang[✉], Yan Li, Qingling Chen, and Guoxian Wang

Heihe University, Heihe, Heilongjiang, China
78623392@qq.com

Abstract. With the advent of the era of globalization and information technology, all aspects of people's lives have been deeply influenced by Internet technologies such as mobile Internet and big data technology. TPACK is presented in this paper under the background of education mode based on network data automation and other related theory, using the Dijkstra algorithm in 31 cities between tourism route design, and through the MATLAB software programming software realization route network shortest route choice, makes the tourists in the process of route choice by according to their actual demand the best travel path. So as to achieve the goal of energy conservation and environmental protection, green travel.

Keywords: Greedy algorithm · Dijkstra algorithm · Route selection

1 Introduction

With the development of economic globalization and tourism market boundaries without borders, tourism market expanded rapidly, consumer demand for the development of transportation and communications and more diverse and more changes, so people for their travel route selection is becoming more and more diversified.It is important of the following several aspects to travel route choice in design based on the Dijkstra algorithm.

First, According to the geographical location (latitude and longitude) design the shortest circuit travel scheme.

Educational Science Research Project of Heihe University: TPACK for mathematics normal university students under normal professional certification standards Research on the cultivation of teaching ability (JYZ202101).

X. Jiang (Ed.): MLICOM 2021, LNICST 438, pp. 48–66, 2022.
https://doi.org/10.1007/978-3-031-04409-0_6

Second, If the traveler starts from Harbin and stays for 3 days in each city, they can choose the air or railway (express sleeper or bullet train) to design the most economical travel booking plan on the Internet.

Third, To take a comprehensive view of money, time and convenience, set up your evaluation criteria, build a mathematical model, revise your program.

2   Application of Dijkstra Algorithm in Optimal Route Selection

In the first problem, the shortest path is related to the longitude and latitude of each city, so the longitude and latitude of each city are listed in the form of matrix, and the Dijkstra algorithm is used to find the shortest path through 31 cities, and the shortest road map is made through MATLAB software [1].

Problem two of the main economic issues related to drive cost, so the use of "timetable" software, through the actual search, getting any a city to the rest of the minimum cost data of 30 cities results when using greedy method. Greedy method is selecting a measure standard, and then pressing measure this sort of input city, a city and a sequential input. If the sum of this input and the partial optimal solution currently constituted in the sense of this measure does not yield a viable solution, the city is not added to the decomposition. This paper is to use this method to solve, and through these datas to do programming, then get about the most economic route. To find the most time-saving route and the most economical approach is the same, To find any city to the other 31 cities in the least time data, and get the most time-saving and the most economic route travel by the greedy method and programming,

2.1   Considering the Shortest Travel Route

It will pass through all the provincial capitals, municipalities directly under the central government, so we choose the longitude and latitude to solve the problem. Latitude and longitude is one of the effective methods to calculate the shortest distance between two points on earth, this article through to the city between latitude and longitude, and latitude and longitude data list matrix, using the Dijkstra algorithm to make the program, it is concluded that the shortest travel route, based on the online survey of 31 provinces data as an example, through the MATLAB software to make the shortest route map. Finally, the shortest travel routes and corresponding road maps for provincial capitals.The shortest path problem can be described as given a directed graph, also known as a network, for each arc, corresponding weights, and given two vertices in, let is a path from, when the weight of the path is defined, the sum of the weights of all the arcs in this path, denoted as. The shortest path is to find the path with the least weight among all the paths from PI to PI, that is, to find a path from PI to PI that minimizes all the paths from PI to PI in D, which is called the shortest path from PI to PI.This method is called Dijkstra's algorithm [2]. The basic principle of Dijkstra's algorithm is that if the shortest path from to, then it must also be the shortest path to. follow the formatting instructions for headings given in Table 1.

Table 1. Latitude and longitude

Number	Province	Capital	Latitude	Longitude
1	Heilongjiang province	Ha erbin	45.44	126.36
2	Jilin	Changchun	43.54	125.19
3	Xinjiang	Wulumuqi	43.45	87.36
4	Liaoning	Shenyang	41.48	123.25
5	Neimenggu	Huhehaote	40.48	111.41
6	Beijing	Beijing	39.55	116.24
7	Tianjin	Tianjin	39.02	117.12
8	Ningxia	Yinchuan	38.27	106.16
9	Hebei	Shijiazhuang	38.02	114.3
10	Shanxi	Taiyuan	37.54	112.33
11	Shandong	Jinnan	36.4	117
12	Qinghai	xinning	36.38	101.48
13	Ganshu	Lanzhou	36.04	103.51
14	Henan	Zhengzhou	34.46	113.4
15	Shanxi	Xian	34.17	108.57
16	Jiangshu	Nanjing	32.03	118.46
17	Anhui	Hefei	31.52	117.17
18	Shanghai	Shanghai	31.14	121.29
19	Sichuan	Chengdu	30.4	104.04
20	Hubei	Wuhan	30.35	114.17
21	Zhejiang	Hangzhou	30.16	120.1
22	Xizhang	Lasha	29.39	91.08
23	Chongqing	Chongqing	29.35	106.33
24	Jiangxi	Nanchang	28.4	115.55
25	Hunan	Changsha	28.12	112.59
26	Guizhou	guiyang	26.35	106.42
27	Gujian	fuzhou	26.05	119.18
28	Yunnan	Hunming	25.04	102.42
29	Guangdong	guangzhou	23.08	113.14
30	Guangxi	Nanning	22.48	108.19

In this paper, in the network, the weight of the arc represents the direct distance from to, through the use of MATLAB programming.

```
program Project1;

findroute.m

points =[
    126.36    45.44
    125.19    43.54
    87.36     43.45
    123.25    41.48
    111.41    40.48
    116.24    39.55
    117.12    39.02
    106.16    38.27
    114.3     38.02
    112.33    37.54
    117       36.4
    101.48    36.38
    103.51    36.04
    113.4     34.46
    108.57    34.17
    118.46    32.03
```

```
117.17    31.52
121.29    31.14
104.04    30.4
114.17    30.35
120.1     30.16
91.08     29.39
106.33    29.35
115.55    28.4
112.59    28.12
106.42    26.35
119.18    26.05
102.42    25.04
121.3     25.03
113.14    23.08
108.19    22.48
114.15 22.28
];
rand('seed',0);
R=6371.11;
for i=1:length(points(:,1))
for j=1:length(points(:,1))
   tabledis(i,j)=distance(points(i,2),points(i,1),points(j,2),points(j,1))*2*R*pi/360;
end;
end;
p=[1:length(points(:,1))]';
optlength=routelength(p,tabledis)


for jjj=1:6
   for kkk=1:60
```

```
    if mod(kkk,20)==0
        disp(['kkk=' num2str(kkk)]);
    end;
    p=randperm(length(points(:,1)))';
    p=optimizeroute(p,tabledis);
    if optlength>routelength(p,tabledis)+1e-10
        figure(1);
        hold off;
        plot([points(p,1); points(p(1),1)],[points(p,2);points(p(1),2)],'k','linewidth',2);
        hold on;
        plot(points(p,1),points(p,2),'r.','markersize',30);
        axis([85 128 15 47]);
        text(95,45,['No. ' num2str(jjj) ' : '
num2str(routelength(p,tabledis))],'fontsize',20);
        drawnow
        optlength=routelength(p,tabledis);
        print('-dpng',['r' num2str(jjj) '.png']);
        break;
    end
  end
end;
firstordercc.m
function r=firstordercc(p,d,tabledis)
lold=routelength(p,tabledis);
lll=length(p(:,1));
lengtharray=zeros(lll,1);
for i=1:lll
    p0=[p;p];
    p0(i:i+d,:)=flipud(p0(i:i+d,:));
    p0=p0(i:i+lll-1,:);
```

```
    lengtharray(i)=routelength(p0,tabledis);
end;
[mmm,i]=min(lengtharray);
  p0=[p;p];
  p0(i:i+d,:)=flipud(p0(i:i+d,:));
  p0=p0(i:i+lll-1,:);
if lold>mmm
  r=p0;
else
  r=p;
end;
optimizeroute.m
function p=optimizeroute(p,tabledis)
for j=1:100
    alength=routelength(p,tabledis);
for i=length(p):-1:1
 p=firstordercc(p,i,tabledis);
end
if alength-routelength(p,tabledis)<1e-10
    break;
end
end;
routelength.m
function r=routelength(p,tabledis)
r=tabledis(p(1),p(end));
for i=1:length(p)-1
    r=r+tabledis(p(i),p(i+1));
end;
```

Draw the following Fig. 1 and get the shortest path of 15591.0705 km.

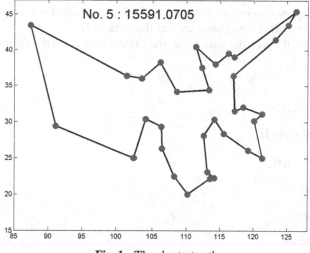

Fig. 1. The shortest path

Namely shortest route is: from Harbin to changchun to shenyang to jinan, tohefei, nanjing to Shanghai to hangzhou to Taipei to fuzhou to nanchang to wuhan, changsha, guangzhou to haikou to nanning to guiyang to chongqing and chengdu to kunming to Lhasa, urumqi, xining to lanzhou, yinchuan to xi'an to zhengzhou, taiyuan to Hohhot to shijiazhuang to Beijing to tianjin to Harbin.

Advantages of the model: since the data used in this problem is only the longitude and latitude of each city, which is not changed by other things, so there are no human and geographical factors, and the result is very accurate.

Disadvantages of the model: the spherical distance is more accurate to calculate the distance between two places, while the actual data used is the straight-line distance between two places, so there will be errors in the results, but it will not affect the travel route.

2.2   Choice of the Cheapest Travel Route by Greedy Algorithm

This paper requires to design a travel booking plan on the Internet for Mr. Zhou to start from Harbin on May 1st, pass through 34 provincial capitals, municipalities directly under the central government, and finally return to Harbin, and stay in each city for 3 days. According to the actual situation, the most economical travel route between any one city and the other 30 cities is first found, and the matrix is listed. Using this matrix, the program is made by greedy method, and then the result is made by C++. The greedy method is an improved grading method. It begins with a travel salesman problem description and selects a metric. The N input cities are then sorted by this metric, one at a time. If the sum of this input and the partial optimal solution currently constituted in the sense of this measure does not yield a viable solution, the city is not added to the decomposition. The hierarchical processing method which can get the optimal solution in a certain sense of measurement is called greedy method, and this paper is to use the greedy method to solve. First of all, use the "train schedule" to find out the most economical travel cost data between any city and other cities, the most time-saving travel data, the most convenient travel data, and list the data table.

List the matrix through the data table, the matrix using greedy algorithm, through C++ editing

```
    program Project1;
#ifndef AdjTWGraph_H
#define AdjTWGraph_H
#include <vector>
#include <iostream>
using namespace std;
const int MaxV=100;
struct Edge
{
  int dest;
  int weight;
  Edge * next;
  Edge(){}
  Edge(int d,int w):dest(d),weight(w),next(NULL){}
};
struct item
{   int data;
  Edge * adj;
};
```

```
class AdjTWGraph
{
private:
   item vertices[MaxV];
   int numV,numE;
public :
   AdjTWGraph();
   ~AdjTWGraph();
   int NumV(){return numV;}
   int NumE(){return numE;}
   int GetValue(const int i);
   int GetWeight(const int v1,const int v2);
   void InsertV(const int & vertex);
   void InsertE(const int v1,const int v2,int weight);
   friend ostream& operator<<(ostream& os,  AdjTWGraph & m)
   {    for (int i = 0; i < m.numV ; i++)    {
        for (int j = 0; j < m.numV; j++)
           os << right << m.GetWeight(i,j) << " ";
        os << endl;
      }
     return os;
   }
   friend istream& operator>>(istream& is, AdjTWGraph & m)
   {    int t;
      for (int i = 0; i < m.NumV(); i++)
        for (int j = 0; j < m.NumV(); j++)
```

```
        {
            is >> t;    m.InsertE(i,j,t);
        }
    return is;
    }
};
AdjTWGraph::AdjTWGraph()
{
    for(int i=0;i<MaxV;i++)    vertices[i].adj=NULL;
    numV=0;numE=0;
}
AdjTWGraph::~AdjTWGraph()
{
    for(int i=0;i<numV;i++)
    {
        Edge * p=vertices[i].adj,*q;
        while(p!=NULL)
        {
            q=p->next;delete p;p=q;
        }
    }
}
 int AdjTWGraph::GetValue(const int i){    return vertices[i].data;  }
 int AdjTWGraph::GetWeight(const int v1,const int v2)
 {
    Edge *p=vertices[v1].adj;
```

```
    while(p!=NULL && p->dest<v2) p=p->next;
    if(v2!=p->dest)    {    return 0;    }
    return p->weight;
}
  void AdjTWGraph::InsertV(const int & v) { vertices[numV].data=v; numV++; }
  void AdjTWGraph::InsertE(const int v1,const int v2,int weight)
  {
    Edge * q=new Edge(v2,weight);
    if(vertices[v1].adj==NULL) vertices[v1].adj=q;
    else
    {
      Edge *curr=vertices[v1].adj,*pre=NULL;
      while(curr!=NULL && curr->dest<v2)    { pre=curr;curr=curr->next;    }
      if(pre==NULL){    q->next=vertices[v1].adj;vertices[v1].adj=q;    }
      else    { q->next=pre->next;pre->next=q;    }
    }
    numE++;
}
#endif
//------------------------------------ tsp.cpp文件----------------------------------------
#include "AdjtwGraph.h"
#include <fstream>
#include <vector>
#include <algorithm>
#include <ctime>
#include <queue>
```

```
using namespace std;
ofstream fout("out.txt");
int N;
AdjTWGraph g;
struct Node
 {   int currentIndex;
   int level;
   Node * previous;
    Node(int L = 0, int V = 0, Node *p = NULL):level(L),currentIndex(V), previous(p) {}
};
class TspBase
 {
protected:
   vector<int> currentPath;
   vector<int> bestPath;
   int cv;
   int bestV;
   Node * root;

   int SumV();
   void EnumImplicit(int k);
   void BackTrackImplicit(int k);

   void EnumExplicit(Node * r);
   void BackTrackExplicit(Node * r);
   void FIFOBB();
```

```
    bool Valid(Node *p,int v)  //
       {    bool flag = true;
          for(Node *r = p; r->level > 0 && v; r = r->previous)  flag = r->currentIndex !=v;
          return flag;
       }

    void StoreX(Node * p) //
       {for(Node *r = p; r->level >0 ; r = r->previous )
  {    currentPath[r->level-1] = r->currentIndex;    }
       }
    void Print();
public:
    TspBase(){currentPath.resize(N);    bestPath.resize(N);    }
  ~TspBase(){currentPath.resize(0);bestPath.resize(0);}


    void TspEnumImplicit();
    void TspBackTrackImplicit();


    void TspEnumExplicit();
    void TspBackTrackExplicit();


    void TspBB();


    void TspGreedy();


    void DataClear(bool flag)
```

```
{   currentPath.resize(N);        bestPath.resize(N);

    if(flag)        { Node * p=root,*q;

             while(p!=NULL) {q=p->previous; delete p; p=q;}

    }

}

};

void TspBase::TspGreedy()

{    fout<<"TspGreedy ........"<<endl;

bestV = 0;

  vector<int> NEAR(N); //

  NEAR[0] = -1;

  for (int i = 1; i < N; i++)

    NEAR[i] = 0;

  bestPath[0] = 1;

  int t;

  for (int s = 1; s < N; s++)

  {

   int j = 1;

   while (j < N && NEAR[j] < 0)

      j++;

   int K = j;

   for (int k = j + 1; k < N; k++)

     if (NEAR[k] >= 0 &&  g.GetWeight(k,NEAR[k]) < g.GetWeight(j,NEAR[j]))

        j = k;

   bestPath[s] = j + 1;

   bestV +=g.GetWeight(j,NEAR[j]);
```

```
    NEAR[j] = -1;

    for (k = K; k < N; k++) //调整NEAR值

      if (NEAR[k] >= 0)

        NEAR[k] = j;

      t = j;

    }

    bestV += g.GetWeight(t,0);

    fout<<"the shortest path is  ";

    for(unsigned w = 0; w < N; w++)

      fout<<bestPath[w] <<"--";

    fout<<"1"<<endl;

    fout<<"minimum money is "<<bestV<<endl;    /* the shortist time  the most
convience */

}

int main(int argc, char* argv[])

  {  int m,n;

     ifstream fin("data.txt");

     if(fin.bad()) return 1;

     fin >> m >> n;

     N = n;

     for(int i=0;i<N;i++) g.InsertV(i);

     fin >> g;

     TspBase it;

     it.TspGreedy();   it.DataClear(false);

     return 0;

}
```

The shortest path is 1--2--3--34--4--29--30--31--32--33--6--5--8--7--25--26--27--28--24--
21--22--23--17--18--19--20--14--15--16--13--10--11--12--9--1

2.3 Choice of the Most Time-Saving Path by Greedy Algorithm

After query to get about any city to the other 33 cities in the bus the least time, with the
data listed matrix, the matrix using greedy algorithm, through C++ editing

TspGreedy ....

The shortest path is 1--3--11--5--8--10--31--30--27--12--6--9--15--16--25--22--19--20--
26--28--21--14--17--18--13--7--4--33--32--34--2--23--29--24--1

The shortist time is 3621.

With the original 31 provincial capital city, municipality directly under the central government, Harbin to shenyang to nanchang, to hefei, to hangzhou to taiyuan to
yinchuan to wuhan to nanjing to xining to kunming, guiyang, chongqing to lanzhou
to xi'an, chengdu, guangzhou to haikou, nanning to changsha to Shanghai to jinanto
Beijing to shijiazhuang to day Beijing to changchun to Lhasa to zhengzhou to urumqi
to Harbin to plus three days stay in each city, a total of 3621 min.

Advantages of the model: the data used in this question are obtained by consulting
the train schedule, the data is more accurate, and the most economical, time-saving and
convenient results of tourism are practical. If you want to travel all over China and save
time, you can start from any starting point according to the travel route in this article
and return to Harbin to ensure time saving, economy and convenience.

Disadvantages of the model: in this problem, a few communication methods are
replaced by aircraft. Since the price of air tickets varies greatly at different times, the
airfare used in this problem is not necessarily accurate and the flight time is not fixed,
which leads to errors in the optimal economic value obtained.

3 A Comparative Study

In the first step, the Dijkstra algorithm is used to program the five programs together,
and the five shortest route diagrams are obtained. The fifth diagram is the most accurate,
with a total length of 15591 km, which means the shortest route of the first step and the
corresponding road map are made. This article has solved the most economical, the most
time-saving and the most convenient travel route, that is, the most economical cost is
11,789 yuan, the most time-saving time is 2431 min. Due to this problem are basic factors
to consider in the process of tourism, so this article petitions walking routes using range
is very wide, such as the first question in the shortest route problem, if you have wanted
to travel around the provinces, municipalities directly under the central government, or
on one section of the route, to walk for the shortest route, can be implemented according
to the result of this paper. Of course, if you want to save time, economy and convenience,
you can choose the route according to the relevant results made in this paper.

In this paper, we use the latitude and longitude data are obtained by the query, the journey time, cost and the number of transfer is done with train schedules and aircraft moment query website of the query, due to the different transit times of the day and month of a year is different, can lead to drive the time error, but the total time of error will not affect tourism, because Mr. Wang to stay for three days in each city, so the whole travel for a long time. The first three questions in this paper use the data investigated, through C++ programming, to make the results, the results are more accurate. It will be cheaper, less time-consuming and more convenient to follow these routes. Based on the survey between the most direct the most economic data, because a lot of data in "timetable", passes through many data are compared to choose the smallest data, which will result in this paper by use of the data has a tiny error, but due to a wide range of tourism, the cost will be very big, so the error of the results won't have influence, not as a problem to consider. Due to the different factors considered in this paper, the tourist routes are also different. These routes are suitable for the problem of time-saving, economic and convenient and the shortest route in the process of tourism. It can be compared with the various walking routes in this paper to take the corresponding tourist routes.

4 Conclusion

This paper takes the cheapest matrix as the equation to establish the model that Mr. Zhou starts from Harbin, travels to provincial capitals, municipalities directly under the central government, and finally returns to Harbin. Namely the most economical, the most time-saving, the most convenient route. This paper uses a lot of computer programming, programming process used in the data error is very small, so after programming to make the route is more accurate.

According to the longitude and latitude of each city, the model lists the relevant longitude and latitude data matrix, and uses MATLAB programming to make the shortest path problem in the first question. According to the investigation of route, ticket price and transfer times, the model lists the cost, time and transfer number between two places into a matrix, and it is convenient to consider the least number of transfer times on the way. Route due to the weather changes, the temporary adjustment, finally there is a certain price volatility, and according to the problem of constraint conditions, to seek the most economical route, between basic train, does not train to replace with aircraft routes, fares will be greatly change, here we only consider the optimal scheme. Findings of the data into a data table, and use Matlab and C++ programming to make the trip route, and the corresponding road map. After the analysis of the problem, this paper designed the corresponding Dijkstra algorithm, MATLAB algorithm, greedy method, etc., and found the corresponding data, in the form of data matrix used in the algorithm, because the accuracy of the data is higher, that is, the reliability of the results is higher. And because the problem of the model is more comprehensive, combined with the actual situation to solve the problem, so the established model can be closely connected with the actual, so that the model has a good universality and generalization.

References

1. Nikolić, M., Teodorović, D.: Transit network design by bee colony optimization. Expert Syst. Appl. **40**(15), 5945–5955 (2013)
2. Nassi, C.D., da Costa, F.C.D.C.: Use of the analytic hierarchy process to evaluate transit fare system. Res. Transp. Econ. **36**(1), 50–62 (2012)

The Wave Filter Design of UFMC Vehicle Communication System

Tengyue Yu[✉], Jingjing Wang, Jiangang Wen, Feng Li, and Jingyu Hua

School of Information and Electronic Engineering, Zhejiang Gongshang University,
Hangzhou 310018, China
19020090017@pop.zjgsu.ecu.cn

Abstract. In recent years, the requirements for low delay and reliability
of vehicular communication are becoming more and more strict, while
the traditional OFDM (Orthogonal Frequency Division Multiplexing)
technology can not meet the above requirements due to high out-of-
band leakage and strict synchronization requirements. Therefore, in this
paper, the UFMC (Universal filtered multi carrier) system is applied to
the Internet of vehicles communication, and the overall performance of
the system is improved through the optimization design of the waveform
filter. The simulation results show that the FIR (finite impulse response)
filter designed in this paper can improve the SER (symbol error rate)
performance of UFMC system compared with DC (Dolph Chebyshev)
filter.

Keywords: Vehicle communication · UFMC · FIR filter · SER

1 Introduction

With the official commercial use of 5G and the popularization of mobile terminal equipment, people gradually have a deeper understanding of the concept of
Internet of things. Three technology scenarios are defined in 5G, which are eMBB
(Enhanced Mobile Broadband), uRLLC (Ultra Reliable and Low Latency Communication) and mMTC (Massive Machine Type of Communication). Among
them, uRLLC can satisfy millisecond level and end-to-end low delay transmission [1,2], which promotes the development of a large number of delay sensitive
mobile applications, such as realtime navigation and autopilot [3,4]. VANET
(Vehicular Ad-hoc Networks), referred to as the Internet of vehicles, is one of
the important applications of 5G system in high reliability and low delay communication scenarios. The Internet of vehicles uses advanced sensor technology,
cloud computing technology, wireless communication technology, etc., which can
fully sense the realtime situation of road and traffic, and connect a certain range
of vehicles, pedestrians and roads to form a special mobile Ad-hoc network [5].
At present, a large number of 5G base stations are integrated into the Internet

© ICST Institute for Computer Sciences, Social Informatics and Telecommunications Engineering 2022
Published by Springer Nature Switzerland AG 2022. All Rights Reserved
X. Jiang (Ed.): MLICOM 2021, LNICST 438, pp. 67–78, 2022.
https://doi.org/10.1007/978-3-031-04409-0_7

of vehicles, which makes the technology of security authentication, interference management and load balancing have further development. To a certain extent, it greatly alleviates the traffic pressure and improves the travel safety.

In the Internet of Vehicles, V2V (Vehicle to Vehicle) communication, V2P (Vehicle to Pedestrian, Vehicle to Person) and other communication services require faster and more reliable information in the transmission process, which puts forward new requirements for basic waveforms [6,7]. If thousands of connections in the Internet of Vehicles scene use the strictly synchronized OFDM system, a large amount of synchronization signaling will appear in the network, which will cause network congestion [8]. As a new multi carrier technology, UFMC suppresses the out of band leakage by filtering the sub-band, so as to reduce the small frequency offset interference and has low synchronization requirements [9]. UFMC uses shorter filter length, which is more suitable for short burst packet transmission with low power consumption [10], such as cognitive M2M (Machine to Machine) communication [11]. These advantages make UFMC system more suitable for vehicle communication.

The current research on UFMC have been carried out. Paper [12] introduces the system model and system principles of UFMC, and analyzes the channel's influence on UFMC when CFO (carrier frequency offset) exists, and at the same time, the robustness of the system against CFO is improved by optimizing the filter parameters. Paper [13] proposes to use two different optimization criteria to optimize the design of FIR filters. The first is to maximize the ratio of signal to out-of-band leakage, and the second is to maximize the ratio of signal and in-band distortion plus out-of-band leakage. The filter optimized by these two criteria can effectively improve the SIR (Signal to Interference) of the system. Paper [14] considers time and frequency offset on the basis of paper [13]. Compared with the UFMC system using DC filtering, the SIR of the optimized UFMC system is increased by 3.6 dB, compared with the traditional OFDM system, the SIR of the optimized UFMC system is increased by 15.1 dB. Paper [15] uses Chebyshev filter, Hamming filter and Hamming filter to filter the UFMC system. The results show that UFMC system is superior to OFDM signal in side lobe attenuation, bit error rate and error vector amplitude. Paper [16,17] proposed a pilot design method to suppress the interference in the UFMC system and effectively reduce the system's bit error rate. Paper [18] proposed a convex optimization method to optimize the filter, and the optimized filter can suppress out-of-band interference to the maximum extent.

Based on the above analysis, it is found that researchers have made some achievements in the research of UFMC system, but most of the researches are based on suppressing the interference of UFMC system, lack of research on the relationship between filters index and system SER. This paper will conduct in-depth research on this problem. Firstly, according to the basic principle of UFMC system, the signal expression after AWGN (Additive White Gaussian Noise) channel is derived, and the interference situation is analyzed. Then the FIR filter is designed according to the CMM (constrained minimum maximum) criterion, and the SER of UFMC system under each index is obtained by traversing the filters index, and the relationship between the filters index and SER is analyzed. Finally, the results show that the FIR filter designed in this paper can improve the SER performance of UFMC system compared with the UFMC system using DC filter.

2 Signal Model of UFMC System

2.1 Transmitter Model of UFMC System

The system model of UFMC is shown in Fig. 1. The overall bandwidth is divided into B sub-bands, and each sub-band can be allocated N_B sub-carriers. With the N-point IDFT operation, the frequency domain signal X_i after equalization is transformed into time domain x_i. Then this output signal is filtered by a filter f_i with the length of L. That results in a symbol length of $N + L - 1$ because of the linear convolution between x_i and f_i.

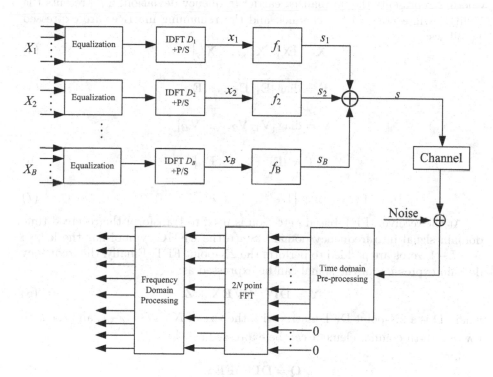

Fig. 1. UFMC system model

Finally, all the filtered sub-band signals $\mathbf{s}_i$ are added together and transmitted. The transmitted signal $\mathbf{s}$ can be expressed as:

$$\mathbf{s} = \sum_{i=0}^{B-1} \mathbf{F}_i \mathbf{V}_i \mathbf{E}_i \mathbf{X}_i \tag{1}$$

where $\mathbf{X}_i$ is a matrix which the element is the signal to be modulated on the i-th sub-band; $\mathbf{E}_i$ is a equalization matrix, where the element is the reciprocal of the amplitude frequency response of the sub-band filter on the current subcarrier; $\mathbf{V}_i$ is the N-point IDFT matrix with the size of $N \times N_B$. The k-th row and n-th column element of $\mathbf{V}_i$ is $\frac{1}{\sqrt{N}} e^{j2\pi \frac{(k-1)[(i-1) \times N_B + n - 1]}{N}}$. $\mathbf{F}_i$ is a Toeplitz matrix with its first column being $\left[f_k(0), f_k(1), \ldots, f_k(L-1), 0_{1 \times (N-1)} \right]^T$, and first row being $\left[f_k(0), 0_{1 \times (L-1)} \right]^T$.

2.2 Derivation of SINR in UFMC System

Considering that the channel is AWGN channel and is affected by CFO, the received time domain signal $\mathbf{r}$ can be expressed as:

$$\mathbf{r} = \mathbf{\Gamma}(\varepsilon)\mathbf{FVEX} + \mathbf{z} \tag{2}$$

where, ε represents the normalized carrier frequency deviation, $\mathbf{z}$ represents the additive white noise in the channel, and the remaining matrices are expressed as follows:

$$\mathbf{X} = \left[\mathbf{X}_1^T, \mathbf{X}_2^T, \ldots, \mathbf{X}_B^T \right]^T \tag{3}$$

$$\mathbf{E} = \mathrm{diag}\left[\mathbf{E}_1, \mathbf{E}_2, \ldots, \mathbf{E}_B \right] \tag{4}$$

$$\mathbf{V} = \mathrm{diag}\left[\mathbf{V}_1, \mathbf{V}_2, \ldots, \mathbf{V}_B \right] \tag{5}$$

$$\mathbf{F} = \left[\mathbf{F}_1, \mathbf{F}_2, \ldots, \mathbf{F}_B \right] \tag{6}$$

$$\mathbf{\Gamma}(\varepsilon) = \mathrm{diag}\left[1, e^{j2\pi \frac{\varepsilon}{N}}, \ldots, e^{j2\pi \frac{\varepsilon(N+L-2)}{N}} \right] \tag{7}$$

At the receiver, FFT-based detection is used to transform the received time domain signal into frequency domain. Since the UFMC symbol has the length $N+L-1$, zeros are padded to perform the 2N-point FFT. Finally, the frequency domain expression of the signal can be expressed as:

$$\mathbf{Y} = \mathbf{D}\mathbf{\Gamma}(\varepsilon)\mathbf{FVEX} + \mathbf{Z} \tag{8}$$

where $\mathbf{D}$ is a 2N-point DFT matrix with the size of $N \times N + L - 1$, and the k-th row and n-th column element can be expressed as $\frac{1}{\sqrt{N}} e^{j2\pi \frac{2(k-1)(n-1)}{N}}$.

Let:

$$\mathbf{Q} = \mathbf{D}\mathbf{\Gamma}(\varepsilon)\mathbf{FEV} \tag{9}$$

For the k-th subcarrier, the useful signal can be expressed as $Q(k,k)X(k)$, the interference signal can be expressed as $\sum_{m \neq k} Q(k,m)X(m)$, then the SINR expression of the k-th sub-carrier can be written as:

$$\mathrm{SINR}_k = \frac{Q^H(k,k)Q(k,k)}{\sum\limits_{m \neq k} Q^H(k,m)Q(k,m) + Z^H(k)Z(k)} \tag{10}$$

3 Design of Waveform Filter

3.1 Filter Optimization Design Model

It can be seen from formula (11) that in order to reduce the SER of the system, it is necessary to suppress interference signals through filters as much as possible. In the design of linear phase filters, CMM criterion is usually considered. In the CMM criterion, it is planned to consider maximum stop-band attenuation of filter, and constraining the pass-band ripple. The mathematical model can be expressed as:

$$\min_{\mathbf{x}} \mathbf{c}_s^T \mathbf{x}$$

$$\text{s.t.} \begin{cases} 1 - \mathbf{c}(\omega)^T \mathbf{x} \le \delta_p^l, \omega \in [0, \omega_p] \\ \mathbf{c}(\omega)^T \mathbf{x} - 1 \le \delta_p^u, \omega \in [0, \omega_p] \end{cases} \quad (11)$$

where $\mathbf{x} = \left[\hat{\mathbf{h}}^T, \delta_s\right]^T$, $\mathbf{c}_s = \begin{bmatrix} \mathbf{0}_{N \times 1} \\ 1 \end{bmatrix}$, $\mathbf{c}(\omega) = \left[2\cos\left(\omega\left(\frac{L-1}{2}\right)\right), \cdots, 2\cos(\omega), 1\right]^T$,

$\mathbf{h}$ is the filter coefficient, δ_p^l represents the lower bound of the pass-band ripple, and δ_p^u represents the upper bound of the pass-band ripple.

The filter design model of formula (11) can flexibly adjust the target requirements to meet special requirements. Figure 2 shows an example, Compared with the DC filter, the FIR filter has a smaller attenuation in the pass-band, and the transition-band is longer than DC, which means that the attenuation of the filter designed in this paper is slower than that of the DC filter in the transition-band.

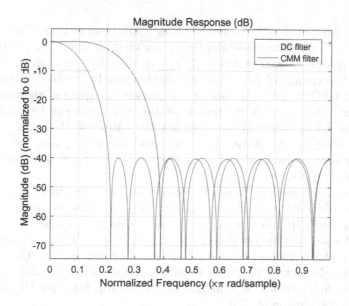

Fig. 2. Magnitude response comparison of DC filter and FIR

3.2   Influence of Filter on Subcarrier Interference of UFMC System

Figure 3 show the comparison of SINR in a sub-band of UFMC system using DC
filter and FIR filter of Fig. 2 when CFO = 0 and 0.05. The simulation results
show that when CFO = 0, the SINR of each sub-carrier is equal, and the gain
of FIR filter is small compared with that of DC filter. When CFO = 0.05, the
SINR of the middle sub-bands are lower than that of the edge sub-bands. The
SINR of the middle sub-bands of FIR filter is about 1 dB higher than that of the
DC filter, but it is lower than that of the edge sub-bands.

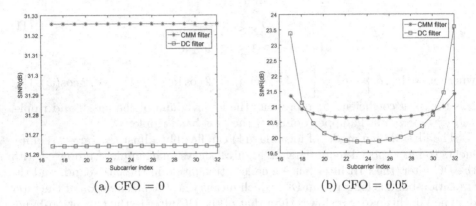

(a) CFO = 0   (b) CFO = 0.05

Fig. 3. Performance comparison of DC filter and FIR filter

Figure 4 show the comparison of SINR in a sub-band of UFMC system when
FIR filters with different pass-band ripple are used at CFO = 0 and 0.05. The
simulation results show that when CFO = 0, the SINR of each sub-carrier is
equal, and the change of pass band fluctuation has little effect on the system
gain. When CFO = 0.05, the smaller the pass-band ripple of the filter is, the
SINR of the sub-carriers in the middle of the sub-bands can be improved. In
addition, the smaller the pass-band ripple of FIR filter is, the smaller the stop-
band fluctuation is, the slower the transition-band drops, and the worse the
interference suppression to the edge sub-carriers, resulting in the worse SINR of
the edge sub-carriers.

From the above analysis, it can be found that the filters index can affect the
performance of UFMC system. According to the amplitude response comparison
of DC filter and FIR filter, it can be inferred that the smaller the pass-band
ripple is, the smaller the interference of the intermediate sub-carriers is; The
more slowly the transition-band decays, the more interference the edge sub-
carriers suffer. In view of the above ideas, this paper intends to use the method
of traversing index to find a more suitable waveform filter for UFMC system
through the comparison of SER.

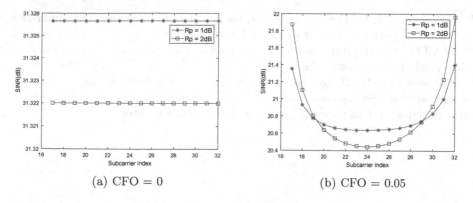

(a) CFO = 0   (b) CFO = 0.05

Fig. 4. Performance comparison of FIR filter with different pass-band ripples

4 Simulation Results and Analysis

The relevant simulation parameters used in this paper are shown in Table 1:

Table 1. Simulation parameter

Parameter	Value1	Value2
Number of sub-carriers	96	96
Number of sub-bands	6	6
FFTsize	128	128
Modulation	16QAM	16QAM
SNR	15 dB	30 dB
CFO	0	0.05

4.1 Performance Analysis of Filter Index Under Large Step Size

The traversable table under large step is shown in Table 2:

Table 2. Traversable table under large step size

Filter parameters	Value
The length of filter	25
The pass-band/stop-band cut-off frequency of filter	0.125/0.2
The pass band ripple of filter	[1 dB:1 dB:6 dB]

Figure 5 shows the SER curves of UFMC system by using FIR filters with different pass-band ripples and the SER curves of UFMC system with DC filters.

It can be seen from the figure that when CFO is 0, there is little difference between the performances of different filters. This phenomenon indicates that when CFO = 0, the interference caused by CFO is very small, and no matter what kind of filter is used, there is little difference in SER. When CFO = 0.05, it can be seen from the figure that with the increase of pass-band ripple, the SER performance of the system is on the rise. In addition, the minimum SER of the filter designed in this paper is less than that of the DC filter.

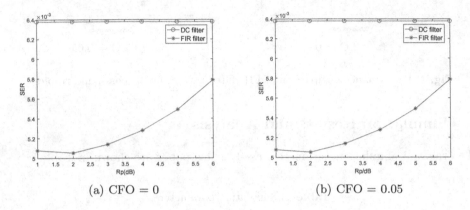

(a) CFO = 0   (b) CFO = 0.05

Fig. 5. SER comparison of UFMC systems with different filters

As can be seen from Fig. 6, with the increase of pass-band ripple, the SER of the intermediate carrier is gradually increasing. As the pass-band ripple increases, the filter stop-band attenuation can be improved. At this time, the filter in the transition-band will attenuate faster, and the interference suppression effect on the edge sub-carriers are better, so the SER on the edge-subcarriers are lower.

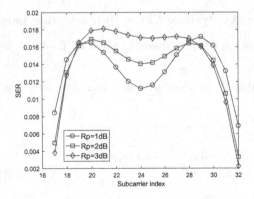

Fig. 6. SER comparison of each subcarrier under different pass-band ripples

4.2   Performance Analysis of Filter Index Under Small Step Size

Section 4.1 analyzes the influence of filter index on SER of UMFC system in large step size. Based on Sect. 4.1, this section narrows the search interval and continues to search for the filter with good performance in small step size. The traversable table is shown in Table 3:

Table 3. Traversable table under small step size

Filter parameters	Value
The length of filter	25
The pass-band/stop-band cut-off frequency of filter	0.125/0.2
The pass band ripple of filter	[0.1 dB:0.1 dB:1 dB]

Figure 7 shows the performance of UFMC system with small step length to traverse the filter pass-band ripple when CFO = 0.05. It can be seen that as the pass-band ripple continues to decrease, the SER is not greatly improved, which indicates that in UFMC system, there is a threshold for the filter pass-band ripple to improve the system performance. Even if the pass-band ripple continues to improve, the performance of UFMC system will not be better, or even worse.

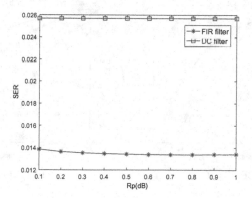

Fig. 7. SER comparison of UFMC systems with different filters

As can be seen from Fig. 8, when the pass-band ripple is 0.1 dB, the SER of the edge subcarrier is the worst, because the pass-band ripple of the filter is the smallest, the stop-band fluctuation of the filter becomes smaller. At this time, the transition-band attenuation is the slowest, so that the interference suppression to the edge sub-carrier is the worst. In addition, the SER of the intermediate-carrier is not improved, which leads to the increase of the overall SER.

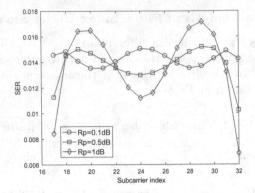

Fig. 8. SER comparison of each subcarrier under different pass-band ripples

4.3   Performance Comparison

It can be seen from Sect. 4.1 and 4.2 that the best filter for UFMC system performance is FIR filter with 1 dB pass band ripple. Figure 9 show that the performance of the FIR filter designed in this paper is better than that of the DC filter in UFMC system regardless of the modulation order with or without CFO.

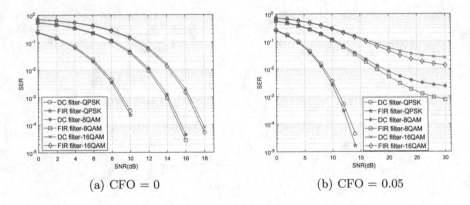

(a) CFO = 0   (b) CFO = 0.05

Fig. 9. SER comparison of FIR filter and DC filter

5   Conclusion

Aiming at the problem that the Internet of vehicles is sensitive to time delay and synchronization, this paper proposes to apply UFMC system to the Internet of vehicles. In order to improve the reliability of UFMC system, this paper analyzes the problem of inter-carrier interference in UFMC system, and gives the detailed derivation process. Then, the interference is suppressed by optimizing the design of waveform filter. The performance of UFMC system using FIR filter and DC filter is compared by MATLAB simulation platform in AWGN channel with or without CFO, The influence of filter index on the performance of UFMC system is analyzed. The results show that the waveform filter designed in this paper is better than the DC filter to a certain extent, and can effectively improve the reliability of the system.

References

1. Li, B., Fei, Z., Zhang, Y.: UAV communications for 5G and beyond: recent advances and future trends. IEEE Internet Things **6**(2), 2241–2263 (2018)
2. Popovski, P., Trillingsgaard, K.F., Simeone, O.: 5G wireless network slicing for eMBB, URLLC, and mMTC: a communication-theoretic view. IEEE Access **6**, 55765–55779 (2018)
3. Ning, Z., Dong, P., Wang, X.: Mobile edge computing enabled 5G health monitoring for internet of medical things: a decentralized game theoretic approach. IEEE J. Sel. Area Commun. **39**(2), 463–478 (2021)
4. Xie, R., Lian, X., Jia, Q.: Overview of mobile edge computing offload technology. J. Commun. **39**(11), 138–155 (2018)
5. Cao, S., Lee, V.C.: An accurate and complete performance modeling of the IEEE 802.11 p MAC sublayer for VANET. Comput. Commun. **149**, 107–120 (2020)
6. Ni, S.J., Zhao, J.H.: Key technologies in physical layer of 5G wireless communications network. Telecommun. Sci. **31**(12), 48–53 (2015)
7. Xie, X.Z.: Key requirements and multi-access multiplexing techniques for 5G. CQU Posts Telecommun. **27**(4), 434–440 (2015)
8. Ma, X., Zhao, J., Sun, X., Gong, Y.: Key technologies in collaborative network based on MEC. Telecommun. Sci. **36**(6), 28–37 (2020)
9. Li, N.Z.: Comparison of new multi carrier transmission technologies for 5G. Commun. Technol. **49**(05), 519–523 (2016)
10. Kibria, M.G., Villardi, G.P., Ishizu, K.: Throughput enhancement of multicarrier cognitive M2M networks: universal-filtered OFDM systems. IEEE Internet Things **3**(5), 830–838 (2016)
11. Helwa, S.S., Ibrahim, M., Elramly, S.: Universal filtered multi-carrier performance analysis with multipath fading channels. In: International Conference on Next Generation Mobile Applications, Security and Technologies, Cardiff, pp. 35–40. IEEE Press (2016)
12. Ambatali, C.D.M., Marciano, J.J.S.: Performance evaluation of the UFMC scheme under various transmission impairments. In: 2016 IEEE International Conference on Communication, Surabaya, pp. 24–28. IEEE Press (2016)
13. Wang, X., Wild, T., Schaich, F.: Universal filtered multi-carrier with leakage-based filter optimization. In: European Wireless 2014, European Wireless Conference, Spain, pp. 1–5. VDE Press (2014)
14. Wang, X., Wild, T., Schaich, F.: Filter optimization for carrier-frequency-and timing-offset in universal filtered multi-carrier systems. In: Vehicular Technology Conference, Glasgow, pp. 1–6. IEEE Press (2015)
15. Geng, S., Xiong, X., Cheng, L., et al.: UFMC system performance analysis for discrete narrow-band private networks. In: IEEE 2015 6th International Symposium on Microwave, Antenna, Propagation, and EMC Technologies (MAPE), Shanghai, pp. 303–307. IEEE Press (2015)

16. Yu, X., Gao, Y., Duan, S.: Channel estimation of UFMC system in multipath channel. Telecommun. Sci. **34**(4), 22–30 (2018)
17. Yang, L., He, P., Wang, S.: Carrier frequency synchronization technology in UFMC. Telecommun. Sci. **32**(11), 50–55 (2016)
18. Tang, M.F., Su, B.: Filter optimization of low out-of-subband emission for universal-filtered multicarrier systems. In: IEEE 2016 International Conference on Communications Workshops (ICC), Kuala Lumpur, pp. 468–473. IEEE Press (2016)

Research on Image Binary Classification Based on Fast Style Transfer Data Enhancement

Shuang Zheng, Junfeng Wu, Fugang Liu$^{(\boxtimes)}$, Jingyi Pan, and Zhuang Qiao

Heilongjiang University of Science and Technology, Harbin 150022, China
liufugang_36@163.com

Abstract. The essence of image classification task is to extract high-level semantic content features of images. The traditional data enhancement methods based on convolutional neural network (CNN) are translation, rotation, clipping, noise adding, etc. These methods have not changed the content and style of image data. This paper proposes a fast style migration data enhancement method, which can quickly apply the style art of one image to another image without changing the high-level semantic content characteristics of the image. Through the experimental comparison, it is found that the method of fast style migration data enhancement proposed here can further improve the accuracy of the model compared with the traditional data.

Keywords: Convolutional neural network · Data enhancement · Style transfer · Image classification

1 Introduction

With the rapid development of the Internet, images have become important data information. For these massive images, it is difficult for people to quickly find the information they expect. This makes people urgently need a way to quickly and effectively obtain the required image content information from a large number of images. With the rapid development of image classification technology [1], convolution neural network has incomparable advantages in image processing based on convolution neural network has become the mainstream of research [2–4].

Data enhancement refers to expanding the number of data sets to increase diversity in the training of convolutional neural networks, especially in the case of insufficient samples, data enhancement becomes more important. On the one hand, popular deep architectures such as AlexNet [7] or VGGNet [8] have millions of parameters, so it is necessary to train a fairly large data set for a specific task, and lack of sufficient data will lead to overfitting [5, 6]. On the other hand, collecting raw data is very time-consuming and expensive in many computer vision tasks. For example, in key tasks such as medical image analysis, industry, and agricultural production, researchers are often limited by the lack of reliable data. Style transfer is a neural network-based image style transfer method proposed by Gatys et al. [7]. It solves the complex process of manual modeling

X. Jiang (Ed.): MLICOM 2021, LNICST 438, pp. 79–89, 2022.
https://doi.org/10.1007/978-3-031-04409-0_8

in traditional methods. The deep learning technique can be used to model the texture features and apply the artistic style of one image to the task of another. However, at the same time, it also has certain drawbacks. It requires constant iteration to generate pictures, which takes too long [8]. This paper proposes a data enhancement method based on rapid style transfer to expand data. Firstly, a fast style transfer network is designed for efficient style transfer, and secondly, the traditional data enhancement method and the style transfer data enhancement method are used to expand the data set. Finally, the data sets expanded by the two methods are divided into data sets, and the image classification network is used for training, and the advantages and disadvantages of the methods proposed in this paper are compared and analyzed through experiments.

2   Image Fast Style Transfer Model

Image conversion network fw and loss network Φ are the parts of the fast style migration network. As shown in Fig. 1, the main structures of fw and Φ are the depth residuals network [9] and the VGG-19 network, respectively. Loss network is defined as feature loss "lfeat" and style loss "lstyle" to measure the gap between content and style.

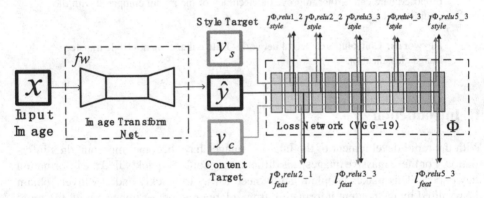

Fig. 1. Image quick style transfer system

2.1   Image Conversion Network

The theory shows that the depth of the network is an important factor in achieving efficient image recognition. This is because the deepening of the network will cause gradient explosion [10, 11] and gradient disappearance [12–14]. In order to solve the above problems and get a good image conversion network, this paper adopts the deep residual network as the backbone of the image conversion network. The deep residual network adds the residual module shown in Fig. 2 to the traditional convolutional neural network, so that the output of the previous layer is directly input to the input of the next layer without convolution operation. Assuming the input of a certain section of convolutional neural network is x and the expected output is $H(x)$. The identity mapping is passed to the next layer, so the learning residual function $F(x) = H(x) - x$.

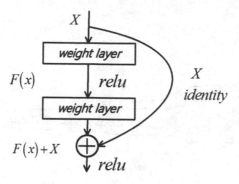

Fig. 2. Residual error module

Formula (1) is the parameter weight parameter W of image conversion network. It completes the conversion of input image x and output image by using $y = fw(x)$, and obtains $l_i(y, y_i)$ by loss function, to measure the difference between the generated image y of the output and the target image y_i.

$$W^* = \arg \min_W E_{x,\{y_i\}} \left[\sum_{i=1} \lambda l_i(f_W(x), y_i) \right] \tag{1}$$

2.2 Loss of the Network

For the loss network, this article defines two perceptual loss functions, content loss function and style loss function, to measure the difference in content and style between two pictures. Although the loss network here is also a convolutional neural network (CNN), the parameters are not updated, and are only used for the calculation of content loss and style loss. In order to ensure that this loss network has excellent extraction capabilities in terms of content and style, this paper uses the VGG-19 network model pretrained in ImageNet [15]. The VGG-19 network structure is shown in Fig. 3.

2.2.1 Content Loss Function

The formula (2) is the content loss function defined in this paper, $\phi_j(x)$ represents the jth layer of the network ϕ, the input is y, and $C_j \times H_j \times W_j$ is the shape of the feature map. This function penalizes the content deviation between the generated image and the target image, and requires the generated image to be very similar to the input target image in content details. The smaller the value of the loss function, the more similar the content of the images before and after processing, and vice versa.

$$l_{feat}^{\phi,j}(\hat{y}, y) = \frac{1}{C_j H_j W_j} \|\phi_j(y) - \phi(y)\|_2^2 \tag{2}$$

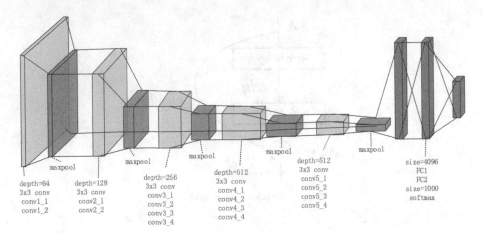

Fig. 3. VGG-19 network structure

2.2.2 Style Loss Function

It is also hoped that the style loss will penalize the deviation in style, such as color, texture, and common mode. In order to achieve this effect, this paper proposes the following style reconstruction loss function as formula (3). $\phi_j(x)$ represents the jth layer of ϕ. The input is x. The shape of the feature map is $C_j \times H_j \times W_j$.

$$G_j^{\phi}(x)_{c,c'} = \frac{1}{C_j H_j W_j} \sum_{h=1}^{H_j} \sum_{w=1}^{W_j} \phi_j(x)_{h,w,c} \phi_j(x)_{h,w,c'} \tag{3}$$

3 Analysis of the Fast Style Transfer Model

All style transfer models in this article are based on the VGG19 pre-training network, using Tensorflow deep learning framework to train coco data set (80000 pieces). The image size is normalized to 256×256, the number of iterations for all models is 20000, batch_size is set to 4, and epoch is set to 1.

3.1 Image Style Transfer

Visualizing the filters of the pre-trained VGG-19 network model will be of great help to the selection of the content and style extraction layer. The visualization of some filters from the low-level to the high-level is shown in Fig. 4.

From the visualization of these filters, it can be seen that the low-level filters extract simple directional edges and color features. As the number of layers deepens, the filter in the convolutional neural network becomes more and more complex, and the feature information that the filter can extract is also richer, such as feathers, leaves, eyes, etc.

In this paper, the higher layer conv5_3 is selected as the content extraction layer, and the lower layer conv1_2 and conv2_2 are selected as the style extraction layer to train

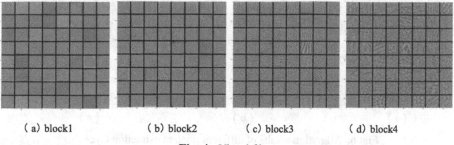

(a) block1   (b) block2   (c) block3   (d) block4

Fig. 4. Visual filter

(a) Target image   (b) Style image   (c) Generated image

Fig. 5. Image migration results

the style transfer model and combine the style transfer network to realize the image style transfer, as shown in Fig. 5.

From the results, when the high-level is only selected as the content extraction layer, and the low-level is used as the style extraction layer, the migration result is completely pixelated. This is because too high a layer contains too much content information, and a too low layer filter almost only extracts some unimportant texture information. So the trained model performs very poorly in style extraction, and it migrates the target image. When the target image is transferred, the single style information is over fitted to make the generated image completely pixelated. This article continues to improve the experiment, adjust the content and style extraction layer, select conv2_1, conv3_3, conv5_3 as the content extraction layer, select conv1_2, conv2_2, conv3_3, conv4_3, conv5_3 as the style extraction layer, train 3 migration models and combine the image conversion network to realize the image Style transfer (from left to right in Fig. 6); select conv3_3 as the content extraction layer, conv1_2, conv1_2, conv2_2, conv1_2, conv2_2, conv3_3, conv1_2, conv2_2, conv3_3, conv4_3, conv1_2, conv2_2, conv4_3, conv5_3 is the style extraction layer, which trains 5 style transfer models and combines the image conversion network to realize image style transfer (from left to right in Fig. 7).

From the results, it can be seen that multiple consecutive layers from the low-level to the high-level are selected as the style extraction layer, and the layer closer to the middle is selected as the content extraction layer can get the best migration effect.

(a)   (b)   (c)

Fig. 6. Migration results of different content extraction layer

(a)   (b)   (c)   (d)   (e)

Fig. 7. Migration results of different style layers

3.2 Image Generation Time

Through the experiment, it is found that when using the style transfer model to transfer the style of the target image, the transfer time of different size of the target image is often different. Use different style images to train a new style transfer model to continue the transfer, and make statistics on the transfer time as shown in Table 1.

Table 1. Timetable for different models.

	67×67	224×224	512×512	1024×1024
Style model 1	1.3742 s	2.5156 s	4.1475 s	9.3756 s
Style model 2	1.3786 s	2.5489 s	4.1549 s	9.3845 s
Style model 3	1.4025 s	2.5132 s	4.1135 s	9.3766 s
Style model 4	1.3812 s	2.6732 s	4.1303 s	9.2524 s
Style model 5	1.3744 s	2.5973 s	4.1387 s	9.3688 s

It can be seen from the statistical data in the above table that under the premise of the algorithm used in this article, the different style transfer models obtained by training are very close to the transfer time of the target image of the same size. With the increase of the size of the target image, the migration time will increase, that is, the migration time of the target image has nothing to do with the style migration model, but only with the size of the target image.

4   Image Binary Classification Based on Fast Style Transfer Feature Enhancement

For image classification tasks, the previous data enhancement only performed simple processing such as translation, cropping, rotation, and noise addition on the image. In this paper, the original image data set will be processed, and the main content features will be retained by using fast style migration technology, and some environment style features will be changed. Then, the training set is added to the image which changes some features to improve the number of samples and help image classification. In order to improve the classification accuracy of the classification model, this paper also verifies the effectiveness of the fast style migration data enhancement compared with the traditional data enhancement.

4.1   Choice of Style Model

Based on the previous work of this article, five style models (waves, feathers and leaves, abstract, animation, Van Gogh starry sky) have been trained. To save the time of image style transfer and ensure conversion effect, we first process the image size to 224×224, and then carry out style transfer. In order to select a suitable style transfer model for data enhancement, this paper uses the class activation algorithm (grad-CAM) to measure the effectiveness of the transfer model for data enhancement. Grad-CAM performs a reverse operation according to the output vector to obtain the gradient of the feature map, that is, the gradient map corresponding to the feature map, and then averages each gradient map. This average value corresponds to the weight of each feature map, and then the weight and feature map are weighted and summed, and the final class activation map is obtained through the activation function. Figure 8 is a diagram showing the class activation performance on the image generated by the style transfer with the target image as the output vector.

It can be seen from the thermal map of class activation after the target image is migrated by five kinds of fast style migration models that for the image whose target image is cat, the effect of wave style activation is the most obvious, and the thermal map of class activation almost covers the whole object; For the image whose target image is dog, the activation effect of abstract style is the most obvious. Therefore, this paper selects ocean wave style and abstract style from 5 style models to enhance the data of cat and dog in the binary image data set.

4.2   Image Classification Network

If the data set used by the pre-training network is large and general enough, the spatial level of the features can effectively serve as a general visual world model. Thus, these features can be applied to various computer vision problems, even if the categories involved in these new problems are completely different from the original tasks. VGG-16 pre-training network is a convolutional neural network with 1000 classes. Therefore, it is necessary to improve the VGG-16 pre-training network to perform two class prediction output. In this paper, the improvement of VGG-16 pre-training network is shown in

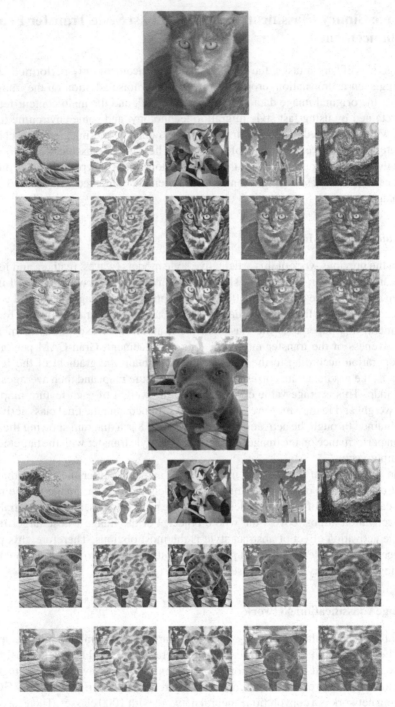

Fig. 8. Style transfer and class activation heat map

Fig. 9. The convolution base trained in the network is retained, all dense connection layers are deleted, and then a two-layer dense connection layer and sigmoid activation function are added after the convolution base.

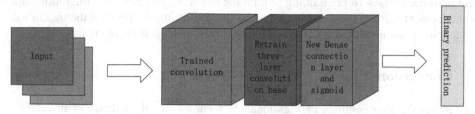

Fig. 9. Improved VGG-16 pre-training network model

4.3 Experiment and Analysis

The data set used in this article is partial data of two categories of cats and dogs in the "kaggle" data set, with 5000 images of cat and dog respectively. The image data of cats and dogs are respectively enhanced by the traditional data enhancement method selected at random and the fast style transfer method proposed in this paper. Two expanded data sets are obtained, and the number of images is 20,000 respectively. Among them, the styles used in the rapid style migration data enhancement methods for cats and dogs are ocean wave style and abstract style respectively. The two expanded data sets are divided into training set, verification set and test set, and the ratio of 6:2:2 is adopted. At the same time, in order to ensure the effectiveness of data enhancement, the enhanced data is also based on the ratio of 6:2:2.

Two expanded data sets are used to train on the improved VGG-16 pre-training network. The parameters are set as: learning rate 1e−5, epochs = 30, batch_size = 20, and loss function as binary_crossentropy. The final training result data is shown in Table 2.

Table 2. VGG-16 binary training data table

Data enhancement method	Training result
No	85.32%
Pan + crop	87.13%
Crop + rotate	86.57%
Rotate + noise	88.35%
Pan + noise	88.59%
Crop + rotate	85.43%
Wave style + abstract style	90.84%

From the statistical data in the above table, we can see that whether it is the traditional data enhancement method or the fast style transfer data enhancement method proposed in this article, the accuracy of classification prediction is relatively good, and both are above 85%.This is because this paper adopts the idea of transfer learning and uses the optimized VGG-16 pre training to train the network. The fast style migration data enhancement method proposed in this paper is significantly better than the traditional data enhancement method, and the maximum increase is 5 percentage points.

5 Conclusion

Based on the shortcomings of traditional data enhancement methods of diversified and single data after enhancement, this paper proposes a method of style transfer data enhancement to help convolutional neural networks in image classification, and addresses the shortcomings of traditional style transfer speed and poor extraction effect. Firstly, a fast style transfer model is designed, which can transfer target images of different sizes in a few seconds to complete a specific style transfer. Secondly, this article uses the grad-CAM algorithm to select appropriate style transfer styles for different data sets, and then selects different data sets Perform style transfer data enhancement. Finally, through experiments, it is found that the fast style transfer data enhancement method proposed here can help convolutional neural networks to classify images and improve the prediction accuracy of the model. The inability to process the data during the training process is one of the shortcomings of this article. The follow-up work of this article will focus on the study of more rapid and effective data enhancement methods, and is committed to improving the accuracy of the classification model.

Acknowledgements. This work has been partially supported by "Heilongjiang Science Foundation Project (LH2021F052)" and "2020 scientific research project of basic scientific research expenses of provincial colleges and universities in Heilongjiang Province (2020-KYYWF-0684)".

References

1. Guo, Y., Rothfus, T.A., Ashour, A.S., Si, L., Chunlai, D., Ting, T.-F.: Varied channels region proposal and classification network for wildlife image classification under complex environment. IET Image Process. **14**(4), 585–591 (2020). https://doi.org/10.1049/iet-ipr.2019.1042
2. Seo, S., Do, W.-J., Luu, H.M., Kim, K.H., Choi, S.H., Park, S.-H.: Artificial neural network for Slice Encoding for Metal Artifact Correction (SEMAC) MRI. Magn. Reson. Med. **84**(1), 263–276 (2020). https://doi.org/10.1002/mrm.28126
3. An, T., et al.: Black tea withering moisture detection method based on convolution neural network confidence. Food Process Eng. **43**(7),(2020). https://doi.org/10.1111/jfpe.13428
4. Qi, Y., Chen, J., Huo, Y., Li, F.: Hyperspectral image classification algorithm based on multiscale convolutional neural network. Infrared Technol. **42**(9), 855–862 (2020). https://doi.org/10.3724/SP.J.7102910261
5. Krizhevsky, A., Sutskever, I., Hinton, G.E.: ImageNet classification with deep convolutional neural networks. Commun. ACM **60**(6), 84–90 (2017)

6. Helmrich, I.R.A.R., van Klaveren, D., Steyerberg, E.W.: Research Note: prognostic model research: overfitting, validation and application. J. Physiother. **65**(4), 243–245 (2019). https://doi.org/10.1016/j.jphys.2019.08.009
7. Gatys, L., Ecker, A., Bethge, M.: A neural algorithm of artistic style. J. Vis. **16**(12), 326 (2016). https://doi.org/10.1167/16.12.326
8. Zhao, X., Zhao, X.-M.: Deep learning of brain magnetic resonance images: a brief review. Methods **192**, 131–140 (2021). https://doi.org/10.1016/j.ymeth.2020.09.007
9. Zhang, Z., Tong Zhou, Y., Zhang, Y.P.: Attention-based deep residual learning network for entity relation extraction in Chinese EMRs. BMC Med. Inf. Decis. Making **19**(S2) (2019). https://doi.org/10.1186/s12911-019-0769-0
10. Chen, J., Xiang, Y.: Summarization of research on gradient instability in deep neural network training. **29**(07), 2071–2091 (2018)
11. Yuexiu, G., Wei, Y., Qi, L., Wang, Y.: Summary of residual network research. Comput. Appl. Res. **37**(05), 1292–1297 (2020)
12. Glorot, X., Bengio, Y.: Understanding the difficulty of training deep feedforward neural networks. J. Mach. Learn. Res. **9**, 249–256 (2010)
13. Tomoyuki, O., Kouyu, S., Naohiko, K.: Proposal and evaluation of pavement deterioration prediction method by recurrent neural network. Int. J. Adv. Res. Eng. **3**(4), 16 (2017)
14. Castillioni, K., Wilcox, K., Jiang, L., Luo, Y., Jung, C.G., Souza, L.: Drought mildly reduces plant dominance in a temperate prairie ecosystem across years. Ecol. Evol. **10**(13), 6702–6713 (2020). https://doi.org/10.1002/ece3.6400
15. Chunshui, C., Yongzhen, H., Yi, Y., et al.: Feedback convolutional neural network for visual localization and segmentation. IEEE Trans. Patt. Anal. Mach. Intell. **41**(7), 1627–1640 (2019)

3DCNN Backed Conv-LSTM Auto Encoder for Micro Facial Expression Video Recognition

Md. Sajjatul Islam[1], Yuan Gao[2], Zhilong Ji[2], Jiancheng Lv[1],
Adam Ahmed Qaid Mohammed[1], and Yongsheng Sang[1(✉)]

[1] College of Computer Science, Sichuan University, Chengdu 610065, China
sangys@scu.edu.cn
[2] TAL Education Group, Beijing 100080, China

Abstract. Facial Micro-Expression recognition in the field of emotional information processing has become an inexorable necessity for its exotic attributes. It is a non-verbal, spontaneous, and involuntary leakage of true emotion in disguise of most expressive intentional prototypical facial expressions. However, it persists only for a split-second duration and possesses fainted facial muscle movements that make the recognition task more difficult with naked eyes. Besides, there are a limited number of video samples and wide-span domain shifting among datasets. Considering these challenges, several video-based works have been done to improve the classification accuracy but still lack high accuracy. This works addresses these issues and presents an approach with a deep 3D Convolutional Residual Neural Network as a backbone followed by a Long-Short-Term-Memory auto-encoder with 2D convolutions model for automatic Spatio-temporal feature extractions, fine-tuning, and classifications from videos. Also, we have done transfer learning on three standard macro-expression datasets to reduce over-fitting. Our work has shown a significant accuracy gain with extensive experiments on composite video samples from five publicly available micro-expression benchmark datasets, CASME, CASMEII, CAS(ME)^2, SMIC, and SAMM. This outweighs the state-of-the-art accuracy. It is the first attempt to work with five datasets and rational implication of LSTM auto-encoder for micro-expression recognition.

Keywords: Micro-expression · Recognition · Deep learning · Transfer learning · Spatio-temporal

1 Introduction

Facial Micro-Expression (ME) discloses true mental state unconsciously while someone is trying to obscure them advertently in a high-stake situation. This transient ME lasts for less than 1/5 s [1] and diminishes under cover of ordinary acted facial expressions. It has a very low intensity [2] due to the tiny movements of facial muscles. It is challenging to create a high-stake situation in a controlled environment and generate ME voluntarily against its spontaneous nature. These reasons impede the real-time [3] implementation of ME recognition (MER) from publicly available ME datasets, while it gives an important

X. Jiang (Ed.): MLICOM 2021, LNICST 438, pp. 90–105, 2022.
https://doi.org/10.1007/978-3-031-04409-0_9

cue for lie or deceitful behavior detection. Though there are only five spontaneous publicly available ME datasets [3], all of them have smaller size of samples. Facial Action Coding System (FACS) coding [4] has also been used in most of the ME databases to identify the action units (AU) that are linked to specific facial muscle movements within facial components. AUs that are pertinent to emotional state help to reduce the subjective biases in recognition of MEs. Despite all of these challenges, ME recognition has gained momentum in the computer vision community in the last few years [5] due to some inescapable practical implications such as business deal negotiation, psychoanalysis, forensic investigation, and homeland securities.

Many handcrafted works for feature descriptions were devised based on appearance-based feature learning for ME recognition. For static and dynamic texture-based ME recognition, LBP and many of its variants have been proposed in [6–12]. Though they are very familiar, they are not innate for AU/motion-based recognition due to LBP features. Hence the geometry or motion-based descriptors [13–17] were introduced to capture the deformation in it with the facial landmarks or optical flow features. These techniques are susceptible to head-pose variations and leaned to face registration. Also, gradient-based feature descriptors [18, 19] were proposed to mitigate lighting variations but still suffer from head-pose variations.

Automatic feature learning methods ignite independent learning from inputs effectively. For that purpose, many deep learning-based models have gain popularity in recent years for ME recognition. The first possible use of the convolutional neural network (CNN) deep model [20] for ME recognition was less prone to better accuracy due to over-fitting. Takalkar and Xu [21] proposed a CNN-based model with data augmentation to combat the over-fitting problem but ended up with minor improvement due to data imbalance and subjective bias in annotations. In [22], temporal interpolation was used with DCNN followed by a support vector machine (SVM) classifier for ME recognition to combat the short duration. Peng. et al. [23] proposed a dual temporal scale convolutional neural network (DTSCNN) for Spatio-temporal feature extractions from optical flow inputs of a composite dataset from two ME datasets. It achieved better performance in comparison to some hand-design methods. In [24], CNN accompanied long-short-term-memory (LSTM) was proposed. It considered the class discrimination, expression states, and persistence of states along with temporal change. It achieved better results but was not strong enough to confront the imbalance sample problem. In TLCNN [25], pre-trained CNN was used to model spatial features from a single frame then fed them to LSTM. It used the combined video samples from three ME datasets. A pre-trained deep network-based method on apex frame was done in [26]. Two-stream optical flow-dependent high level features extractions and classification network was introduced in [27]. In [28], dual-stream shallow CNN was proposed to combat with over-fitting and saliency map. Deep recurrent-CNN (R-CNN) based-model trained from scratch for spatiotemporal feature learning were presented in [29]. In [30] shallow R-CNN model was designed and experimented on composite dataset samples. VGGNets and LSTM discriminative attention model were proposed in [31]. Deep learning-based approaches and models have shown a strong and reliable representation of discriminative features from ME.

Numerous researches have been carried out based on handcrafted feature engineering, automatic spatial features extractions, and temporal correlation among spatial features to classify the ME from SMIC [32], CASME [33], CASMEII [34], CAS(ME)^2 [35], and SAMM [36] datasets. There is some resemblance between macro-expressions (MACE) and MEs in terms of some facial dynamics. In addition, MACE datasets (e.g., CK+ [37], MUGFE [38], and OULU-CASIA [39]) have a large number of samples, which facilitate taking advantage of transfer learning in recognition of ME from limited samples using deep learning models. Automatic ME recognition from frame sequences is quite challenging due to the persistence in a small number of frames. Moreover, ME videos contain some/many redundant and neural frames that increase the computational cost as well as the influence of irrelevant feature extractions. Despite this, video-based end-to-end deep ME recognition is more resilient as it models the spatio-temporal features against the illumination, head-pose, and subtle motion variations. Though composite ME samples from multiple ME datasets make the solution even harder due to inconsistency among them, it helps to model ME to a greater extent from a diverse and large group of samples possessing different intrinsic factors that might be a set/subset in the wild samples. That paves the way to realistic categorization of ME from more spontaneous and natural ME samples.

We propose a method to extract spatio-temporal features from composite samples of five spontaneous ME datasets [32–36] through the 3D CNN in the residual network as backbone and LSTM auto-encoder for de-noising and fine-tuning the high-level feature maps comprising the temporal deformation of spatial features and followed by a native structural regularizer accompanied with a soft-max classifier. Two cross-validation strategies, Leave-One-Subject-Out (LOSO) and Stratified 5-Fold cross-validations (CV) have been designed and tested on the combined samples to estimate standard accuracy, unweighted average recall (UAR), and un-weighted average F1-Score (UF1). Two-stage transfer learning has been used based on three benchmark MACE datasets[37–39]. Our model shows superior recognition accuracy on three metrics that surpass the state-of-the-art methods.

The main contributions to this work are summarized below:

- We propose an automatic ME recognition method based on the 3DCNN-18 residual network as a backbone for spatio-temporal feature extractions followed by a conv-LSTM auto-encoder with the size of 2-1-2 for fine-tuning the temporal correlation among spatial features and de-noising them. Finally, a structural regularizer is appended for aggressive summarization to feed the final vector to a soft-max classifier.
- Macro-to-micro transfer learning has been revitalized to deal with over-fitting due to the lower number of ME video samples.
- Construction of a composite ME video dataset with three class samples (e.g., negative, positive, and surprise) from five publicly available ME datasets.
- Validation with two CV techniques, LOSO and Stratified 5-fold, to measure effectiveness and verify the generalization of the model using cross samples and cross subjects. That shows the very high effectiveness of the proposed method that outweighs the state-of-the-art MER approaches.

The rest of this paper is organized with methodology in Sect. 2, experiments in Sect. 3, and results and discussion in Sect. 4, and conclusions in Sect. 5.

2 Methodology

This section systematically presents our proposed method. The approach encompasses the pipeline, model architecture, evaluation metrics, and loss function, and transfer learning mechanism from macro to micro expressions.

2.1 Process Pipeline

General pipelines show the flow of input video processing steps, 3DCNN-18 residual [40] backbone for spatio-temporal feature extractions, 2D Conv-LSTM auto-encoder inspired by [41], and a structural regularizer followed by a soft-max classifier. It covers the input to emotional class label predictions from a sequence of spontaneous ME frames, which is depicted in Fig. 1.

Faces in ME video frames are detected and aligned with a deep-based reliable face alignment network [42] along with a real-time and robust single-shot-scale invariant face detector (S3FD) [43] to correct head-pose. It reduces the negative influence on ME recognition. The face has been cropped based on the detected bounding box to eliminate the irrelevant area from images. The facial images are then normalized to 64 × 64, which makes training faster for video sequences by reducing the computational cost. Then it is augmented using vertical flipping and 8° counter-clockwise rotation to triple the original samples. It helps to reduce over-fitting to some extent. Furthermore, the frame sequences have been padded with last frame which is the onset frame in our case for all ME datasets except SMIC, as the apex frame is not annotated in it. We restrict the ME video length to 12 frames for batching to reduce the computational cost and unnecessary redundancy. As the datasets samples are highly imbalanced, we have calculated the class weights for sampling in weighted random sampler for batching to ensure the representative samples for each class for recognition. After all of these preprocessing, augmentation and batching steps, the frame sequences have been fed into the model depicted in Fig. 2 for saptio-temporal feature extractions and classification. The model is described in the following section.

2.2 Model Architecture

It encompasses a residual 18 3DCNN backbone network, a 2-1-2 LSTM auto-encoder with 2D convolution, a 3DCNN layer followed by a structural regularizer, and a soft-max classifier. Here 3DCNN is for convolutions in spatial and temporal dimensions of ME frame sequence concurrently. It is implemented in a residual framework with 18 layers to capture the dynamic changes in spatial ME features from faces. The elicited spatio-temporal features with the dimension (**channel × length × height × width**) have been transferred as input to the convolutional LSTM two-layer auto-encoder for compact representation of features by reducing noises and fine-tuning the subtle spatial changes. It unrolls both LSTM encoder cells for the length dimension. We have considered the vanilla LSTM cell with 2D convolutions, which are formulized in the following set of equations-

$$i_t = \sigma(W_{xi} \; conv \; x_t + W_{hi} \; conv \; h_{t-1} + W_{ci} * c_{t-1} + b_i) \qquad (1)$$

$$f_t = \sigma\left(W_{xf} \; conv \; x_t + W_{hf} \; conv \; h_{t-1} + W_{cf} * c_{t-1} + b_f\right) \qquad (2)$$

$$c_t = f_t * C_{t-1} + i_t * tanh(W_{xc} \; conv \; x_t + W_{hc} \; conv \; h_{t-1} + b_c) \qquad (3)$$

$$o_t = \sigma(W_{xo} \; conv \; x_t + W_{ho} \; conv \; h_{t-1} + W_{co} * c_t + b_o) \qquad (4)$$

$$h_t = o_t * \tanh(c_t) \qquad (5)$$

In Eqs. (1), (2), (3), (4), and (5), it is the input, f_t is the output from forget gate, C_t current state, o_t output, and H_t is the hidden state at current time step t. Again, conv represents the convolution operation and * for Hadamard product. LSTM cell is iteratively unrolled for the activated feature map sequence obtained from the 3DCNN backbone. Conv-LSTM encoder mapped the input as a compact representation to an encoded vector. Here, it is the hidden vector h_2 from the 2nd LSTM encoder cell for the last featured frame in the high-level features frame sequence. Conv-LSTM decoder with two LSTM cells has been used to reconstruct the fine-grained, smooth spatio-temporal transient evolution. Here 3×3 convolutional filter is used for both the decoder and encoder parts. Regenerated ME features stacked on h_3 through **length** iterations from the decoder part are fed into a 3DCNN layer with kernel $1 \times 3 \times 3$. It converts the feature maps from regressive to actual class form to categorize ME expression sequence into three labels negative, positive, and surprise. Then a native structural regularizer with adaptive average pooling is used for aggressive summarization to generate a vector of three predicted values. It reduces the trainable parameters to alleviate the over-fitting. A finishing soft-max classifier is used to ensure the predicted of three values is 1.

2.3 Evaluation Metrics and Loss Functions

To evaluate the model on composite ME samples, three metrics have been used to observe the influence of data organization, preprocessing, augmentation, and frame rate setup, as well as to measure the effectiveness of the proposed model. Here standard accuracy, balanced accuracy, i.e., UAR and UF1 macro metrics, have been represented in Eqs. (6), (7), and (8).

$$Standard \; Accuracy = \frac{TP + TN}{TP + FP + TN + FN} \qquad (6)$$

$$Un\text{-}weighted \; Average \; Recall = \frac{\sum per \; class \; accuracy}{C} \qquad (7)$$

$$Un\text{-}weighted \; Average \; F1 \; Score = \frac{2TP}{2TP + FP + FN} \qquad (8)$$

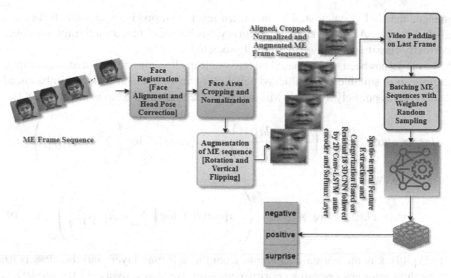

Fig. 1. ME recognition pipeline comprising preprocessing of input video to class label prediction.

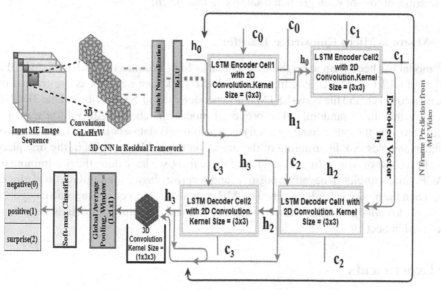

Fig. 2. Model architecture composed of 3D ResNet18 and Conv-LSTM auto-encoder appended with structural regularizer.

In Eqs. (6), (7), and (8), TP, TN, FP, FN, and C represent True Positive, True Negative, False Positive, False Negative, and the number of classes, respectively.

As the target ME datasets are highly imbalanced, we have considered these metrics to reduce the bias of the model to higher sample classes on accuracy. Model sensitivity is measured with UAR by averaging the recall on each predicted class of a ME video sequence, and UF1 is calculated at the macro level from precision and recall for each predicted sample. Also, the standard accuracy has been estimated on the total number of correctly classified samples out of total predicted samples.

The model has been trained based on cross-entropy loss function on predicted output. Therefore, it is suitable for multiclass label classification and for highly imbalanced datasets such as publicly available ME datasets. The analytical form is given in Eq. (9).

$$loss(x, class) = -log\left(\frac{exp(x[class])}{\sum_j exp(x[j])}\right) = -x[class] + log\left(\sum_j exp(x[j])\right)$$

For class weights-

$$loss(x, class) = weight[class]\left(-x[class] + log\left(\sum_j exp(x[j])\right)\right) \qquad (9)$$

In Eq. (9), x is the normalized output from the soft-max layer, and the class is [0, 1, 2] for three categories negative, positive, and surprise, respectively. As the model has been trained on a batch of ME frame sequence, the loss has been calculated based on the average of loss of each predicted sample in that batch.

2.4 Macro to Micro Knowledge Transfer

The model has been trained on three benchmarks MACE datasets, CK+ [37], MUGFE [38], and OULU-CASIA [39]. In our model, the backbone network is pre-trained on kinetics-400 [44], and the conv-LSTM auto-encoder with 4 LSTM cells and the 3DCNN layer are initialized randomly. The proposed model has about 37.6 million trainable parameters. On the other hand, publicly accessible ME datasets have a lower number of video samples. So, the training of the model on target ME samples in the first place must be a cause of over-fitting. Considering these facts, we have done the pre-training on MACE video samples in negative, positive, and surprise classes for similar knowledge of ME. Then the model is further trained on ME composite samples in the same categories for target knowledge MER. Datasets organization and experimental details have been discussed in Sect. 3.

3 Experiments

This section describes the organization of data samples into three discrete categories negative, positive, and surprise for both MACE and ME. It also represents the data set summaries, model implementation, and design and implementation of cross-validations LOSO and Stratified-5Fold.

3.1 Macro and Micro Datasets Organization

Three benchmark MACE datasets have been used for the transformation of knowledge about ordinary prototypical facial expressions. The widely used extended Cohn-Kanade

(CK+) [37] is one of them. The other two MUGFE [38] and OULU-CASIA [39] are also very relevant datasets for MACE video samples. We have considered frame sequences for the expressions of anger, disgust, sadness, happiness, and surprise in all three datasets. In CK+, the respective MACE videos have been reduced to the range of 6 to 50 frames by manually eliminating some early neutral frames but preserving the last one as a peak in each sequence. For MUG facial expression dataset, we have kept the video length is less than or equal to 62 frames by discarding the neutral and less expressive frames. Videos of OULU-CASIA have been restricted to 20 frames in the same way. Only the samples of the strong visible lighting part of this dataset are taken for our transfer learning. All the samples from these datasets are categorized into three classes negative (anger, disgust, and sadness), positive (happiness), and surprise (surprise). So, it results in a composite MACE three class dataset for pre-training. Samples from these representative datasets are summarized in Table 1.

We have considered five spontaneous ME datasets mentioned in Table 2 for ME recognition in negative, positive, and surprise categories. A composite dataset comprising of ME video samples from those ME datasets has been constructed. Here the negative one has been formed with anger, disgust, and sadness, where happiness and surprise for positive and surprise respectively. The number of samples in each class is tabulated in Table 1. To the best of our knowledge, this is the first attempt to recognize ME on five ME datasets. To reduce the subjective bias, all ME samples except SMIC enlisted in Table 1 have been reclassified based on AUs [45].

Table 1. Macro expressions and micro expressions video samples summary from three MACE datasets and five publicly available spontaneous ME datasets

Dataset	Negative	Positive	Surprise	Total video samples	
				Before augmentation	After augmentation
Macro expressions video samples					
CK+ [37]	133	69	83	285	1140
MUGFE [38]	376	163	143	682	2728
OULU-CASIA [39]	208	69	69	346	1384
Micro expressions video samples					
SMIC [32] (HS & VIS)	93	79	63	235	705
CAMSE [33]	80	6	14	100	300
CASMEII [34]	145	25	15	185	555
CAS(ME)^2 [35]	19	6	6	31	93
SAMM [36]	31	23	13	67	201

As ME videos have many redundant frames, which have a detrimental effect on recognition accuracy, we have eliminated many irrelevant frames by keeping only the frames in between onset and apex frames, including these two. Thus, the ME video sequences have been reduced to the intervals 6 to 13, 5 to 12, 7 to11, and 11 to 12 for CASME, CASMEII, CAS(ME)^2, and SAMM, respectively. The last frame in each ME sample is the frame with the highest peak. As SMIC is not annotated with apex frames, so we have kept the original video length. Only high-speed (HS) and visual (VIS) samples have been considered for SMIC. But this composite dataset has introduced a domain shifting challenge due to subject diversities and different disparate attributes among the ME datasets. But a larger number of samples facilitates to alleviate over-fitting and model generalization, which has been supported by the results in Sect. 4. Preprocessing and augmentation except smoothing are like those that have been discussed in Sect. 2.1. In the case of the MACE dataset, image smoothing has also been used for augmentation.

3.2 Experimental Settings

The proposed model has been trained on a composite macro dataset summarized in Table 1. The sequence length of each video is made equal to 12 frames by selecting the frames at equal interval and is padded with the last frame. Then the padded sequences have been used for pre-training. The hyper-parameters such as batch_size and initial learning rate are set to 64 and 0.0001, respectively. Learning rate is scheduled with patience 5 for equal validation loss in five consecutive epochs. An early stopping regularizing is used based on degraded or unchanged validation loss for 10 consecutive epochs. Learnable parameters have been optimized using Adam optimizer. The dimension of a batch of videos is $64 \times 3 \times 12 \times 64 \times 64$. For training and testing on ME composite target samples, we have considered the initial learning rate as 0.001, and the early stopping epoch is 8. For both cases, a weighted random sampler is configured and used to combat the bias towards the larger sample classes. But all other settings remain the same. The model is trained and tested on a platform with Windows 10 Pro, Intel Core I5 7400 CPU 3GHz, 8 GB DDR4 RAM, and NVIDIA GeForce RTX 2070 with 8 GB memory. The widely used Pythonic deep learning framework PyTorch has been used to accomplish the experiment.

3.3 Model Evaluations

The proposed model has been aligned with similar domain knowledge through the hold-out evaluations (80%:20%) on MACE composite samples. Here the model is trained and validated against three classes. The resulting confusion matrix is given in Fig. 3. Then the pre-trained model has been evaluated on our composite ME dataset in Table 1.

For this purpose, two validation strategies have been carefully considered and tuned for evaluating the model under three classes negative, positive, and surprise. One is LOSO CV, and the other one is Stratified-5 fold. Many challenges have been induced in the composite ME dataset due to the domain transition, especially the subjective diversities and the larger variations in temporal and spatial- frequencies along imbalance problem are notable. These cause a bias towards a specific group of ME video samples. LOSO and Stratified-5 fold are there to reduce biases for such data distributions. In LOSO, 87 subjects have been used to validate the model, where each subject is tested in each split during one epoch. On the other hand, each fold-out of 5 equal folds has been used as test samples in each split during one epoch. The metrics such as standard accuracy, UAR, and UF1 have been estimated from these validations. Figure 4 demonstrates the confusion metrics of best accuracies for both the tests. Also, the evolution of model convergence has been recorded in Fig. 5 and 6.

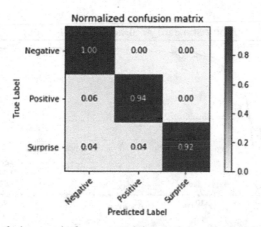

Fig. 3. Confusion matrix from pre-training on the composite MACE dataset

Table 2. Disparate spatio-temporal properties of five Publicly available spontaneous ME datasets. Here, HS-High Speed, VIS-Visual Camera, NIR- Nearly Infrared.

Spatial/Temporal properties	SMIC HS/VIS/NIR [32]	CASME [33]	CAMSEII [34]	CAS(ME)^2 [35]	SAMM [36]
Spatial resolution	640 × 480	640 × 480, 720 × 1280	640 × 480	640 × 480	2040 × 1088
Temporal frequency	100/25/25	60	200	30	200

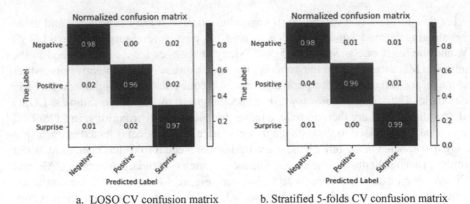

a. LOSO CV confusion matrix   b. Stratified 5-folds CV confusion matrix

Fig. 4. Confusion matrix for LOSO CV and Stratified 5-folds on composite ME dataset

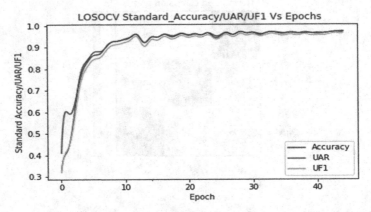

Fig. 5. LOSO CV standard accuracy, UAR, and UF1 scores

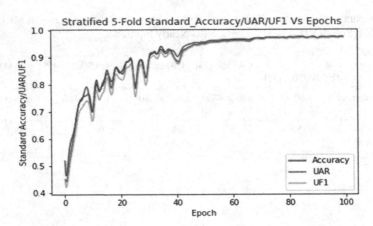

Fig. 6. Stratified 5-fold CV standard accuracy, UAR, and UF1 scores

4   Results and Discussion

We have constructed and used a composite ME dataset from the five spontaneous ME datasets mentioned in Table 3 for LOSO and Stratified 5-fold CV to categorize ME video sequence in three classes negative, positive, and surprise. Our proposed method and evaluations on this ME combined dataset show superiority to the state-of-the-art methods. It achieves significantly higher effectiveness standard accuracy, UAR, and UF1 metrics for both CVs, which is clear from the results in Table 3 and Fig. 4, 5, and 6. Table 3 has recorded the results for similar tasks base-on recent methods. CapsuleNet based on apex frame [46] has achieved about 65% UAR, and UF1 which is lower by 32% and 31%, respectively, compared to our proposed method. In RCN-A [30], the score has been improved up to 71% and 74% for both metrics. However, it is also far behind our estimated results. In macro assisted network MicroNet [47], there is a reasonable gain for both the metrics. It is ended up with scores less than 86% and 87%, respectively. Our proposed method has demonstrated a remarkable gain in terms of three metrics standard accuracy, UAR, and UF1. The estimated score is about 97% for all three metrics in the stratified CV. In the case of LOSO CV, our approach shows consistent scores of 97%, 97%, and 96%, respectively. We have covered both LOSO and stratified CV, but other approaches have done evaluations on the first one.

To lessen the over-fitting due to small size ME datasets, our composite ME dataset with larger video samples put a positive impact on all three accuracies by confronting the domain shifting challenge. Transfer learning on the integrated MACE dataset is another contributing factor to it. Subjective bias reduction with the objective categorization of ME samples, length of frame sequence reduction to 12 frames with apex frame as the last one, augmentation, and small spatial size of each frame have influenced the model prediction approvingly. With these facts, model design with spatio-temporal backbone in 3D residual framework and de-noising the five-dimensional activated feature maps with two encoders convolutional LTM layers and two accompanied LSTM decoder layers. This auto-encoder has facilitated further abstraction of relevant spatial changes in the ME frame sequence. Final structural regularization has subsidized the parameters.

The collaborative positive effects of our method on accuracies have also demonstrated the model generalization in-terms of a myriad of attributes in ME datasets, which has been captured by normalized confusion matrices and shown in Fig. 4. Some irregular weight updates have caused the minor drifting before the epoch 20 and epoch 42 in Fig. 5 and 6 respectively, which is due to the random initialization of parameters of auto-encoder and the last 3DCNN layer. After that points model is started to converge for all three metrics in both CV.

Table 3. LOSO CV ME recognition results based on contemporary methods for negative, positive and surprise classes in different compositions of ME datasets.

Methods	Composite datasets	CV	Accuracy	UAR	UF1
CapsuleNet on apex frame [46]	SMIC, CASMEII and SAMM	LOSO	–	0.651	0.652
RCN-A [30]	SMIC, CASMEII and SAMM	LOSO	–	0.719	0.743
MicroNet [47]	SMIC, CASMEII and SAMM	LOSO	–	0.857	0.864
Ours	SMIC, CAMSE, CASMEII, CAS(ME)^2 and SAMM	LOSO	**0.973**	**0.971**	**0.966**
		Stratified 5-Fold	**0.976**	**0.976**	**0.973**

5 Conclusions

Our work has proposed a method and model for ME recognition on composite ME video sequences from spontaneous datasets SMIC, CASME, CASMEII, CAS (ME)^2, and SAMM. To the best of our knowledge, it is the first attempt for ME recognition on five ME datasets. The proposed model combines the synergies of 3DResNet 18 and conv-LSTM auto-encoder. Two exhaustive cross-validations LOSO and Stratified 5-fold, have been experimented on the composite dataset. Our method shows remarkable accuracies compared to state-of-the-art methods. From our model evaluation, it is evident that the model is generalized, highly effective across domain shifting among ME datasets. In the future, this will help to classify the ME frame sequence from diverse ME samples in the wild.

Declarations.

Conflict of Interests. The authors declare that they have no known competing financial interests or personal relationships that could have appeared to influence the work reported in this paper.

Funding. This work was supported by the National Key R&D Program of China (Grant No. 2020AAA0104500), and was partially supported by Sichuan Science and Technology Major Project (Grant No. 2019ZDZX0006).

References

1. Zhang, M., Fu, Q., Chen, Y.H., Fu, X.: Emotional context influences micro-expression recognition. PLoS ONE **9**(4), 95018 (2014)
2. Yan, W.-J., Wu, Q., Liang, J., Chen, Y.-H., Fu, X.: How Fast are the leaked facial expressions: the duration of micro-expressions. J. Nonverbal Behav. **37**(4), 217–230 (2013). https://doi.org/10.1007/s10919-013-0159-8

3. Takalkar, M., Xu, M., Wu, Q., Chaczko, Z.: A survey: facial micro-expression recognition. Multim. Tools Appl. **77**(15), 19301–19325 (2017). https://doi.org/10.1007/s11042-017-5317-2

4. Ekman, P., Cohn, J.F., Ambadar, Z.: Observer-based measurement of facial expression with the facial action coding system. Handbook Emot. Elicit. Assess. **1**(3), 203–221 (2007)

5. Goh, K.M., Ng, C.H., Lim, L.L., Sheikh, U.U.: Micro-expression recognition: an updated review of current trends, challenges and solutions. Vis. Comput. **36**(3), 445–468 (2020). https://doi.org/10.1007/s00371-018-1607-6

6. Pfister, T., Li, X., Zhao, G., Pietikäinen, M.: Recognising spontaneous facial micro-expressions. In: Proceedings of the IEEE International Conference on Computer Vision, pp. 1449–1456 (2011)

7. Wang, Y., See, J., Phan, R.-W., Oh, Y.-H.: LBP with six intersection points: reducing redundant information in LBP-TOP for micro-expression recognition. In: Cremers, D., Reid, I., Saito, H., Yang, M.-H. (eds.) ACCV 2014. LNCS, vol. 9003, pp. 525–537. Springer, Cham (2015). https://doi.org/10.1007/978-3-319-16865-4_34

8. Zhao, G., Pietikäinen, M.: Dynamic texture recognition using local binary patterns with an application to facial expressions. IEEE Trans. Pattern Anal. Mach. Intell. **29**(6), 915–928 (2007)

9. Pietikinen, G.Z.M., Huang, X., Wang, S.J.: Facial micro_expression recognition using spatiotemporal local binary pattern with integral projection. In: ICCV Workshop on Computer Vision for Affective Computing, pp. 1–9 (2015)

10. Huang, X., Zhao, G., Hong, X., Zheng, W., Pietikäinen, M.: Spontaneous facial micro-expression analysis using Spatiotemporal Completed Local Quantized Patterns. Neurocomputing **175**(PartA), 564–578 (2015)

11. Huang, X., Wang, S.J., Liu, X., Zhao, G., Feng, X., Pietikainen, M.: Discriminative spatiotemporal local binary pattern with revisited integral projection for spontaneous facial micro-expression recognition. IEEE Trans. Affect. Comput. **10**(1), 32–47 (2017)

12. Zong, Y., Huang, X., Zheng, W., Cui, Z., Zhao, G.: Learning from hierarchical spatiotemporal descriptors for micro-expression recognition. IEEE Trans. Multimed. **20**(11), 3160–3172 (2018)

13. Chaudhry, R., Ravichandran, A., Hager, G., Vidal, R.: Histograms of oriented optical flow and Binet-Cauchy kernels on nonlinear dynamical systems for the recognition of human actions, pp. 1932–1939 (2009)

14. Liu, Y.J., Zhang, J.K., Yan, W.J., Wang, S.J., Zhao, G., Fu, X.: A main directional mean optical flow feature for spontaneous micro-expression recognition. IEEE Trans. Affect. Comput. **7**(4), 299–310 (2016)

15. Xu, F., Zhang, J., Wang, J.Z.: Microexpression identification and categorization using a facial dynamics map. IEEE Trans. Affect. Comput. **8**(2), 254–267 (2017)

16. Liong, S.T., See, J., Wong, K.S., Phan, R.C.W.: Less is more: micro-expression recognition from video using apex frame. Signal Process. Image Commun. **62**, 82–92 (2018)

17. Happy, S.L., Routray, A.: Fuzzy histogram of optical flow orientations for micro-expression recognition. IEEE Trans. Affect. Comput. **10**(3), 394–406 (2019)

18. Polikovsky, S., Kameda, Y., Ohta, Y.: Facial micro-expressions recognition using high speed camera and 3D-Gradient descriptor. In: IET Seminar Digest, vol. 2009, no. 2 (2009)

19. Li, X., et al.: Towards reading hidden emotions: a comparative study of spontaneous micro-expression spotting and recognition methods. IEEE Trans. Affect. Comput. **9**(4), 563–577 (2017)

20. Patel, D., Hong, X., Zhao, G.: Selective deep features for micro-expression recognition. In: Proceedings - International Conference on Pattern Recognition, vol. 0, pp. 2258–2263 (2016)

21. Takalkar, M.A., Xu, M.: Image based facial micro-expression recognition using deep learning on small datasets. In: DICTA 2017 - 2017 International Conference on Digital Image Computing: Techniques and Applications, vol. 2017, pp. 1–7 (2017)
22. Mayya, V., Pai, R.M., Pai, M.M.M.: Combining temporal interpolation and DCNN for faster recognition of micro-expressions in video sequences. In: 2016 International Conference on Advances in Computing, Communications and Informatics, ICACCI 2016, pp. 699–703 (2016)
23. Peng, M., Wang, C., Chen, T., Liu, G., Xiaolan, F.: Dual temporal scale convolutional neural network for micro-expression recognition. Front. Psychol. 8 (2017). https://doi.org/10.3389/fpsyg.2017.01745
24. Kim, D.H., Baddar, W.J., Jang, J., Ro, Y.M.: Multi-objective based spatio-temporal feature representation learning robust to expression intensity variations for facial expression recognition. IEEE Trans. Affect. Comput. 10(2), 223–236 (2017)
25. Wang, S.J., et al.: Micro-expression recognition with small sample size by transferring long-term convolutional neural network. Neurocomputing 312, 251–262 (2018)
26. Li, Y., Huang, X., Zhao, G.: can micro-expression be recognized based on single apex frame? In: Proceedings - International Conference on Image Processing, ICIP, pp. 3094–3098 (2018)
27. Gan, Y.S., Liong, S.T., Yau, W.C., Huang, Y.C., Tan, L.K.: OFF-ApexNet on micro-expression recognition system. Signal Process. Image Commun. 74, 129–139 (2019)
28. Khor, H.Q., See, J., Liong, S.T., Phan, R.C.W., Lin, W.: Dual-stream shallow networks for facial micro-expression recognition. In: Proceedings - International Conference on Image Processing, ICIP, vol. 2019, pp. 36–40 (2019)
29. Xia, Z., Feng, X., Hong, X., Zhao, G.: Spontaneous facial micro-expression recognition via deep convolutional network. In: 2018 8th International Conference on Image Processing Theory, Tools and Applications, IPTA 2018 – Proceedings (2019)
30. Xia, Z., Peng, W., Khor, H.Q., Feng, X., Zhao, G.: Revealing the invisible with model and data shrinking for composite-database micro-expression recognition. IEEE Trans. Image Process. 29, 8590–8605 (2020)
31. Yang, B., Cheng, J., Yang, Y., Zhang, B., Li, J.: MERTA: micro-expression recognition with ternary attentions. Multim. Tools Appl. 80(11), 1–16 (2019). https://doi.org/10.1007/s11042-019-07896-4
32. Li, X., Pfister, T., Huang, X., Zhao, G., Pietikainen, M.: A Spontaneous Micro-expression Database: Inducement, collection and baseline. In: 2013 10th IEEE International Conference and Workshops on Automatic Face and Gesture Recognition, FG 2013 (2013)
33. Yan, W.J., Wu, Q., Liu, Y.J., Wang, S.J., Fu, X.: CASME database: a dataset of spontaneous micro-expressions collected from neutralized faces. In: 2013 10th IEEE International Conference and Workshops on Automatic Face and Gesture Recognition, FG 2013 (2013)
34. Yan, W.J., et al.: CASME II: An improved spontaneous micro-expression database and the baseline evaluation. PLoS One 9(1), e86041 (2014)
35. Qu, F., Wang, S.J., Yan, W.J., Li, H., Wu, S., Fu, X.: CAS(ME)2: a database for spontaneous macro-expression and micro-expression spotting and recognition. IEEE Trans. Affect. Comput. 9(4), 424–436 (2018)
36. Davison, A.K., Lansley, C., Costen, N., Tan, K., Yap, M.H.: SAMM: a spontaneous micro-facial movement dataset. IEEE Trans. Affect. Comput. 9(1), 116–129 (2018)
37. Lucey, P., Cohn, J.F., Kanade, T., Saragih, J., Ambadar, Z., Matthews, I.: The extended Cohn-Kanade dataset (CK+): a complete dataset for action unit and emotion-specified expression. In: 2010 IEEE Computer Society Conference on Computer Vision and Pattern Recognition - Workshops, CVPRW 2010, pp. 94–101 (2010)
38. Papachristou, C., Aifanti, A.D.N.: The MUG facial expression database. In: 11th International Workshop on Image Analysis for Multimedia Interactive Services WIAMIS 10, pp. 1–4 (2010)

39. Zhao, G., Huang, X., Taini, M., Li, S.Z., Pietikäinen, M.: Facial expression recognition from near-infrared videos. Image Vis. Comput. **29**(9), 607–619 (2011)
40. Tran, D., Wang, H., Torresani, L., Ray, J., Lecun, Y., Paluri, M.: A closer look at spatiotemporal convolutions for action recognition. In: Proceedings of the IEEE Computer Society Conference on Computer Vision and Pattern Recognition, pp. 6450–6459 (2018)
41. Shi, X., Chen, Z., Wang, H., Yeung, D.-Y., Wong, W., Woo, W.: Convolutional LSTM Network: A Machine Learning Approach for Precipitation Nowcasting. Adv. Neural Inf. Process. Syst. **2015**, 802–810 (2015)
42. Bulat, A., Tzimiropoulos, G.: How far are we from solving the 2D & 3d face alignment problem? (and a Dataset of 230,000 3D Facial Landmarks). In: Proceedings of the IEEE International Conference on Computer Vision, vol. 2017, pp. 1021–1030 (2017)
43. Zhang, S., Zhu, X., Lei, Z., Shi, H., Wang, X., Li, S.Z.: S3FD: Single Shot Scale-Invariant Face Detector. In: Proceedings of the IEEE International Conference on Computer Vision, vol. 2017, pp. 192–201 (2017)
44. W. Kay *et al.*, "The Kinetics Human Action Video Dataset," May 2017
45. Davison, A.K., Merghani, W., Yap, M.H.: Objective classes for micro-facial expression recognition. J. Imaging **4**(10), 119 (2018)
46. Van Quang, N., Chun, J., Tokuyama, T.: CapsuleNet for micro-expression recognition. In: Proceedings - 14th IEEE International Conference on Automatic Face and Gesture Recognition, FG 2019 (2019)
47. Xia, B., Wang, W., Wang, S., Chen, E.: Learning from Macro-expression: a Micro-expression Recognition Framework. In: Proceedings of the 28th ACM International Conference on Multimedia, pp. 2936–2944 (2020)

Research on Charge and Discharge Control Strategy of Supercapacitor

Wanjuan Cong[✉] and Guanghua Yu

College of Computer and Information Engineering, Heihe University, Heilongjiang 164300, China
724045551@qq.com

Abstract. This paper introduced four common methods to improve the voltage balance of supercapacitor. Because of the advantages of high efficiency and high speed, the flyover capacitor method is selected to solve the problem of different charging and discharging speed of supercapacitor caused by different parameters of supercapacitor. In order to further improve the efficiency of the supercapacitor charging and discharging control system, a fuzzy control algorithm is designed based on the balance strategy of the flyover capacitor to further improve the efficiency of the supercapacitor charging and discharging control system. Finally, the validity of the design is verified by PSIM simulation software.

Keywords: Supercapacitor · Charge and discharge control · Flyover capacitor method

1 Introduction

With the development of society and the progress of science and technology, the electronic industry urgently needs high-performance, lightweight, environmental protection energy storage devices to achieve sustainable renewable energy [1]. For the utilization of renewable energy, supercapacitor has become one of the most promising candidate power sources because of its fast charging ability, high power density and good cycle performance [2]. However, in practical applications, the voltage of single supercapacitor is only 1 V–4 V, so multiple supercapacitor units need to be used in series [3]. In the process of series use, because the parameters of each single supercapacitor are different, it is very easy to cause the voltage imbalance at both ends of the supercapacitor in the process of charging and discharging, which affects the service life of the supercapacitor [4]. Therefore, in order to reduce the damage of supercapacitor during charging and discharging and prolong its service life, it is an urgent problem to study and solve the voltage balance setting of series supercapacitor during charging and discharging.

This paper introduced four common methods to improve the voltage balance of supercapacitor, and designs the charging and discharging control system of supercapacitor by using the flyover capacitor method. In order to further improve the efficiency

Foundation item: School level project (KJY202102).

X. Jiang (Ed.): MLICOM 2021, LNICST 438, pp. 106–116, 2022.
https://doi.org/10.1007/978-3-031-04409-0_10

of the supercapacitor charging and discharging control system, a fuzzy control algorithm is designed based on the flyover capacitor equalization technology to improve the efficiency of the supercapacitor charging and discharging control system.

2 Common Equalization Techniques

2.1 Parallel Resistance Method

According to the characteristics of each supercapacitor in series and the charging current, the parallel resistance method selects the appropriate resistance to parallel with each supercapacitor, so as to realize the consumption of excess energy on the supercapacitor unit [5]. The principle is shown in Fig. 1.

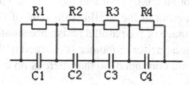

Fig. 1. Schematic diagram of the principle of parallel resistance method

When charging the supercapacitors C1, C2, C3 and C4 in the figure, the resistors R1, R2, R3 and R4 in parallel with each supercapacitor are discharging. The supercapacitor with high voltage has faster discharging speed than that with low voltage. Thus, in the process of charging and discharging the supercapacitor bank, the balanced protection of the supercapacitor unit is realized. The selection principle of resistance is to ensure that when the single super capacitor reaches the rated voltage, the current flowing through the parallel resistance is equal to the constant current, and the single super capacitor is not charging, so the super capacitor will not overcharge, so as to achieve the effect of equalization and protection. It can be seen from the schematic diagram that the circuit structure of parallel resistance is simple, no control module is needed, and the cost is low. However, this method is only suitable for low power applications because of its serious heating and high loss in the charging process.

The supercapacitor of 4 rated voltages is 2.7 V, capacitance values of 200 F, 220 F, 240 F, 260 F and initial voltage of 1.8 V, 1.5 V, 1.2 V, 0.9 V are connected in series under the condition of constant current of 3 A, and the blocking value of parallel resistance is 0.9 Ω. After 1000 s, the simulation results are shown in Fig. 2. It can be seen from the figure that the voltage of supercapacitors is rising and gradually approaching during the charging process, and the charging rate is gradually decreasing. Finally, the voltage of each supercapacitor reaches the rated voltage of 2.7 V.

2.2 Switch Resistance Method

The switch resistance method is based on the parallel resistance and a switch connected in series with the parallel resistance [6]. The parallel switch works when the super

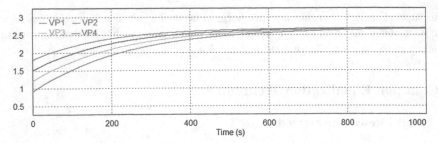

Fig. 2. Simulation effect of parallel resistance

capacitor is charging, and the voltage collected by the voltage sensor is equal to the reference voltage of the pre-set super capacitor rated voltage, the switch is turned on, so that the current flows through the resistor and the switch, and then reaches the super capacitor. The schematic diagram of the equilibrium state of the capacitor is shown in Fig. 3. The value of the resistance of the parallel resistance should be the current flowing of the resistor when the supercapacitor monomer is charged to the rated voltage, and the supercapacitor monomer is not continued, so that there is no overvoltage.

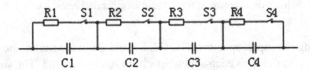

Fig. 3. Schematic diagram of switch resistance

The supercapacitor of 4 rated voltages is 2.7 V, and the capacitance values are 200 F, 220 F, 240 F, 260 F, in the case where the constant current is 3 A. The initial voltage value is set to 0 V, the reference voltage is set. For 2.4 V, the parallel resistance tissue is selected 0.9 Ω for simulation, and the simulation time is 800 s, the result is shown in Fig. 4. It can be seen from Fig. 3 that the switch resistance method is more flexible than the parallel resistance method. When the switch is disconnected at the beginning of charging, the parallel resistance can't be shunted, and the loss is lower than that of the parallel resistance method. However, when the reference voltage is reached, the switch turns on, and the rising rate of supercapacitor voltage gradually decreases significantly, and gradually approaches the rated voltage. In this process, there is still energy loss, at the same time, the structure of the circuit is also complex.

2.3 Voltage Stabilizing Diode Method

The voltage stabilizing diode method is a diode which replaces the parallel resistance in the parallel resistance method into a diode of the breakdown voltage equal to the rated voltage, which is shown in Fig. 5.

When charging the supercapacitor C1, C2, C3 and C4, if C2 reaches the rated voltage, the voltage stabilizing diode D2 associated with the inverse is reverse, and the current

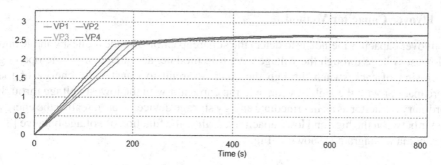

Fig. 4. Simulation effect of switch resistance

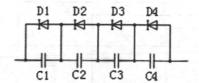

Fig. 5. Schematic diagram of Zener diode

flows through D2, thereby consuming the excess energy, and stopping charging the supercapacitor C2 to achieve the effect of voltage equalization. As can be seen from the schematic, the circuit of this method is simple and the cost is low, but there is also a phenomenon of energy loss and fever. If heating is serious, the parameters of the diode will be affected, or even damaged.

Connect four supercapacitors with a rated voltage of 2.7 V and capacitance values of 200 F, 220 F, 240 F, and 260 F in series with a constant current of 3 A. The initial voltage value is set to 0 V. The breakdown voltage is set to 2.7 V, and the result is shown in Fig. 6 after the simulation for 350 s. It can be seen from the figure, when the constant current is charged, the voltage of each supercapacitor presented a linear upward trend. When a supercapacitor reached the rated voltage of 2.7 V, the voltage didn't rise and remained unchanged at the rated voltage of 2.7 V, and there will be no overshooting.

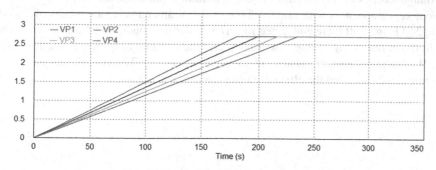

Fig. 6. Simulation effect of Zener diode

2.4   Flyover Capacitor Method

The flyover capacitor method is to detect the supercapacitor with the highest voltage and the lowest voltage through the voltage detection module, and then control the opening and closing of each switch through the control circuit to transfer the energy of the supercapacitor with the highest voltage to the capacitor with the lowest voltage through an ordinary capacitor as an intermediate energy storage device, so as to realize the energy transfer between the high and low capacitors, realize the function of voltage balance [8]. The schematic diagram is shown in Fig. 7.

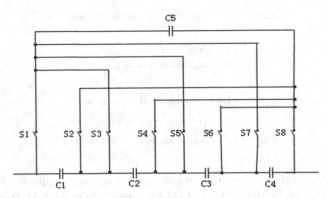

Fig. 7. Schematic diagram of flyover capacitor

Suppose that in the schematic diagram, the voltage detection module detects that the voltage of C1 is the highest and that of C3 is the lowest, the energy of the C1 having a high voltage is required to transfer the C3 of the lowest voltage. By controlling the switch network, S1 and S2 are closed, so that C1 with the highest voltage charges the intermediate energy storage device C. when the voltage of C is equal to that of C1, S1 and S2 are opened, S5 and S6 are closed, so that C charges C3 until the voltage of C3 is equal to that of C, and S5 and S6 are opened, The detection circuit re detects the supercapacitor with the highest and lowest voltage, and repeats the above process until the voltage reaches the equilibrium state.It is assumed that in the schematic.

Four supercapacitors with rated voltage of 2.7 V and capacitance values of 200 F, 220 F, 240 F and 260 F are connected in series under the condition of constant current of 3 A. the initial voltage value is set to 0 V and the capacity of flyover capacitor is set to 1 MF. The simulation effect after 60s is shown in Fig. 8. The voltage value of each capacitor is balanced and the effect of voltage balance is achieved.

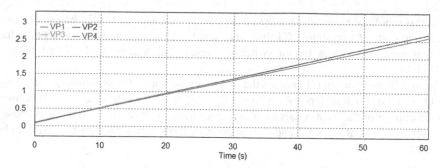

Fig. 8. Simulation diagram of flyover capacitance

3 The Choice of Equalization Technology

Through the above analysis, it can be clearly seen that the advantages of direct parallel resistance method, switching resistance method and voltage stabilized diode method are relatively simple structure and relatively low cost, but they have the disadvantages of large energy loss and serious heating, which makes the above schemes have great limitations. The flyover capacitor method has advantages over the above methods in balancing speed and efficiency, so the flyover capacitor method is used as the system balancing strategy in this design. In this design, the flyover capacitor equalization technology is used to realize the energy transfer between supercapacitor and flyover capacitor. In order to improve the rate of charging and discharging in the process of energy transfer,

The switch in Fig. 7 is changed to a series of MOS transistors that can be bidirectional on and bidirectional off. One switch is replaced by every two MOS transistors, and each conduction path contains four MOS transistors. The obtained balanced topology is shown in Fig. 9. In the process of principle analysis, it is assumed that the supply voltage is basically unchanged in a switching cycle, and the parasitic parameters of components and circuits are ignored.

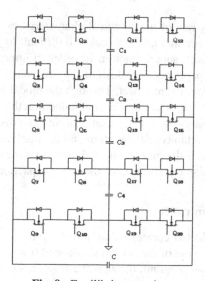

Fig. 9. Equilibrium topology

In this topology, assuming that the power of C1 is transferred to C3, the equalization process consists of two stages, C1 discharge and C3 charging, and the switch tube has different conduction states. Let the switching cycle of MOS transistor be T and the duty cycle be D.

In [0, DT] time, when C1 charges the flyover capacitor C, the switches Q_{11}, Q_{12}, Q_3 and Q_4 turn on, C1 transfers energy to the flyover capacitor C through the MOS tube, and the current of the flyover capacitor increases linearly. According to the hypothesis, the discharge current i_{c1} of C1 and the variation of flyover capacitor current Δi_c can be obtained.

$$i_{C_1}(t) = i_C(t) = \frac{1}{C} \int_0^t v_C dt + i_C(0) = \frac{V_{C_1}}{C} t + i_C(0) \tag{1}$$

$$\Delta i_C = i_C(DT) - i_C(T) = \frac{V_{C_1}(D)}{Cf} \tag{2}$$

In [DT, t] time, when the flyover capacitor charges C3, the switches Q17, Q18, Q5 and Q6 are on, and the energy in the flyover capacitor is released to C3. The voltage at both ends of the flyover capacitor is equal to the voltage at both ends of C3. It can be concluded that the discharge current of the flyover capacitor is C3, and the changes of the charging current and the flyover capacitor current are as follows:

$$i_{C_3}(t) = i_C(t) = \frac{1}{C} \int_{DT}^T v_C dt + i_C(DT) = -\frac{V_{C_3}}{C}(t - DT) + \frac{V_{C_1}D}{Cf} + i_C(0) \tag{3}$$

$$\Delta i_C = i_C(DT) - i_C(T) = \frac{V_{C_3}(1 - D)}{Cf} \tag{4}$$

4   Design of Fuzzy Control Algorithm

Due to the different decay rate of the chemical characteristics of each supercapacitor, there are differences between them, which makes it difficult to get the voltage, current and other parameters of each supercapacitor. In order to improve the balance performance of the system, this paper not only designs the hardware circuit, but also adds the algorithm design from the software aspect. Through the modal analysis of the equalization technology in the previous section, it is concluded that the duty ratio of the switch tube plays an important role in the equalization charging and discharging process of the system. In view of the uncertainty of the system and the nonlinear characteristics of the complexity, this paper selects the fuzzy control algorithm as the control core to optimize the charging and discharging equalization of the super capacitor.

4.1   Design of Fuzzy Controller

This paper takes the collected current value and the pre-set deviation value and the current change rate as the input of the system's balanced fuzzy controller, and then calls the fuzzy control algorithm program, through the fuzzy controller processing, outputs clear control amount and the time response current variation, and adjusts the output pulse width of the corresponding PWM signal through the control amount. The high and low of PWM signal is used to control the closing and opening of MOS transistor, so as to realize the voltage balance of supercapacitor in the process of charging and discharging.

The fuzzy controller is the core of the fuzzy control system in this system, so the design of the fuzzy controller in this system will be described from the three processes of fuzzification, fuzzy reasoning and clarity introduced in the second chapter.

1. Fuzzification

The fuzzy controller in this paper adopts the Mamdani type "double input single output" control structure, which has the advantages of less information, no overshoot, fast response and less errors, the deviation e and current change rate ec obtained by subtracting the set value 1.2 from the collected current i are used as input parameters, and the duty cycle D of MOS switch is output. In order to improve the accuracy of the control, the value of e is divided into seven fuzzy sub states in the universe $[-6, 6]$, and the language values are: NS, NM, NL, ZE, PS, PM, PL. Similarly, the fuzzy sub states of the current change rate ec and the duty cycle D value of MOS switches can also be divided into the above seven fuzzy sub states, and the fuzzy control rules of the system can be obtained as shown in Table 1.

Table 1. Fuzzy control rules

ec \ D\e	NS	NM	NL	ZE	PS	PM	PL
NS	NS	NS	NS	NS	NM	NL	ZE
NM	NS	NS	NM	NM	NL	ZE	ZE
NL	NS	NM	NM	NL	ZE	ZE	PS
ZO	NM	NL	NL	ZE	PS	PS	PM
PS	NL	ZE	ZE	PS	PM	PM	PL
PM	ZE	ZE	PS	PM	PM	PL	PL
PL	ZE	PS	PM	PL	PL	PL	PL

2. Fuzzy Inference

According to the analysis, the fuzzy control rules in this paper can be expressed in the following form: if $\{(e) = A_i$ and $(ec) = B_j\}$ then $D = C_{ij}$, $(i, j = 1, 2, \cdots, n)$, A_i, B_j and C_{ij} are all fuzzy sets in their respective domains in the process of fuzzification.

Suppose that there are n fuzzy rules in a fuzzy controller, and each fuzzy rule in the fuzzy controller corresponds to a fuzzy relation R_i. Then the sum of the fuzzy relations R_j $(j = 1, 2,\ldots N)$ corresponding to the N fuzzy rules is the total fuzzy relation R of the fuzzy control system.

$$R = R_1 \cup R_2 \cup \cdots \cup R_8 \cup R_n = \bigcup_{i=1}^{n} R_j \qquad (5)$$

Substituting R into approximate reasoning rule:

$$U^* = \left(\overrightarrow{A}^* \right)^T \circ R \tag{6}$$

The total output of approximate reasoning is:

$$U^* = \left(\overrightarrow{A}^* \right)^T \circ \bigcup_{j=1}^{n} R_j \tag{7}$$

Or

$$U^* = \overset{n}{\underset{j=1}{Y}} \left(\left(\overrightarrow{A}^* \right)^T \circ R_j \right) = \overset{n}{\underset{j=1}{Y}} U_j \tag{8}$$

In the above formula "$\circ$" Represents the synthesis algorithm, and A^* is the input quantity matrix.

According to the above introduction, there are two calculation orders. Formula 7 calculates each R_j from 1 to N, and then calculates their union, it is calculated by substituting it into the synthesis rule. Then the formula (8) first calculates each U_j from 1 to N, then calculates their union, and substitute them into the synthesis rule.

Because in a certain sampling period, one input of the input controller can not activate all fuzzy relations at the same time, that is to say, it can't activate all fuzzy control rules [9]. Therefore, it is necessary to optimize the activation of fuzzy control rules, so this paper chooses formula (8) for fuzzy reasoning. In this way, in a certain sampling period, the activated fuzzy relations can be calculated first, and then their union can be calculated, which can greatly reduce the amount of calculation and improve the corresponding ability of the controller.

3. Clarify

In this paper, the weighted average method, which is convenient, intuitive and reasonable for calculation, is selected to carry out the deblurring calculation. The weighted average method, also known as the area center method, first calculates the integral of the membership function curve of the fuzzy set in the corresponding abscissa range, that is, the area surrounded by them, and calculates the abscissa value of the area center [10], this value is the accurate value after clear calculation. Let $Z(u)$ be the membership function of fuzzy subset Z on the universe M, and u belongs to M. The abscissa of the center of the area is X, defined by:

$$X = df(u) = \frac{\int_M uZ(u)du}{Z(u)du} \tag{9}$$

4.2   Simulation of Fuzzy Controller

In order to verify whether the fuzzy controller designed above meets the requirements of this design and whether it can achieve the objective of membership function optimization,

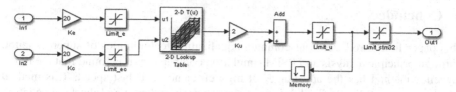

Fig. 10. Fuzzy control simulation block diagram

it is simulated by using Simulink. The simulation block diagram of fuzzy control is shown in Fig. 10.

Figure 11 shows the simulation effect of supercapacitor charge discharge balance under fuzzy algorithm. Compared with the equalization effect diagram of the supercapacitor without fuzzy control before (Fig. 8), in the process of charging and discharging, the battery pack with fuzzy control achieves the equalization effect in 40 s, while in Fig. 8, it takes 60 s for the supercapacitor to achieve the equalization effect without fuzzy control. Through the above analysis, it can be concluded that the charging time of supercapacitor can be optimized by using fuzzy control system. The comparison between this method and the previous charging and discharging strategy is shown in Table 2. It can be seen that the charging and discharging speed of this method is higher than that of other methods.

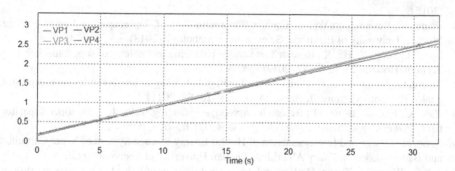

Fig. 11. Effect diagram of charge discharge equalization under fuzzy algorithm

Table 2. Time comparison of each charging strategy.

Charge discharge strategy	Time/s
Parallel resistance method	800
Switch resistance method	600
Voltage stabilizing diode method	350
Flyover capacitor method	60
Simulation of fuzzy controller	35

5 Conclude

This paper first introduced four common equalization technologies of supercapacitor. Through principle analysis and PSIM simulation comparison, it is found that the flying capacitor method has the advantages of high efficiency and fast speed. This method is used as the equalization technology of supercapacitor charge and discharge control. Secondly, in order to further improve the efficiency of the supercapacitor charging and discharging control system, a fuzzy control algorithm is designed based on the balance strategy of the flying capacitor to further improve the efficiency of the supercapacitor charging and discharging control system.

References

1. Jinlei, Y.: Research on Constant Power Charge and Discharge Control System of Super Capacitor. Dalian University of Technology (2015)
2. Shang, Y., et al.: Synthesis of hollow $ZnCo_2O_4$ microspheres with enhanced electrochemical performance for asymmetric supercapacitor. Electrochim. Acta **286**, 103–113 (2018)
3. Haidong, L.: Research on Modular Technology of Supercapacitor. Graduate School of Chinese Academy of Sciences (Institute of Electrical Engineering) (2006)
4. Suryawanshi, S.R., et al.: Pt-nanoparticle functionalized carbon nano-onions for ultra-high energy supercapacitors and enhanced field emission behavior. RSC Adv. **5**, 80990–80997 (2015)
5. Wang, X.: Research on Voltage Equalization Technology of Supercapacitor Energy Storage Module. University of Electronic Science and Technology (2018)
6. Luo, M., Song, Y., He, X.: Research on voltage balancing technology of supercapacitor. Sci. Technol. Horizon **25**, 133–137 (2017)
7. Zhang, L., Zhang, N., Li, C., et al. Design of voltage balancing system for series supercapacitor banks. Electron. Measure. Technol. **34** (009), 8–10, 53 (2011)
8. Yan, X., Liu, B., Dong, H.: Research on voltage balancing technology of super capacitor bank. Power Capac. React. Power Compens. **36**(03), 62–67 (2015)
9. Song, H.: Design and Implementation of Hybrid Energy Storage System of Super Capacitor and Battery Based on Fuzzy Algorithm. Taiyuan University of Technology (2014)
10. Xu, C., Wang, X., Zhang, Q.: Research on control strategy of hybrid energy storage system based on fuzzy algorithm. J. Shenyang Inst. Eng. (Nat. Sci. Ed.) **15** (02), 100–105 + 188 (2019)

Intelligent Wheelchair Based on Medical Health Examination

Fucong Tan[✉], Yu Wei[✉], Hongzhang Zhou, Honglan Li, and Jiacheng Zhong

Wuzhou University, Wuzhou, China
2242594011@qq.com

Abstract. The acceleration of the population ageing and the frequent accidents have caused the rapid growth of the number of the elderly and the disabled in our country. The Traditional Electric Wheelchair can no longer meet the diversified needs of the elderly and the disabled in the new era, therefore, it is necessary to research and develop the intelligent wheelchair according to this demand. In this paper, an intelligent wheelchair based on medical health detection is designed. The system is mainly divided into three parts: lower computer, Web end and mobile end. It is mainly composed of STM32 main control chip, 4g communication module, GPS module, sensor module, alarm module and motor driving module, with the function of detecting human health indicators, after experimental testing, the system can effectively remind obstacle avoidance and detect health indexes such as blood pressure, heart rate, body temperature, PM2.5, temperature and humidity.

Keywords: Health index · Intelligent wheelchair · Blood pressure and heart rate · STM32 · GPS

1 Introduction

With the continuous improvement of modern people's living standards and the gradual acceleration of the aging process of our country's population, how to solve the daily life of the elderly is an important contemporary issue. Due to the influence of the childbirth policy of the last century, most contemporary families are single-child families. One family often needs to support multiple elderly people. It is difficult for children to take care of the elderly on both sides while working [1], so the elderly need to have a certain degree of self. Survival skills. Among them, the elderly and some disadvantaged groups with leg disabilities have severely reduced physical functions or loss of motor functions and require the assistance of external media to carry out their daily lives. Therefore, it is very important to design a smart wheelchair to meet the above needs.

In the daily life of the elderly or the disabled, traditional wheelchairs or crutches are usually used to assist travel. Traditional wheelchairs are mainly controlled manually, and there are many problems. For example, manual assistance is still required when using them, and traditional wheelchairs are only a means of transportation for users, and

X. Jiang (Ed.): MLICOM 2021, LNICST 438, pp. 117–127, 2022.
https://doi.org/10.1007/978-3-031-04409-0_11

cannot understand the user's physical condition in time. In order to be able to understand the physical condition of wheelchair users at any time, this article adds some functions to the original basis of traditional wheelchairs, such as adding sensors that can detect human blood pressure, heart rate, body temperature and ambient temperature, humidity, and pm2.5 in modern traditional wheelchairs. Real-time collection of environment and human body information, and can generate the user's path map. Install a 4G module on a traditional wheelchair to act as a client, upload it to the designated cloud server via TCP/IP, and the upper computer receives the information collected by the sensor to analyze the user's environment and physical health, and provide corresponding diagnostic solutions. When these data reach the upper limit set in advance, the manager can be pushed by a short message or forced to occupy the front desk (similar to an alarm clock) to remind the manager, and the device can also be located by calling the Baidu map API. It is helpful for managers to understand the user's location in real time, and to check the information, which effectively protects the personal safety of users. Compared with the current traditional wheelchairs, our products have great advantages, for example, it can detect health indicators (blood pressure, heart rate, body temperature) and the temperature, humidity, pm2.5, etc. of the environment in which it is located, so This is a smart wheelchair that can meet the needs of contemporary people, and can bring great convenience to mankind.

2 Related Work

Intelligent unmanned wheelchair technology is to extend the wide application of electric robot intelligent technology to electric unmanned wheelchairs, integrating technical research in a variety of key areas, including electric robot intelligent vision, robot intelligent navigation and automatic positioning, pattern recognition, multi-function sensors and A variety of user interaction interfaces, etc., the key technical fields involved include electromechanical, control, sensors, artificial intelligence, etc., which can also be called artificial intelligence unmanned wheelchair mobile robots.

Intelligent driving wheelchairs may usually be added a tablet computer and some temperature sensors on the basis of the functions of the electric driving wheelchair, or may be added a power seat system on the basis of the functions of a mobile robot to carry out technological research and development. In 1986, British workers began to use computer vision technology to automatically carry out wheelchair navigation, and developed the first electric wheelchair, which was later called ibm. TJwatsonresearchcenter's chconnell and ooviola can set the mobile seat on a mobile robot working platform. Thus, it is possible to use electric joysticks, ultrasonic laser sensors and various infrared laser sensors to directly realize the three-dimensional walking and mobile obstacle avoidance functions of the mobile robot. After more than 20 years of research and development, many countries have invested more funds to develop smart wheelchairs [3]. At present, the United States [4], Germany, Japan, France, Canada, Spain, China and other countries have begun to conduct in-depth research on various types of smart electric wheelchair technologies, so that smart electric wheelchairs can have the following functions: Assisted map, automatic assisted obstacle avoidance [5], automatic assisted walking, interaction with other users, etc. In 2009, Ulm University in Germany re-developed a wheelchair navigation robot namaid on the basis of a commercial wheelchair. According to the different regional environment of the machine navigation, he subdivided the operation mode of the wheelchair machine into: nan (small Regional deep navigation) and nawan (wide regional deep navigation), which greatly effectively improves the accuracy of machine navigation [6]. Together with two researchers from the Hokkaido Institute of Industrial Design, we have jointly developed an intelligent voice-controlled electric wheelchair that can be operated mechanically without requiring any manual labor. The researcher uses a ut as a voice chip that senses the voice of the system. It is installed in a wheelchair. After a user speaks his request aloud to the phone microphone, the sensor voice system has the opportunity to follow his request. Directly start the mobile phone to operate the wheelchair. In addition to the wheelchair being able to walk upwards, forwards, backwards, left and right, and moving speed, the back of the chair is also designed to tilt backward or forward, which makes it more convenient for the user to rest. In the technological development of new smart electric wheelchairs, although my country has developed later than other developed countries [7], at present, Chinese wheelchair developers have already developed and produced many products based on their own advanced technology research and development advantages and application characteristics. Featured new intelligent electric wheelchair [8]. Researchers at home and abroad have also achieved good research results after more than 20 years of in-depth research. In 1998, Fan Xiaochun's paper proposed a new automatic control system method for electric driving wheelchairs, that is, the automatic driving direction and movement rate of this wheelchair are automatically controlled through the wheelchair joystick, and the system temperature is manually adjusted to achieve a certain movement. Stability [9]. In 2011, Sun Dongyuan proposed a smart wheelchair controller with a FREESCALE 8-bit microprocessor as the core, thus realizing the high performance and low cost of the smart wheelchair. The multi-modal interactive smart wheelchair and embedded smart wheelchair of the Institute of Automation of the Chinese Academy of Sciences, the multi-functional smart wheelchair of Shanghai Jiaotong University, and the smart wheelchair based on head movements of the Shenzhen Institute of Advanced Technology of the Chinese Academy of Sciences [10]. The Electrical Engineering Department of Chung Cheng University in Taiwan uses an industrial-grade PC as the control center, which drives the amplifier through the motor control, and uses the joystick to control the operation of the electric wheelchair, etc. [11].

In terms of the structure and design form of the machine tool automatic control system, in fact, most large-scale machine tools currently adopt a master-slave automatic control operating system design method. To control the electric driving mode, the smart electric vehicle generally can use three modes to control the electric mode on the wheelchair, namely, all the three modes of automatic mode, semi-automatic mode, and manual intelligent control. Each model will be formulated for different groups of people. According to the different interface modes of the automobile rolling control system, its interfaces can be divided into two types: the setting human-machine interface and the natural human-machine interface. Among them, the stable human-machine interface that is naturally used on the device is mainly used for patients. Physically disabled medical people who have physical disability or have a low degree of illness and death but have relatively high requirements for their own physical disability movement control ability and have a strong sense of self-protection, including the use of car rolling joystick button scrolling control, button button scrolling control, Steering wheel button scroll control, touch screen button scroll control, menu button scroll control, etc. [12]. The wide-spread use of natural human-machine interfaces is mainly aimed at special groups of people who have a high degree of physical disability and low physical mobility, including the use of voice operation control, breathing operation control, head operation control, gesture operation control, and biological control. Information signal processing control and other operation methods.

3   Overview of Smart Wheelchair Control System

This research project will be used to design a smart medical wheelchair for medical health detection based on stm32 single-chip microcomputer to realize the four major functions of manual autonomous driving navigation, automatic safe obstacle avoidance, fast automatic human-computer interaction, and multi-functional health services, Can greatly improve the quality of healthy daily life and health work management of urban elderly and severely disabled people, so that they can greatly strengthen their daily life self-care ability and fully integrate into a healthy society. The system is mainly divided into three parts: the lower computer, the Web terminal, and the mobile terminal. With four stm32 as the core of the automatic control system, it is mainly composed of four stm32 master control chips, 4gps communication control module, gps communication module, sensor control module, alarm control module, motor circuit drive control module and other parts.

The main research of this project is a smart wheelchair that can effectively remind obstacle avoidance and detect blood pressure, heart rate, body temperature, PM2.5, temperature and humidity and other health indicators through STM32 single-chip microcomputer, and display the data on the host computer and analyze the results. On the basis of the smart wheelchair, the function of health detection is added, and the user can detect the three health indicators of body temperature, blood pressure, and heart rate anytime and anywhere, which brings great convenience to the user. The design of the entire frame structure is shown in Fig. 1:

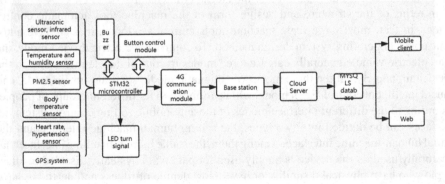

Fig. 1. The design of the entire frame structure

3.1 Introduction to the Lower Computer

The lower computer is composed of stm32 single-chip microcomputer, 4gps communication control module, gps communication module, temperature and humidity change sensor, heart rate graph and hypertension temperature sensor, body temperature and humidity sensor, ultrasonic laser sensor, infrared laser sensor, pm2.5 sensor, noise buzzer and The alarm module is composed. The stm32 microcontroller first reads the data randomly collected by each signal sensor and then processes the collected data. After the data processing is generated, it is sent to the 4g mobile phone communication control module through the serial port, and then the 4g mobile phone communication control module sends the collected data to two Mobile phone communication client and web. In order to better protect the safety of users in the wheelchair, we control the obstacle avoidance module through the STM32 single-chip microcomputer. When encountering obstacles, the signal of the obstacle in front is quickly sent to the STM32 single-chip microcomputer through the ultrasonic sensor and the infrared sensor. After the signal is transmitted to the buzzer, an alarm will be issued quickly to remind the user that there is an obstacle in front. The specific functions are shown in Fig. 2:

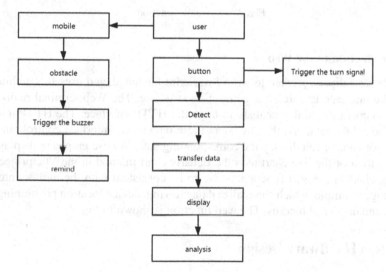

Fig. 2. The specific functions

3.2 Introduction to Android

The mobile development client will be developed based on the mobile development platform with androids, using the new androidstudio mobile development tool, and implemented in the java application language. In addition to being able to view the detected data, the mobile client can perform intelligent analysis on the data. It can draw a line chart by referring to the Android chart view library MP Android Chart and display it in a discounted manner. When the data is abnormal, the guardian will be reminded by means of pop-up windows. Due to the user-oriented particularity, the mobile client interface will strive to be concise, intuitive, and easy to use, making it convenient for users to view data. Guardians or users can log in to the mobile client and can view the operation of the device in real time. Its overall function is shown in Fig. 3:

Fig. 3. Its overall function

3.3 Introduction to the Web

Web end uses eclipse software to write JavaScript language, and uses B/S architecture mode. The interface is a tree-like connection structure. The Web terminal realizes the connection operation of the database through the HTTP interface. The HTTP interface obtains the JSON data, and then transfers these data to the interface control, and then the interface control can display the corresponding data. We use graphs to display data. The realization of the line chart uses the Echarts chart method in the Vue project, and draws the chart in the Vue function. Strive to be consistent with the mobile interface, and the page is simple, which can realize data viewing, device location positioning, data analysis, and historical records. The web function is shown in Fig. 4:

4   System Hardware Design

4.1 Positioning and Communication Module

The 4g network module network is an important communication carrier between mobile connected things and one of the core components of the integrated access network of mobile terminal equipment and the Internet of Things. The positioning and wireless communication engine module selects a multifunctional wireless communication module that integrates four high-performance frequency gnss communication engines and four same-band frequency gsm/gprs communication engines. gmc20 [2]. Connect MC20's UART serial port transmitter TXD with MCU's UART1 receiver RXD (PA10), MC20 UART serial port receiver TXD with MCU's UART1 transmitter RXD (PA9), then GPS data can be sent to the MCU, STM32F103 will The data is transferred to the MYSQLS database and then transferred to the Android mobile platform.

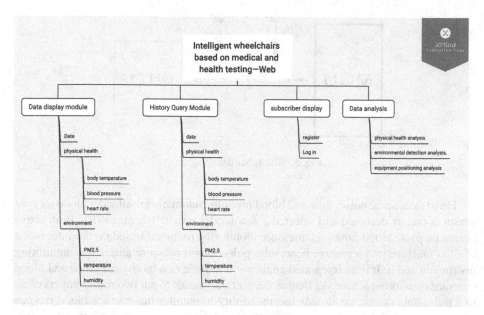

Fig. 4. The web function

4.2 Sensor Module

The main products of the temperature sensor laser module of this technical project include human body temperature and humidity laser sensor, heart rate graph and hypertension temperature sensor, body temperature and humidity sensor, ultrasonic laser sensor, infrared laser sensor, pm2.5 sensor.

The temperature and humidity sensor uses the DHT11 model. The sensor includes a resistive humidity sensing element and an NTC temperature measurement element, and is connected to a high-performance 8-bit single-chip microcomputer. The product has the advantages of excellent quality, ultra-fast response, strong anti-interference ability, and high cost performance. The DHT11 sensor is calibrated in an extremely accurate humidity calibration room. The calibration coefficients are stored in the OTP memory in the form of a program, and these calibration coefficients are called during the processing of the detection signal inside the sensor. The single-wire serial interface makes system integration easier and faster. Ultra-small size and low power consumption, the signal transmission distance can reach more than 20 m, so DHT11 is a better choice. The schematic diagram is shown in Fig. 5:

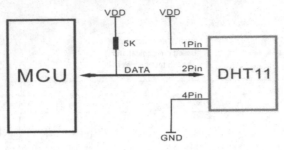

Fig. 5. The schematic diagram

Heart rate, aorta, pulse, flow and blood pressure automatic monitoring blood oxygen sensor is mainly designed and selected a new model mxa30102, max30102 is an active heart rate pulse blood flow high pressure monitoring oximeter based on the integration of man-machine and a passive heart rate, pulse, blood pressure automatic monitoring instrument and it. It is an integrated application module of a biological pulse and blood pressure monitoring sensor. As long as the user only needs to put two round fingers close to a pulse data sensor, he already has the ability to monitor the average blood oxygen concentration and thermal saturation in the pulse data in real time through calculation and output (spo2). And can monitor the pulse in real time. Small neutral red blood cells that carry a large amount of other oxygen can usually only absorb a certain amount or more of long-distance infrared light (850–1000 nm) at the same time, and large neutral red blood cells that are not breathing or carry a small amount of other oxygen at the same time usually also It also can only absorb more ultraviolet light and red light (600–750 nm) at the same time, so the design of pupupulseoximeterr is a mini design for analyzing the refraction of blood oxygen fluorescence, so that we can make full use of two red blood cells with different types of fluorescence. The different refraction principles of the blood oxygen refraction spectrum absorbed at the same time are used to accurately analyze the refraction saturation of different types of blood oxygen light. In other words, it can directly detect the average exercise heart rate of the human body in the world and the blood pressure of normal people. Therefore, we use max30102 blood oxygen sensor not only to directly detect the user's heart rate and blood pressure, but the host computer receives the information collected by the sensor to detect whether the user can reach the health indicators. When the data reaches the upper limit set in advance, it can be managed The user carries out a short message push or forced occupation of the front desk (similar to an alarm clock) to remind, and also analyzes the user's environment and physical health, and provides the corresponding diagnosis plan and sends it to the mobile phone [13], for this reason This project has increased the detection of health indicators, which brings great convenience. The measurement standards of nitric oxide and unsaturated chemical factor gas concentrations in blood oxygen are defined as follows:

$$SaO_2 = \frac{C_{HbO2}}{C_{HbO2} + C_{Hb}} \times 100\%$$

4.3 Obstacle Avoidance Module

Ultrasonic sensors use ultrasonic waves to detect object distances, and infrared sensors use photosensitive objects to measure object distances [14]. The combination of the two can better avoid obstacles. In order to better protect the safety of users in wheelchairs, we use STM32 single-chip microcomputer to connect ultrasonic sensors and infrared sensors to control the obstacle avoidance module. When an obstacle is encountered, the signal of the obstacle in the front is quickly sent to the STM32 MCU through the ultrasonic sensor and the infrared sensor, and then the signal is transmitted to the buzzer alarm, and then an alarm is quickly issued to remind the user that there is an obstacle in front, and then By driving the L298N motor to control the straight stop, left and right rotation and other actions. The design logic of obstacle avoidance program is shown in Fig. 6:

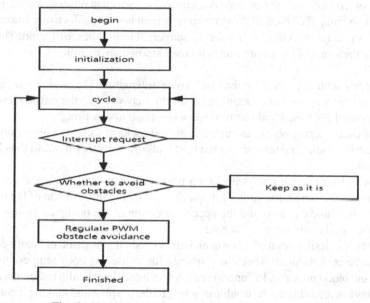

Fig. 6. The design logic of obstacle avoidance program

5 Results

This project is based on electric wheelchair equipment. A turn signal controlled by STM32 is added to an ordinary electric wheelchair. When the user reaches a dangerous distance from an obstacle, a buzzer will be used to remind the user. Here the user can press the button to detect body temperature, blood pressure, heart rate, temperature, humidity, pm2.5, and the data collected by the sensor is sent to the cloud server through the 4G module, and finally to the host computer. The administrator can view the data through the Web terminal, locate the user's real-time location, and provide related services for the monitor or user. The mobile client can not only view and locate the data, but also analyze the data in the background and push the medical rehabilitation plan suitable for the user. When the health factor is higher than a critical point, you can directly push the text message or occupy the phone interface to warn, so as to remind the user and make the user aware of their own health problems.

6 Summary

With the rapid development of the Internet of Things, embedded technology and sensor technology, people's daily life has been greatly improved [8]. Our project "Smart wheelchair based on medical health detection" cleverly combines the development of smart wheelchairs with remote monitoring. In combination, a smart wheelchair suitable for patients with inconvenient legs and the elderly is designed.

This system integrates all modules on the wheelchair, which is easy to operate and has strong practicability. The real-time detection of sensors can observe the status of the wheelchair and map the status of the occupants, which not only effectively improves the safety and convenience, And also give the passengers' families peace of mind. Therefore, the main innovations of the smart wheelchair we studied are as follows:

(1) Equipped with a control system and voice interaction [7], which can not only increase the way users communicate with the network and the outside world, but also control the functional status of the wheelchair at any time;
(2) When encountering obstacles such as pits and rocks ahead, the voice module will broadcast a sound and tell the user the next walking trajectory to avoid the obstacles in front.
(3) The wheelchair is equipped with a GPS positioning module. While the occupant is using the wheelchair, the family can check the location information of the occupant at any time, and can also find the specific location of the occupant at any time, so that the family can feel more at ease.
(4) The biggest design point of this wheelchair is to add the function of health detection on the basis of its smart wheelchair, mainly for measuring body temperature, heart rate, and blood pressure. Its function can detect these three health indicators anytime and anywhere, reducing the trouble of going to the hospital and making it convenient for users.

References

1. Xiao, R., Zhang, Y.: Research and Exploration of Smart Wheelchairs. Shanghai Medical College of Health, Shanghai (2021)
2. Xiang, Z.: Research on BCI Human-Machine Interface Technology of Smart Wheelchair. Tianjin University, Tianjin (2007)
3. Bourhis, G., Hom, O., Habert, O., Pruski, A.: An autonomous vehicle for people with motor disabilities. IEEE Robot. Autom. **8**, 20–28 (2001)
4. Mazo, M.: The research group of the SIAMO project, "Anintegral system for assistedmobility". IEEE Robot. Automat. **8**, 46–56 (2001)

5. Chujie, S.: Research on Intelligent Wheelchair Motion Control and Automatic Obstacle Avoidance System. Hubei University of Technology, Hubei (2020)
6. Zhi, Q.: Research on the Control System of Smart Wheelchair. Harbin Engineering University, Harbin (2012)
7. Xiao, Q.: Design and Research of Voice Interaction System for Smart Wheelchair Bed. Tianjin University of Technology, Tianjin (2021)
8. Kui, Z.: Research on Intelligent Wheelchair Control System. Graduate Office of Anhui University of Science and Technology, Anhui (2018)
9. Xiaohong, C., Hong, P., Feifei, B.: Research on the System Structure of Smart Wheelchairs. Shaanxi Institute of Clothing Engineering, Shaanxi (2019)
10. Biyao, S.: Hardware Design and Control System of Smart Wheelchair Based on STM32. Nanjing Normal University, Nanjing (2018)
11. Shuai, S.: Intelligent Wheelchair Navigation Based on Information Fusion. Chongqing University of Posts and Telecommunications, Chongqing (2011)
12. Lu, F.: Go to the Chinese University of Hong Kong to conduct collaborative research on robot experiments. Int. Acad. Trends 4 (2006)
13. Lin, J., Chang, F., Chen, D., Qiu, B., Jia, M., Meng, Y.: Multifunctional self-service smart wheelchair. School of Electronics and Information Engineering. Liaoning University of Science and Technology, Liaoning (2021)
14. Bojing, M., Xiaodong, X.: Design of an Outdoor Monitoring System for Electric Wheelchairs Based on STM32. Zhejiang University of Science and Technology, Hangzhou, Zhejiang (2020)

Research on Forest Fire Image Recognition System in Northeast Forest Region Based on Machine Vision

Yan Li[✉], Guagnhua Yu, and Fengling Wang

Heihe University, Heihe 164300, Heilongjiang, China
495287146@qq.com

Abstract. As a large forest region in Northeast China, forest fire prevention has always been an important matter concerned by Heilongjiang Province. The emergence of fire, the damage to the ecology and environment is inestimable. Therefore, it is particularly important to use the intelligent image recognition technology to monitor the forest fires in northeast China in real time to ensure that the forest areas in northeast China are not damaged by fire. In fact, in the field of forest fire prevention, many scholars at home and abroad have done a lot of forest fire research, mainly in the field of forest fire monitoring, a lot of research and practical application. The forest fire detection and recognition system based on machine vision can effectively reduce the impact of forest fire, reduce the loss, and improve the real-time and accuracy of forest fire recognition.

Keywords: Forest fire · Machine vision · Fire recognition

Northeast forest region is the largest natural forest region in China. This area is very rich in forest resources, forest area of nearly 700 million mu, in the national forest area of more than one-third, the amount of wood savings more than 3 billion cubic meters, in China's total wood savings of more than 33% [1]. At present, most of the defense schemes used in fire monitoring in northeast China are human normal patrol, UAV and satellite monitoring. Subject to the influence of the changeable seasonal climate and the imperfect monitoring technology and high monitoring costs and other factors, the real-time monitoring and early warning of forest fire prevention can not be better achieved by the human ground patrol forest protection, remote control UAV patrol and satellite monitoring.

With the continuous improvement of image and pattern recognition technology, it has become more and more important to use video image recognition technology to distinguish forest fire in forest fire prevention and prevention, and it has become a very important research trend for image video recognition of forest fire [2]. In view of the northeast forest safety protection, the researchers of our country have carried out special research and actual monitoring of the northeast forest fire prevention. However,

School-level topics (KJZ202102); School-level topics (XJGY201923); School-level topics (2020-KYYWF-0885).

X. Jiang (Ed.): MLICOM 2021, LNICST 438, pp. 128–133, 2022.
https://doi.org/10.1007/978-3-031-04409-0_12

due to the high cost of key control equipment, high area and narrow coverage, and the influence of seasonal climate in northeast China, the timeliness and monitoring distance of the monitoring system are insufficient. In view of the above problems, this project is committed to the study of forest fire image recognition and classification in the northeast forest region, and to build an intelligent real-time fire monitoring platform in the northeast forest region, which is of great significance for strengthening the protection and restoration of forest resources in the region.

Forest fire image recognition system plays an important role in forest fire prevention in northeast China. Its two main functions are to identify the physical properties of fire and smoke in time and to solve forest problems by studying the system. In order to ensure the accuracy and efficiency of forest image recognition system in northeast China, technical problems such as fire, light, seasonal weather and the influence of various interference factors on the system should be considered in system design. The forest fire recognition system in northeast China mainly adopts pattern recognition technology.

1 Image Pattern Recognition Technology

1.1 Dynamic Change Feature Extraction

Smoke produced by forest fires tends to rise or move under the influence of air currents. With the increase of smoke volume, the shielding range becomes larger and the thickness of smoke increases [3]. The whole process is changing, and the pixels in the video image are changing. The approximate range of forest fire can be judged by the displacement change of video pixels. Generally speaking, according to the comparison between the original image and the current image, the larger the overlap area of contrast, the greater the similarity value of the determined image. Usually, image area signal-to-noise ratio formula is used to calculate. The SNR formula of image area is:

$$SNR = 10LOG10\left[\frac{\sum\limits_{I-1}^{M}\sum\limits_{J-1}^{N}G(I,J)^2}{\sum\limits_{I-1}^{M}\sum\limits_{J-1}^{N}[G(I,J)-F(I,J)]^2}\right] \tag{1}$$

In the SNR formula, I and J respectively represent horizontal rows and vertical columns in the image where the pixels in the image are located, M and N respectively represent the total number of horizontal rows and vertical columns in the computed pixel range, G (I, J) is the original image, and F (I, J) is the compared image. The larger the SNR value is, the higher the overlap degree of the image is.

1.2 LBP Texture Feature Extraction

LBP is a $3 \times 3 \times 3 \times 3$ window, which takes the center pixel as the threshold and compares the gray value of 8 pixels. If the peripheral pixel value is larger than the center pixel value, the position is binary 1. Otherwise, it is binary 0 [4]. Through this method, an eight-bit binary can be obtained, which can be used as the value of the LBP of the center pixel of the window, and finally obtain the texture information of this area.

$$LBP_{(M,N)} = \sum_{L=1}^{8} S(I(L) - I(C)) * 2^L \qquad (2)$$

Here, L represents the L pixel excluding the center point in the 3×3 window; I(c) represents the gray value of the center point, and I(L) represents the gray value of the L pixel point within the range. The formula of S (M) is as follows:

$$S(M) = \begin{cases} 1, \ M \geq 0 \\ 0, \ otherwise \end{cases} \qquad (3)$$

By modifying the circular LBP operator, the range can be extended to any neighborhood, that is, the neighborhood radius can be extended to meet the requirements of texture features of different sizes in this way, so as to achieve gray scale and rotation invariance [3].

1.3 Smoke Classification Model Based on SVM

Support Vector Machine (SVM) is to establish the optimal classification surface to maximize the interval between two types of samples, and achieve the correct classification of positive samples and negative samples. The computational complexity is low, which is helpful to solve problems such as small sample learning, nonlinear and high-dimensional pattern recognition. A total of 5,544 forest fire smoke areas in all videos were selected as positive samples, while 1,470 typical non-smoke areas, including clouds, cars and pedestrians, were selected as negative samples. LBP features were extracted as the INPUT of SVM, and k-fold cross validation (K-CV) was used to obtain the optimal parameters of the model. The kernel function was set as radial basis kernel function (RBF), which mapped the data nonlinearly to the high-dimensional space and processed the nonlinear relations between features and their attributes. The penalty factor C is 100, and the coefficient γ is 0.001. 70% of the original samples were taken as the training set and 30% as the test set. The SVM classification model was trained and tested by using the optimal parameters. Then, the trained SVM classification model was used to classify the suspected smoke area and distinguish the smoke area from the non-smoke area. Classification algorithm evaluation index, accuracy rate M, recall rate N and F1, calculation formula is as follows:

$$M = \frac{T_M}{T_M + F_M} \qquad (4)$$

$$N = \frac{T_M}{T_M + F_C} \qquad (5)$$

$$F_1 = 2 \times \frac{M \times N}{M + N} \qquad (6)$$

where, represents the number of image blocks predicted as smoke and actually as smoke; Represents the number of image blocks predicted to be smoke but actually non-smoke;

Represents the number of image blocks predicted to be non-smoke but actually smoke; M is the accuracy rate. For the prediction result, here represents the proportion of the sample predicted as smoke that is actually smoke. N is the recall rate, which represents the proportion of smoke samples accurately predicted as smoke [5]. Is the harmonic mean of accuracy rate and recall rate.

1.4   Technical Segmentation of Dynamic Images

By segmenting the image region, the quality of video recognition can be guaranteed more clearly. Image segmentation technology refers to the process of dividing the distribution points, boundary regions, textures, shapes and color features of an image into non-overlapping regions. Image segmentation is a key step in the process of image pattern recognition. This process provides a basis for the next step of image feature extraction. Because the color image contains a lot of information, it needs to carry on the complex segmentation operation. Generally speaking, in order to study the problem of low color attribute, we will use the technology of transforming color image into gray image, which greatly reduces the difficulty of replacement technology. The commonly used methods are region growth method, edge detection method, threshold segmentation method and so on [6] (Fig. 1).

Fig. 1. The Python segmentation plot

2   Research Methods

The northeast forest area image acquisition system mainly realizes the operation of image processing algorithm on hardware circuit. With MATLAB image processing software, the recognition and separation of flame, smoke, temperature and other features of forest fire video images can be realized, and the pattern recognition technology of images can be used to identify the fire in northeast forest region, find the fire in time and display it in real time (Figs. 2 and 3).

Fig. 2. The original picture of the fire

Fig. 3. Fire division diagram

3 Research Content

The fuzzy C-means clustering algorithm based on unsupervised learning was used to segment forest fire images. In view of the problem that the fuzzy C-means clustering algorithm could not solve nonlinear segmentation, an improved fuzzy C-means clustering algorithm, namely the kernel fuzzy C-means clustering algorithm, was proposed to segment forest fire images.

Aiming at the problem that the initial clustering center of the kernel fuzzy C-means clustering algorithm is difficult to determine, an intelligent algorithm is used to optimize the kernel fuzzy C-means clustering algorithm to overcome its deficiency in image segmentation.

Whale optimization algorithm has excellent performance in intelligent optimization algorithm, has a strong ability to search for optimization, this topic will make some improvements to the whale optimization algorithm, and design experiments to prove the improved whale optimization algorithm in performance. Then the improved whale optimization algorithm is used to optimize the kernel fuzzy C-means clustering algorithm to obtain more accurate segmentation threshold and higher segmentation efficiency. The intelligent real-time fire monitoring platform in donglin forest area is realized by using MATLAB and Visual C++ software.

Donglin forest fire intelligent real-time monitoring platform is composed of acquisition front end, processing algorithm and carrier. Among them, the front end of collection is to install a camera to collect video images, and then carry out image processing or video image information processing. The intelligent monitoring of forest fires in northeast China is realized by using image feature extraction technology and classification technology through real-time monitoring of forest areas in northeast China to identify whether there are forest fire characteristics in the monitoring area (Fig. 4).

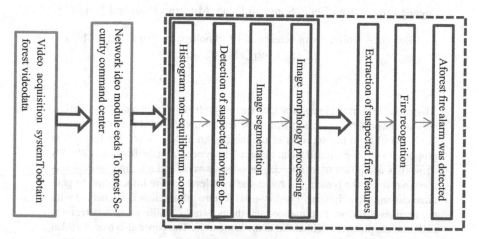

Fig. 4. Map of fire monitoring function module in Northeast Forest Area

Forest fires do great harm to human beings and ecological resources. The prevention and monitoring of forest fire has been paid great attention to all over the world. Video image monitoring and recognition based on visible distance is an important new research direction in forest fire prevention field. The forewarning of forest fire concerned by researchers of various countries has strong practical significance. Based on the research of image processing and pattern recognition technology, a forest fire automatic recognition and detection system applied to forest video surveillance system is proposed. At the same time, the image features are extracted by image preprocessing and motion sensing segmentation, and then the technical analysis, algorithm design and the judgment process of MATLAB simulation experiment are systematically carried out by image classifier recognition technology.

References

1. Wencheng, Z.: Investigation and analysis of forest fire prevention system in Baise, Guangxi. Guangxi University (2017)
2. Peixun, L.: All Weather Fire Detection System Based on Video Surveillance, pp. 40–50. Jilin University, Jilin (2011)
3. Jiyun, Z.: Forest fire smoke detection technology based on video analysis. Nanjing University of Aeronautics and Astronautics (2017)
4. Qi, Z.: Research on automatic monitoring and recognition technology of forest fire based on video image. University of Electronic Science and technology (2017)
5. Xue, Z.: Forest fire recognition system based on machine vision. Forest. Mach. Woodwork. Equipm. **12**, 2095–2953 (2020)
6. Baolin, C., Enron, D.: Modeling and prediction of forest fire mortality in Daxinganling. Mod. Econ. Inform. **08**, 339–340 (2017)

Research on Face Image Restoration Based on Improved WGAN

Fugang Liu$^{(\boxtimes)}$, Ran Chen, Songnan Duan, Mingzhu Hao, and Yang Guo

Heilongjiang University of Science and Technology, Harbin 150022, China
`liufugang_36@163.com`

Abstract. This article focuses on the face recognition model in real life scenarios, because the possible occlusion affects the recognition effect of the model, resulting in a decline in the accuracy of the model. An improved WGAN network is proposed to repair occluded facial images. The generator in the improved WGAN network is composed of an encoder-decoder network, and a jump connection is used to connect the bottom layer with the high-level feature information to generate missing facial images. The low-level feature information is connected with the deep-level feature information, and the network's ability to extract features and generate pictures is enhanced at the same time. The paper also uses a global discriminator and a local discriminator, taking all the restored pictures as input to measure the overall authenticity, and taking the restored part of the pictures as input to judge whether the content structure is reasonable. After comparison and analysis of experiments, the improved face image has a complete structure and clear content, which is helpful for face recognition with partial occlusion.

Keywords: WGAN · Face recognition · Face image inpainting

1 Introduction

Face recognition model has high recognition effects, such as Deep face [1], FaceNet [2], DeepID [3], etc. However, problems such as jewelry, illumination and hand occlusion may occur in complex environments, resulting in poor recognition effect of face recognition system and difficult to authenticate identity information. As early as the 20th century, the research on image restoration has begun. Image restoration mainly removes the occluded part or restores the missing part of the image, and the semantics and structure of the repaired image are consistent. The repaired image is reasonable and realistic, and it is difficult for the observer to see the repair trace or find that it has been damaged.

Bertalmio and Sapiro [4] proposed a digital image restoration technology for small-scale missing images, simulating the way that professional painters repair damaged or missing parts of images. The main idea of decomposition based image algorithm [5] is to divide the image into two parts: structure and texture for image processing, and finally add the two sub parts to reconstruct the repaired image. The texture synthesis algorithm

© ICST Institute for Computer Sciences, Social Informatics and Telecommunications Engineering 2022
Published by Springer Nature Switzerland AG 2022. All Rights Reserved
X. Jiang (Ed.): MLICOM 2021, LNICST 438, pp. 134–146, 2022.
https://doi.org/10.1007/978-3-031-04409-0_13

based on image block [6] as a whole is to find a pixel according to the texture feature information at the image position to be repaired, select the image block centered on the pixel, search the similar sample block in the unobstructed area, and replace the most similar image information with the area to be repaired.

Traditional face restoration methods based on texture and structure basically learn the image block information close to the junction of occluded and non occluded parts of the face, and then fill in the missing or occluded parts of the image. The disadvantage is the lack of context structure information. How to use the information associated between occluded and unobstructed areas is the key of research. The face restoration algorithm based on deep learning solves this problem. For example, the face restoration method based on context coding [7], but this method has some problems, such as the repaired face image is not clear enough and it is difficult to repair large-area occlusion.

Therefore, this paper proposes a face image restoration algorithm based on deep learning, which uses the improved WGAN network to repair the partially occluded face image. The generator network is built by encoder and decoder, and the jump connection is used to integrate the bottom features and deep features. The discriminator adopts a global discriminator and a local discriminator, Finally, the repaired image generated by the model has clear texture and reasonable structure, and the repaired face image is used for subsequent face recognition tasks, which can effectively improve the accuracy of partially occluded faces.

2   Related Models and Algorithms

2.1   Revolutionary Neural Networks

Revolutionary Neural Networks [8] is one of the important branches of deep learning model. Especially in the field of image processing, CNN is more widely used, and CNN has better image processing ability. The processing of two-dimensional images by revolutionary neural network is invariant to displacement, scale size and rotation. At the same time, CNN has the characteristics of local connection and weight sharing. There is a certain correlation between local images. The weight sharing uses the same convolution kernel in each layer. These two characteristics can improve the generalization ability of model feature extraction and reduce the amount of parameters.

Generally, CNN network usually includes the following parts: convolution layer, activation function, pooling layer and full connection layer. The basic structure of CNN is shown in Fig. 1.

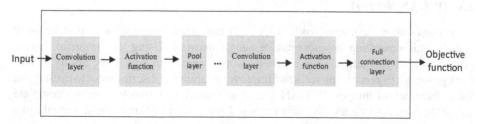

Fig. 1. CNN network structure

2.2 Generative Countermeasure Network

The generic countermeasure network is mainly composed of a generator (G) and a discriminator (D) [9]. As shown in Fig. 2, the uniform distribution Z is trained by the generator G to generate a false sample G(z), judge whether it is true by the discriminator D, and measure the difference between the generated data and the true data distribution, so as to optimize the generator G. The two start to iterate and update each other. Generator G hopes that the generated result can deceive D, and discriminator D hopes to judge G(z) as false, so that generator G can be continuously optimized to generate target samples through each round of confrontation optimization.

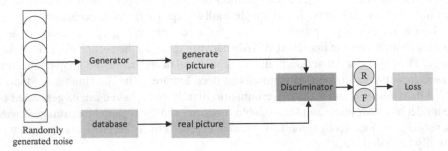

Fig. 2. Generative confrontation network structure

The loss function of Gan network is shown in formula (1):

$$\arg \min_{G} \max_{D} V(G, D) = E_{x \sim P_{\text{data}}}[\log(D(x))] + E_{x \sim P_G}[\log(1 - D(G(x)))] \quad (1)$$

In formula (1), $\arg \min_{G} \max_{D} V(G, D)$ means maximizing the discriminator loss function and minimizing the generator loss function; When x obeys the distribution of real data P_{data} is input into the discriminator, the expectation of $\log(D(x))$ is $E_{x \sim P_{\text{data}}}[\log D(x)]$; When x obeys the distribution of generated data P_G, the expectation of $\log(1-D(G(x)))$ is $E_{x \sim P_G}[\log(1 - D(G(x)))]$.

According to formula (1), the essence of the model is to optimize the discriminator D first, then to optimize generator G. So given a generator, maximize $V(G, D)$, the optimal solution D^* of the discriminator is obtained.

2.3 DCGAN Network

Deep convolution neural network (DCGAN) combines convolution neural network (CNN) with generation countermeasure neural network. Using the powerful feature extraction ability of convolution neural network, we can strengthen the ability of network generator to generate pictures and improve the ability of discriminator to distinguish the authenticity of images. DCGAN uses transpose convolution to generate complete image data. In 2010, Zeiler [9] first proposed the concept of transposed convolution. Transpose convolution and standard convolution can be regarded as mutual inverse processes. Convolution describes a many to one process in which the features of the input image are extracted through the convolution kernel, while transpose convolution, on the contrary, is a one to many process. The low-dimensional feature vector is mapped to the high-dimensional feature vector by transpose convolution to generate a picture.

As shown in Fig. 3(a), in the standard convolution process, the size of the input characteristic image is 3×3, convolution kernel of 2×2. The step size is 1, no filling, and the size of the output feature map is 2×2.

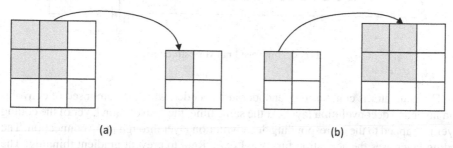

(a)   (b)

Fig. 3. Standard convolution process and transposed convolution process

2.4 WGAN Network

WGAN solves the problems of gradient disappearance and model collapse of KL divergence and JS divergence in the process of GAN network model training by introducing Wasserstein distance [10] into GAN network model. Wasserstein distance is shown in formula (2):

$$W(P, Q) = \inf_{\gamma \in \prod(P,Q)} E_{(x,y) \sim \gamma}[\|x - y\|] \tag{2}$$

In formula (2), $W(P, Q)$ means the lower bound of all possible distance expectations of joint distribution γ; $\prod(P, Q)$ means a set of joint distributions between P distribution and Q distribution; $E_{(x,y) \sim \gamma}[\|x - y\|]$ represents the expectation of the distance between (x, y) samples with joint distribution γ.

3 Network Design

3.1 Improved WGAN Network

The improved WGAN network structure consists of two parts (three networks), one is the generator model G, which is used to generate images; The other part is composed of two discriminator model D, which is used to distinguish whether an image is a real image or a generated image. The discriminator consists of a global discriminator and a local discriminator. The overall structure of the network is shown in Fig. 4.

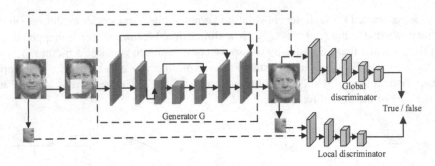

Fig. 4. Improved network structure

The generator is composed of encoder and decoder, which is composed of convolution layer and deconvolution layer. At the same time, the convolution layer of the coding layer is mapped to the corresponding deconvolution layer through jump connection. The coding layer uses the activation function Leaky-Relu to prevent gradient thinning; The rewind layer uses the ReLu activation function, and the last output layer uses the Tanh activation function. The specific structure of the generator is shown in Fig. 5.

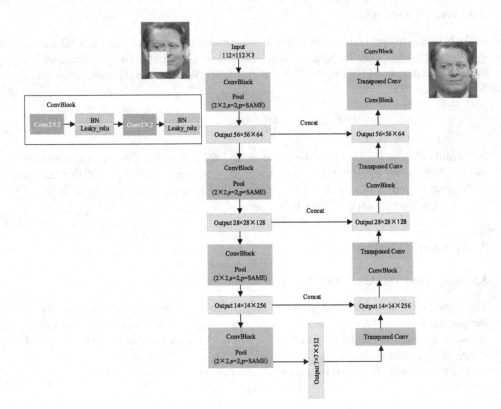

Fig. 5. Generator network structure

The discriminator is composed of Convolutional neural network. By constantly learning against the generator, the ability of the model to distinguish real pictures and generate pictures is improved. The local discriminator inputs the repaired complete image to identify whether the global image is consistent; The local discriminator inputs the image of the repaired part to judge whether the parts are consistent. The specific structure of the discriminator is shown in Fig. 6.

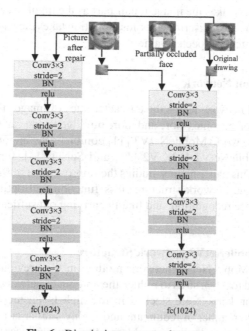

Fig. 6. Discriminator network structure

In the previous section, the loss function of the generator is formula (3), while the generator in this paper is composed of coder and decoder. The coder extracts the picture hidden features and inputs them to the decoder to generate face pictures. Therefore, the loss function generated in this paper is:

$$L_G = -E_{z \sim P(x,y)}[D(G(Z))] \tag{3}$$

In formula (3), L_G represents the Generator loss function, $P(x, y)$ is the feature extracted from the image to be repaired by the encoder; $D(G(Z))$ is the image generated by the generator.

The purpose of discriminator is to distinguish the authenticity of real data and generated data. In this paper, both global and partial discriminators use Wasserstein distance. Therefore, the loss function of the discriminator is mainly composed of two parts. The global discriminator uses the Wasserstein distance to measure the distance between the generated face and the face to be repaired, and some discriminators use the Wasserstein distance to measure the distance between the repaired part and the sample occlusion area. Therefore, the loss function of the discriminator is listed as follows:

$$
\begin{aligned}
L_D &= L_g + L_l \\
&= E_{z\sim Pg(x,y)}[D(G(z))] - E_{z\sim Pgdata}[D(x)] \\
&\quad + E_{z\sim Pl(x,y)}[D(G(z))] - E_{z\sim Pldata}[D(x)]
\end{aligned}
\tag{4}
$$

In formula (4), L_D means the discriminator loss function; L_g represents the global discriminator loss function takes the image repair part as the input to calculate its expected value; L_l represents the local discriminator loss function takes the whole repaired picture as the input to calculate its expected value.

3.2 Face Recognition Network

Convolutional neural network learns the characteristics of images through convolution layer and pooling layer, becomes more and more intelligent, and can well liberate human beings from repetitive work. MobileNetV3 [11] combines the important network structure modules of MobileNetV1 [12], V2 [13] and SeNet [14], further improving the effect of the model. This paper mainly studies the improvement of MobileNetV3_small, including adjusting the network structure, loss function and optimizer, applying the improved model to face recognition, and finally carrying out sufficient experiments and result analysis.

Improvement of MobileNetV3 Network Structure
Combined with the MobileNetV3 network module in the previous section, the input image size is changed to 3 * 3, so as to reduce the amount of network operation. Because too many convolution kernels are stacked in the high layer, the effect of the model is reduced and a large number of redundant and highly similar convolution kernels are caused. Therefore, aiming at the above problems, this paper reduces the number of layers of the network and effectively reduces the amount of parameters. In order to reduce the memory access of the network, this paper adopts the deep separable convolution network, improves the running speed of the network by reducing the channel expansion coefficient in the module, reduces the amount of parameters and redundancy of the model, and enhances the attention of the model channel by using compression and activation blocks.

Convolutional neural networks no longer use global average pooling, but 7×7 globally separable convolution substitution. If global pooling is used for feature extraction of the whole picture, it means that the feature importance of the corner is consistent with that of the middle. This is obviously wrong. The corner part of the image only includes the features of a small part of the face, and the middle part is the important feature of the face. In this paper, global separable convolution will be used instead of global pooling to give different importance to different receptive fields. The improved network structure is shown in Table 1, where n represents the number of repetitions of this operation.

Joint Loss Function Based on CenterLoss and Softmax
The loss function consists of two parts, which are model parameters. The Softmax loss function is used as a classifier, and the network iteratively trains and optimizes the loss

Table1. Improved MobileNetV3 network model structure

Input	Operator	exp size	out	SE	NL	s	n
$112 \times 112 \times 3$	conv2d,3×3	-	64	-	RE	2	1
$56 \times 56 \times 64$	depthwise, 3×3	16	64	$\checkmark$	RE	1	1
$56 \times 56 \times 64$	Bneck, 3×3	128	64	$\checkmark$	RE	2	3
$28 \times 28 \times 64$	Bneck, 3×3	512	128	-	RE	2	1
$14 \times 14 \times 128$	Bneck, 3×3	256	128	$\checkmark$	HS	1	3
$14 \times 14 \times 128$	Bneck, 3×3	512	128	$\checkmark$	HS	2	1
$7 \times 7 \times 128$	Bneck, 3×3	256	128	$\checkmark$	HS	1	2
$7 \times 7 \times 128$	Bneck, 3×3	256	512	$\checkmark$	HS	1	1
$7 \times 7 \times 512$	LinearGDConv7 $\times$ 7	-	512	$\checkmark$	-	1	1
$1 \times 1 \times 512$	Linearconv1 $\times$ 1	-	128	$\checkmark$	-	1	1

function to obtain the global optimal solution. In the second half, CenterLoss calculates the distance between the sample features and the middle features as the loss function. At the beginning of network training, the feature center is randomly selected. After the network optimizes the loss function, the feature center is updated, and the network model is continuously updated until the network reaches the optimum. When the super parameter is, the loss function is Softmax loss function, and it can play the constraint ability of the loss of the control center.

$$L_{loss} - L_{soft \max} + L_{centerloss}$$

$$= -\frac{1}{n} \sum_{i=1}^{n} \log \frac{e^{W_{y_i}^T x(i)}}{\sum_{l=1}^{k} e^{W_l^T x(i)}} + \lambda \cdot \frac{1}{2} \sum_{i=1}^{n} \|x_i - c_{y_i}\|_2^2 \tag{5}$$

4 Experiment and Result Analysis

The training set of face restoration experiment in this paper adopts the large-scale CelebA face data set published by the Chinese University of Hong Kong, which contains a total of 10177 celebrity face images, a total of about 202599 face images, and the size of the original face image is 178 * 218. The images in face data have done a lot of labeling work, including face key point labeling, face rectangle labeling and face attribute labeling information. Therefore, CelebA data set is widely used in various tasks related to face in the field of computer vision, such as face attribute recognition, face detection and key point detection.

The detected partial face images are uniformly scaled to size $112 \times 112 \times 3$. We process the pictures of CelebA data set, add rectangular box occlusion, simulate the occlusion that may occur in the real situation, and then use this data set for network training, including the following examples of facial occlusion (Fig. 7):

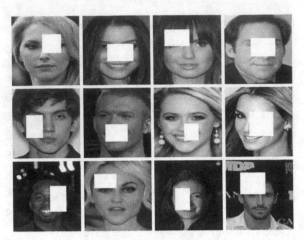

Fig. 7. The processed data set

Peak signal-to-noise ratio measure (PSNR). It mainly calculates the difference between the pixel values of the original picture and the two pictures after occlusion repair. It can measure whether the repaired image has distortion and the difference between images. The calculation process is as follows (6).

$$PSNR = 10 \times \log_{10}[\frac{(2^n - 1)^2}{MSE}]$$

$$MSE = \frac{1}{HW} \sum_{i=1}^{H} \sum_{j=1}^{W} \left\| f(i,j) - f(\hat{i}, j) \right\|^2 \tag{6}$$

In formula (6), n is the number of bits of the pixel value (generally is 8), that is, the gray scale of the pixel value is 256; MSE is mean square error between the repaired image and the original image; H and W represent the Height and width of image respectively.

Structural similarity index (SSIM) is an index to calculate whether the structure of the original image is similar to that of the image after occlusion repair. It is mainly measured from three aspects: brightness, contrast and structure。As shown in Eq. (7) for the calculation of SSIM, The larger the calculated SSIM value, the more similar the two images are.

$$SSIM(x, y) = \frac{(2u_x u_y + C_1)(2\sigma_{xy} + C_2)}{(u_x^2 + u_y^2 + C_1)(\sigma_x^2 + \sigma_y^2 + C_2)} \tag{7}$$

In formula (7), u_x, u_y represent the mean of image x and y, respectively; σ_x, σ_y represent the variance of image x and y, respectively; σ_{xy} is the Covariance of X and Y.

Experiment 1

The face data set CelebA is divided into training set and test set according to 9:1. Before using the training set to train the network model, the image is processed to add occlusion, and then the original network and the improved network model are trained respectively.

After the model is trained, the same test set is used, and the repaired images and the original images are evaluated by PSNR and SSIM indicators. The calculation results are shown in Table 2.

Table 2. Comparison between the original algorithm and the improved algorithm

Evaluating indicator	Original algorithm	This paper improves the algorithm
SSIM	0.88	0.92
PSNR	27.48	29.58

For the comparison between the repaired images of the original algorithm and the improved algorithm, see Fig. 8. From left to right, there are occluded images, repaired images and original face images. The above three images are the face repaired by the original algorithm, and the lower half is the improved face repair image. It can be directly seen from the figure that the effect of the face repair algorithm repaired in this paper is clearer and more complete than that of the original algorithm.

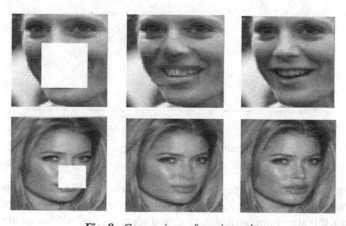

Fig. 8. Comparison of repair results

Experiment 2

It mainly proves the performance of face recognition under occlusion of different area sizes. The experiment uses LFW public data set for evaluation. On the test data set samples, four area sizes of occlusion of 10%, 20%, 30% and 40% are used respectively, as shown in Table 3:

Table 3. Results of face recognition with different occlusion areas

Occlusion area algorithm	10%	20%	30%	40%
Improved mobilnetv3_ Small + joint loss function	93.86%	91.21%	87.23%	82.3%
Paper algorithm	94.56%	93.65%	92.35%	90.07%

Draw a broken line diagram according to the data in Table 2, as shown in Fig. 9.

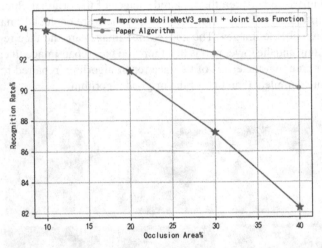

Fig. 9. The recognition accuracy of different occlusion areas

As can be seen from the experimental results shown in Fig. 9, the appearance of occlusion increases the difficulty of face recognition algorithm. With the increasing occlusion area, this algorithm can maintain a good accuracy, and still has a stable accuracy when the occlusion area is greater than 20%. Therefore, this algorithm is more robust to face recognition with partial occlusion.

5   Conclusion

In order to make face recognition still have a high recognition rate in the case of occlusion, this paper uses the improved WGAN network to repair the partially occluded area and increase the image face features, which can effectively improve the accuracy of face recognition.

(1)   The process of mutual confrontation learning between GAN network generator and discriminator is applied to the problem of face restoration. The improved

WGAN generator adopts the structure of encoder and decoder. The network learns the global information of the picture by extracting the image features, and the generated picture semantic information is more complete.

(2) At the same time, the generator uses jump connection to map the convolution layer of the coding layer to the corresponding deconvolution layer, and fuse the bottom feature information with the deep feature information, which will make the generated picture clearer.

(3) The discriminator adopts global discriminator and local discriminator, which can ensure the correctness of global information and local repair information at the same time。

(4) Through the experimental comparison and the comparison of the generated repaired images, the images repaired by the face repair algorithm proposed in this paper are clearer and semantically complete.

Acknowledgements. This work has been partially supported by Heilongjiang Science Foundation Project (LH2021F052).

References

1. Taigman, Y., Yang, M., Ranzato, M., Wolf, L.: DeepFace: closing the gap to human-level performance in face verification. In: 2014 IEEE Conference on Computer Vision and Pattern Recognition, pp. 1701–1708 (2014). https://doi.org/10.1109/CVPR.2014.220
2. Schroff, F., Kalenichenko, D., Philbin, J: FaceNet: a unified embedding for face recognition and clustering. IEEE (2015)
3. Ouyang, W., Zeng, X., Wang, X., et al.: Deformable Deep Convolutional Neural Networks for Object. arXiv:1412.5661v2 (2015)
4. Bertalmof, M., Sapiro, G., Caselles, V., et al.: Image Inpainting. In: Proceedings of Annual Conference on Computer Graphics & Interactive Techniques, pp. 417–424 (2000)
5. Li, P., Wang, H., Li, X., Zhang, C.: An image denoising algorithm based on adaptive clustering and singular value decomposition. IET Image Process. **15**, p. 3 (2021)
6. Drori, I., Cohen-Or, D., Yeshurun, H.: Fragment-based image completion. ACM Trans. Graph. **3** (2003)
7. Angah, O., Chen, A.Y.: Removal of occluding construction workers in job site image data using U-Net based context encoders. Autom. Constr. **119** (2020),
8. Sun, Y., Wang, X., Tang, X: Deep learning face representation from predicting 10,000 classes. In: Proceedings of the IEEE Conference on Computer Vision and Pattern Recognition, pp. 891–1898 (2014)
9. Yonghao, M., Ming, Z., Jing, L., Yaguo, L.: Application of an improved maximum correlated kurtosis deconvolution method for fault diagnosis of rolling element bearings. Mech. Syst. Signal Process. **92**, 173–195 (2017)
10. Arjovsky, M., Chintala, S., Bottou, L: Wasserstein GAN. CoRR,abs (2017)
11. Howard, A., Sandler, M., Chen, B., et al.: Searching for MobileNetV3. In: 2019 IEEE/CVF International Conference on Computer Vision, IEEE (2020)
12. Sandler, M., Howard, A., Zhu, M., et al.: MobileNetV2: inverted residuals and linear bottlenecks. In: 2018 IEEE/CVF Conference on Computer Vision and Pattern Recognition (2018)

13. Howard, A.G., Zhu, M., Chen, B., et al.: MobileNets: efficient convolutional neural networks for mobile vision applications. Int. J. Intell. Sci. **11** (2017)
14. Liu, Y.F., Meng, L., Qiu, D., et al.: Multi-task squeeze-and-excitation networks for pedestrian attributes recognition. Sci. Techno. Eng. **19**(24), 237–241 (2019)

Research on Text Communication Security Based on Deep Learning Model

Guanghua Yu[1,2(✉)] and Wanjuan Cong[1,2]

[1] Heihe University, Heihe, Heilongjiang, China
Ygh2862@163.com
[2] School of Computer and Information Engineering College, HeiHe University, Heihe, China

Abstract. In response to the current spam flooding problem, this paper uses Python language machine learning and natural language processing technology to study the identification classification of spam messages. The Jieba algorithm is used to distinguish the Chinese word, and the TF-IDF algorithm is used to conduct feature extraction. On the basis of the analysis of the classifier algorithm, the experimental data is finalized. The results show that the classification effect of the polynomial plain Bayes classifier is optimal, and the identification of garbage text is best optimized.

Keywords: Spam message · Naive Bayesian Model

1 Preface

With the wide application of social media, text message service has developed rapidly. At the same time, a large number of junk information and fraud information are added to it, which brings different degrees of harassment and serious security risks to people's lives, and adds unstable factors to the development of a harmonious society. Therefore, the use of information technology to establish the ability to identify, correct and deal with spam text information is particularly important. In this paper, the deep learning algorithm and python language are used to identify and classify spam text messages. Jieba Chinese word segmentation tool and TF-IDF feature extraction are used to analyze the principles of naive Bayes, Gaussian distribution, random forest and other classifier algorithms. Finally, according to the experimental data, the classification effect is compared [1].

2 Correlation Theory

There are three methods to effectively identify spam messages, which are black and white list method, rule-based method and SMS content-based method [2–5]. The blacklist and rules is relatively simple, but the disadvantage is that the number list and keywords need

Foundation item: School-level topics (KJZ202102); School-level topics (XJGY201923) Project of Heilongjiang Provincial Department of Education (2019-KYYWF-0462).

X. Jiang (Ed.): MLICOM 2021, LNICST 438, pp. 147–154, 2022.
https://doi.org/10.1007/978-3-031-04409-0_14

to be added manually, and the number that can be added is relatively limited and difficult to be comprehensive, resulting in poor recognition effect. In view of the limitations of the two methods, the current research on spam SMS identification technology mainly focuses on the content of SMS, using text classification technology to transform spam SMS recognition problem into a supervised learning problem. Text classification technology is based on machine learning algorithm. Firstly, it extracts the features of the manually marked text, and then using the algorithm to classify the text automatically.

2.1 Chinese Participle

In text data mining, word or phrase is usually used as feature to segment words. Therefore, we need to extract the original text data by word segmentation to obtain the corresponding feature list before text classification and feature extraction. Therefore, high accuracy of text segmentation has a great impact on the subsequent text analysis and text classification. At present, English and Chinese are the main text segmentation methods. Due to the different grammatical structures, the two languages have different word segmentation methods. However, English word segmentation is much easier than Chinese word segmentation in practical point, because English word results and punctuation are relatively clear, while Chinese text is relatively vague. This paper uses Chinese text, and uses Jieba Chinese word segmentation to segment Chinese text.

1   The construction principle of prefix dictionary: Prefix dictionary is constructed by using statistical dictionary algorithm. For example: "Heihe College" is a word in the statistical dictionary. The prefix of the word is {"Hei", "Heihe", "heihexue"}, and the prefix of the word "College" is {"Xue"}. By analogy, we can get the prefix Dictionary of the Chinese text to be segmented.
2.   The construction principle of directed acyclic graph based on prefix dictionary is shown in Fig. 1.

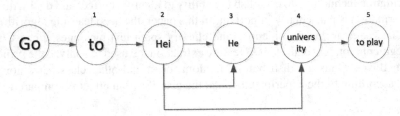

Fig. 1. An example of directed acyclic graph based on prefix dictionary

From Fig. 1 can be seen, there are three ways to divide "Hei" into "Hei", "Heihe" and "Heihe College", while for "Qu", there is only one way to divide "Qu". The reason is that the word "Qu" has no prefix. Similarly, the combination of "Xue" and "play" can be obtained. Based on this, a directed acyclic graph is constructed.

3. The algorithm principle of using dynamic programming algorithm to find the maximum probability path: the maximum probability path of the front drive node must be calculated for every node found by the dynamic programming. The core condition of dynamic programming algorithm is to have repeated subproblems and optimal substructures. For the problem of finding the maximum probability path in directed acyclic graph, the repetitive subproblem and the optimal substructure are as flows:

(1) Repetitive subproblem: In a directed acyclic graph, any node di may have some successor nodes dj or dk, and it is necessary to repeatedly calculate the probability value of the path to di for each successor node. The mathematical expressions are 1 and 2.

$$P(i) -> j = P(i) + weight(j) \qquad (1)$$

$$P(i) -> k = P(i) + weight(k) \qquad (2)$$

(2) The optimal substructure is as follows: For the end node dx of a directed acyclic graph, there may be multiple precursor nodes di and dj. The maximum probability paths for DK to reach these precursor nodes are respectively $P_{max(i)}$, $P_{max(j)}$ and $P_{max(k)}$. According to this, the maximum probability path is $P_{max(x)}$, and the calculation formula is 3.

$$P_{max(x)} = max\{(P_{max(i)}, P_{max(j)}, P_{max(k)}.....) + weight(dx)\} \qquad (3)$$

2.2 Feature Representation and Extraction of Text Data

TF IDF algorithm is used to express and extract text data features, that is, the frequency of a word appearing in text. Because word frequency has a great influence on the classification of original text data, the greater the word frequency of a word, the greater its contribution to text recognition. The frequency of words is shown as 4:

$$tfij = \frac{nij}{\sum nkj} \qquad (4)$$

nij is the number of times that the word appears in the file dj, and the denominator is the total number of times that all words appear in the file dj.

$$idf_j = \log(|D|/|\{k:t \in dk\}|) \qquad (5)$$

|D| is the total number of files in the corpus. |{k:t ∈ dk}| denotes the number of files containing the word ti (i.e. the number of files with ni, j ≠ 0).

The TF-IDF algorithm process takes five groups of Chinese text data as examples, as shown in Table 1:

1. Calculate the inverse document frequency of Chinese text data: The algorithm counts the number of different words appearing in the text. For example, from the text data

Table 1. Five groups of Chinese text data content

Number	Content
1	Pets have pets, pets, pets, pets, pets
2	Pets include dogs, cats, hamsters, hedgehogs and squirrels
3	The animals are lovely. I like lions best
4	Dogs are loyal pets
5	Lovely pets are dogs, cats, chinchillas, other pets are hamsters and lizards

content in Table 1, we can see that "pet" is quoted in text 1, 2, 4 and 5, it appears in 4 places, so the reverse document frequency of "pet" is 4. Similarly, the reverse document frequencies of other nouns are: pet = 4, dog = 3, cat = 2, hamster = 2, cute = 2, hedgehog = 1, beast = 1, lion = 1, loyalty = 1, chinchilla = 1, lizard = 1. Therefore, "pet" and "dog" are the two most important words in the five sets of texts. Remove text 1 and text 3.

2. Calculate the word frequency of Chinese text data: After the algorithm calculation of inverse document frequency, text 2, text 4 and text 5 are selected. Because the frequency of words in text has a significant impact on text classification, "pet" is the core word in the text. Through calculation, it is found that the word appears twice in the fifth text, and only once in the second and fourth text. Therefore, the final ranking result is shown in Table 2.

Table 2. Five groups of sorted Chinese text data content

Sort	Content
1	Lovely pets are dogs, cats, chinchillas, other pets are hamsters and lizards
2	Pets include dogs, cats, hamsters, hedgehogs and squirrels
3	Dogs are loyal pets
4	Pets have pets, pets, pets, pets, pets
5	The animals are lovely. I like lions best

2.3 Segmentation of Training Set and Test Set

The paper uses train_test_split method of sklearn.model_selection is used to segment the data. According to 75% and 25% segmentation ratio, the text data is divided into training data set and test data set.

3 Naive Bayesian Recognition Model

Firstly, the text data is extracted, and then the prior probability belonging to the feature value is calculated. According to the obtained prior probability, the Bayesian formula is used to calculate the posterior probability. The flow chart of naive Bayesian algorithm is shown in Fig. 2.

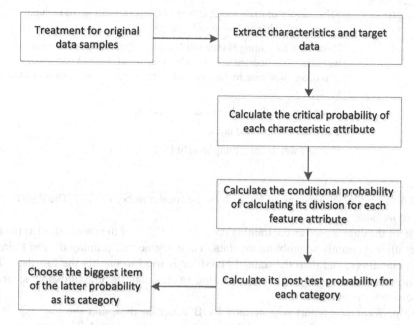

Fig. 2. Flow chart of naive Bayes algorithm

The sample space of test E is Ω. Suppose that "B1, B2,..., Bn" is a partition of Ω, A is an event of R, and P (A) > 0, P (Bi) > 0 (i = 1, 2, ..., n), then the Bayesian formula is expressed as [6]:

$$P(Bi \mid A)\frac{P(Bi)P(A \mid Bi)}{\sum_{j=1}^{n} P(Bj) P(A \mid Bj)} \tag{6}$$

4   Experiment and Result Analysis

4.1   Experimental Environment

The programming language is python 3.6. The framework of deep learning is Tensorflow1.0. The internal storage is 8 GB. The operating system is windows 10.

4.2   Data Analysis

The wiki Chinese corpus used for text data contains 863000 Chinese texts. There are more than 80000 pieces of data belonging to spam SMS category, accounting for 10% of the total number of data. There are more than 720000 pieces of data belonging to

Table 3. The format of Chinese text data

Number	Category	SMS text content
1	0	"The secrecy of trade secret is one of the preconditions to maintain its commercial value and monopoly position."
2	1	Thank you for calling Hangzhou Xiaoshan Quanjin kettle Korean barbecue shop, located at XXX Jincheng Road. Korean barbecue, etc., affordable, welcome to patronize [Korean barbecue restaurant of Quanjin kettle]
3	0	Bring us a grand visual feast in Changzhou
4	0	There are unexplained urinary stones, etc.
5	0	Feel self weight loss, jump weight loss Aerobics

normal SMS category, accounting for 90% of the total number of data. The data format is shown in Table 3.

75% of the data is used as the training data set, and 25% of the data is used as the test data set after randomly scrambling the data. Then segmented training data to training various classifiers, and then the trained classifier is used to predict the test data. The prediction results are compared with the actual results, and the classification accuracy of the classifier is obtained.

The performance report is generated by B function in a, and the learning curve analysis is constructed when the model parameters are determined. The training speed is shown in Fig. 3.

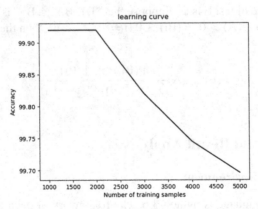

Fig. 3. Learning curve of naive Bayes classifier with prior Gaussian distribution

4.3 Interpretation of Result

The classification model trained by the training data set and the test data are used to predict the results. The performance reports generated are shown in Table 3 and Table 4. Because of the computational power 10074 data were selected for model training.

Table 4. Performance report of naive Bayes classifier 1

Category	Precision	Recall	f1_score	Support
Normal	93%	100%	96%	3925
Garbage	100%	29%	45%	412

Table 5. Performance report of naive Bayes classifier 2

Accuracy			93%	4337
Macro avg	97%	64%	70%	4337
Weighted avg	94%	93%	91%	4337

From the data in Table 4 and Table 5, it can be seen that 10074 data sets are used as raw data, and then the original data sets are divided into training data sets according to 75% of the comparison columns, and 25% of the comparison columns divide the original data sets into test data sets, the accuracy of naive Bayesian classifier reaches 93%. If the calculation force allows, the accuracy of naive Bayesian classifier can reach 93%, According to the actual situation, the training data set and the test data set data set data can be improved to some extent.

5   Conclusion

It is a social problem that spam SMS flooding has always plague people's life. In order to effectively identify spam messages, this paper proposes to use naive Bayes model to train samples from wiki Chinese corpus. To a certain extent, it solves the problems of sparse data, high dimension and difficult modeling of semantic relationship between words. However, when the number of features in the text is large or the correlation between the features is large, the classification effect has some limitations. At the same time, the prior probability needs to be known in the prediction, and the calculation of the prior probability depends on the assumptions of the model, which increases the difficulty of the prediction efficiency. Therefore, further research should be done to improve data classification and efficiency.

References

1. Bhat, S.Y., Abulaish, M.: Community-based features for identifying spammers in Online Social Networks. In: IEEE/ACM International Conference on Advances in Social Networks Analysis & Mining (2013)
2. Baozhong, Z.: Application of various classification methods in garbage ports, pp. 5–45. Huazhong Normal University (2017)
3. Mountain, X.: Study on word vector classification, pp. 15-16. Jilin University (2019)

4. Ruiqi, C.: Research on the study of text acquisition analysis based on strengthening learning, pp. 11–12. Beijing University of Posts and Telecommunications, Beijing (2019)
5. Sone, S.F.: Spam identification application based on machine. Anhui Comput. Knowl. Technol. **16**(3), 202–204 (2020)
6. Huangyu, L.: Discussion on the application of Bayesian formula. Chengdu Sci. Technol. Econ. **28**(8), 165 (2020)

Elimination of Network Intrusion Using Advance Data Mining Technology

Dhulfiqar Saad Jaafar[1]([✉]) and Hoshang Kolivand[2]

[1] Ministry of Education, Baghdad, Iraq
ghaffoori15@itu.edu.tr
[2] Department of Computer Science, Liverpool John Moores University, Liverpool L3 3AF, UK
h.kolivand@ljmu.ac.uk

Abstract. Advancements of data mining and machine learning have paved the road for establishing an efficient attack prediction paradigm to protect large scaled networks. In this study, computer network intrusions had been eliminated using smart machine learning algorithm to eliminate network intrusion. Referring a big dataset named KDD computer intrusion dataset which includes large number of connections that diagnosed with several types of attacks; the model is established for predicting the type of attack by learning through this data. Feed forward neural network model is outperformed over the other proposed clustering models in attack prediction accuracy.

Keywords: Network intrusion · Data mining · Machine learning · FFNN · KDD · K-means · DB Scan · Intrusion · Attack

1 Introduction

It has been realized from the literature survey that internet as a public network imposes plenty of challenges on data security. The solutions proposed in the literature involves using of virtual; private network in the standard format to secure the data over such public networks [1]. The advancement of software technology and electronic component manufacturing led to the invention of software defined network. Intrusion detection systems are used to identify irregularities in the flow of data from the host to the client or across the network [3]. Any malicious packet injection can be detected and deleted using an intrusion detection system, which can discover security problems on a network [2]. These systems work by examining the sender's and receiver's digital signatures and certificates. Any infractions of the rules are tracked and reported to the network administrator, who is alerted to the likelihood of a network assault. Packets are sometimes transmitted after decrypting and examining their contents for far more secure transmission [4]. Networks are using data technology such as machine learning algorithms for detection the attack and hence feedback signal can be transmitted to the firewall for blocking the suspicious inward request discovered by the machine learning algorithm.

X. Jiang (Ed.): MLICOM 2021, LNICST 438, pp. 155–161, 2022.
https://doi.org/10.1007/978-3-031-04409-0_15

2   Previous Work

One of the big issues that has been realized from the current approaches of virtual private network is that: using the same paradigm cannot be used to prevent all types of attacks and to secure whole web application. More likely, this is done applying the ordinary virtual private network that securing the two connections through the internet in personal computer into the data security in companies or institution (campus) networks. From the other hand, it was realized that virtual private networks protocols are sensitive for particular attacks or malwares whereas the other malwares or attacks are remained untraceable in virtual private network [5]. Some other tools are proposed for protection purposes by prevention the foreign requests unless it is pre-defined in the routing data. The same can stand with the case of data flooding applications such as ecommerce and social applications. Intermediate gates and software could be used to prevent the malfunctioning requests, the same is realized having negative impact on the network performance from the throughput, time delay, packets drop rates point of views. The main task of virtual private network is imposing the security over the network while the other aspects alike network performance guaranties are not gain their priority level in the research [6]. The number of nodes can be varied from two nodes and can be extended further according to the networking constrains. The security of data is remained disputed even over the virtual private networks which make the last (virtual private network) unable to face this security threat. The term virtual is standing for assumable (imaginary) connections that made as a part of plenty of connections involved in a real (physical) network [9, 11]. Firewalls and other software defined networks are tended to enhance the security and to ensure more privacy to the users' data.

3   Method

3.1   Dataset Description

Our internet network datasets were sourced from the UCI machine learning repository [8]. Intrusion is a famous challenge that can access any network especially those with large number of users such as internet network. Over the internet there are tons of the software defined networks which are linking a plenty of users from different locality in the globe. However, users are getting access into the internet network through smaller networks that acts as relay. So-to-say, routing log data was obtained from open-source database inventory where one thousand inward web requests were recorder. Each request is representing an incoming web connection for a particular network operating over the internet [10, 11].

Each connection is representing a type of attack that aimed for network penetration. The dataset is made by monitoring some features for each connection aiming to classify the said connection according to the type of attack it represents. The last column of the dataset is represented as the target or the classes that made according to understand each attack features.

3.2 Pre-processing Model

The data cells on the dataset are being observed in order to prepare it for the so-called pre-processing. The data is included of large number of entries which represents the connection properties of large number of users (one thousand user). Each user is demonstrated by set of connection features as stated above. The challenges that might be addressed through the pre-processing model can be enlisted as following:

a> data might be included with missing cells that are raised due to several aspects including the storage of bad sector which lead to damage some data and hence it looks alike missing data. All the missing data are usually substituted with question marks, hashes, or even terms alike "missing".

b> missing data are to be recovered using the method of column values averaging which means each column with missing data is to be treated by adding all the columns values together and dividing the result of the summation by the number of elements situated in the column except those which said as missing. Equation 1 demonstrates the missing values substitutionary values; Algorithm 1 shows the model structure of missing values recovery.

Let column "A" witnessing three missing values that denoted as question marks in their particular cells;

Let "S" is the summation of total column elements;

Let "N" is the total count number of column elements;

Let "M" is the total number counts the missing values.

Hence, the missing value will be retained by fulfilling the Equation 1.

$$R(A) = \frac{\sum_{N=1}^{N=x} A(N)}{X} = \frac{S}{X} \tag{1}$$

Algorithm 1: Missing values evaluation and substitution

Select the column (Ci), L=Len(A), i=0
While! (A(i)∈ /#, &,?, !/)
    A(i)=Aver(A)
    i++
  End while

From the other hand, data normalization is the last step that was conducted during the per-processing task. The dataset after the decoding will appear with codes stated where no other unknown alphabets or numbers is longer existed. At the end of the encoding stage, data will be ready to be in warded into the machine learning paradigms. However, one more step can be performed for enhancing the performance of training by normalizing the data. Data in each cell over the dataset can be normalized by fining the peak value of every column and then dividing the entire column elements by that value. The same is yielding new appearance of the data which has value of "one" as the maximum value (new peak) and all other values are divisions of this new peak. However, the process of normalization is made to enhance the training performance by minimizing the variance of the overall values in dataset.

4 Intrusion Sensing

Machine learning as well as deep learning approaches were used to perform data clustering tasks in order to predict the intrusion attack. In the first stage of processing, the dataset is made ready for this process as the data can be feed into the algorithm and the algorithm can decided wither this connection is an attack or not. However, four type of classes are being associated with the test dataset as listed in Table 1.

Table 1. Target classes illustrating the number of classes the target vector

Class name	Class code
normal	0
snmpgetattack	1
Xlock	2
Smurf	3

Figure 1 demonstrates the role of the clustering technology performed by both machine learning and deep learning approaches for detecting of the attack.

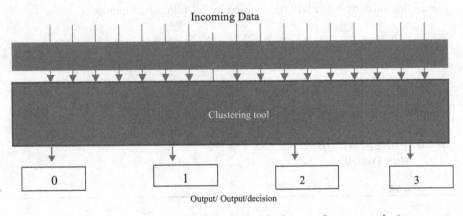

Fig. 1. Decision making in clustering method (general representation).

In order to safe safeguard the network against any malicious attack, a Feed Forward neural Network is utilized to develop a smart attack prevention paradigm. This paradigm may predict occurrence of attack depending of the attitude of each attack before it is actually taking place. Model employing the feed forward neural network for predicting the malicious activities [11, 12].

In order to use this model, the feed forward neural network is being trained using a dataset of network attacks attitudes. Data set is included with large number of connections, those connections included with attack (malicious connection) as well as safe connection [14]. Every connection was diagnosed and accordingly the target column is made to classify the data according to the nature of connection. The attack prevention model is working according to the Algorithm 2.

Algorithm 2: Attack prevention model

Step 1: network attacks dataset is downloaded from open access data bank and used in the further steps of the system.

Step 2: dataset is pre-processed in order to convert any alphabetic entry into numerical entry. From the other hand, all the values (numbers) in the dataset are being normalized in order to reduce the variance between the data cells which may enhance the performance of model training in hereinafter.

Step 3: there was no missing values in the dataset entries so-no missing value recovery program was made.

Step 4: Feed Forward Neural Network model is used for implementing the model of attack prevention. A prediction process is made firstly by letting the model training using eighty percent of the data.

Step 5: after successful training of the model, model is tested using the remained twenty percent of the dataset.

The performance of the feed forward neural network model is compared with baseline clustering technologies namely: Agglomerative clustering algorithm, DB scan clustering algorithm, K-means clustering and Mini batch K-means clustering. All the mentioned algorithms are made to produce the decision of attack type and performs the operations that similar to the process done by feed forward neural network [15, 16]. FFNN model is first initiated by preforming of fifty iteration with random wright allotment (ordinary FFNN model). Hence after, model is optimized using the weight freezing method which involved selecting the optimal weight coefficients out of the iterated weight in the ordinary model to be the permanent weight of the model. The Freeze FFNN model is eventually observed to be outperformed over the other clustering techniques.

5   Results and Discussion

Each clustering algorithm is made to perform the task of attack clustering so that the attack can be predicted foreach incoming web request before it is actually taking place. The performance of each algorithm is determined using three performance metrics namely: mean absolute error, mean square error and accuracy of clustering. However, the Table 2 below illustrates the performance metrics for each algorithm.

Table 2. Performance metric for the attack clustering

Clustering	MAE	MSE	Accuracy
Agglomerative clustering	1.8653	3.7714	51
DB scan	2.1395	7.7128	13.3
K-means	1.9666	4.2407	46
Mini batch	1.8897	3.8897	50.1
FFNN (Freeze model)	0.9172	2.6142	98

6 Conclusion

Networks are highly susceptible for malware and malicious attacks since it is operating over a public network like internet. The cost of attack prevention machinery and network components is far expensive than network itself in some applications. Hence, the current trends of network protection alike virtual private networks are also can't stand to face the fluctuation on the attacks which are developed a lot due to the software and computer advancement in the current research. In this project, a smart attack prediction approach is proposed in which predicting the attack by learning through the behaviors of each incoming connection. However, big dataset issues which involves a thousand connections, each connection is being featured by several properties such as connection duration, service protocol, number of errors, etc. two approaches of learning are used namely deep learning approach (e.g., Feed Forward Neural Network) and machine learning clustering approaches' (e.g., Agglomerative clustering algorithm, DB scan clustering algorithm, K-means clustering and Mini batch K-means clustering). Results shown that Feed Forward neural network has outperformed for attack clustering and attack prediction with prediction performance of 98 percent. On the other hand, the second-best prediction performance is realized on Agglomerative clustering followed by mini batch, K-means and DB Scan respectively. The other performance metrics are also revealed the same point that is feed forward neural network is the optimum intrusion prediction algorithm.

References

1. Habibzadeh, H., et al.: A survey on cybersecurity, data privacy, and policy issues in cyber-physical system deployments in smart cities. Sustain. Cities. Soc. **50**, 101660 (2019)
2. Clarke, N., Li, F., Furnell, S.: A novel privacy preserving user identification approach for network traffic. Comput. Secur. **70**, 335–350 (2017)
3. Haripriya, L., Jabbar, M.A.: Role of machine learning in intrusion detection system. In: 2018 Second International Conference on Electronics, Communication and Aerospace Technology (ICECA), pp. 925–929. IEEE (2018)
4. Azwar, H., Murtaz, M., Siddique, M., Rehman, S.: Intrusion detection in secure network for cybersecurity (2018)
5. Panetta, K.: Gartner's Top 10 Security Predictions 2016. Сайт компанії «Gartner» (2016). http://www.gartner.com/smarterwithgartner/top-10security-predictions2016

6. Arshad, J., et al.: A review of performance, energy and privacy of intrusion detection systems for IoT. Electronics **9**(4), 629 (2020)
7. Ande, Ruth, et al. "Internet of Things: Evolution and technologies from a security perspective." Sustainable Cities and Society 54 (2020): 101728
8. Blake, C.L., Merz, C.J.: UCI Repository of Machine Learning Databases. University of California, vol. 55. Department of Information and Computer Science, Irvine (1998). http://www.ics.uci.edu/?mlearn/MLRespository.html
9. Riahi, A., Challal, Y., Natalizio, E., Chtourou, Z., Bouabdallah, A.: A systemic approach for IoT security. In: Proceedings of the 2013 IEEE International Conference on Distributed Computing in Sensor Systems (DCOSS), Cambridge, MA, USA, 20–23 May 2013
10. Jesus Pacheco, S.H.P.: IoT security framework for smart cyber infrastructures. In: Proceedings of the IEEE International Workshops on Foundations and Applications of Self* Systems, Augsburg, Germany, 12–16 September 2016
11. Dorri, A., et al.: Blockchain for IoT security and privacy: the case study of a smart home. In: 2017 IEEE International Conference on Pervasive Computing and Communications Workshops (PerCom Workshops), IEEE (2017)
12. Yao, X., et al.: A lightweight multicast authentication mechanism for small scale IoT applications. IEEE Sens. J. **13**(10), 3693–3701 (2013)
13. Mamdouh, M., Elrukhsi, M.A., Khattab, A.: Securing the internet of things and wireless sensor networks via machine learning: a survey. In: 2018 International Conference on Computer and Applications (ICCA), pp. 215–218. IEEE (2018)
14. Debar, H., Dacier, M., Wespi, A.: Towards a taxonomy of intrusion-detection systems. Comput. Netw. **31**(8), 805–822 (1999)
15. Meng, G., Liu, Y., Zhang, J., Pokluda, A., Boutaba, R.: Collaborative security: a survey and taxonomy. ACM Comput. Surv. **48**, 1:1-1:42 (2015)
16. Zaidan, M.R.: Power system fault detection, classification and clearance by artificial neural network controller. In: Global Conference for Advancement in Technology (GCAT), Bangalore (2019)

Automatic Detection and Classification of Anti-islamic Web Text-Contents

Rawan Abdullah Alraddadi[1]([⊠]) and Moulay Ibrahim El-Khalil Ghembaza[2]

[1] Department of Computer Science, College of Computer Science and Engineering, Taibah University, Medina, Saudi Arabia
rawanalradadi3@gmail.com
[2] Department of Computer Science, College of Engineering and Information Technology, Onaizah Colleges, Qassim, Saudi Arabia
mghembaza@oc.edu.sa

Abstract. The aim of this research is to use the sentiment analysis techniques to deal with large dataset corpus, which has been collected, to detect and classify anti-Islamic online contents. Anti-Islamic websites have spread a lot in the last decade causing a lot of hate toward the Muslims communities; there have been many websites that attack Islam and Muslims and insult the Messenger, blessings and peace be upon him. We have gathered our proper dataset from different sources into a large corpus, and we have produced two datasets (balanced and non-balanced) for the English language. The framework of our proposed methodology has been described. Two approaches are used in this framework, the first one is based on supervised Machine Learning (ML) approach using Support Vector Machines (SVM) model as classifier and Term Frequency-Inverse Document Frequency (TF-IDF) as feature extraction; the second one is a hybrid approach combining lexicon-based dictionary and TF-IDF as feature extraction with SVM algorithm. We conducted different experiments and we compared the obtained results. We first use TF-IDF on word level, and then we have improved the model using tri-gram level. The experimental results show that the ML approach is the best approach for both datasets that produces high accuracy of 97% applied on the non-balanced English dataset using SVM with tri-gram level TF-IDF as feature extraction. Additionally, SVM with word-level TF-IDF also provides excellent results regardless of the type of dataset.

Keywords: Web text mining · Text analysis · Text classification · SVM · Sentiment analysis · Fake news · Hate speech · Toxicity detection

1 Introduction

In the last decade, there was a lot of hate in the world toward Islam, Muslims and even some have insult the Prophet Muhammad, peace be upon him. For some people, the

---

The original version of this chapter was revised: The author's last name and first name order has been corrected as "Ghembaza, Moulay Ibrahim El-Khalil". The correction to this chapter is available at https://doi.org/10.1007/978-3-031-04409-0_33

X. Jiang (Ed.): MLICOM 2021, LNICST 438, pp. 162–181, 2022.
https://doi.org/10.1007/978-3-031-04409-0_16

hate has gone beyond verbal and physical assaults, and some have committed murders and hate crimes against Muslims and Islam. The hate crime against Islam has increased and in the Al-Noor Mosque in New Zealand, 51 people were killed just because they were Muslims [1]. Moreover, one of the recent incidents occurred in September 2020 in France is the insult to the Prophet Muhammad, peace be upon him, by a history teacher named Samuel Patti who showed some caricature that offend the Prophet [2]. Furthermore, Muslims get a lot of abuse and insults through the Internet. In recent times, there have been many websites that attack Islam and Muslims and insult the Messenger, blessings and peace be upon him, and some other websites contain information that promotes hated and terrorism toward Islam and Muslims, and publish misleading, false, and fake news.

The hate toward Islam has increased due to different reasons including the tragedy that took place in America on September 11, 2001, and the terrorist acts that are taking place in the world and the Middle East in the name of Islam [3]. Due to these incidents, the media have focused on Islam and show the terrorist acts that are done by some radicals and claimed that this is what Islam is calling for. Some peoples have believed these claims, which yield some anti-Islamic websites where they express their thoughts and spread hate towards Islam and Muslims.

Anti-Islamic websites have spread a lot in the last decade causing a lot of hate toward the Muslims communities especially people who live in foreign countries or any places containing extremists who are against Islam. Therefore, we need to stop this as it affects many people and gives a bad image for Islam. This can be done by many ways; one of them is detecting and classifying those websites to try limiting their existence. These websites will be gathered into a database to be processed and validated, then analyzed using sentiment analysis techniques. Using this method will allow us to extract the meaning from a large text corpus, which contains opinions, attitude, thoughts and emotions to detect and classify whether the webpage is anti-Islamic or not. Anti-Islamic websites real-time detection will be considered as a new research topic, where it is worth for researchers to take it into consideration since there are about 1.8 billion Muslims in the world[1].

The social impact of this research is attempting to limit the spread of false information about Islam and Muslims by detecting and classifying hostile websites against Islam. This may help to stop the wrong perception about Islam and spreading correct information about this religion to all the humanity, without including any form of extremist views and ideas of some bad people. Therefore, the need of real-time detection of anti-Islamic online content, using machine learning-based sentiment analysis techniques, or any other techniques, is necessary to prevent any terrorist acts towards Islam and Muslims.

To the best of our knowledge, there is no previous research prior to our research that addresses this issue and provides an automatic detection method of anti-Islam online contents. Unfortunately, we did not find papers that discuss this issue; therefore, we will give an overview of the existing detection methods in different related fields like fake news detection, racism and hate speech detection, and toxicity detection.

This research focuses on detecting anti-Islamic websites using machine learning (ML) techniques. Our main contribution is to provide a huge dataset for anti-Islamic

---

[1] According to Wikipedia, the free encyclopedia, 2021.

websites to help governments and researchers in the future. In addition, we identify the features that can be used for this purpose and develop a system that will classify the webpages based on their contents.

The remainder of the paper is structured as follows: Section two provides the necessary background. In section three, we review some related work. Section four demonstrates our proposed framework along with the data collection and the various stages of our methodology. Section five includes experimental results and discussion. Finally, section six concludes the paper with a summary and future work.

2   Background

2.1   Sentiment Analysis and Classification

Sentiment Analysis or opinion mining is a natural language processing (NLP) technique that deals with a large text corpus, which contains opinions, attitude, thoughts and emotions to measure the polarity (positive, negative or neutral) in a given document. The process consists of different steps including pre-processing of the document; this may include tokenization, stop-words removal, special symbol removal and other pre-processing techniques. Then, extracting features, which is the process of converting the text in the dataset into a feature set that can be used by the classifier. There are different feature extraction techniques including Term Frequency-Inverse Document Frequency (TF-IDF), N-gram, Bag of Words and other techniques. Then, the training process of the ML model involves the learning algorithm with the training data to learn from. The next step is the classification of the sentiment as positive, negative or neutral; and the aggregation of them. Finally, evaluating the performance of the model using one of various measures such as, Cosine Similarity, Jacquard Similarity, Perplexity and Word Error Rate.

The sentiment classification can be done in different methods as shown in Fig. 1, the first group of methods is lexicon-based that uses sentiment lexicons to assign to each word their sentiment orientation (positive or negative). This method is divided into two approaches: dictionary-based and corpus-based. In dictionary-based the classification relies on a predefined dictionary of terms, while corpus-based does not rely on a predefined dictionary, it uses the statistical analysis of the contents of documents [4]. This group of methods has some limitations and drawbacks because sometimes the domain is not considered, also some new vocabulary and informal language are not considered in addition to other issues.

The second group of methods is based on ML techniques, which finds associations between features extracted from documents and sentiments. It has proved that it is very useful in classification [5]. Sentiment Analysis uses ML techniques that learn and improve based on previous experience, in order to help in classification and predictions of sentiments as positive, negative or neutral. ML is usually categorized as supervised, unsupervised and semi-supervised learning algorithms [5].

Supervised ML algorithms use pre-labeled classes to predict future results based on the past data; the algorithm classifies the dataset with the support of trained classifiers. Supervised algorithms are grouped into classification and regression. In classification, the output variable is a category of various classes; whereas in regression, the output variable is a real value. The algorithms that are most widely used in supervised learning are Linear Regression, Random Forest and Support Vector Machines (SVM).

Unsupervised ML algorithms use unlabeled input data to find the hidden structure or pattern using different algorithms because they do not have a pre-labeled class to be used in the training of classifiers. Unsupervised algorithms are grouped into clustering and association. A clustering is when we need to discover the inherent grouping in the data; whereas an association is when we need to discover rules that describe huge portions of data. The algorithms that are most widely used in unsupervised learning are K-Means and Apriori Algorithms.

Semi-supervised ML algorithms combine both labeled and unlabeled datasets. It combines a small set of labeled data with a huge dataset of unlabeled data to train the classifier. With the help of supervised and unsupervised ML algorithms, we can predict whether or not a giving website contain information that promotes hated and racism toward Islam and Muslims.

The third group of methods uses deep learning techniques consisting of multiple layers with a middle hidden layer to solve complex problems. It is an evolution of ML techniques, where the features are learned and extracted automatically, and provide better performance and accuracy [4]. There are different algorithms that are widely used in deep learning techniques such as Deep Neural Networks (DNN), Convolution Neural Networks (CNN) and Recurrent Neural Networks (RNN) [4].

The fourth group of methods is the methods based on ontology, where they model the concepts and terms in the domain knowledge based on the interest and the relations among these terms. The ontology model consists of entities, objects, properties of objects, and relations between them; as well as the common vocabulary in a domain [6]. The use of ontology helps in making the knowledge easier to understand for the people and the software agents, and also differentiate between words which have the same meaning [7].

Other sentiment analysis methods exist, namely the hybrid method where it combines different approaches to proposed new methods that can optimize the result. This method takes the advantage of the combined approaches to achieve the classification goal with a high accuracy. Some proposed hybrid methods combine lexicon-based approach and ML approach; others combine symbolic approach where it models structured domains and relations among objects, and statistical approach, which can model uncertainty in a robust manner and take advantage of both approaches [8, 9].

2.2 Fake News

Fake news is a long-lasting problem that has existed since the beginning of the printing press in 1493. Fake news is known as news articles that contain false information about a particular subject to mislead the readers to think that the presented information is true. Unfortunately, most of this news are intentionally and verifiably false, and detecting that fake news is considered a hard task due to the speed of spreading this wrong information and the availability of its content, which makes it hard to control [10].

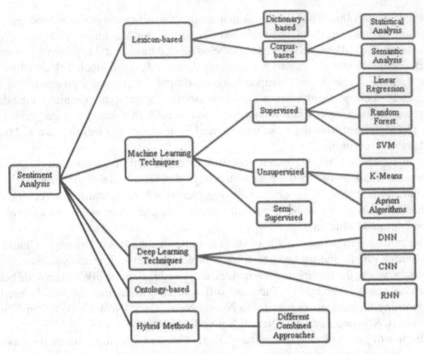

Fig. 1. Sentiment analysis methods.

2.3 Hate Speech

As the number of Internet users increase and the anonymity of their personal information increases, they have the freedom of speech where they can express their thoughts freely, but some of them misuse this by spreading hate and offending others [1, 11]. The number of articles containing hate and racist speeches towards a certain society or type of person has increased. Some jokes and comments can be considered as hate speech as it spreads wrong and hateful information about a particular subject, company or a specific community or even a person. In some counties such as Germany and Iceland, this type of comment and speech are punishable by the law, therefore, detecting and classifying hate crime, racism, hate speech, abuse, harassment, and toxic language online contents are considered important tasks in the NLP field.

3   Related Work

3.1   Fake News Detection

Automatic detection attracts the attention of several researchers; Ghosh and Shah [12] proposed and developed a generalized method based on DNN. They used two databases based on the length and structure of the sentences. Their model starts by classifying the topics using a modular approach in order to detect if the news is fake or true. The model consists of different sub-modules that categorize the instances based on predefined features including the authenticity of the source, style, natural language features and other features, to predict the credibility of the news. They have combined different techniques from information retrieval, NLP, and deep learning to compare two main sub-modules. The first sub-module uses information retrieval relevant, knowledge base and word-level features; whereas the second sub-module uses a DNN. Their classification model has an accuracy of up to 82.4% by combining the two models. The accuracy of their model is not that good therefore; it needs to be improved [12].

In another research, Barbosa et al. [13] proposed an automatic detection and classification method that uses a Multi-layer Perceptron (MLP) neural networks algorithm called AuFa. They obtained the dataset from a Kaggle repository called "Fake News-Build a system to identify unreliable news". The dataset has 20,800 news but 39 of them are null. The model is divided into three layers: classification, web search and database. In the classification layer, the content of the document goes through a preprocessing process, where the unnecessary words are removed and only the unique and meaningful words stay and turned into lowercase without double spacing. After preprocessing, the data are converted into numeric values to check the credibility of the document and if it is less than 90%, it will move to the second layer. In the web layer, the document is checked using a similarity grouping technique to search for similar results on the web. Whilst, in the database layer, the new data is saved in the database. Comparing their MLP Classifier algorithm with Naïve Bayes, Stochastic Gradient Descent (SGD) Classifier, and SVM algorithms, the results showed that their classifier has a better accuracy with 96.44%, but still needs to be improved [12].

Some research, instead of proposing and developing a new method, they improved an existing method by combining the existing method with new data mining techniques. Rukavitsyn et al. [14] proposed several webpage categorization methods using neighboring webpages. The first method classifies the page based on text data by filtering the page based on "correctly predicted". The second method classifies the page based on two level keywords. The third method is based on neighboring pages, where the main page has links to other subpages depending on their distance; this method is considered complex and produces a low accuracy rate. The last proposed method was the best one, which is a hierarchical classification method; it links different classifiers that are trained with different attributes and algorithms. They compare k-Nearest Neighbors (k-NN), SVM, Logistic Regression, Decision Tree, and Bagging Random Forest, and the results have shown that the SVM model had the highest accuracy. The open issue in this research is how to classify a webpage that doesn't contain text content but only contains images.

Vaibhav et al. [15] proposed a graph neural network-based model because of the diverse interaction between words on different websites containing long text. They used three databases: Satirical and Legitimate News Database (SLN), Random Political News Dataset (RPN) and Labeled Unreliable News Dataset (LUN). They implemented three neural baselines: CNN layer, Long Short-Term Memory layer (LSTM) and Bidirectional Encoder Representations from Transformers (BERT). The contents of the page are represented by a fully connected graph, where the nodes represent the sentences in the page, and the edges between those nodes are similar. Their experiment was done on two types of graph neural networks. The first one is Graph Convolution Network (GCN) where it predicts the relationship between two nodes in the graph [16]; and the second one is Graph Attention Network (GAT), which is developed to improve the GCN, and it focuses on computing the hidden representations of each node without depending on the graph structure [17]. Their proposed methods outperform the three best baselines.

The research conducted by Ahmed et al. [18] showed that most of the people in the US depend on online news articles, which may contain fake news rather than mainstream media. Therefore, the authors proposed a detection model using word-based n-gram analysis. The purpose of this model is to represent the word in the article and generate features so that it can classify the article. Their dataset was collected by their team, and collected publicly available news articles. They also test their model on the publicly available dataset Horne and Adali[2]. They presented and compared two features selection methods that are Term Frequency (TF) and TF-IDF. TF counts the number of words appearing in the article to calculate the similarity between articles while TF-IDF is based on the importance of the words in the article where it increases whenever it appears in the article. The detection model also uses six machine classification techniques, that is, SGD, SVM, Linear Support Vector Machines (LSVM), Logistic Regression, k-NN, and Decision Tree. The experiment showed that the best performance as a feature extraction technique was TF-IDF, while the best performance as classification techniques was LSVM with an accuracy of 92%.

Also in a newer paper published in 2020, Yazdi et al. [19] used a feature selection method combined with K-means clustering and SVM approaches. They used different datasets with different features to evaluate their method, namely, BuzzFeed News[3] including 1627 papers, BS Detector[4] and LIAR[5] including 12836 brief statements. Their method has four steps; the first one calculates the similarity between all the features in the dataset. The second step categorizes those features into clusters using the k-means clustering method based on similarities. The third step chooses the final features of clusters based on the appropriateness of the features to reduce the size of the dataset. The final step detects fake news using the SVM algorithm. The results have shown that their proposed method has a better classification compared to other methods that use a feature extraction approach [19].

Aphiwongsophon and Chongstitvatana [20] used the normalization rules for cleaning data before using ML methods for classification. They used three ML methods: SVM, Naïve Bayes and Neural networks. Their experiment started by collecting data from Twitter, then applying normalization rules and removing the unnecessary data, and finally classifying the data using ML methods. The experimental results showed that Naïve Bayes has the lowest accuracy between them with 96.08%, whereas SVM and Neural networks have equal accuracy with 99.90%.

Moreover, another research has been done on Twitter by Mahir et al. [21], where they proposed a model for identifying fake news from the tweets. They used Chile earthquake 2010 Datasets consisting of 20,360 Twitter data posts in the dataset. They also compared five ML algorithms: SVM, Naïve Bayes Method, Logistic Regression, and RNN models. The experiment results showed that SVM and Naïve Bayes had a better performance

---

[2] https://github.com/BenjaminDHorne/fakenewsdata1.

[3] https://github.com/BuzzFeedNews.

[4] https://github.com/thiagovas/bs-detector-dataset.

[5] https://paperswithcode.com/dataset/liar.

with 94% for both of them in terms of F1 score that is the average weight of Precision and Recall.

Another approach has been adopted where the algorithm depend on the subjectivity of the language proposed by Libanio et al. [22]. Their dataset of legitimate news consists of 207,914 articles collected between 2014 to 2017 from two news sites in Brazil, namely Estadão and Folha de São Paulo. They used semantic distances as features between the document, and the five subjectivity lexicons, which are argumentation, presupposition, sentiment, valuation and modalization. Each document will have a vector to calculate the Word Mover's Distance, where it calculates the minimum distance for a word to reach another word in the embedding space for the classification. The results showed that this approach has better results than classical text classification. As well, it is good when the training and testing domains are different [22].

Ozbay and Alatas [23] adapted two metaheuristic optimization algorithms. The first one is the Grey Wolf Optimization (GWO), where it has a candidate solution that is divided into four groups for the problem. The second one is Salp Swarm Optimization (SSO) and has a number of n-dimensional random candidate solutions. The fitness values for these solutions are calculated and the best one is chosen. They used three datasets: BuzzFeed Political News, Random Political News and Liar Benchmark. Their approach consists of three steps, the first one was data preprocessing, the next step was adapting the GWO and SSO to construct a model for fake news detection, and the last step was testing the proposed model. Their experiment has been constructed using three datasets and compared with seven supervised artificial intelligence algorithms. The results have shown that GWO has the highest accuracy with 96.5% between them all, but SSO has a better performance in terms of precision with 100% between them all, within two out of three datasets. However, the algorithms need to be improved.

3.2 Hate Speech Detection

Asmi and Sanaj [11] proposed a word embedding approach and deep learning techniques to automatically classify toxic speech. They combined three feature extraction methods: TF-IDF, fastText Embedding and BERT Embedding. They later extracted the feature from the converted text into numerical form. They used a DNN classifier including CNN and BiLSTM. Perform their classification on binary and multi-class corpus extracted from Twitter and Facebook. In addition, they gave a brief review of the different existing techniques that detect different kinds of speech. Unfortunately, they did not give enough details about the data cleaning and data collection process or their implementation.

In paper [24], D'Sa et al. proposed the same approach as mentioned in paper [11] where they used word embedding representations and deep learning techniques. Their proposed approach used in two ways feature-based and fine-tuning approaches. They used an available dataset that consisted of 24883 tweets and annotated by CrowdFlower, which is the leader in enterprise crowdsourcing, that provide different services for companies. Their pre-processing techniques include removing numbers and special characters except some characters like exclamation mark, question mark and other characters. They also removed the user names and any word connected to the symbol @, and they removed "RT" which refers to re-tweet. Then, they split the hash tags into multiple words. Moreover, they used fastText embedding and BERT embedding as feature extraction. In addition, they performed their classification on binary and multi-class corpus extracted from Twitter only. The difference compared with [11] is that they used two approaches, in the first approach, they extracted the word embedding and then used a DNN classifier, and in the second approach, they performed fine-tuning of the pre-trained BERT model. Their experimental results showed that BERT fine-tuning outperformed feature-based approaches, where the first one can detect the hate speech up to 53% whereas the feature-based detects only 31% [24].

Fortuna et al. [25] discussed in depth the publicly available datasets that have been introduced to the field of hate speech classification. The authors analyzed six different publicly available datasets based on their similarity and compatibility, and have clarified the categories of the datasets. They referred to the datasets as Waseem, Davidson, Amievalita, Hateval, TRAC, and Toxkaggle. They have conducted two different experiments. In the first experiment, the pre-processing techniques used are to lowercase all words in the corpus, removing IPs, hashtags and usernames. They also removed all the stop-words in the corpus. They trained the word embedding using fastText word vectors and pertained embedding. They compared the classes based on the similarity to other classes in the dataset and their homogeneity. In the second experiment, they used the Perspective API Toxicity classifier, where the classifier calculated the score of the class, which is between 0 to 1. The classifier uses trained CNNs with GloVe word embedding fine-tuned. They performed binary classification and the evaluation is done based on how well the classification algorithm can detect the harmful messages from non-harmful messages. To evaluate the performance of the classifier on the different datasets, they used the F1 metric. The results of their first experiment showed that hate speech categories are very close and similar as well as the aggression categories. However, the categories that contain pejorative speech like toxicity are not related to each other. The results of their second experiment showed that using generic categories data samples or inconsistent annotation can cause a variety and divergence of the classifier performance [25].

4   Proposed Methodology

The main focus in this research is to use sentiment analysis techniques to deal with large dataset corpus which was collected to detect and classify anti-Islamic webpages. The gathered data can be from texts like books, articles, journals, newspapers, and magazines or via oral such as interviews and speeches, to understand the language and predict the meaning of the text or audio-visual materials. We mainly analyzed written text rather than oral or visual materials. Most of the data we have collected were from articles, journals and some of them are from personal blogs. These data are collected and arranged to create a clean database that has a huge amount of data about anti-Islamic websites to be used in the model that we are developing. Figure 2 shows the framework of our proposed methodology, which consists of five stages.

The first stage is data collection, where we collect the data from different sources into a large corpus, and then produce two datasets (balanced and non-balanced datasets). The second stage is data pre-processing, where we prepare the data by applying some techniques such as normalization, stop-words removal, steaming and lemmatization. The third stage is the stage of selecting the features to be used in the next stage. The fourth stage is the process of training the ML models, where we provide the ML algorithm with the training data to learn from. The last stage is the evaluation of our ML models.

The models used in this research are based on supervised ML approach using SVM algorithm, and hybrid approach combining dictionary-based with SVM algorithm.

In the first model, we used only TF-IDF as feature extraction technique with SVM as classifiers. For the second model, we implemented a hybrid method that uses a lexicon-based dictionary from the Natural Language Toolkit (NLTK) called Valence Aware Dictionary for sEntiment Reasoning (VADER) [26], to analyze the word sentiment meaning. VADER is a simple rule-based model that contains 7517 words and emoticons with their own sentiment polarity for analysis. It was validated by 10 different independent human judges.

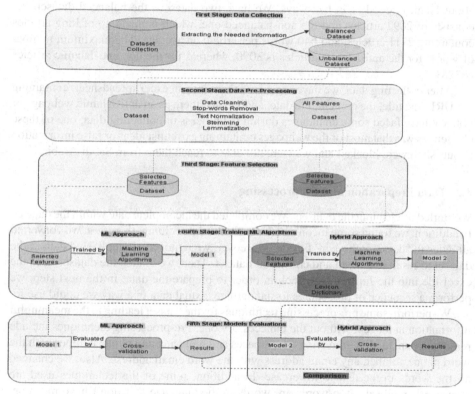

Fig. 2. Framework of the proposed methodology.

4.1 Data Collection and Annotations

We target to create a general benchmark dataset that contains a huge dataset for anti-Islamic websites. The dataset for this research consisted of anti-Islamic websites as well non anti-Islamic websites. The collection of data was mainly done through qualitative data collection methods. The collected data were from articles, journals and some of them are from personal blogs. The main reason for choosing these types of data is because we are interested in the formal English language used to write academic content and not informal English used in social media. We gathered these data from the Internet using Yahoo and Google search engines. The collection of data started from July 2020 until the end of February 2021.

At first, the data was manually collected, and then we switched to a web-scraping tool called Octoparse. This tool takes the URL of the webpage we want to extract data from, and then we select the target data to be extracted and run the scraping to get the data as CSV, Excel, Application Programming Interface (API), or save them to a database.

The collected data are in English language. The main keywords used in collecting data were: Anti-Islam, Anti-Muslims, Islamophobia, Cyber-Islamophobia, Islamization, Eurabia, Racism, and Islam are false. These keywords help to find the desired content and to decrease the amount of search, due to the enormous quantity of articles that talk about Islam in good or in bad ways. We have two datasets, the balanced dataset that consists of 2092 articles and the non-balanced one, which is made up of long articles containing 2711 articles, and 640 words per article on average. The maximum number of words for the anti-Islamic articles is 3090, whereas for the non anti-Islamic articles is 3281.

After collecting data, we have organized them into an excel spreadsheet, containing the URL, the title, the content, the date, and labeled them as an anti-Islamic webpage or not. We have faced some challenges during the process of collecting data, one of these challenges was that most of the webpages containing extremist ideas or false information about Islam were blocked and we were not able to reach them from Saudi Arabia.

4.2 Data Preparation and Preprocessing

We started by cleaning the datasets. We completed the incomplete date within the dataset. In addition, we found some inconsistent data in the date column; therefore, we converted all dates to "day-month-year" format. Moreover, we removed all duplicated data in the dataset to result in a clean and consistent dataset. Then, we loaded the dataset from the excel file into the Jupyter Notebook in order to prepare the data. In the next step, we perform a sequence of procedures to standardize textual data in a way we could use it.

We perform some pre-processing techniques for the dataset leading to the meaningful information in the text without the unnecessary one. Pre-processing techniques include removing punctuation, removing whitespaces and replacing any phone number with the word phone number, any email address with the word email address. Also, we changed all the words in the text to lowercase. In addition, some of the techniques used are stop-words removal. Stop-words are words in the language that don't have meaning. Removing all stop-words in each article, this will reduce the corpus and speed up the classification process. This method is simple and produces quick and accurate results.

Furthermore, we perform a tokenization, which is the process of dividing the text into a list of tokens that can be either sentences or individual words.

Stemming and lemmatization are a little bit similar; there is not that much difference between them. Using stemming enabled us to save a lot of time as stemming returned the words into their original form, and therefore, a group of words can be reduced to the same stem. Removing word suffixes and/or prefixes can result in a word which is not actually a word in the language.

For the English stemming, we have used Porter stemmer, which was developed in 1979; and then included in the NLTK library; the algorithm removes suffixes to produce the original form of the word. Moreover, for the English lemmatization, we used WordNet Lemmatizer to group different forms of the word to the basic form to be analyzed as the same form. Lemmatization consider the context of the words where it groups the word, which has similar meaning to one word; whereas stemming does not consider the context of the words. Lemmatization can produce accurate results but it require more computation compared to stemming.

4.3 Feature Selection

For feature extraction, we used TF-IDF weighting in both models (ML and hybrid). TF-IDF shows the frequency of a word in the dataset which means that this word has strong sentiment. The value of a word increases with the count but decreases with the frequency of the word in the dataset. In this method, the document contains scores for each word instead of just 0 and 1. The scores can be produced by multiplying the term frequency and inverse document frequency. The term frequency is the frequency of a word in the dataset [27].

Term frequency is calculated by the following equation:

$$TF(word, doc) = \frac{FrequencyOfWord}{NumberOfwords} \tag{1}$$

Inverse document frequency is calculated by the following equation:

$$IDF(word) = log_e \left(\frac{NumberOfDoc}{NumberOfDocWithWord} \right) \tag{2}$$

Therefore, the TF-IDF will be calculated using the following equation:

$$TF - IDF = TF(word, doc) * IDF(word) \tag{3}$$

We have used TF-IDF with word level, where we consider the frequency of a single word in the dataset. Moreover, we have also used TF-IDF with N-gram, which is a model that depends on the sequence of words with a predefined length N to predict the next word. N-gram is another feature extraction technique that is well known used in NLP for language modeling also. There are different popular models for N-gram, the most widely used are word-based and character-based. In our experiment, we used tri-gram, where we consider the frequency of three words in the dataset.

For the second model (hybrid approach), we have used the "SentimentIntensityAnalyzer" from NLTK to categorize each article through VADER sentiment lexicon as positive, negative or neutral using the polarity scores method to get the sentiment for each article. Each word is assigned with its score, and then we used them to conclude the sentiment score for the entire article. We consider the sentiment score results with compound values greater than (0.1) as positive and less than (−0.1) as negative. After that, we used TF-IDF to calculate the weight for each article based on the result from the lexicon. This final result is used as the training data and then fed to our classifier to detect the anti-Islamic content in websites.

4.4 Training and Classification

To achieve our goal in detecting and classifying the anti-Islamic content, we used the SVM classifier for defining the ML model. SVM is a supervised learning algorithm used for classification; the task of the algorithm is to determine which category a new data belongs to based on certain features in the dataset. We choose this algorithm because it is the most suitable algorithm for our dataset as it is less than 100K data. Moreover, this algorithm requires less data for the training to achieve accurate results and produce these results faster than other algorithms.

The dataset is divided into: training, and testing sets. We used the training data to train our model. Furthermore, we used the testing data to confirm that the trained model performs well for the hidden data. We split the data into 70% for training data and 30% for testing data, which will be used in the end when the train of the model is completed.

5 Experimental Results and Models Evaluation

We perform the experiments using 10-fold cross-validation to overcome the overfitting problem in the dataset especially in the non-balanced dataset where a set of partitions for training and testing are used to produce k-classification models. The following metrics are used to evaluate the performance of our model: namely, Confusion Matrix, Precision, Recall, F1 Score, and Accuracy.

Confusion Matrix summarizes the number of correct and incorrect predictions for each class. In the confusion matrix, the row is the actual class, while the column is the predicted class. The four measures, i.e. True Positive (TP), True Negative (TN), False Positive (FP), and False Negative (FN) are used to calculate the following Eqs. (4, 5, 6, and 7) in order to obtain the precision, recall, F1 score, and accuracy:

$$Precision = \frac{TruePositive}{(TruePositive + FalsePositive)} \tag{4}$$

$$Recall = \frac{TruePositive}{(TruePositive + FalseNegative)} \tag{5}$$

$$F1score = \frac{(2 * Precision * Recall)}{(Precision + Recall)} \tag{6}$$

$$Accuracy = \frac{(TruePositive + TrueNegative)}{(TruePositive + TrueNegative + FalsePositive + FalseNegative)} \tag{7}$$

5.1 TF-IDF Vector as Feature

We have used TF-IDF as a feature in our models. We first use it on word level, where it calculates the TF-IDF for each word in the document (article in our case). Then, we have improved the model using tri-gram level, where it calculates the TF-IDF for each three words in the document.

5.1.1 Word Level TF-IDF

Figure 3 shows the confusion matrix using the ML model with a non-balanced dataset, whereas Fig. 4 shows the confusion matrix using a hybrid model with non-balanced dataset. When we use TF-IDF, the True Positive (TP) which is the number of predictions is 699 for the ML model, which is better than 619 for the hybrid model. For the True Negative (TN), which is the correct prediction for the class, the ML model produces 1134, while the hybrid model achieves 1012 correct predictions. For the False Positive (FP), the number of predictions in the ML model is 30, whereas in the hybrid model is 99. For the False Negative (FN), which is the false prediction for the class, the ML model produces 34, but the hybrid model achieves 114 correct predictions.

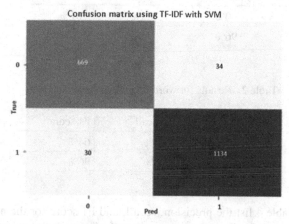

Fig. 3. Confusion matrix using ML model and non-balanced dataset.

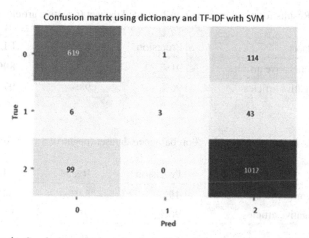

Fig. 4. Confusion matrix using hybrid model and non-balanced dataset.

Table 1 lists the different results between using TF-IDF with SVM (for ML model) and using dictionary and TF-IDF with SVM (for the hybrid model) on a non-balanced dataset. The experimental results shown in Table 1 indicate that the recall and accuracy difference between the two models is close. However, for the two others measurements: Precision and F1 score, the differences are very huge. In Table 2, the accuracy difference between the two models is close. However, for the rest of the measurements, the differences are very huge.

Table 1. Results for word level on non-balanced dataset.

Non-balanced dataset	Precision	Recall	F1 score	Accuracy
Hybrid model	60%	82%	61%	86%
ML model	96%	94%	95%	96%

Table 2. Results for word level on balanced dataset.

Balanced dataset	Precision	Recall	F1 score	Accuracy
Hybrid model	66%	63%	64%	82%
ML model	96%	96%	96%	96%

Table 3 and Table 4 list the precision, recall, and F1 score for the negative articles on the non-balanced and balanced datasets respectively.

Table 3. Results for word level on non-balanced dataset (negative articles only).

Non balanced dataset	Precision	Recall	F1 score
Hybrid model for negative articles	91%	87%	89%
ML model for negative articles	96%	98%	97%

Table 4. Results for word level on balanced dataset (negative articles only).

Balanced dataset	Precision	Recall	F1 score
Hybrid model for negative articles	48%	84%	84%
ML model for negative articles	96%	95%	96%

Consequently, the experimental results show that for our balanced and non-balanced datasets, the best algorithm that produces high accuracy is SVM with word level TF-IDF as feature extraction (see Fig. 5).

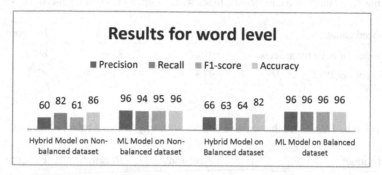

Fig. 5. Results for word level on the two models.

5.1.2 N-gram Level TF-IDF

When we use tri-gram for the hybrid model with SVM, the result has not been modified in all metrics even in the confusion matrix. For the ML model with TF-IDF, the False Positive (FP) becomes 34 and the False Negative (FN) becomes 30. The True Positive (TP) and True Negative (TN) stayed the same. For the negative articles in the ML model, the recall has increased but the precision decreases by one, and the F1 score stays the same.

Table 5 and Table 6 list the different results between using N-gram on the training models with non-balanced and balanced datasets.

Table 5. Results for tri-gram on a non-balanced dataset.

Non-balanced dataset	Precision	Recall	F1 score	Accuracy
Hybrid model	60%	82%	61%	86%
ML model	96%	96%	96%	97%

Table 6. Results for tri-gram on a balanced dataset.

Balanced dataset	Precision	Recall	F1 score	Accuracy
Hybrid model	63%	78%	66%	82%
ML model	79%	85%	78%	85%

Table 7 and Table 8 list the precision, recall and F1 score for the negative articles on the non-balanced and balanced datasets respectively.

Table 7. Results for the negative articles with tri-gram on a non-balanced dataset.

Non-balanced dataset	Precision	Recall	F1 score
Hybrid model for negative articles	91%	87%	89%
ML model for negative articles	97%	97%	97%

Table 8. Results for the negative articles with tri-gram on a balanced dataset.

Balanced dataset	Precision	Recall	F1 score
Hybrid model for negative articles	85%	87%	86%
ML model for negative articles	58%	100%	73%

The experimental results show that for our balanced and non-balanced datasets, the best algorithm that produces high accuracy is SVM with tri-gram level TF-IDF as feature extraction (see Fig. 6).

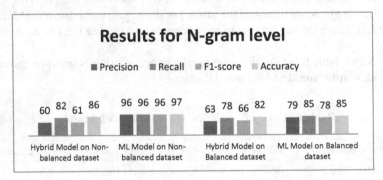

Fig. 6. Results for N-gram level on the two models.

We conducted our experiments on a DELL laptop. The processor is Intel(R) Core (TM) i7-4510U CPU @ 2.60 GHz, the RAM is 8.00 GB, on a 64-bit Operating System. For the non-balanced dataset, the training time for SVM with TF-IDF as feature extraction was 0.096946 s, and the prediction time was 0.001999 s. While the training time for SVM with dictionary and TF-IDF as feature extraction was 0.287853 s, and the prediction time was 0.003998 s. For the balanced dataset, the training time for SVM with TF-IDF as feature extraction was 0.110935 s, and the prediction time was 0.002004 s. While the training time for SVM with dictionary and TF-IDF as feature extraction was 0.660602 s, and the prediction time was 0.003999 s.

6   Conclusion and Future Work

In this research, we have proposed an automatic detection and classification of anti-Islamic websites using sentiment analysis techniques. These websites are considered kind of toxic online contents that encourage spreading hate speech toward Islam and Muslims. Our first objective was to collect our proper dataset and use it to detect and classify the anti-Islamic webpages, to identify the features that can be used in this issue and to create a general benchmark dataset containing a huge amount of data for anti-Islamic and non anti-Islamic websites to help the researchers having and using such corpus.

Some of the limitations that we faced during the process of achieving our goals were the absence of a database that contains anti-Islamic websites neither in English nor in Arabic or other languages. In addition, we have faced some challenges when we were collecting the data, one of the challenges was that a number of webpages that contain extremist ideas or false information about Islam were blocked, and we were not able to reach those webpages from Saudi Arabia. This problem slowed the process of collecting the data and made it harder to find different webpages that contain this kind of information.

We have described the framework of our proposed methodology, which consists of five stages, namely, the data collection, the data pre-processing, the features selection, the training process, and the evaluation of our models. The models used in this research are based on supervised ML approach using SVM algorithm, and hybrid approach combining dictionary-based with SVM algorithm.

The experimental results show that for our datasets, the best algorithm that produces high accuracy with 97% is SVM as classifier with tri-gram level TF-IDF as feature extraction. Additionally, SVM with word-level TF-IDF also provides excellent results regardless of the type of dataset (balanced or non-balanced). This confirm that the SVM algorithm produces high accuracy compared to other algorithms and also it can learn the parameters and produces good results even when the training data are small and this is in a fast training time.

In the future, we continue adding more data to our datasets. We propose to implement a translation-based approach to deal with non English contents such as Arabic or French anti-Islamic text contents; and compare it with standard approaches. Moreover, we will introduce some concepts using NLP techniques to study the effect of a semantic analysis approach and to deal with Arabic texts as well.

Another track to search is exploring different social media to collect data and compare their contents with our dataset, and discover what the experiment's results will show.

References

1. Christchurch shootings: The people killed as they prayed - BBC News. https://www.bbc.com/news/world-asia-47593693. Accessed 26 Jan 2021
2. France Muhammad cartoon row: What you need to know l News l DW l 27.10.2020. https://www.dw.com/en/france-muhammad-cartoon-row-what-you-need-to-know/a-55409316. Accessed 26 Jan 2021

3. Kavakli, K.C., Kuhn, P.M.: Dangerous contenders: election monitors, Islamic opposition parties, and terrorism. Int. Organ. **74**(1), 145–164 (2020)
4. Dang, N.C., Moreno-García, M.N., de la Prieta, F.: Sentiment analysis based on deep learning: a comparative study, arXiv (2020)
5. Becker, K., Harb, J.G., Ebeling, R.: Exploring deep learning for the analysis of emotional reactions to terrorist events on Twitter. J. Inf. Data Manag. **10**(2), 97–115 (2019)
6. Yaakub, M.R., Latiffi, M.I.A., Zaabar, L.S.: A review on sentiment analysis techniques and applications. IOP Conf. Ser.: Mater. Sci. Eng. **551**(1), 012070 (2019)
7. Thakor, P., Sasi, S.: Ontology-based sentiment analysis process for social media content. Procedia Comput. Sci. **53**(1), 199–207 (2015)
8. Nandi, V., Agrawal, S.: Political sentiment analysis using hybrid approach. Int. Res. J. Eng. Technol. **3**(5), 1621–1627 (2016)
9. Alrefai, M., Faris, H., Aljarah, I.: Sentiment analysis for Arabic language: a brief survey of approaches and techniques. arXiv (2018)
10. Shu, K., Sliva, A., Wang, S., Tang, J., Liu, H.: Fake news detection on social media: a data mining perspective. arXiv, vol. 19, no. 1, pp. 22–36 (2017)
11. Asmi, P., Sanaj, M.S.: Online Toxic Speech : Automatic Detection Methods and Techniques, vol. 6, no. 6, pp. 3353–3356 (2020)
12. Ghosh, S., Shah, C.: Toward automatic fake news classification. In: Proceedings of 52nd Hawaii International Conference on System Sciences, vol. 6, pp. 2254–2263 (2019)
13. Barbosa, V., de Oliveira, C., Braga, R.B.: AuFa-automatic detection and classification of fake news using neural networks. In: 8th International Workshop on ADVANCEs in ICT Infrastructures and Services (ADVANCE 2020), Cancún, Mexico, pp. 1–8, January 2020
14. Rukavitsyn, A.N., Kupriyanov, M.S., Shorov, A.V., Petukhov, I.V.: Investigation of website classification methods based on data mining techniques. In: 2016 XIX IEEE International Conference on Soft Computing and Measurements (SCM), St. Petersburg, Russia, pp. 333–336 (2016)
15. Vaibhav, V., Mandyam, R., Hovy, E.: Do Sentence Interactions Matter? Leveraging Sentence Level Representations for Fake News Classification, pp. 134–139 (2019)
16. Wang, Z., Zheng, L., Li, Y., Wang, S.: Linkage based face clustering via graph convolution network. In: Proceedings of IEEE Computer Society Conference on Computer Vision and Pattern Recognition, vol. 2019-June, no. c, pp. 1117–1125 (2019)
17. Veličković, P., Casanova, A., Liò, P., Cucurull, G., Romero, A., Bengio, Y.: Graph attention networks. In: 6th International Conference on Learning Representations, ICLR 2018 - Conference Track Proceedings, pp. 1–12 (2018)
18. Ahmed, H., Traore, I., Saad, S.: Detection of online fake news using n-gram analysis and machine learning techniques. In: Traore, I., Woungang, I., Awad, A. (eds.) ISDDC 2017. LNCS, vol. 10618, pp. 127–138. Springer, Cham (2017). https://doi.org/10.1007/978-3-319-69155-8_9
19. Yazdi, K.M., Yazdi, A.M., Khodayi, S., Hou, J., Zhou, W., Saedy, S.: Improving fake news detection using k-means and support vector machine approaches. Int. J. Electron. Commun. Eng. **14**(2), 38–42 (2020)
20. Aphiwongsophon, S., Chongstitvatana, P.: Detecting fake news with machine learning method, pp. 528–531 (2018)
21. Mahir, E.M., Akhter, S., Huq, M.R.: Detecting fake news using machine learning and deep learning algorithms, pp. 1–4 (2019)
22. Libanio, C., Jeronimo, M., Campelo, C.E.C., Veloso, A., Sales, A.: Fake News Classification Based on Subjective Language (2019)
23. Ozbay, F.A., Alatas, B.: A novel approach for detection of fake news on social media using metaheuristic optimization algorithms. Elektron. ir Elektrotechnika **25**(4), 62–67 (2019)

24. D'Sa, A.G., Illina, I., Fohr, D.: BERT and fasttext embeddings for automatic detection of toxic speech. In: Proceedings of 2020 International Multi-Conference on Organization of Knowledge and Advanced Technologies, OCTA 2020 (2020)
25. Fortuna, P., Soler, J., Wanner, L.: Toxic, hateful, offensive or abusive? What are we really classifying? An empirical analysis of hate speech datasets, no. May, pp. 6786–6794 (2020)
26. Hutto, C.J., Gilbert, E.: VADER : a parsimonious rule-based model for sentiment analysis of social media text, pp. 216–225 (2014)
27. Das, B., Chakraborty, S.: An improved text sentiment classification model using TF-IDF and next word negation, arXiv (2018)

Deep Learning Technique for Desert Plant Classification and Recognition

Najla Alsaedi$^{(\boxtimes)}$, Hanan Alahmadi, and Liyakathunisa Syed

Madinah, Saudi Arabia
nalsaedi@taibahvalley.com.sa

Abstract. Recognition of desert plants has been a difficult activity for both human and computers due to similarities between these plants. In this paper, we propose an approach for recognizing desert plants by images of the bark. This approach depends on deep learning techniques for image recognition. The recognition process depends on texture of the bark. Therefore, we use Prewitt edge detection and Hough transform to detect the bark from original image. Further, we build a bark dataset for desert plants; this dataset consists of 1660 bark images for five species of desert plants. Each species in the dataset has 332 images. These species are Palm Dates, Mimosa Scabrella, Sidr, Lemon and Pomegranate. Convolutional Neural Network (CNN) is a deep learning technique that used in image classification tasks. Therefore, we test CNN on our dataset, and it gives an accuracy of 99.8%. Performance of CNN is very high, hence CNN can be adapted for recognition of desert plants.

Keywords: Bark texture · Deep learning techniques · Prewitt edge detection

1 Introduction

There are hundreds of desert plant species that grow in Saudi Arabia, as it has one of the wide deserts of the world. Due to the similarity between these plants, the recognition process of desert plant has been a difficult activity for both humans and computers, since they geographically share the same area and receive similar climate conditions.

Leaves, stems, and trunk are the main parts of desert plants. What distinguishes desert plants from other plants is their leaves, which are typically small and are not present on the tree throughout the year. Desert plants lose their leaves almost five times throughout the year [1]. The trunk of the tree is covered by a texture known as bark [2]. Unlike leaves, barks can be found on a tree at any time of year. Moreover, they can be photographed effortlessly because they

This research is supported by AI Research group, Department of Computer Science, College of Computer Science and Engineering, Taibah University.

The original version of this chapter was revised: an error in the title of the paper was corrected. The correction to this chapter is available at https://doi.org/10.1007/978-3-031-04409-0_32

Published by Springer Nature Switzerland AG 2022. All Rights Reserved
X. Jiang (Ed.): MLICOM 2021, LNICST 438, pp. 182–194, 2022.
https://doi.org/10.1007/978-3-031-04409-0_17

are easy to reach [3]. For these reasons, several studies on recognizing trees by their bark have been conducted [2–5]. To our knowledge, however, none of these researches have focused on desert plants, especially those that are grown in Saudi Arabia. The goal of this study is to investigate if desert plants can be classified based on the texture of their bark. Recognition of desert plants by their bark could be useful for desert applications, such as using flying drones in the desert to perform autonomous desert plants inventory.

In this study, we present an approach to determine desert plants relying on the texture of their bark. The bark is detected from the original image using Prewitt edge detection and Hough transform. We created a desert plant bark texture dataset. We photograph five desert plant species that are being studied. Palm Dates, Mimosa Scabrella, Sidr, Lemon, and Pomegranate are among the species. Experiments are performed using deep learning techniques for classifying the desert plants by their bark images. For classification, we applied Convolutional Neural Network (CNN) as a deep learning technique for our desert plants dataset. In Deep learning, feature extraction and classification are handled together.

The following is how the rest of the paper is organized: In Sect. 2, you'll find information on related work. In Sect. 3 the proposed methodology is presented. Evaluation metrics are presented in Sect. 4. Section 5 provides experimentation and results. Finally, in Sect. 6, we conclude our paper.

2   Related Work

The topic of plant species identification has attracted many researchers in this field. Most of these researches used some parts of the plant, e.g. leaves [6,7], flowers [8,9] and bark [2–5], for identifying plant species. These research studies vary in the type of plants depending on the geographical area, where the study is performed. For example, some studies targeted Austrian plants [5], while other studies targeted Canadian plants [4]. In this paper, we target desert plants from Saudi Arabia.

In the field of leaf classification, many papers target plant species identification using leaf images. In 2013, Suvarna et al. have provided a method for identifying plants using their leaves images [6]. They have extracted geometrical features of the leaf, such as base angle, apex angle, and margin type. First, they have used Adoptive Otsu threshold to segment the leafy parts from the background. After that, the geometrical features for about 900 leaf images were extracted and stored in the dataset. Their dataset contains 18 plant species with 50 images for each species. For classification, Neural Network with one input layer, three hidden layers, and one output layer was used. The average classification accuracy obtained was 98%.

In 2011, plant identification using leaves was proposed in [7]. In this work, three types of features were extracted. These features are shape, color, and texture features. Before features were extracted, segmentation using adaptive threshold was performed to separate the leaf image from the background. Flavia dataset was used to test the method. This dataset contains 32 plant species with 50 images per species. Probabilistic Neural network (PNN) was used as a classifier, which gave them an accuracy of 93%.

In 2018, Kolivand et al. have presented a paper to describe a feature extraction technique based on phenetic features of the leaf for identifying plant species [10]. Centroid Contour Distance is used to detect local maxima and minima, with the north and south regions used to recognize the apex and base. The leaf shape and margin are measured using digital morphology. For the dataset, they used two different datasets, Flavia and Acer, 32 leaf images of tropical plants were analyzed and evaluated. This approach has resulted in an identifying rate of 94.76% and 82.6% respectively.

In paper [11], an approach to identify plant species and classify the leaf shape using venation detection was presented. The proposed approach consists of five main steps to extract the leaf venation, including canny edge detection, remove leaf boundary, extract curve, and produce hue normalization image and image fusion. Two different datasets, Flavia and Acer, are used to analyze and evaluate thirty-two leaf images of Malaysian plants. The average accuracy for the Flavia and Acer datasets is 98.6% and 89.83%, respectively.

Plant species identification for flower species detection and recognition was proposed in 2017 [8]. In this paper, an automated system was proposed to recognize flower species from their images. First, the flower part was segmented using region growing segmentation. Then, shape, color, and texture features were extracted. After that, a dataset for 19 flower species was built. The total number of images in this dataset was 513 flower images. For classification, Stochastic Gradient Descent(SGD) was used, and the resulted accuracy was 92%.

In 2018, a technique for classifying desert plant species based on their flowers was presented. [9]. The study focused on plant species from the Sonoran Desert. First, the image of the desert plant flower was preprocessed using Median filter to remove the noise. After that, texture and color features were extracted and integrated into the classification step, where a Cascade-Forward Neural Network was used. The dataset used contains 609 images for 25 species of desert plants. The resulted accuracy was 96.8%.

The most relevant topic to our work is identifying plant species relying on the texture of their bark. There are few studies in this field, particularly on desert plants. On the other hand, other types of plants, such as Austrian plants [5] and Canadian plants [4], have been the subject of some studies.

A technique for identifying tree species is presented in 2013, based on 3D geometry analysis [2]. Further, the geometric 3D texture was also converted into a 2D deviation map, from which roughness and shape features were computed and utilized as classification features by the Random Forest classifier. They used a dataset containing 265 samples to obtain the findings, 53 samples were considered for each species. The accuracy achieved was 98.06%.

Automatic tree species identification from photos of bark and leaves was presented in [5]. On grayscale images, the local texture descriptor was calculated. SVM had been used for classification. They used a leaf image dataset of 134 images of leaves from the five most popular Austrian large leaf trees. They also employed another bark image dataset, which has 1183 bark photos for 11 different trees. The leaf dataset had a classification accuracy rate of 93.6%, whereas the bark dataset had a rating of 69.7%.

In paper [4], a pre-trained CNN was used on the ImageNet dataset. ResNet architecture was used to identify tree species from 20 Canadian tree bark pictures. The method's accuracy ranged from 93.88% to 97.81%. They have also produced a wide public dataset that contains labeled images for the bark of Canadian trees.

In 2019, a wild bark recognition approach was introduced [3]. This technique relied on two essential features: histograms of color and texture. They suggested a method for estimating Late Statistics from texture histograms. They also offered a new method for determining color based on domain priors. They combined the obtained histograms to take advantage of both texture and color features. They tested their method on four publicly available datasets: 1) BarkTex, NewBark-Tex, which consists of six bark classes, 2) AFF, which consists of eleven bark classes, and 3) Trunk12, which consists of twelve bark classes, as well as their own dataset 4) Bark-101, a collection of 101 bark classes which were published for public. This dataset includes 2592 images of the bark. They tested two classifiers KNN and SVM, respectively 34.2% outer performance and 41.9% accuracy. Table 1 provides an overview of these approaches and the proposed approach.

3   Proposed Methodology

The proposed methodology is presented in Fig. 1, each component of the framework is discussed in the following sections.

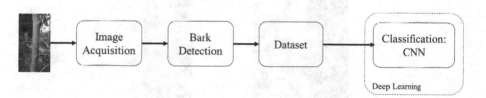

Fig. 1. The step by step process in our proposed approach

3.1   Image Acquisition

The bark images of desert plants are obtained by video of the bark from top to bottom. Five different species of desert plants are captured on videos: Lemon, Palm Dates, Mimosa Scabrella, Pomegranate, and Sidr. To collect images of the bark, we additionally extract frames from the video.

Table 1. Overview of existing approaches and the proposed approach

Paper	Recognition part	Plant type	Dataset size	Classification method	Result
[6]	Leaves	Medicinal plants	900	ANN	98%
[7]	Leaves		1600	PNN	93%
[8]	Flowers	Jordan flowers	513	SGD	92%
[9]	Flowers	Desert plants	609	Cascade-forward NN	96.8%
[2]	Bark	Forest plants	256	Random forest	98.06%
[5]	Leaves and Bark	Austrian plants	1183	SVM	69.7%
[4]	Bark	Canadian plants	23616	CNN	97.81%
[3]	Bark	Wild plants	2592	KNN SVM	34.2% 41.9%
Proposed approach	Bark	Desert plants	1660	CNN	99.8%

3.2 Bark Detection

After acquiring the images of the bark from the videos, a series of detection techniques are applied to crop the image and keep only the part where the bark is visible. Assuming that bark is visible in the image's central section, the image is cropped from left and right sides at 25% and 75% of the original image width, to reduce the image's size to half of its original size. Figure 2 shows the image before and after resizing.

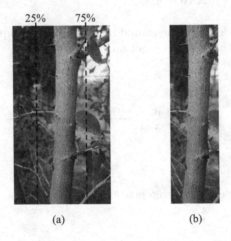

(a)   (b)

Fig. 2. (a) cropping the original image at 25% and 75% of its width. (b) Image after resizing

After that, Prewitt edge detection is used to extract edges of the bark. However, non-relevant edges are detected. Therefore, an area opening operation is performed to remove all points that are less than 60 pixels, resulting in a binary image that has the line boundaries of the bark, as shown in Fig. 3.

Hough transform is used to extract lines from the resulted image. Hough transform converts points from Cartesian space (x, y) to (ρ, θ) space. ρ is a function on θ that returns a set of points lie on the same line segment. Hough transform applies a voting mechanism to select points (ρ, θ) corresponding to the straight line passing through them [14]. Figure 4(a) shows the Hough space (ρ, θ) that is obtained after applying Hough transform to the bark image. Lines

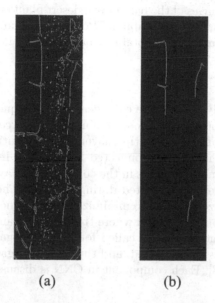

(a)   (b)

Fig. 3. (a) Prewitt edge detection of the bark image. (b) Removing non-relevant edges from Prewitt edge detection image

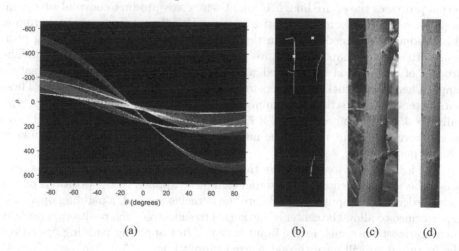

(a)   (b)   (c)   (d)

Fig. 4. (a) Hough transform of the bark image. (b) Lines extracted by Hough transform. (c) Bark image before obtaining the bark. (d) Cropping bark image at the area enclosed by Hough lines

extracted by Hough transform are shown in Fig. 4(b). Finally, we crop the image at the area enclosed by these lines, as shown in Fig. 4(d).

3.3 Dataset

The dataset includes Images of the bark of five desert plant species. These species are Lemon, Palm Dates, Mimosa Scabrella, Pomegranate, and Sidr. Each species is presented with 332 images. The total number of images in the dataset is 1660.

3.4 Classification Using CNN

CNN is the most widely used image classification technique. CNN mainly consists of three components: convolution, pooling, and fully connected layers. The architecture of CNN consists of multiple layers of Convolution and pooling layers followed by one or more fully connected layer(s). An important concept in CNNs is weight adjustment. Weights in the convolutional layer(s) and weights in the fully connected layers are adjusted during learning. Therefore, the learning process in CNN optimizes weights to minimize the difference between predicted output and actual output. The track where the input is transformed throughout layers and converted into output is called forward propagation. After the output is produced, the loss is computed, and the backpropagation starts to adjust kernels and weights [13]. Each component in CNN is discussed as follows.

Convolution Layer
Convolution is a special linear operation used for feature extraction, where the kernel is applied to the input. The kernel is a small 2D array of numbers. The kernel processes the entire image, element-wise cross-product convolution operations are performed across the entire image with different kernels. Furthermore, this product is summed to obtain the output result in the corresponding position of the feature map. The feature map is the output of the convolution. The process of convolution is repeated with many kernels to obtain many feature maps. Therefore, kernel parameters must be set before learning is started. These parameters are size, stride, and number of kernels. The size of the kernel is typically 3×3, but it can be 5×5 or 7×7. The stride is the step that the kernel takes to slide over the input image. The number of kernels determines the number of feature maps [15].

The feature map may not have the same size as the input image. This issue occurs because the center of the kernel cannot be applied to the positions on the four borders of the input image. Before the kernel is applied, a padding operation is performed to allow the center of the kernel to slide over each position, especially the outermost positions, in the input image. After applying padding operation, the feature map will have the same size of input image [15].

There are two types of padding zero padding and the same padding. Zero padding adds rows and columns of zeros on each side of the input image, while the same padding adds rows and columns of the same values of each side in the input image [13].

As convolution is a linear operation, it is followed by a nonlinear activation function that allows the classifier to learn nonlinear data. The output of convolution operation is passed to a nonlinear activation function, such as sigmoid or hyperbolic tangent (tanh). The most commonly used activation function is Rectified Linear Unit (ReLU), which is given by Eq. 1 [13].

$$f(x) = max(0, x) \tag{1}$$

Pooling Layer

In order to reduce the dimensional size of the feature maps, down-sampling operations were performed. Pooling is a down-sampling operation that uses a small 2D filter, as in the convolution layer, to go through each feature map and downsamples its dimension. Parameters must be set for pooling, such as filter size, stride, and padding. Pooling has two types-max pooling and average pooling. Max pooling is the most popular type of pooling, which divides the input feature map into regions. For each region, the maximum value is taken as an output, and other values are discarded. Therefore, the width and height of the feature map are minimized, as shown in Fig. 5 [13].

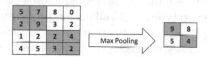

Fig. 5. Max pooling operation

Fully Connected Layer

The last convolution or pooling layer's output is turned into a 1D vector. This vector is connected to one or more fully connected layers, where the classification task is performed. Each feature vector is mapped to output through the fully connected layer. The number of neurons in the last fully connected layer equals the number of classes. Therefore, this layer has a special activation function that computes the probabilities for each class and assigns the input to the class that has the highest probability. Each probability ranges between 0 and 1, and the sum of all probabilities is equal to 1. The softmax activation function is one of the most often used activation functions for this purpose [15].

In this research work, our implementation of the CNN architecture is shown in Fig. 6.

4   Evaluation Metrics

The confusion matrix is used to show the performance of each classifier, which is also called the error matrix. Confusion matrix is a simple tool used for analyzing the performance of a classification model. A set of test data with known labels

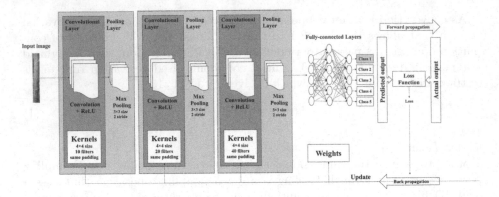

Fig. 6. CNN architecture

are used in order to compare between actual class and predicted class. Confusion Matrix allows describing the performance of an algorithm. Moreover, it can be used to calculate many performance measures, such as accuracy and precision [16].

The shape of the confusion matrix varies depending on the type of classification problem. There are two types of classification problems: binary and multiple classification problems. Binary classification problems are those problems that classify data into two classes only. On the other hand, multiple classification problems classify data into more than two classes [17].

The binary confusion matrix is shown in Fig. 7, where there are only two classes, one is positive and the other is negative. Therefore, the binary confusion matrix has four terms:

- True Positive, the number of items in positive class that are correctly classified,
- True Negative, the number of items in negative class that are correctly classified,
- False Positive, the number of items in positive class that are incorrectly classified, and
- False Negative, the number of items in negative class that are incorrectly classified [18].

In contrast, the multiclass confusion matrix has more than one class. Multiclass confusion matrix is shown in Fig. 8. The diagonal of the matrix, T1, T2, . . . , Tn, shows how many items the classifier has classified correctly. Where N is the number of classes. Entries upper and lower the diagonal present the number of items that are incorrectly classified by the classifier. These entries are presented in Fig. 8 by the symbol Fxy, where x is the predicted class and y is the actual class. For example, F12 is the number of items from class 2 that are incorrectly classified as class 1.

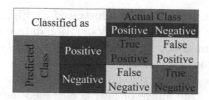

Fig. 7. Binary confusion matrix for performance analysis

Classified as		Actual Class				
		1	2	3	...	N
Predicted Class	1	T1	F12	F13	...	F1n
	2	F21	T2	F23	...	F2n
	3	F31	F32	T3	...	F3n
	:	:	:	:		:
	N	Fn1	Fn2	Fn3	...	Tn

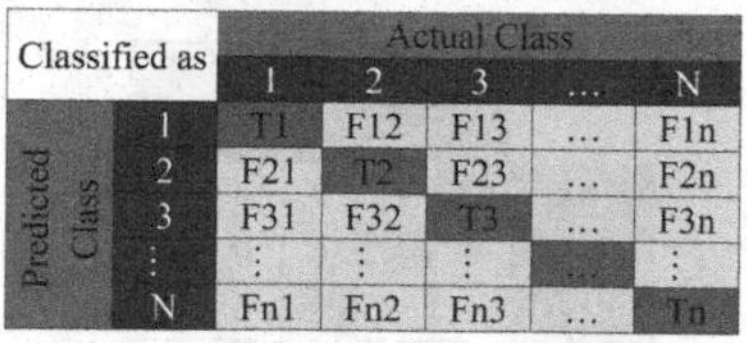

Fig. 8. Multiple confusion matrix for performance analysis

We used accuracy as a performance measure to evaluate the classifiers. The ratio of correct classifications to the total number of images is referred to as accuracy, shown in Eq. 2 [12].

$$Accuracy = \frac{T_1 + T_2 + T_3 + ... + T_n}{total\ number\ of\ images} \times 100 \qquad (2)$$

Accuracy is positively oriented, meaning that a higher value is better. As we have more than two classes, evaluation of Accuracy is calculated based on multiple confusion matrix that is shown in Fig. 8.

In addition, we consider Precision and Recall, another two performance measures, to evaluate the performance for each class individually.

Precision is known as the ratio of correct classifications divided by the total number of images that are predicted by the classifier and classified to the positive class under consideration, given by Eq. 3 [17].

$$Precision(c) = \frac{T_c}{F_{c1} + ... + F_{c(c-1)} + T_c + F_{c(c+1)} + ... + F_{cn}} \qquad (3)$$

On the other hand, Recall is the ratio of correct classifications divided by the total number of actual images for each class under consideration, given by Eq. 4 [17]. Evaluation of Precision and Recall is calculated based on a multiclass confusion matrix that is shown in Fig. 8.

$$Recall(c) = \frac{T_c}{F_{1c} + ... + F_{(c-1)c} + T_c + F_{(c+1)c} + ... + F_{nc}} \qquad (4)$$

5 Experimentation and Results

Our dataset consists of 1660 images. For simplicity, we assign a number from 1 to 5 for each desert plant species which represents the desert plant category.

The confusion matrix for CNN is illustrated in Fig. 9. It summarizes the performance of CNN on validation data. Validation data represents 25% of data. The total data is 1660 images with 332 images for each class. Therefore, 25% of the data represents 83 images for each class. As we can see from Fig. 9, CNN predicts almost all images correctly. The confusion happens only in predicting Sidr and Pomegranate. One image of Sidr is classified as Pomegranate. This is the reason behind the high accuracy of CNN, namely 99.80%.

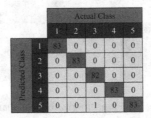

Fig. 9. Confusion matrix for CNN

Precision and recall are calculated for each class. The calculation of precision and recall is performed according to Eq. 3 and Eq. 4. Table 2 presents the performance of each desert plant species using precision and recall. Figure 10, presents CNN performance evaluation graph for each desert plant species. As we mentioned previously, the confusion occurs in the classes Sidr and Pomegranate, as we can see from Fig. 10. This confusion maybe because of the similarities between the bark texture of these two species, as presented in Fig. 11.

Table 2. Precision and recall evaluation for each desert plant species

ID	Desert plant species	Precision (%)	Recall (%)
1	Palm Dates	100	100
2	Mimosa Scabrella	100	100
3	Sidr	100	98.8
4	Lemon	100	100
5	Pomegranate	98.8	100

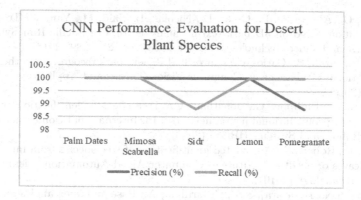

Fig. 10. CNN performance evaluation for desert plant species

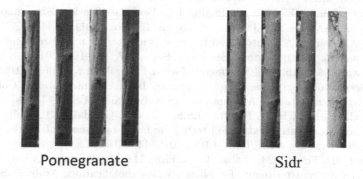

Fig. 11. The similarities between Sidr and Pomegranate species

6 Conclusion

The purpose of this study is to investigate the possibility to classifying desert plant species relying on the texture of their bark. The bark was detected using Prewitt edge detection and Hough transform. A dataset for desert plant bark images was built, which includes 1660 photos for five desert plant species. For classification, we used CNN with our dataset, and it gave a very high accuracy, e.g. 99.8%. Therefore, for classifying desert plants, CNN is thought to be an efficient classifier. As future work, we plan to enhance our dataset by adding more different species of desert plants. In addition, adding more images per class. Finally, we plan to use different techniques in bark detection and compare them.

References

1. Jim, J.: How Do Desert Plants Adapt to Their Environment?. Sciencing (2018). https://sciencing.com/do-desert-plants-adapt-environment-6526946.html. Accessed 15 Nov 2020

2. Ahlem, O., Alexandre, P., Oscar, D., Nicolas, L., Said, M., Yan, V.: Tree species classification based on 3D bark texture analysis. In: 6th Pacific-Rim Symposium on Image and Video Technology (PSIVT 2013), pp. 279–289 (2013)

3. Remi, R., Sarah, B., Carlos, C., Laure, T.: Efficient bark recognition in the wild. In: International Conference on Computer Vision Theory and Applications (VISAPP 2019) (2019)

4. Mathieu, C., Philippe, G., Jonathan, G.: Tree species identification from bark images using convolutional neural networks. In: International Conference on Intelligent Robots and Systems (IROS) (2018)

5. Stefan, F., Robert, S.: Automated identification of tree species from images of the bark, leaves or needles. Institute of Computer Aided Automation, Vienna University of Technology (2010)

6. Suvarna, S.N., Basavaraj, S.A., Govardhan, A.: Base and apex angles and margin types-based identification and classification from medicinal plants' leaves images. Int. J. Comput. Vis. Robot. **3**, 197–224 (2013)

7. Abdul, K., Lukito, E., Adhi, S., Paulus, I.S.: Leaf classification using shape, color, and texture features. Int. J. Comput. Trends Technol. (2011)

8. Aalaa, A., Ashraf, A.: Automated flower species detection and recognition from digital images. Int. J. Comput. Sci. Netw. Secur. **17**, 144–151 (2017)

9. Thilagavathi, M., Abirami, S.: Cascade-forward neural network in identification of plant species of desert based on wild flowers. In: IEEE International Conference on System, Computation, Automation and Networking (ICSCA) (2018)

10. Kolivand, H., Fern, B.M., Rahim, M.S.M., Sulong, G., Baker, T., Tully, D.: An expert botanical feature extraction technique based on phenetic features for identifying plant species. PLoS ONE **13**(2), e0191447 (2018)

11. Kolivand, H., Fern, B.M., Saba, T., Rahim, M.S.M., Rehman, A.: A new leaf venation detection technique for plant species classification. Arab. J. Sci. Eng. **44**(4), 3315–3327 (2019)

12. Shai, S., Shai, B.: Understanding Machine Learning: From Theory to Algorithms (2014)

13. Abien, F.A.: An Architecture Combining Convolutional Neural Network (CNN) and Support Vector Machine (SVM) for Image Classification (2017)

14. Abhijeet, R., Ankit, A.R., Yohei, H., Takanori, E., Yukinori, K.: On a hopping-points SVD and hough transform-based line detection algorithm for robot localization and mapping. Int. J. Adv. Robot. Syst. **13**, 98 (2016)

15. Rikiya, Y., Mizuho, N., Do, R.K.G., Kaori, T.: Convolutional neural networks: an overview and application in radiology. Insights Imaging **9**, 611–629 (2018)

16. Anupama, J., Meenu, D., Supriya, M.: Comparison of binary class and multi-class classifier using different data mining classification techniques. In: International Conference on Advancements in Computing and Management (ICACM-2019) (2019)

17. Liyakathunisa, S., Saima, J., Manimala, S., Abdullah, A.: Smart healthcare framework for ambient assisted living using IoMT and big data analytics techniques. Futur. Gener. Comput. Syst. **101**, 136–151 (2019)

18. Syed, L., Jabeen, S., Manimala, S., Elsayed, H.A.: Data science algorithms and techniques for smart healthcare using IoT and big data analytics. In: Mishra, M.K., Mishra, B.S.P., Patel, Y.S., Misra, R. (eds.) Smart Techniques for a Smarter Planet. SFSC, vol. 374, pp. 211–241. Springer, Cham (2019). https://doi.org/10.1007/978-3-030-03131-2_11

Sparse Algorithm for OFDM Underwater Acoustic Channel Estimation

Tieliang Guo, Wenxiang Zhang$^{(\boxtimes)}$, Zhijun Li, and Xue Sun

College of Electronics and Information, Wuzhou University, Wuzhou 543002, China
zhang_wenxiang@126.com

Abstract. Channel estimation is very important and challenging for underwater acoustic (UWA) systems that use orthogonal frequency division multiplexing (OFDM) technique. The conventional methods are not appropriate to the severe frequency selective fading channel; also current channel estimation algorithms do not use the sparse characteristics of the UWA channel efficiently. In this paper, a novel algorithm about channel estimation is addressed that applies channel sparse features. First, Least Square (LS) algorithm is used to get the pilot channel valuation. Secondly, the sparse degree of channel is estimated through DFT for noise reduction processing. Then the autocorrelation matrix of the channel is obtained approximately. Finally a preliminary calculation of the error threshold is acquired, and the high quality data subcarrier channel impulse can be estimated by the pilot symbols through using the orthogonal matching pursuit (OMP) algorithm. In terms of simulating, we study the performance of the system through bit error rate (BER) and the constellation diagram, and it is indicated that the new method has excellent performance at less computation. So it is very important that the method can be implemented in OFDM systems.

Keywords: Underwater acoustic communications · OFDM · Channel estimation · OMP algorithm

1 Introduction

Due to the large delay, time-varying and multipath, the channel of UWA is one of the most challenging wireless channels [1]. Recently the UWA channels are proved to have sparse feature, namely that the most energy of the channel is focused on a few channels. Considering the sparse nature of the channels, many sparse methods about the channel estimation have been addressed. OFDM technique has low computation cost and can resist frequency selective fading. This promotes the application of OFDM in wireless underwater acoustic communication systems. Over the past decade, the sparse estimation methods based compressed sensing (CS) are widely employed. There are many algorithms about CS. Basic Pursuit (BP) and OMP methods belong to greedy algorithms among them, and the two ways studied as a solution to the UWA channel estimation [2, 3]. In the literature [4], through exploiting the sparse feature of the channel, some estimation algorithms described have been mainly proposed. In the works [5, 6], BP and

© ICST Institute for Computer Sciences, Social Informatics and Telecommunications Engineering 2022
Published by Springer Nature Switzerland AG 2022. All Rights Reserved
X. Jiang (Ed.): MLICOM 2021, LNICST 438, pp. 195–202, 2022.
https://doi.org/10.1007/978-3-031-04409-0_18

other OMP methods have been verified, and through simulating and experimenting, it was indicated that BP has better performance than OMP for the UWA channel. However, the BP method has much higher computational complexity. In [7], through comparing conventional CS methods, a field test have been done by exploiting joint sparse nature about the continuous OFDM blocks. In the experiment, the authors verified the superiority of the method. In addition, the LS method used is greatly affected by noise for channel estimation in the system [8]. To solve the above problems, this paper proposes an optimization algorithm based on CS about the noise of the LS method. Combined with CS algorithm, pilot data are used to optimize the LS channel estimation at the receiving end. Simulation results and theoretical analysis indicate that the impact of Gaussian white noise can be reduced in the process of the channel estimation.

This thesis will make the following structure arrangement. In the second part of the paper, we will introduce the model of signal and system. Section 3 briefly explores the error threshold values about OMP approach and the details proposed method for estimating UWA channel. The results of simulation will be contained in Sect. 4. Conclusions are summed up in Sect. 5.

2   Signal and System Model

2.1   UWA Sparse Channel Model

We usually use the model of time-varying channel for underwater acoustic communication [9]

$$h(t) = \sum_{k=0}^{L-1} A_k(t) e^{j\beta_k(t)} \delta(t - \tau_k(t)) + g(t) \tag{1}$$

where, let's say there are L paths in the channel. A_k and τ_k denote the gain and delay of the kth path respectively. β is related to the Doppler shift, and g denotes noise. In addition, the gain and delay of the propagation path will vary greatly over a long period of time [10], it is assumed that the path delay remains constant in several adjacent OFDM blocks, and that Doppler scale factor and the path gain are stable in one block, but different from one block to another.

2.2   OMP Algorithm Model

OMP is one algorithm about CS theory that is given in the form as follows

$$v = \Phi u = \Phi \Psi \theta \tag{2}$$

where, Φ represents $M \times N$ measurement matrix and $\mathbf{v}$ the $M \times 1$ measurement vector; $\Psi = [\psi_1, \psi_2, \cdots, \psi_N]$ is $N \times N$ orthonormal basis matrix and $u \in R^N$ the $N \times 1$ column vector. Usually in vector ϑ, there are some K non-zero elements that $K \ll N$. In addition, $\mathbf{v}$ can be acquired from a K-sparse u by using Φ. Due to $M \ll N$, Eq. (2) is underdetermined. Therefore, in order to search for the optimal one in the solution space, an appropriate algorithm is needed.

BP algorithm and OMP algorithm are two typical search optimization algorithms in common use [11]. For the second algorithm, in order to achieve sparse recovery, the minimum sparse estimation can be obtained by optimizing the constrained norm problem [12].

$$\hat{\theta} = \arg\min \|\boldsymbol{\vartheta}\|_1 \ s.t. \ \|\boldsymbol{\Phi\Psi\vartheta} - v\|_2 \le \varepsilon \tag{3}$$

where, ε is the l_2 norm threshold value.

2.3 System Model of OFDM

In one OFDM cycle, $X(k)$ represents the complex information code to be transmitted on the kth subcarrier. Doing N point IDFT, the following time domain expression will be got

$$x(n) = \frac{1}{N} \sum_{k=0}^{N-1} X(k)e^{j2\pi nk/N}, \quad n = 0, 1, \cdots, N-1 \tag{4}$$

Then the discrete baseband data in the receiver will be obtained in the following form

$$y(n) = h(n) * x(n) + g(n) \tag{5}$$

Next, the frequency domain model matrix of Eq. (1) will be as follows

$$H = Fh + G \tag{6}$$

where F is $N \times L$ DFT matrix. Therefore, the frequency domain data of the pilot subcarrier in the following receiver will be obtained

$$Y_p = diag(X_p)F_ph + G_p \tag{7}$$

where F_p is $N_p \times L$ DFT matrix and X_p denotes pilots data transmitted.

When the number N_p is less than L, Eq. (7) is a problem to solve the underdetermined equation. Then h can be calculated through knowing ε.

$$\hat{h} = \arg\min \|h\|_1 \ s.t. \ \|diag(X_p)F_ph - Y_p\|_2 \le \varepsilon \tag{8}$$

To the OMP algorithms, the sparse degree is unknown, so we need to know the threshold value ε that determines the time of iterations. On the basis of LS algorithm, this paper proposes an innovative algorithm which uses pilot frequency to set threshold.

3 Estimation of Error Threshold Values

The pilot channel estimation is obtained by LS channel estimation.

$$\hat{H}_p(k) = \frac{Y_p(k)}{X_p(k)}, \quad k = 0, 1, 2, \cdots, N_P - 1 \tag{9}$$

These data are then carried out N_P point IDFT to obtain the point time domain sequence as fellows

$$\hat{h}_{\mathrm{p}}(n) = \frac{1}{N_{\mathrm{P}}} \sum_{k=0}^{N_{\mathrm{P}}-1} \hat{H}_{\mathrm{p}}(k) e^{j\frac{2\pi k}{N_{\mathrm{P}}}n} \tag{10}$$

Then denoising is performed for Eq. (10), and L effective paths are reserved for each response value and the rest are set as "0". If the delay information of the channel is unknown, the circular prefix can be retained or the value of L can be determined by setting noise threshold. The N_p point time domain sequence is obtained after denoising is given by

$$h_{\mathrm{p}}(n) = \begin{cases} \hat{h}_{\mathrm{p}}(n) \, n = 0, 1, \cdots, L-1 \\ 0 \, n = L, L+1, \cdots, N_p - 1 \end{cases} \tag{11}$$

Then Let $\hat{h}_{\mathrm{p}}(n)$ be the sequence acquired by using the N_{p}-IDFT, the channel response estimation at the pilot frequency after denoising is finally obtained as

$$H_{\mathrm{P}}(k) = \sum_{n=0}^{N_{\mathrm{P}}-1} h_{\mathrm{p}}(n) e^{j\frac{2\pi k}{N_{\mathrm{P}}}n} \tag{12}$$

M denotes the sum of channel estimation error and Gaussian white noise, and it can be acquired

$$M = diag(X_{\mathrm{P}})\left(H_{\mathrm{P}} - \hat{H}_{\mathrm{P}}\right) + G_{\mathrm{P}} \tag{13}$$

where, H_{P} and $\hat{H}_{\mathrm{P}}$ denote true value and estimated value of LS at the pilot frequency response respectively.

Then let $C = H_P - \hat{H}_P$, Eq. (13) becomes

$$M = diag(X_{\mathrm{P}})C + G_{\mathrm{P}} \tag{14}$$

The noise M can be assumed a multivariable normal distribution with zero mean value, and its covariance matrix can be expressed by the following equation

$$R_{MM} = diag(X_{\mathrm{P}})R_{CC}diag(X_{\mathrm{P}})^{\mathrm{H}} + \sigma^2 I_{N_{\mathrm{P}}} \tag{15}$$

where, σ^2 denotes the variance of Gaussian white noise and it can be obtained based on LS channel estimation; R_{CC} denotes the covariance matrix of C, which is calculated by the following formula

$$R_{CC} = R_{H_P H_P} - R_{H_P H_P}\left(R_{H_P H_P} + \frac{\beta}{SNR}I_{N_P}\right)^{-1} R_{H_P H_P} \tag{16}$$

where, β is a constant, and its value is related to the specific modulation mode; SNR represents the signal-to-noise ratio, and $I_{N_{\mathrm{P}}}$ is $N_{\mathrm{P}} \times N_{\mathrm{P}}$ unit matrix; $R_{H_P H_P}$ denotes the channel autocorrelation $N_P \times N_P$ matrix at pilot frequency. Since it is difficult to obtain the channel autocorrelation matrix, this paper adopts DFT transform domain denoising processing on the basis of LS algorithm to obtain the approximate autocorrelation matrix. According to Eq. (15), the following types can be calculated [13]

$$E\left(\|M\|_2^2\right) = trace(R_{MM})$$ (17)

$$E\left(\|M\|_2^4\right) = \sum_{i=1}^{N_P} \sum_{j=1}^{N_P} \left[R_{MM}(i,i)R_{MM}(j,j) + \|R_{MM}(i,j)\|^2 \right]$$ (18)

where, $trace(\cdot)$ indicates tracing of a matrix; $R_{MM}(i,j)$ represent the element at the position of row i and column j of the matrix. Then the standard deviation of $\|M\|_2^2$ is calculated by Eqs. (17) and (18)

$$std\left(\|M\|_2^2\right) = \sqrt{E\left(\|M\|_2^4\right) - \left(E\left(\|M\|_2^2\right)\right)^2}$$ (19)

According to the knowledge of probability theory, $\|M\|_2^2$ generally satisfies the following formula

$$\|M\|_2^2 \leq E\left(\|M\|_2^2\right) + 2 \cdot std\left(\|M\|_2^2\right)$$ (20)

To sum up, the error tolerance value ε can be approximated as fellows

$$\varepsilon \approx \sqrt{E\left(\|M\|_2^2\right) + 2 \cdot std\left(\|M\|_2^2\right)}$$ (21)

4 Simulation Results

The detailed system specifications of the simulation are shown in Table 1. In the simulation process, the performance of the new method is tested mainly by detecting the BER curve and constellation diagram. Assume that time synchronization and frequency synchronization is ideal. In addition, in order to highlight the performance of the new algorithm, the additive white Gaussian noise is the only factor affecting the performance of the algorithm in UWA channel.

Table 1. Specifications of OFDM system

Parameter	Value	Parameter	Value
FFT size	2048	Cyclic prefix duration	10.7 ms
Carrier frequency	20 kHz	Modulation order	16-QAM

The OMP algorithm proposed in this paper can use the sparse characteristics of UWA channel to overcome the noise. In order to verify the performance of the new algorithm in channel estimation, Fig. 1 shows the bit error rate curve comparison of the results of the LS algorithm and the OMP algorithm. Because the traditional LS method cannot eliminate the Gaussian noise of the receiver, the bit error rate of the system will be reduced seriously. In addition, the above conclusion can be verified according to the constellation diagram in Fig. 3 and Fig. 4.

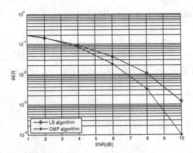

Fig. 1. BER performance of different algorithms

Fig. 2. BER performance of different pilots

Pilot subcarriers are applied to roughly estimate the channel based on OMP algorithm, so the number of pilot subcarriers has some influence on the new algorithm. The influence of bit error rate curve on the number of different pilot subcarriers will be simulated and analyzed. As can be seen from Fig. 2, the system performance will decrease with the reduction of pilot frequency. This is because the frequency interval of the pilot frequency has a great influence on the LS algorithm, that is, the LS algorithm will affect the calculation of the threshold ε.

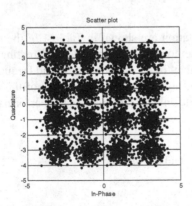

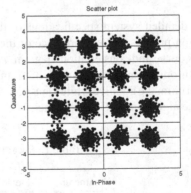

Fig. 3. Constellation diagram of LS algorithms

Fig. 4. Constellation diagram of OMP algorithms

5 Conclusions

In this paper, a new UWA channel estimation method based on OMP algorithm is proposed by using the sparsity of UWA channel and CS processing method, combined with LS method. The algorithm can make the receiver estimate the channel pulse accurately and greatly reduce the Gaussian noise. Both theoretical analysis and simulation results indicate that the algorithm is effective in reducing Gaussian noise, and the complexity is low. In conclusion, compared with the traditional LS method, the improved method is more practical for high-speed real-time OFDM communication on the underwater acoustic system.

Acknowledgement. This work was supported in part by the second batch of New Engineering Research and Practice Projects of the Ministry of Education of China, under Grant E-DZYQ20201426; in part by the undergraduate teaching reform Project of Guangxi Higher Education, under Grant 2021JGZ159; in part by the Project Program of Scientific Research and Technology Development of Wuzhou Science and Technology Bureau, Wuzhou, China, under Grant 201902035, 201902038; in part by the Project Program of Scientific Research of Wuzhou University, Wuzhou, China, under Grant 2018A005, 2018A006, 2018A007; in part by the Project Program of Teaching Reform of Wuzhou University, Wuzhou, China, under Grant Wyjg2020A011, Wyjg2019A035, Wyjg2019B025.

References

1. Li, B., Zhou, S., Stojanovic, M., et al.: Multicarrier communication over underwater acoustic channels with nonuniform Doppler shifts. IEEE J. Oceanic Eng. **33**(2), 198–209 (2008)
2. Li, W., Preisig, J.C.: Estimation of rapidly time varying sparse channels. IEEE J. Oceanic Eng. **32**(4), 927–939 (2008)
3. Berger, C.R., Member IEEE, et al.: Sparse channel estimation for multicarrier underwater acoustic communication: from subspace methods to compressed sensing. In: Oceans. IEEE (2009)
4. Stojanovic, M.: OFDM for underwater acoustic communications: adaptive synchronization and sparse channel estimation. In: IEEE International Conference on Acoustics, Speech and Signal Processing, 2008, ICASSP 2008. IEEE (2008)
5. Yu, F., Li, D., Guo, Q., et al.: Block-FFT based OMP for compressed channel estimation in underwater acoustic communications. IEEE Commun. Lett. **19**(11), 1937–1940 (2015)
6. Huang, J., Berger, C.R., Zhou, S., et al.: Comparison of basis pursuit algorithms for sparse channel estimation in underwater acoustic OFDM. In: Oceans. IEEE (2010)
7. Zhou, Y.H., Tong, F., Zhang, G.Q.: Distributed compressed sensing estimation of underwater acoustic OFDM channel. Appl. Acous. **117**(PTA), 160–166 (2017)
8. Lee, S.D., Jung, S.: An adaptive control technique for motion synchronization by on-line estimation of a recursive least square method. Int. J. Control Autom. Syst. **16**(3), 1103–1111 (2018)
9. Qiao, G., Song, Q., Ma, L., et al.: Sparse Bayesian learning for channel estimation in time-varying underwater acoustic OFDM communication. IEEE Access **6**, 56675–56684 (2018)
10. Qarabaqi, P., Stojanovic, M.: Statistical characterization and computationally efficient modeling of a class of underwater acoustic communication channels. IEEE J. Oceanic Eng. **38**(4), 701–717 (2013)

11. Huang, J., Berger, CR., Zhou, S, et al.: Comparison of basis pursuit algorithms for sparse channel estimation in underwater acoustic OFDM. In: Oceans, pp. 1–6 (2010)
12. Panayirci, E., Altabbaa, M.T., Uysal, M., et al.: Sparse channel estimation for OFDM-based underwater acoustic systems in Rician fading with a new OMP-MAP algorithm. IEEE Trans. Signal Process. **67**(6), 1550–1565 (2019)
13. Mohammadnia-Avval, M., Ghassemi, A., Lampe, L.: Compressive sensing recovery of non-linearly distorted OFDM signals. In: IEEE International Conference on Communications. IEEE (2011)

Improvement of CL Algorithm
in MIMO-OFDM System

Xiaolin Jiang[1], Yu'e Li[2(⊠)], and Tian Han[1]

[1] Teacher-Student Relationship, Jinhua Advanced Research Institute, Zhejiang 321000, China
hantian@hrbust.edu.cn
[2] Heilongjiang University of Science and Technology, Harbin 150000, China
1185142481@qq.com

Abstract. The sphere detection algorithm is a low SNR algorithm in the MIMO-OFDM system with low complexity, but it still has a certain complexity. It is challenging to choose its initial radius and determine whether a point is in the ball. The improved algorithm is to find the CL algorithm's initial radius by the particle swarm algorithm's optimization ability. Then the convergence factor is given to speed up the shrinkage speed of the CL algorithm's radius. The improved algorithm is compared with the CL algorithm. The simulation results clear that when the SNR ratio is below 16 dB, the enhanced algorithm significantly affects algorithm complexity. The improvement of the algorithm is proved to be effective and reliable.

Keywords: MIMO-OFDM system · Spherical detection algorithm · Convergence factor

1 Introduction

MIMO-OFDM technology can remove the influence of inter-symbol interference and solve the problem of frequency selective fading to improve frequency band utilization. It can also increase the data transmission rate and increase channel capacity [1]. Compared with other technologies, it is more Advantage. The MIMO-OFDM system can use the multiple input multiple output system's signal detection algorithms on the narrowband orthogonal sub-channels of the orthogonal frequency division multiplexing system to complete the signal detection research of the system [2].

Among the signal detection algorithms, the ML algorithm is the best detection algorithm [3]. It is the best signal detection algorithm when the number of transmitting antennas and modulation order is low, and it is not applicable when the two are higher [4]. The proposed CL detection algorithm's performance tends to the implementation of the ML detection algorithm, and the complexity is lower [5]. Still, the CL algorithm's complexity will gradually increase with the decrease of SNR, so it is more difficult at low SNR Large, not suitable for use. In order to solve this phenomenon, the particle swarm algorithm is first used to obtain the optimal solution to find the CL algorithm's

X. Jiang (Ed.): MLICOM 2021, LNICST 438, pp. 203–213, 2022.
https://doi.org/10.1007/978-3-031-04409-0_19

initial radius. The MMSE detection algorithm is then combined with the CL detection algorithm to reduce the complexity of the CL detection algorithm at low SNR. There is still high complexity, so the convergence factor β is set to accelerate the shrinkage of the CL detection algorithm radius, reduce the number of search grid points required by the CL algorithm when the SNR is low, and improve the complexity of the CL algorithm [6].

2   MIMO-OFDM System Model

The MIMO-OFDM system model is shown in Fig. 1 below. The input signal is split after serial/parallel conversion to form an Nt layer data stream and $x = [x_1, x_2, x_3 \cdots x_{Nt}]$ represents its transmit signal. IFFT modulates the movement for OFDM, which means that low-speed multiple parallel data streams are simultaneously modulated onto Nt orthogonal sub-carriers. Then add a cyclic prefix CP before the output data stream to reduce the influence of channel delay spread.

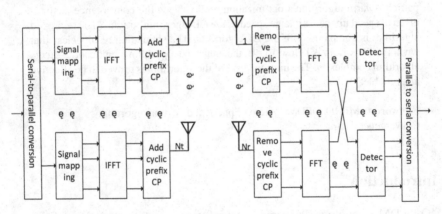

Fig. 1. MIMO-OFDM system model

The receiving end performs the reverse signal processing process of the transmitting end. First, the modulated signal is sent to Nr receiving antennas. The data streams received by different receiving antennas simultaneously are all linearly combined by Nr noisy data streams. The received signal of the system is represented by $y = [y_1, y_2, y_3 \cdots y_{Nr}]$, and the expression is:

$$y = Hx + n \tag{1}$$

The channel matrix is represented by H, and H can be represented as $H = \left[h_{ij}\right]_{Nt \times Nr}$; each element h_{ij} in the channel matrix is represented as the channel gain between antennas, i is the transmitting antenna, and j is the receiving antenna. N is expressed as Gaussian white noise with mean 0 and variance [7]. After the CP is removed, the remaining signal is demodulated by FFT; finally, the parallel data flow is detected by the detector. The data is recovered by the parallel/serial converter.

3 CL Algorithm Implementation

3.1 CL Algorithm Description

The sphere detection algorithm assumes an initial search radius d in a given search area, searches for grid points in a multi-dimensional sphere with the received signal vector r as the center of the globe, and finds the nearest grid point to the received signal [8]. The sphere decoding (SD) algorithm can be divided into depth-first strategy and breadth-first strategy. The sphere detection algorithm based on the depth-first approach restricts the search radius by the size of the Euclidean distance to obtain the maximum likelihood performance. The representative algorithms include the VB algorithm and the CL algorithm. The breadth-first strategy is to perform a one-way search by layer by limiting search grid points. Usual algorithms have the K-Best algorithm and the FSD algorithm [9].

The VB algorithm searches for the next signal grid point in the new search area after searching each time after a signal grid point is searched. Therefore, the search will be repeated many times, which increases the calculation amount of the algorithm and makes the algorithm difficult. Increased, and the key to the VB algorithm is the selection of the radius. Too small a radius will affect the experiment's accuracy, while too large a radius will result in too many search grid points and slower computing speed [10].

An improved CL algorithm of the VB algorithm appears in this case, and the CL algorithm proposed by A.M. Chan and I. Lee is an improvement of the VB algorithm [11]. The CL algorithm will update the candidate symbol set and its upper and lower bounds after searching for the signal grid point and then search from the breakpoint from the new reduced radius. So there is no repeated search, thereby reducing the investigation required time cases the CL algorithm's complexity [12].

3.2 CL Detection Algorithm Based on Particle Swarm Optimization

The particle swarm algorithm is a swarm optimization algorithm proposed by simulating a flock of birds' foraging behavior. Each particle represents a solution of the algorithm. They all have a speed expressing the direction and distance of the search path, and then the particle is at the optimal particle. Search in the solution space. Particle swarm can ensure the accuracy and sharing of information and find the best position through continuous improvement [13].

The optimization of particle swarm optimization is mainly accomplished through continuous iteration. First, the number of populations is initialized, and the system randomly generates the parameters, and each repeated loop mainly completes the optimization. The next iteration is to search by each particle's characteristics and their learning factors and keep the particles with better performance for the next search until the best position is obtained. At the end of each cycle, its particle in the particle swarm must update its speed and position until the end of the cycle. The update formula of the particle swarm algorithm is:

$$V_{id} = \omega V_{id} + C_1 random(0, 1)(P_{id} - X_{id}) + C_2 random(0, 1)(P_{gd} - X_{id}) \quad (2)$$

$$X_{id} = X_{id} + V_{id} \tag{3}$$

among them: ω—— Inertia factor, indicating the influence of the inertial speed on the current speed update;

C_1, C_2—The acceleration constant, usually a value of 2, is used to measure the degree of learning of the particle to the position with the best global performance and the best part of itself;

P_{id}—Represents the d-the dimension of the extreme individual value of the I-th variable;
P_{gd}—Represents the D-th dimension of the optimal global solution.

First, the optimal radius is obtained by the particle swarm algorithm. The channel matrix H is QR decomposed to receive $H = QR$, where Q is an orthogonal matrix, and R is a $Nt \times Nt$ dimensional upper triangular matrix. Using Q^T, the following formula can be obtained:

$$\|y - Hx\|^2 = \|y - QRx\|^2 = \left\|Q^T y - Q^T QRx\right\|^2 = \left\|Q^T y - Rx\right\|^2 = \|\bar{y} - Rx\|^2 \tag{4}$$

among them: $\bar{y} = Q^T y$.
Expand to:

$$\left\| \begin{bmatrix} \bar{y}_1 \\ \bar{y}_2 \\ \vdots \\ \bar{y}_{Nt-1} \\ \bar{y}_{Nt} \end{bmatrix} - \begin{bmatrix} R_{11} & R_{12} & \cdots & & R_{1Nt} \\ 0 & R_{22} & \cdots & & R_{2Nt} \\ \vdots & \cdots & \vdots & & \cdots \\ 0 & \cdots & R_{Nr-1,Nt-1} & R_{Nt-1,Nt} \\ 0 & \cdots & & & R_{Nr,Nt} \end{bmatrix} \begin{bmatrix} x_1 \\ x_2 \\ \vdots \\ x_{Nt-1} \\ x_{Nt} \end{bmatrix} \right\|^2$$

It can be seen from the expansion that the optimization idea of the particle swarm algorithm is used to solve the optimal solution. Each particle's path will produce a set of solutions. Under the modulation of P-QAM, each particle has P selection paths.
It can be inferred from solution $\hat{x}_{ML} = \arg\min_{X \in C_{NT}} \|y - Hx\|^2$ of the ML algorithm,

$$\bar{x} = \arg\min_{X \in C_{NT}} \sum_{j=1}^{Nr} \left\| \bar{y}_i - \sum_{j=i}^{Nr} R_{ij} X_j \right\|^2 \tag{5}$$

Suppose the distance from the I-th layer to the J-th node is

$$d_{ij} = \bar{y}_i - \sum_{j=i}^{Nr} R_{ij} X_j^2 \tag{6}$$

When the particle swarm completes the first search and performs the next examination, the particle swarm formula is updated. When the termination condition of the algorithm is reached, the particle swarm will produce an optimal solution. The distance between the generated solution and the received signal is taken as The search radius of the sphere detection algorithm. The CL detection algorithm is searched according to the search radius determined by the particle swarm algorithm. The detection points of the sphere detection algorithm meet the following conditions:

$$\|y - Hx\|^2 \le d^2 \tag{7}$$

After QR decomposition of the channel matrix H, Eq. 7 can be written as $\|\bar{y} - Hx\|^2 \le d^2$, which is expanded as

$$d^2 \ge \sum_{j=1}^{Nr} \left\| \bar{y}_i - \sum_{j=i}^{Nr} R_{ij}X_j \right\|^2 \tag{8}$$

Further expand into

$$d^2 \ge \left\| \begin{bmatrix} \bar{y}_1 \\ \bar{y}_2 \\ \vdots \\ \bar{y}_{Nt-1} \\ \bar{y}_{Nt} \end{bmatrix} - \begin{bmatrix} R_{11} & R_{12} & \cdots & & R_{1Nt} \\ 0 & R_{22} & \cdots & & R_{2Nt} \\ \cdots & \cdots & & \vdots & \cdots \\ 0 & \cdots & R_{Nr-1,Nt-1} & R_{Nt-1,Nt} \\ 0 & \cdots & & & R_{Nr,Nt} \end{bmatrix} \begin{bmatrix} x_1 \\ x_2 \\ \vdots \\ x_{Nt-1} \\ x_{Nt} \end{bmatrix} \right\|^2$$

The analysis of the above formula expands to:

$$d^2 \ge \left\| \bar{y}_{N_T} - R_{N_T,N_T} x_{N_T} \right\|^2 + \left\| \bar{y}_{N_T-1} - R_{N_T-1,N_T} x_{N_T} - R_{N_T-1,N_T-1} x_{N_T-1} \right\|^2 + \cdots \tag{9}$$

The above formula is only related to $\left\| \bar{y}_{N_T} - R_{N_T,N_T} x_{N_T-1} \right\|^2$ and x_{N_T}, so

$$\left\lceil \frac{-d + \bar{y}_{N_T}}{R_{N_T,N_T}} \right\rceil \le x_{N_T} \le \left\lfloor \frac{d + \bar{y}_{N_T}}{R_{N_T,N_T}} \right\rfloor \tag{10}$$

Among them: $\lceil \ \rceil$—the upper bound is rounded, $\lfloor \ \rfloor$—the lower bound is rounded.

From Eq. (10), the value of x_{N_T} can be obtained, and the radius can be updated. Let $d^2_{N_T-1} = d^2 - (\bar{y}_{N_T} - R_{N_T,N_T} x_{N_T})^2$ and $\bar{y}_{N_T-1} = (\bar{y}_{N_T} - R_{N_T-1,N_T} x_{N_T})^2$ be substituted into Eq. (10) to obtain

$$\left| \bar{y}_{N_T-1} - R_{N_T-1,N_T-1} x_{N_T-1} \right|^2 \le d^2_{N_T-1} \tag{11}$$

Expand to interval form as

$$\left\lceil \frac{-d_{N_T-1} + Y_{N_T-1}}{R_{N_T-1,N_T-1}} \right\rceil \le x_{N_T-1} \le \left\lfloor \frac{d_{N_T-1} + \bar{y}_{N_T-1}}{R_{N_T-1,N_T-1}} \right\rfloor \tag{12}$$

Obtain the value of x_{N_T-1} from Eq. (11), and then calculate other values of x in turn. In this process, each time a value of x is obtained in this process, the radius will be updated once. Secondly, the MMSE detection algorithm is used to reduce the interference caused by noise. The linear operator G can ensure that there is at least one grid point in the search area when the search radius of CL is too small [14]. Then use the attenuation factor to accelerate the convergence speed of the spherical algorithm radius. The shrinkage factor β is used to accelerate the convergence speed of the radius. When a valid grid point is found, the radius is updated. To avoid the search area being empty, the updated radius is:

$$\overline{d}^2 = e^{-\beta \times n_{SNR}} d^2 + (1 - e^{-\beta \times n_{SNR}}) d^2 \tag{13}$$

Among them: d— initial radius; β—compression factor;

Also, the relationship between the algorithm performance loss p and the radius d:

$$p = 1 - \exp\left(-\frac{d^2}{\sigma^2}\right) \sum_{j=0}^{N_t} \frac{1}{j!} \left(\frac{d^2}{\sigma^2}\right)^j \tag{14}$$

4   Performance Simulation and Analysis of CL Algorithm

This simulation software uses Matlab for simulation, the modulation method used is 16QAM, the number of antennas is configured as 2×2, and the noise type is Gaussian white noise.

Figure 2 below shows the comparison of the complexity of the VB and CL algorithms. It can be seen from Fig. 2 that the computational complexity of the CL algorithm is obviously lower than that of the VB algorithm under the same conditions, so this article chooses to improve and optimize the CL detection algorithm.

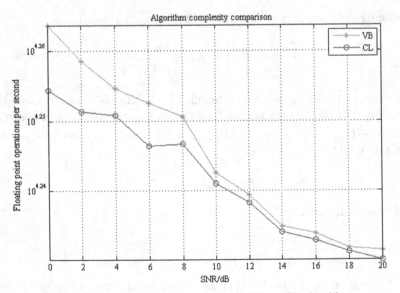

Fig. 2. Comparison of the complexity of VB and CL algorithms

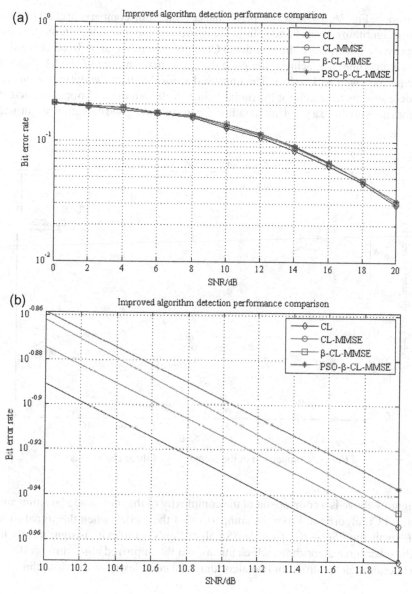

Fig. 3. (a) Comparison of detection algorithm detection performance. (b) Comparison of detection algorithm detection performance

The above Fig. 3(a, b) shows the performance simulation comparison chart of the four detection algorithms. It can be seen from the figure that the error rate difference between the improved algorithm and the traditional CL algorithm is not large. In other words, the improved algorithm can achieve the good detection performance of the CL algorithm, but the performance will be lost. The improved algorithm uses the optimization ability of particle swarms to search for the initial radius. Although the traditional CL detection algorithm does not have a good initial radius, it can still have good detection performance.

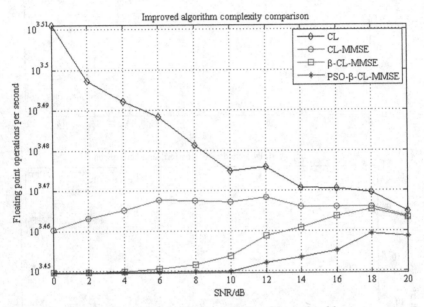

Fig. 4. Comparison of the complexity of three algorithms

Figure 4 above is a comparison of the complexity of the improved algorithm and the traditional CL algorithm. From the comparison of the model, when the signal-to-noise ratio is small, the $PSO - \beta - CL - MMSE$ algorithm's complexity is significantly lower than the other three algorithms, which means that the improved algorithm is effectively more inferior than the different two algorithms the complexity of the algorithm.

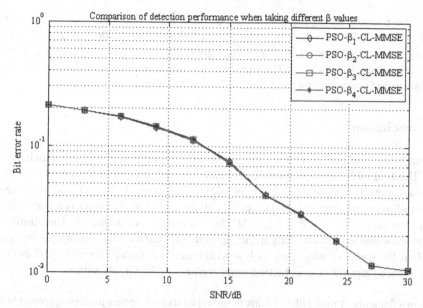

Fig. 5. Improved algorithm's detection performance under different β values

The above Fig. 5 is a simulation comparison of the bit error rate of the $PSO - \beta - CL - MMSE$ improved algorithm when different values of β are taken. Among them, the importance of β_1, β_2, β_3, β_4 are 0.5, 0.1, 0.04, 0.02, and the difference can be seen from the figure. The convergence factor of β is consistent in detection performance.

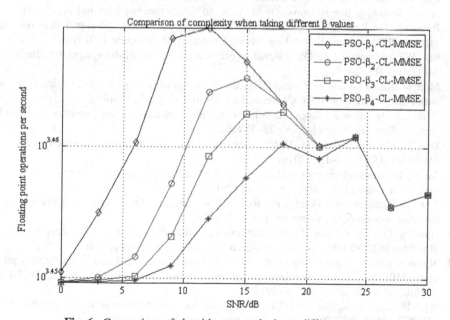

Fig. 6. Comparison of algorithms complexity at different β values

Figure 6 above shows the complexity of the $PSO - \beta - CL - MMSE$ algorithm when β takes different values. It can be seen from the figure that as the value of β decreases, the complexity of the algorithm gradually decreases, and as the signal-to-noise ratio gradually increases, The impact of the importance of β on the complexity of the algorithm is slowly falling.

5 Conclusion

The purpose of this paper is to find a low-complexity sphere detection algorithm based on the MIMO-OFDM system to improve the detection performance of the algorithm. Given the sphere detection algorithm's high complexity, the general solution is to improve the initial radius or speed up the shrinkage. The method used in this paper is a combination of the two, so the $PSO - \beta - CL - MMSE$ algorithms are proposed. The simulation results show that the improved algorithm dramatically reduces the algorithm's complexity when the signal-to-noise ratio is low while retaining better detection performance. The enhanced algorithm is a practical improvement in the CL algorithm.

Acknowledgments. I would like to thank the anonymous commenters for their responsible attitude and helpful suggestions. Thanks to the tutor for guiding me and the students who helped me in the research process.

References

1. Jing, S.: Research on channel estimation and signal detection algorithms in MIMO_OFDM system Shen Jing. Beijing University of Posts and Telecommunications, Beijing (2012)
2. Jingpeng, G.: Research on joint method of channel estimation and signal detection in MIMO_OFDM system. Harbin Engineering University, Heilongjiang (2014)
3. Rui, W.: An improved ZF-OSIC signal detection algorithm in MIMO system. Inf. Technol. **34**(4), 165–168 (2017)
4. Men, H., Jin, M.: A low - complexity ML detection algorithm for spatial modulation systems with PSK constellation. IEEE Commun. Lett. **18**(8), 1375–1378 (2014)
5. Zhibin, X., Weichen, Z., Tongsi, X.: A low-complexity sphere detection algorithm for MIMO systems. Ship Sci. Technol. **35**(8), 28–33 (2013)
6. Dan, W., Chao, S.: Improved MIMO system ball decoding and detection algorithm. Sensors Microsyst. **35**(8), 123–126 (2016)
7. Jiejun, W.: Research on improved algorithm of SM system signal detection based on signal vector. Chongqing University, Chongqing (2016)
8. Nan, L., Qianzhu, W., Deling, H.: Research on low-complexity massive MIMO signal detection algorithm. Inf. Commun. **1**, 32–34 (2017)
9. Jianqing, C., Lijia, G., Hui, H., et al.: Performance simulation comparison of sphere decoding algorithm in MIMO system. Antenna Servo Technol. **38**(6), 38–41 (2012)
10. Nguyen, V.H., Berder, O., Scalart, P.: On the efficiency of sphere decoding for linearly precoded MIMO systems. In: Wireless Communications and Networking Conference (WCNC), pp. 4021–4025. IEEE, Shanghai (2013)
11. Ngo, H., Larsson, E., Marzetta, T.L.: Energy and spectral efficiency of very large multiuser MIMO systems. IEEE Trans. Wirel. Commun. **61**(4), 1436–1449 (2012)

12. Diyuan, G.: Improved research on sphere decoding and detection algorithm in MIMO system. Northeastern University, Liaoning (2014)
13. Chunmeng, G.: Research on spatial modulation signal detection algorithm based on particle swarm optimization. Harbin Institute of Technology, Heilongjiang (2015)
14. Rui, L., et al.: Research on the application of sphere decoding algorithm in signal space diversity system. Comput. Appl. Res. **34**(5) 1452–1454 (2017)

SD-Based Low-Complexity Signal Detection Algorithm in Massive MIMO

Zhang Lihuan[1(✉)] and Jiang Xiaolin[1,2]

[1] Heilongjiang University of Science and Technology, Harbin 150000, China
2655517184@qq.com

[2] Jinhua Advanced Research Institute, Jinhua 321000, China

Abstract. The steepest descent algorithm (SD) itself can find a better convergence direction, but its own convergence speed is relatively slow, resulting in multiple iterations to approach the true solution. This paper proposes an improvement method for this problem. The principle is to improve the approximate solution obtained after every time the steepest descent algorithm is performed, so as to change the iterative formula and speed up the convergence speed of the algorithm, and then divide the constellation into four regions based on the idea of region division. The points are extracted directly for judgment and no longer participate in subsequent iterations. It is proved by simulation that when the number of iterations of the improved algorithm is consistent with the number of iterations of the steepest descent method, the improved algorithm has an order of magnitude higher detection performance than the original SD algorithm. The improved SD iterative algorithm has 2 iterations and a signal-to-noise ratio greater than 4 dB. The bit error rate is lower than that of the Minimum Mean Square Error (MMSE) detection algorithm, and its own complexity is only 67.4% of that of the SD iterative algorithm 2 iterations. The greater the difference between the number of user antennas and the number of base station antennas, the complexity of the improved algorithm can be even greater low.

Keywords: Steepest descent method · Approximate solution · Minimum Mean Square Error · Number of iterations · Complexity

1 Introduction

With the increase of mobile smart terminals, the traditional MIMO system has been unable to meet the user's demand for data services [1–3], thus a massive MIMO system is proposed. The massive MIMO system improves the channel capacity and spectrum utilization of the entire communication system by configuring a large number of antennas in the base station to serve multiple users. In the traditional algorithm, the Maximum Likelihood (ML) [4] detection algorithm finds the optimal estimation value by traversing all the constellation points, so the bit error rate is the lowest but its complexity is exponentially related to the modulation order and the number of antennas. Although the Sphere Decoding algorithm [5] can reduce the complexity of the algorithm by reducing

X. Jiang (Ed.): MLICOM 2021, LNICST 438, pp. 214–225, 2022.
https://doi.org/10.1007/978-3-031-04409-0_20

the number of traversed constellation points, the detection performance is close to the detection performance of the ML algorithm, it is still relatively complex compared to other algorithms, while the Zero Forcing (ZF) detection algorithm and The Minimum Mean Square Error (MMSE) [6] detection algorithm as a linear detection algorithm involves matrix inversion. Due to the rapid increase in the number of antennas in a massive MIMO system, the four detection algorithms mentioned are too high complex to be implemented in a massive MIMO system, so searching for low-complexity signal detection algorithms has become a research hotspot in massive MIMO wireless communication technology.

As the number of antennas increases, the channel matrix in the wireless communication system will have channel hardening characteristics, and each sub-channel will gradually be orthogonal [7]. Therefore the MMSE detection algorithm has better detection performance, but the algorithm involves matrix inversion operation. The complexity is too high and is not suitable for using in massive MIMO systems, so it is generally used as a comparison standard for detection performance. In order to reduce the complexity of the algorithm, many scholars have proposed many improved algorithms based on MMSE. At present, the more frequently used MMSE optimization algorithms can be divided into two categories, they are iterative method and approximation method.

The more common iterative methods are: Jacobi iteration method, Gauss-Seidel iteration method [8], Steepest descent method, Relaxation iteration method [9], Conjugate gradient algorithm [10], etc. The iteration method was previously used for linear equations. The principle of solving is to continuously loop through the iterative formula, so that the value obtained in each iteration continuously approaches the real solution, it can avoid matrix inversion. The approximation method is mainly the Neuman Series expansion method [11]. The approximation method generally uses the expanded polynomial to approximate the matrix inversion, but the Neuman Series also has larger defects. When the number of expansion items is 2 or less, although the computational complexity of the algorithm is lower than the complexity of calculating matrix inversion, the bit error rate is higher. When the number of expansion items is greater than 2, the detection performance is improved but the algorithm complexity is increased. Therefore the Neuman Series expansion method generally takes the expansion term as 1 as the approximate matrix inverse, and the solution obtained in this way is used as the initial value of the iterative method to accelerate the iteration.

In response to the above problems, this paper proposes an improved algorithm based on the steepest descent method. This algorithm uses the solution of linear equations, the final exact solution will be equal to the sum of the rough solution and the residual solution, and the idea of region division is used further improvement, If a certain component of the estimated value x obtained after iteration falls into the reliable region, it is directly extracted for judgment and no longer participates in subsequent iterations, so that the matrix dimension of the next iteration will be reduced, and the complexity will also be reduced. Simulation proves that when the number of iterations of the improved algorithm is lower than that of the original algorithm, the detection performance is very close. When the number of iterations of the improved algorithm is consistent with the number of iterations of the original algorithm, the detection performance of the improved algorithm is better than that of the original algorithm.

2 System Model

The object of this paper is the uplink of a massive MIMO system. The system model can be expressed as:

$$y = Hx + n = h_1 x_1 + h_2 x_2 + \cdots + h_K x_K + n \tag{1}$$

The base station in this system is configured with N antennas, and K single antenna users. Since K << N in the massive MIMO system, the sub-channels also tend to be orthogonal. The user sending vector and the base station receiving vector are arrespectively: $x = [x_1, x_2, \cdots, x_K]^T y = [y_1, y_2, \cdots, y_N]^T$, Where x_j represents the signal transmitted by the j-th user, y_i and represents the signal received by the i-th antenna. $n = [n_1, n_1, \cdots, n_N]^T$ Represents the Gaussian white noise that obeys the Gaussian distribution, and the Mathematical Expectation is 0.variance isσ^2.

Where H represents the channel matrix with dimension N * K, h_j represents the j-th column of the channel matrix.

The ZF detection algorithm eliminates interference between users through a weighted matrix. The weighting matrix is the inverse of the signal matrix and can be expressed as:

$$W_{ZF} = (H^H H)^{-1} H^H \tag{2}$$

The user transmitted vector estimated from the received signal vector can be expressed as:

$$x_{ZF} = W_{ZF} y = x + n_{ZF} \tag{3}$$

Since the ZF detection algorithm does not consider the influence of noise, its detection performance has a great relationship with the power of n_{ZF}. In the case of low signal-to-noise ratio, the error detection rate of the ZF detection algorithm is not very ideal. In order to reduce noise interference, the MMSE detection algorithm makes noise compensation on the basis of ZF. The weighting matrix of MMSE is:

$$W_{MMSE} = (H^H H + \sigma^2 I)^{-1} H^H \tag{4}$$

I is the identity matrix, and the estimated user transmission vector can be expressed as:

$$x_{MMSE} = W_{MMSE} y \tag{5}$$

Since the MMSE detection algorithm has made up for noise in the weighting matrix, the performance of the MMSE detection algorithm is better than that of the ZF detection algorithm. we can convert the MMSE detection algorithm into the form of solving linear equations, it can be expressed as:

$$Ax = b \tag{6}$$

Among them $A = H^H H + \sigma^2 I$, $b = H^H y$.

3   Improvement of SD Iterative Algorithm

3.1   Application of SD Algorithm

The iterative algorithm is to make the estimated value gradually close to the signal vector sented by the user through multiple iterations, so as to avoid the inversion of the matrix and reduce the complexity. Compared with other iterative algorithms, SD iterative algorithm can find a better iterative direction, but its own convergence speed is poor.

Theorem 1: Assuming that the matrix A is a symmetric matrix, the quadratic function $f(x) = (Ax, x) - 2(b, x)$, if and only if x is the solution of the equation system $Ax = b$, point x makes the quadratic function take the minimum value.

Theorem 2: Assuming that the matrix A is a symmetric matrix, and the quadratic functional method $f(x) = (Ax, x) - 2(b, x)$, if and only if x is the solution of the equations, x is the center of the ellipsoid $f(x) = c$.

Since C is symmetric and positive definite, according to Theorem 1 and Theorem 2, the solution of the equation system $Ax = b$ is the center of $f(x) = c$ of the ellipsoid, which also makes the quadratic function $f(x) = (Ax, x) - 2(b, x)$ obtain the minimum value.

Take a random point x0 as the initial value, x0 must be on the spherical surface of the ellipsoid $f(x) = (Ax0, x0) - 2(b, x0)$, passing through the point x0 along the fastest descending direction r0 to make a straight line $x = x0 + t * r0$, and then look for the point x1 on this straight line that can make f(x) the minimum value. Assuming that the function f(x) can get the minimum value when $t = a$, Then there is $x = x0 + a * r0$, so only a need be required., which becomes the problem of solving the minimum value of the function $f(x0 + t * r0)$ on the variable t. Derivation the function $f(x0 + tr0)$ can be expressed as:

$$\frac{df(x_0 + tr_0)}{dt} = 2t(Ar_0, r_0) - 2(r_0, r_0) = 0 \tag{7}$$

$$t = \frac{(r_0, r_0)}{(Ar_0, r_0)} = a \tag{8}$$

So we can get the next approximate solution

$$r_0 = b - Ax_0 \tag{9}$$

$$a_0 = \frac{(r_0, r_0)}{(Ar_0, r_0)} \tag{10}$$

$$x_1 = x_0 + a_0 r_0 \tag{11}$$

3.2   Neuman Series Expansion Algorithm

In order to avoid solving the inverse of matrix A directly, Neuman series expansion is used to approximate the inverse of A, when X and A are close and satisfy the condition:

$$\lim_{n \to \infty} (I - AX)^n = 0 \tag{12}$$

Then the inverse of matrix A can be expressed as:

$$A^{-1} = \sum_{n=0}^{\infty} X(X^{-1} - A)^n X \tag{13}$$

Decompose matrix A into $A = D + E$, where D is the matrix formed by the main diagonal of matrix A. Taking the first t term instead of the inverse of matrix A

$$A^{-1} = \sum_{n=0}^{t-1} (-D^{-1}E)^n D^{-1} \tag{14}$$

3.3 Improvements to the Iterative Structure of the SD Algorithm

Assuming that x1 is an approximate solution of the equation $Ax = b$, then $r1 = b - A * x1$ represents the residual vector. Solving the equation $A * d1 = r1$ obtains the residual solution as $d1 = A^{-1}r1$, $x2 = x1 + d1$ then x2 is the equation $Ax = b$ exact solution. Because the complexity of matrix inversion is too high when we solve d1, Neuman series expansion can be substituted matrix inversion to reduce the complexity. Although the exact value cannot be obtained directly, x2 is more accurate than x1.

$$x_1 = x_0 + a_0 r_0 \tag{15}$$

Then improve the approximate value obtained when the number of Neuman series expansion items is 1:

$$r_1 = b - Ax_1 = b - A(x_0 + a_0 r_0) = r_0 - a_0 A r_0 \tag{16}$$

$$x_2 = x_1 + D^{(-1)}r_1 = x_1 + D^{(-1)}(r_0 - a_0 A r_0) \tag{17}$$

x2 as the initial value of the next iteration,
  Improvement when the number of Neuman series expansion items is 2:

$$x_2 = x_1 + A_2^{(-1)}r_1 = x_1 + A_2^{(-1)}(r_0 - a_0 A r_0) \tag{18}$$

where A_2 represents the approximate inverse of the matrix when the number of Neuman series expansion items is 2. It is also possible to use when the expansion series is 3, but when the expansion series is 3, the complexity is too high and not applicable.

3.4 Further Improvement Based on the Idea of Area Division

In the actual iteration process, the speed at which the estimated value of each user approaches the true value is inconsistent. The estimated value of some users is already very close to the true value. The estimated value continued iteration will not change much, and these values can be directly judged. The estimated value of some users is still far from the true value, for the overall accuracy, the estimated value of the user who is already close to the true solution must continue to iterate with the estimated value of other users, which causes unnecessary calculations. In order to reduce the complexity

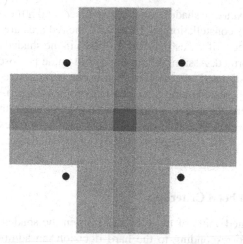

Fig. 1. Schematic diagram of 4QAM modulation area division

and detection performance of the algorithm, this paper divides the constellation map area into four different areas: reliable area, normal iteration area, mildly unreliable area, and unreliable area.

Figure 1 is a schematic diagram of the 4QAM modulation area division. The black dots represent the constellation points, the white area represents the reliable area, the cyan area represents the normal iteration area, the shaded area represents the mildly unreliable area, and the red area represents the unreliable area. The user's estimated value falling in the reliable area means that it does not need to iterate, these values can be directly judged. The user's estimated value falls in the normal iterative area, we don't do any disposal and let it continue to iterate. The user's estimated value falls in a mildly unreliable area, indicating that the estimated value is not much different from the two surrounding constellation points, which means that these two values may be the true value of the user's send vector. In order to reduce the possibility of misjudgment, the point with the smallest cost function is selected as the estimated value by traversing these two points. The user's estimate falls in the unreliable area, indicating that all four surrounding points may be true solutions, so all four surrounding points are traversed, and the point with the smallest cost function is selected as the estimated value.

The two thresholds used in this paper to distinguish each region are 0.04 and 0.198 respectively. The red area indicates that the real and imaginary parts of the estimated value are both less than 0.04, the cyan area indicates that the real or imaginary part is less than 0.04, the white area indicates that both the real and imaginary parts are greater than 0.19, and the rest are shaded parts.

After each iteration of the SD-NM algorithm, the estimated value obtained is divided into regions. If the estimated value falls in the reliable area, the value can be directly judged, and the corresponding rows and columns are deleted. If the estimated value falls in the continuous iteration area, no processing is done and the iteration continues. When the iteration is completed, if the estimated value falls in the shadow area, the two constellation points next to the shadow area are traversed, and if the estimated value falls in the red area, the four constellation points around the red area are all traversed.

In the iterative process, if the estimated value falls in the shaded area or the red area, no processing is performed. Assuming that the initial value is close to 1-i and the true solution is $1 + i$, the estimated value obtained after one iteration may falls in the shaded area or red area, the estimated value after one iteration continue iterate, the estimated value may be in the reliable area. In order to avoid this situation, the points that fall in the shadow area or the red area after each iteration are not processed. Only after the iteration is completed, if the estimated value falls in the shaded area or the red area, it will be processed.

3.5   Maximum Likelihood Criterion

Assuming that estimated value of the j-th user falls in the shaded area, it means that excepting the point corresponding to the hard decision, an additional point must be traversed. Due to $Hx = h_1 x_1 + h_2 x_2 + \cdots + h_k x_k$, the extra traversed points are the same as the points corresponding to the hard decision, except for x_j, the other values are the same. In order to reduce the amount of calculation, the minimum cost function can be transformed as:

$$x_{ML} = argmin\|y - Hx\|^2 = argmin\|y - \sum\nolimits_{i=1, i \neq j}^{k} h_i x_i - h_j x_j\|^2 \tag{19}$$

$$x_{ML} = argmin\|y - h_j x_j\|^2 \tag{20}$$

In formula (19), the $y - \sum_{i=1, i \neq j}^{k} h_i x_i$ is the same, the only difference is $h_j x_j$, this means that formula (19) is equivalent to formula (20).

Among them, using formula (20) to calculate the maximum likelihood cost function can greatly reduce the complexity of the algorithm. The formula (19) must first calculate Hx, and then calculate the inner product. The calculation of Hx can be regards as a 2k * 2k matrix multiplying a 2k * 1 vector. The complexity of multiplying the two is $4k^2$. The calculation of the inner product can be regarded as the multiplication of two 2k * 1 vectors. The complexity is 2k. Using Using formula (20) replace formula (19), the complexity of calculation the maximum likelihood cost function is only 4k. Therefore, every time a constellation point is traversed, the added complexity is 4k.

4   Simulation Results and Analysis

This section gives the MATLAB simulation result graph, and analyzes and explains the simulation result graph. In the simulation, the number of users is 16, the number of base station antennas is 64, and the size of channel matrix is 64 * 16. If there is no additional statement in the subsequent analysis, the default channel size is 64 * 16. The t in the simulation diagram represents the number of iterations of the detection algorithm, and n represents the number of items expanded by the Neuman series (Fig. 2).

The performance of the MMSE detection algorithm in the traditional algorithm is better, but it is only used as a standard to measure the detection performance of other

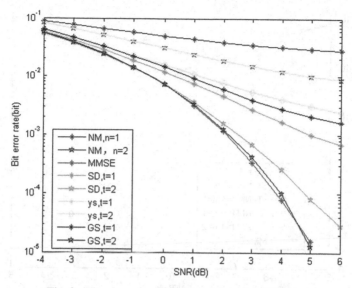

Fig. 2. Bit error rate of traditional detection algorithm

iterative algorithms. When the number of iterations of the Gauss Seidel iteration method is 2, the detectability can approach the performance of the MMSE detection algorithm. The detection performance of the SD algorithm when the number of iterations is 1 is better than the detection performance of the Gauss Seidel iteration method when the number of iterations is 1, Due to the problem of convergence speed, the detection performance of the SD algorithm is poor when the number of iterations of both is 2. The detection performance is not very good when the number of expansion items of the Neuman series expansion method is 1 and 2. When the signal-to-noise ratio is 6 dB, the bit error rate is still 10^{-2}. When the expansion item is 3, the complexity of Neuman series is close to complexity of the MMSE algorithm, so the Neuman series expansion method still has big flaws.

Figure 3 shows that SD is the iteration of the steepest descent method, and SD-NM is an improved algorithm for improving the approximate solution obtained in each iteration of SD, where t represents the number of iterations, and n represents the number of items expanded by the Neuman series. The simulation results show that the SD-NM iterative algorithm has detection performance is close to the detection performance of the traditional SD iterative algorithm when the number of iterations of SD-NM is 1, and the number of items expanded by the Neuman series is 1, the number of iterations of SD iterative algorithm is 2. This shows that improving the approximate solution obtained after each iteration of SD can speed up the convergence speed of the original algorithm. The signal-to-noise ratio is 5 dB, the bit error rate of SD-NM iterative algorithm at $t = 1$ and $n = 2$ is $8.9 * 10^{-4}$, and the bit error rate is $1.25 * 10^{-4}$ when $t = 1$ and $n = 1$, and when $t = 2$ and $n = 1$ bit error rate is $1.25 * 10^{-5}$. Therefore, when the difference in the number of receiving and transmitting antennas is more small, the number of Neuman series expansion items should be selected as 2, so that the iterative algorithm can converge faster.

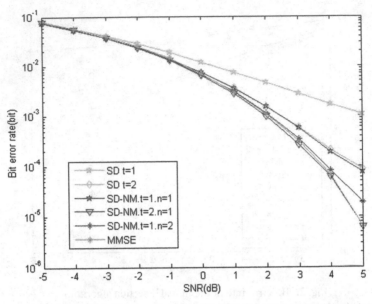

Fig. 3. Comparison of bit error rate between SD-NM algorithm and original algorithm

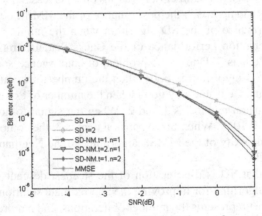

Fig. 4. The influence of the number of antennas on the detection performance of SD-NM algorithm

Figure 4 shows the comparison of the detection performance of each algorithm when the number of receiving and transmitting antennas is 128 * 16. As shown in Fig. 4, the detection performance of $t = 1$, $n = 1$ and $t = 1$, $n = 2$ in the SD-NM algorithm are consistent with the detection performance of the MMSE algorithm, but when the number of items expanded by the Neuman series is 2, the algorithm complexity is higher. Therefore, when the number of receiving and transmitting antennas differ greatly, the number of items in the Neuman series expansion should be selected as 1.

SD-NM-RC in Fig. 5 represents an algorithm that uses the idea of area division to further improve SD-NM. When the signal-to-noise ratio is lower than 2 dB, the

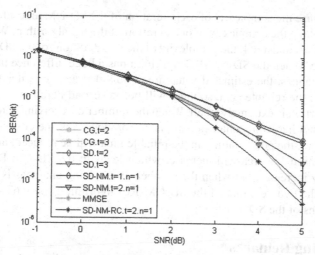

Fig. 5. Comparison of bit error rate between SD-NM-RC algorithm and other algorithms

detection performance of each algorithm is not much different. Because the SD-NM-RC algorithm uses the ML criterion for the unreliable area to traverse the surrounding points, the detection performance of the SD-NM-RC detection algorithm is better. when the signal-to-noise is greater than 3 dB, the bit error rate of SD-NM-RC at t = 2 and n = 1 is lower than that of the MMSE detection algorithm and SD-NM algorithm (Fig. 6).

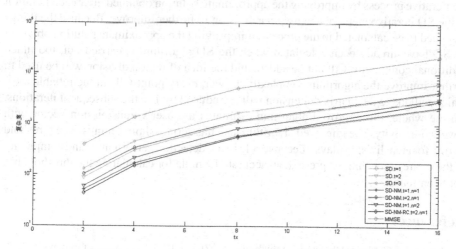

Fig. 6. Comparison of the complexity of each algorithm

Since the signal-to-noise ratio has an impact on the complexity of the SD-NM-RC algorithm, but has no effect on the complexity of other algorithms, in this simulation, the signal-to-noise ratio is set to 5 dB and the number of receiving antennas is fixed to 64. Change the number of transmitting antennas to compare the complexity of each algorithm. Because the complexity of each iteration of the SD-NM algorithm when n = 1 is only higher than the complexity of one iteration of the SD algorithm. When the SD-NM algorithm t = 2 and n = 1, the complexity of the two iterations of the SD algorithm is almost the same. When the SD-NM-RC algorithm has a large difference in the number of receiving antennas, the estimated value area is divided after one iteration. Almost all values fall in the reliable area, so there will be no second iteration or x need to be iterated. The portion is extremely small. When the number of receiving antennas is very close, the channel hardening characteristic is not obvious, and the convergence speed is slow. Therefore, the points falling in the reliable area will be reduced, and the points falling in the unreliable area will increase, which leads to the SD-NM-RC algorithm The complexity increases, but when the number of receiving antennas is 64 * 16, the complexity of the two iterations of the SD-NM-RC algorithm is only 67.4% of that of the two iterations of the SD algorithm.

5 Concluding Remarks

Due to the large number of antennas in the Massive MIMO system, the dimensionality of the channel matrix is high, while the traditional ZF detection algorithm and the MMSE detection algorithm are more complex. Aiming at this problem, this paper proposes an improved algorithm based on the steepest descent method. The algorithm can consider estimating the vector sent by the user as solving a linear equation set and solving it in an iterative manner, which avoids the inversion of a high-dimensional matrix and reduces the complexity. The improved algorithm is to change the iterative formula to speed up the iterative process by improving the approximate solution obtained after each iteration of the SD iterative method, and use area division to further improve. Because the things that need to be calculated in the process of improving the approximate solution obtained by SD have already been calculated when the SD algorithm is carried out, too much additional complexity will not be added, and the idea of region division will be used to further improve the algorithm complexity. Lower, every point falls in the reliable area, which will make the matrix dimension will be reduced by 1 in the subsequent iterations. On the whole, the improved algorithm estimates the user's transmission vector with lower complexity. The improved algorithm also has certain shortcomings. The threshold setting for area division plays a decisive role in the detection performance and complexity of the entire algorithm. At present, an accurate formula for calculating the threshold has not been found.

References

1. Lu, L., Li, G., Swindlehurst, A., Ashikhmin, A., Zhang, R.: An overview of massive MIMO: benefits and challenges. IEEE J. **8**, 742–758 (2014)
2. Wu, M., Yin, B., Wang, G., Dick, C., Cavallaro, J., Studer, C.: Large-scale MIMO detection for 3GPP LTE: algorithms and FPGA implementation. IEEE J. **8**, 916–929 (2014)
3. Nakamura, T., et al.: Trends in small cell enhancements in LTE advanced. IEEE Commun. Mag. **51**(2), 98–105 (2013)
4. Noh, H., Myoungseok, K., Jaesang, H., Chungyong, L.: A practical MMSE-ML detector for a MIMO SC-FDMA system. IEEE Commun. Lett. **13**, 902–904 (2009)

5. Nguyen, V.-H., Berder, O., Scalart, P.: On the efficiency of sphere decoding for linearly MIMO systems. In: Wireless Communications and Networking Conference (WCNC), pp. 4021–4025. IEEE, Shanghai (2013)
6. Tran, X.N., Le, A.T., Fujino, T.: Performance comparison of MMSE-SIC and MMSE-ML multiuser detectors in a STBC-OFNM system. In: Proceedings of the IEEE 16th International Symposium on Personal, Indoor and Mobile Radio Communications, pp. 1050–1054. Berlin, Germany, 11–14 Sept 2005
7. Narasimhan, T.L.: Channel hardening-exploiting message passing (CHEMP) receiver in large-scale MIMO systems. IEEE J. Select. Top. Sign. Process. 8(5), 847–860 (2014)
8. Zhou, J., Ye, Y., Hu, J.: Biased MMSE soft-output detection based on Jacobi method in massive MIMO. In: 2014 IEEE International Conference on Communication Problem-Solving, pp. 442–445. IEEE (2014)
9. Wang, F., Zhang, C., Liang, X., et al.: Efficient iterative soft detection based on polynomial approximation for massive MIMO. In: 2015 International Conference on Wireless Communications and Signal Processing (WCSP). IEEE (2015)
10. Zhou, J., Hu, J., Chen, J., et al.: Biased MMSE soft-output detection based on conjugate gradient in massive MIMO. In: 2015 IEEE 11th International Conference on ASIC (ASICON), pp. 1–4. IEEE (2015)
11. Rosario, F., Monteiro, F.A., Rodrigues, A.: Fast matrix inversion updates for massive MIMO detection and precoding. IEEE Sign. Process. Lett. 23(1), 75–79 (2016)

Improved YOLOv4 Infrared Image Pedestrian Detection Algorithm

Jin Tao[1(✉)], Jianting Shi[2], Yinan Chen[2], and Jiancai Wang[3]

[1] Graduate College, Heilongjiang University of Science and Technology, Harbin 150022, China
taojin@usth.edu.cn
[2] School of Computer and Information Engineering, Heilongjiang University of Science and Technology, Harbin 150022, China
[3] Academic Affairs Office, Heilongjiang University of Science and Technology, Harbin 150022, China

Abstract. Because pedestrians are always in the active state, each target is at a different distance from the camera, resulting in a certain difference in the size of similar targets in the figure. Therefore, an infrared pedestrian detection algorithm is proposed in the paper based on Yolov4 algorithm. Aiming at the problems of low recognition rate and high background influence in infrared image downlink human small target detection, the network structure of YOLOv4 is optimized. Compared with YOLOv4 and YOLOv3, the mean Average Precision is improved by 0.53% and 1.05%, which improves the detection accuracy in a certain extent.

Keywords: Infrared image · YOLOv4 · Pedestrian detection · Network structure · YOLOv3

1 Introduction

With the development of artificial intelligence technology and deep learning, computer vision is becoming more and more mature, and pedestrian detection technology has entered people's life. There is a broad prospect in the fields of security monitoring, vehicle unmanned driving and human behavior analysis etc. [1–12].Pedestrian detection technology is to study and judge the given image or verify whether there are pedestrians to be detected in each frame of video sequence, and the specific location of the target can be found accurately and quickly.

The traditional visible light technology can't be applied in the fields of night or unmanned driving. Infrared thermal image is based on the relative temperature information of the object, compared with the traditional situation, which is less affected by various additional factors and can be applied in many aspects. But there is no color in the image collected by infrared equipment, so the accuracy of pedestrian detection is low. Pedestrian detection algorithm can be divided into traditional algorithm and deep learning algorithm. The traditional algorithm mainly uses the artificial design to extract the image features, combined with machine learning to recognize and classify the image

X. Jiang (Ed.): MLICOM 2021, LNICST 438, pp. 226–233, 2022.
https://doi.org/10.1007/978-3-031-04409-0_21

features, so that to detect the target. However, the traditional algorithm is complex, sometimes it is difficult to design a reasonable method in the complex scene, and the weight parameter is difficult to get a more accurate value, so the generalization ability is poor.

In recent years, Convolutional Neural Network (CNN) [7] has made a significant breakthrough in pedestrian detection. Convolutional Neural Network (CNN) can learn the original features of the target through a large number of data automatically. Compared with the manually designed features, CNN has stronger abilities in discrimination and generalization [8]. In the meanwhile, the deep learning algorithm not only improves the detection efficiency, but also improves the detection speed, which is better than traditional method. Before the appearance of YOLO, the detection speed of deep learning was not very fast, and the real-time performance could not be guaranteed, especially in the future unmanned driving technology. Redmon et al. [5] proposed YOLO (you only look once, unified, real-time object detection) algorithm, which entered the field of one stage target detection. The idea of one stage solves the problem of speed in target detection, and improves the real-time performance with a certain accuracy greatly. Although the speed is improved, but the accuracy is not more precisely than other algorithms. After that, there are YOLOv2, YOLO9000 and YOLOv4. The network structure of YOLOv4 is simple and efficient, so it's easy to deploy and widely used. It is one of the preferred algorithms in many commercial fields. Combined with the practical application scenarios, it is applied to large-scale outdoor monitoring to detect the areas where pedestrians are forbidden. Moreover, YOLOv4 has great application prospects in infrared images of small object detection and pedestrian detection. The backbone network is better used in the network structure such as DarkNet or RESNET classifier, but also detected quickly. The most important thing is to build a simple environment, reduce the background detection error and make a strong generalization. Although YOLOv4 network has great advantages in multi-scale prediction and better classifier, there are several disadvantages that the accuracy of object recognition is poor and the recall rate is low, compared with other RCNN series detection algorithms.

To solve the above problems, the YOLOv4 algorithm is improved in the paper. The pedestrian detection accuracy (MAP) of infrared image is improved by 0.04%, compared with the original YOLOv4 algorithm.

2 Algorithm Structure of YOLOv4 Network

YOLO algorithm is the first work of one-stage detection. It is a target detection system based on single neural network proposed by Redmon and Ali Farhadi in 2015. In CVPR in 2017, Redmon and Ali Farhadi published YOLOv2 and YOLOv3, which further improved the accuracy and speed. After further improvement, YOLOv4 algorithm appeared. YOLOv4 is mainly introduced in three aspects: network input, structure and output, the network structure is shown in Fig. 1.

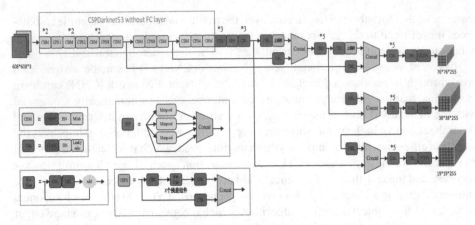

Fig. 1. YOLOv4 network structure.

3 Improved Infrared Pedestrian Detection Algorithm Based on YOLOv4

In the night vision infrared pedestrian detection and location task, first, the sampling machine is in the high spot to make the volume of the pedestrian target smaller; Second, because of the active pedestrians, each target is at a different distance from the camera, resulting in the differences of similar targets in the images. These two factors lead to a certain deviation between the final detection results and the actual situation. So the structure of the feature extraction network is optimized to enhance the ability of the network to capture the target position.

In the feature extraction network CSPDarknet adopted by YOLOv4, standard convolution of 3 × 3 size is mainly used for feature extraction. Because the shape and size of the receptive field of standard convolution are fixed, it will also extract the features of non-target areas when detecting small targets, which leads to more interference factors in the features extracted by final convolution and more interference effects on the prediction of the detector. So in the actual detection situation, deformation convolution is used as the core component, the deformation feature extraction module is constructed to improve the effectiveness of target feature extraction based on the standard convolution of YOLOv4. Compared with standard convolution, deformable convolution has the following advantages: firstly, the efficiency of receptive field is improved, that is, the feature map is more accurate in mapping target information; Secondly, the effectiveness of feature extraction in convolution kernel is improved. Convolution kernel can adapt to the position of the target for sampling, and the extracted feature information matches the target better; In addition, the deformable convolution can extract features more specifically for the region of the target, the stability of the feature graph (that is, the weight parameter will not change) is better than the standard convolution. When the feature graph is transferred in the network, the deformation process during model training can be expressed by the following formula and the deformation convolution used in the paper.

$$y(p) = \sum_{k=1}^{K} w_k \cdot x(p + p_k + \Delta p_k) \cdot \Delta m_k \tag{1}$$

p—Convolution kernel coordinates.

k—The number of convolution kernels (for example, 3×3 convolution kernels with 9 kernels).

w—Weight.

p_k—The offset of the Kth kernel.

Δp_k—The offset of the model needs to learn.

Δm_k—Offset control parameters that the model needed to learn.

The feature extraction network module is optimized based on deformation convolution. The composition of the optimized deformation feature extraction module is shown in Fig. 2.

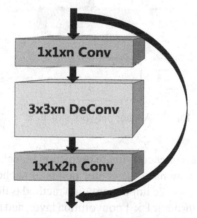

Fig. 2. Deformation feature extraction module.

Compared with the module before optimization, the optimized module mainly uses 3×3 deformation convolution to replace the standard convolution, and uses 1×1 convolution layer to construct feature channel for dimension reduction and dimension elevation. In the beginning, a 1×1 standard convolution layer is used to reduce the dimension of the input feature map, at the same time, the redundant features are deleted; Then, the feature map is extracted by 3×3 deformation convolution; Finally, 1×1 standard convolution is used to enhance the dimension of the extracted feature to increase the amount of information. In order to enhance the reuse of target location information, coordinate attention mechanism module is added based on the attention mechanism of YOLOv4 to enhance the coordinate information. Coordinate attention mechanism module optimizes based on SE channel attention mechanism, extracts the horizontal and vertical feature weight information of feature graph, and achieves accurate target position coordinate saliency mark through aggregation.

In order to optimize the location accuracy of the anchor, the "Guided Anchoring" mechanism is added in the detection layer of YOLOv4 to improve the quality of the anchor and the candidate region through the adaptive generation of the network anchor. The core principle of guided anchoring is to decompose the location attribute, the location attribute of a target is usually by four parameters (x, y, w, h) to represent location and size. That is to say, if the position information of a target can be expressed as $p(x, y, w, h|F)$ in the feature graph F, it can be decomposed into $p(x, y|F)p(w, h|x, y, F)$. This decomposition method shows that the definition of the position information of a target is to determine the existing region firstly, the shapes and sizes are closely related to the regional coordinates. Guided Anchors includes two branches, one is responsible for the prediction of anchor center coordinates, and the other is responsible for the prediction of anchor shape. The structure of anchor generator is shown in Fig. 3.

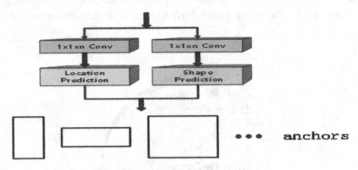

Fig. 3. Anchor network structure.

The main function of the center coordinate prediction branch is to determine whether regions in the feature map may have the center points of anchors, which is the binary classification problem. The specific implementation method is that the input feature map is converted into score map through 1×1 convolution layer, and then the final probability map is obtained by activating the sigmoid function of the elements on the map in the way of element-wise. At the same time, the threshold value ε_L is set to select the area where there may be anchors center point. Taking the point on the feature graph F as the anchor center point (i, j), the probability value is $p(i, j|F)$, and mapping it back to the coordinates in the input image is $((i + 1/2)s, (j + 1/2)s)$, S is the down sampling step of the feature graph related with the original image, by which the point on the feature graph can be mapped to the size of the original image for detection and output.

4 Experimental Results and Analysis

4.1 Evaluating Indicator

The related performance indicators of the infrared pedestrian detection algorithm, such as intersection and union ratio, IOU, precision and recall, are used to evaluate the advantages and disadvantages of infrared pedestrian detection. According to the size of the corresponding value to judge the quality of the model.

$$IOU = 2 * area(S_1 \cap S_2)/(area(S_1) + area(S_2)) \tag{2}$$

$$Recall = TP/(TP + FN) \tag{3}$$

$$P = TP/(TP + FP) \tag{4}$$

S1—Pedestrian area predicted by infrared image.
S2—Pedestrian area marked by people;
TP—The correct prediction of infrared image downlink;
FN—The situation of wrong prediction;
FP—It's not a pedestrian area, but it's predicted to be pedestrian.

4.2 Experimental Steps and Innovation Analysis

The data sets used in the experiment is from the OSU Thermal Pedestrian Database. Before used, the data set is cleaned, and 1500 ordinary samples, 400 difficult samples, and 200 negative samples are selected to form a 2100 training set; 300 ordinary samples and 200 difficult samples are used as 500 test sets.

According to the two training models, the improved YOLOv4, YOLOv4and YOLOv3 are compared and tested. The test results are shown in Table 1.

Table 1. Model checking performance comparison

Indexes	Precision	Recall	F2-1 score	IOU	mAP
YOLOv3	0.90	0.77	0.83	64.75%	82.04%
YOLOv4	0.92	0.78	0.86	63.92%	82.56%
Improved YOLOv4	0.89	0.85	0.87	64.86%	83.09%

Among them: the meaning of each index in Table 1 is as follows: precision represents the proportion of the part that the classifier considers to be a positive class and is indeed a positive class in all classifiers. Recall represents the proportion of the part that the classifier thinks is a positive class and is a positive class in all the positive classes. F1score calculation formula: 2 * precision * recall/(precision + recall). IOU (intersection and union ratio) represents the overlap ratio of the candidate bound and the ground truth bound, that is the ratio of their intersection and union. The ideal situation is complete overlap, that is, the ratio is 1. The mean accuracy (mAP) represents the average value of each category of AP. From the analysis in Table 1, the column F2-1score shows that the overall robustness and recall rate of the improved YOLOv4 algorithm are better than YOLOv3, which comprehensively reflects that the optimization of backbone network and detection network is of great help in improving network performance. The improved YOLOv4 algorithm is used for pedestrian detection, and the test results are shown in Fig. 4.

Fig. 4. Test results with improved YOLOv4 algorithm.

In order to verify the comprehensive performances, three algorithms are compared with the same training sets and the same testing sets to obtain the ROC curve. The comparison of improved YOLOv4(Im-YOLOv4), YOLOv4 and YOLOv3 are shown in Fig. 5.

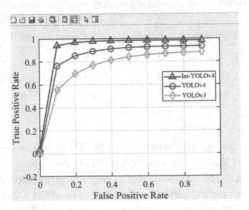

Fig. 5. The comparison of comprehensive performances.

5   Conclusion

In the paper, an improved infrared pedestrian detection algorithm based on YOLOv4 is proposed. The optimized algorithm improves the detection ability of gray image, small target, and the practicability of infrared detection. The deformation convolution is used as the core component, and the deformation feature extraction module is constructed to enhance the effectiveness of target feature extraction, to strengthen the ability of feature information transmission, and effectively improve the detection accuracy.

Acknowledgements. This work has been partially supported by "The National Key Research and Development Program of China (2018 YFC0810500)" and "2020 scientific research project of basic scientific research expenses of provincial colleges and universities in Heilongjiang Province. (2020-KYYWF-0680)".

References

1. Jensen, M.B., Nasrollahi, K., Mocslund, T.B.: Evaluating state-of-the-art object detector on challenging traffic light data. In: Proceedings of the IEEE Conference on Computer Vision and Pattern Recognition Workshops, pp. 9–11 (2017)
2. Girshick, R: Fast R-CNN. In: Proceedings of the IEEE International Conference on Computer Vision, pp. 1440–1448 (2015)
3. Ren, S., He, K., Girshick, R., et al.: Faster R-CNN, towards real-time object detection with region proposal networks. In: Advances in Neural Information Processing Systems, pp. 92–199 (2015)
4. Liu, W., et al.: SSD: single shot multibox detector. In: Leibe, B., Matas, J., Sebe, N., Welling, M. (eds) Computer Vision – ECCV 2016. ECCV 2016. (LNCS), vol. 9905. Springer, Cham (2016). https://doi.org/10.1007/978-3-319-46448-0_2
5. Redmon, J., Divvala, S., Girshick, R., et al.: You only look once: unified, real-time object detection. In: Proceedings of the IEEE conference on computer vision and pattern recognition, pp. 779–788 (2016)
6. Mukai, L., Tao, Z., Wennan, C.: Research on infrared pedestrian small target detection technology based on YOLOv4. In: Infrared Technology, pp. 1002–18891 (2020)
7. Dalal, N., Triggs, B.: Histograms of oriented gradients for human detection. In: International Conference on Computer Vision & Pattern Recognition (CVPR 2005), IEEE Computer Society, vol. 1, pp. 886–893 (2005)
8. Yao, Y., Wang, N.: Fault diagnosis model of adaptive miniature circuit breaker based on fractal theory and probabilistic neural network. Mech. Syst. Signal Process. **142**, 106772 (2020)
9. Sandler, M., Howard, A., Zhu, M., et al.: MobileNetV2: inverted residuals and linear bottlenecks. In: 2018 IEEE/CVF Conference on Computer Vision and Pattern Recognition (CVPR), IEEE (2018)
10. Lecun, Y., Bottou, L., Bengio, Y., et al.: Gradient-based learning applied to document recognition. Proc. IEEE **86**(11), 2278–2324 (1998)
11. Felzenzwalb, P.F., Grishick, R.B., Mcallister, D., et al.: Object detection with discriminatively trained part-based models. IEEE Trans. Pattern Anal. Mach. Intell. **32**(9), 1627–1645 (2010)
12. Shi, J., Zhang, G.: Improved infrared pedestrian detection algorithm based on YOLOv3. J. Heilongjiang Univ. Sci. Technol. 21–37 (2020)

Research on ECG Classification Method Based on Convolutional Neural Network

Jin Tao[1(✉)], Jianting Shi[2], and Rongqiang Wu[2]

[1] Graduate College, Heilongjiang University of Science and Technology, Harbin 150022, China
taojin@usth.edu.cn

[2] School of Computer and Information Engineering, Heilongjiang University of Science and Technology, Harbin 150022, China

Abstract. The electrocardiogram reflects the temporal changes in the body's cardiac potential; This is also an important technology for diagnosing cardiovascular disease, so the classification of electrocardiogram has gradually become the focus of many scholars. This paper designs an ECG classification algorithm based on convolutional neural network, which aims to automatically classify ECG using artificial intelligence algorithm. The algorithm has the characteristics of less parameters and more layers, and the classification speed is faster and has very strong real-time performance. The experimental results show that the accuracy of the algorithm reaches 98.1%, which has strong advantages in medical diagnosis and application.

Keywords: Convolutional neural network · Electrocardiogram · Classification · Convolution kernel scale

1 Introduction

An electrocardiogram (ECG) is a visualization of the electrophysiological activity of the human heart recorded by electrodes placed on the skin. The data of heart rate, S-T segment, P wave, QRS complex shape and appearance position exhibited by the electrocardiogram can be use to diagnose the arrhythmia such as sinus tachycardia, sinus arrhythmia, ventricular premature beats and atrial fibrillation. Medical specialists have accumulated a large number of rules for ECG diagnosis in long-term practice, but since the large number of rules and empirical knowledge accumulated in ECG analysis, it is quite time-consuming to learn ECG analysis skills. Currently, The number of professional ECG analysis doctors is insufficient to cope with massive ECG data, so the computer-aided diagnostic classification is needed to improve diagnostic efficiency [1]. Based on this demand, various ECG automatic classification algorithms based on medical experience knowledge are proposed. KTateno et al. proposed an analysis of atrial fibrillation based on the sequence of R peak intervals; SONG Li and MENG Qingjian extracted five time domain features, 32 wavelet domain features and 18 high-order statistic features based on wavelet transform and QRS heartbeat detection algorithm,

X. Jiang (Ed.): MLICOM 2021, LNICST 438, pp. 234–242, 2022.
https://doi.org/10.1007/978-3-031-04409-0_22

and used support vector machine to conduct classification. FA Elhaj, N Salim et al. used wavelet analysis and QRS complex group detection algorithm to extract linear and non-linear waveform features and then use support vector machine and neural network for classification [2]. However, such methods are extremely dependent on the accuracy of the extracted features. The existing waveform feature recognition algorithms perform well on the public dataset, but do not satisfactorily meet the requirements in terms of clinical data performance [3]. In recent years, some scholars have proposed automatic classification algorithms based on deep neural networks. For example, UR Acharya, H Fujita and others use convolutional neural networks to classify ECG signals on 2–5 s, which reduces the need for medical prior knowledge, but ECG signal processed by this method, since those time of data are too short and the data samples are small, resulting the classification effect is not very ideal [4].

2 Related Technology

2.1 Basic ECG Knowledge

Human heart activity is regular, such as the generation of electrical stimulation, the ECG signal occurs before the mechanical contraction of the heart, and can be transmitted to many parts of the body through the body tissue. If the human myocardium is stimulated, it will cause positive and negative ion movement inside and outside the membrane, so that different potential changes occur at different positions on the body surface, thereby forming an electrocardiogram of the human body. Therefore, the electrode information can be collected from the body surface, and the time, direction change of the information is Called electrocardiogram. When the data collecting electrodes are placed at different positions, different types of ECG signals are generated, and according to this division principle, 12 leads are divided. Usually, we have 6 limb leads, I, II, III, aVR, aVL, aVF; Six chest leads, V1–V6, usually, the ECG of the hospital examination also uses this 12-lead system. Electrocardiogram can reflect the related changes in human heart potential, so it has become an important technical means for doctors to diagnose cardiovascular disease. However, due to the complexity of the ECG data and the long analysis time, the traditional analysis method has low accuracy and long time; Therefore, in order to improve the accuracy of heart beat classification and shorten the analysis time, many scholars have proposed to introduce advanced pattern recognition, machine learning and other technologies, in order to use artificial intelligence technology to improve the analysis level for the heart beats, and provide strong support for medical diagnosis.

2.2 Convolutional Neural Networks

Convolutional neural network (CNN) is a deep feedforward artificial neural network that has been successfully applied to image recognition. CNN consists of two basic structures. The first is the feature extraction layer. The input of each neuron is locally connected with the previous layer. The local features of this part can be extracted. Once the local features are extracted, it is possible to determine the positional relationship between these features and other features; The second is the feature mapping layer. Each computing layer of the network can be composed of multiple feature maps. Each feature map can be described as a plane, and all the neurons on the plane have the same weight [5]. The mapping structure feature of CNN is to use the Sigmoid function as the activation function of the convolution network, in this way, the displacement of the feature maps can be made invariant, and the neurons on the same plane can share the weights; thus, the setting of the free parameters can be greatly reduced. Each convolutional layer of the convolutional neural network can be followed by a computational layer for local averaging and quadratic extraction, which can greatly reduce the feature resolution [6]. The CNN model has been known for many years and has not received enough attention in the years since it was reported; until recently, people intend to use the trained CNN model to achieve image classification, which can accurately distinguish each local feature. This result makes CNN technology widely accepted and applied in the fields of image classification, face recognition, and target detection. CNN's weight has common characteristics, which is convenient for high-dimensional data processing by reducing the number of training of free parameters. These characteristics are in line with the requirements of remote sensing images, and its classification calculation can obtain higher accuracy. The CNN structure is shown in Fig. 1.

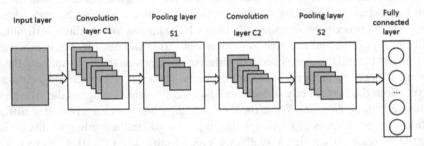

Fig. 1. CNN structure.

The main role of the input layer is to preprocess the original image data.

The convolution layer generally contains two operations. The first is to perform local associations, treating each neuron as a filter; the second is to perform window sliding, and the filter calculates local data. The key role of the convolutional layer is to acquire the local features of the image. Each convolutional layer can be used as a feature extraction layer, and the convolution accuracy can be improved by reducing the number of parameters set [7].

The main role of the pooling layer is to compress the amount of data and parameters and reduce overfitting. In other words, the pooling layer is used to compress images [8]. Based on the image features extracted by the convolutional layer, the pooling layer can calculate the average value of a local convolution feature, and can also calculate the maximum or minimum value; by reducing the dimension of the convolution layer feature, the classification can be continuously reduced. The computational complexity of the device reduces the burden on the classifier and also avoids over-fitting of the classifier.

The fully connected layer can output the classification result and function as a classifier, which can output the trained operation model so that the features of the image can be extracted.

3 Algorithm Design of Lead ECG Heart Beat Classification Based on Convolutional Neural Network

3.1 Algorithm Description

The electrocardiogram classification uses a convolutional neural network algorithm to include three key steps. First, it is necessary to obtain all the data images of the electrocardiogram, perform effective pre-processing operations on the data, and then perform electrocardiographic filtering and denoising operations to normalize the electrocardiogram so as to ensure that the results of the classification operation of the electrocardiogram are as Accurate and reliable. Secondly, the preprocessed data is input to the convolutional neural network, and the data features can be acquired through a series of convolution operations and pooling operations. Finally, the operation results of the convolutional neural network are output to form a classification result.

The convolutional neural network proposed in this paper consists of eight layers, five convolutional layers, two Pooling layers and one full connected layer. The setting parameters of the convolutional layer include the convolution kernel and the moving step size. For example, the convolutional layer C uses a convolution kernel of 7 * 1, the moving step size is set to 2, and the output result is 32X 18 * 1 feature vectors. The setting parameters for the pooling layer include the pooling kernel and the moving step size. For example, the pooling kernel used by the pooling layer B is 3 * 1, the moving step size is set to 2, and the output result is 32X 6 * 1 feature vectors. The fully connected layer uses the softmax classifier to output classification results. Detailed parameter settings are shown in Table 1. The convolutional neural network proposed in this paper consists of eight layers, five convolutional layers, two Pooling layers and one full connected layer. The setting parameters of the convolutional layer include the convolution kernel and the moving step size. For example, the convolutional layer C uses a convolution kernel of 7 * 1, the moving step size is set to 2, and the output result is 32X 18 * 1 feature vectors. The setting parameters for the pooling layer include the pooling kernel and the moving step size. For example, the pooling kernel used by the pooling layer B is 3 * 1, the moving step size is set to 2, and the output result is 32X 6 * 1 feature vectors. The fully connected layer uses the softmax classifier to output classification results. Detailed parameter settings are shown in Table 1.

3.2 Algorithm Design

The algorithm implementation proposed in this paper includes two key links. The first is the stage of training and learning for convolutional neural networks. The second is to test and verify the trained convolutional neural network. The specific description of each stage is as follows.

Table 1. Convolutional neural network structure

Name	Type	Number of convolution kernels	Step size	Feature vector	Output feature vector
1	Convolution layer	11 * 1	2	32	93 * 1
2	Convolution layer	9 * 1	2	32	85 * 1
3	Pooling layer	3 * 1	2	32	42 * 1
4	Convolution layer	7 * 1	2	32	18 * 1
5	Convolution layer	5 * 1	2	32	18 * 1
6	Pooling layer	3 * 1	2	32	6 * 1
7	Convolution layer	6 * 1	2	32	1 * 1
8	Fully connected layer			2048	11 * 11 * 256

(1) Training and learning stage.

The first step is forward calculation, and the selected training sample data D can be input into the network. The data is calculated by the convolution layer A, the convolution layer B, the pooling layer C, the convolution layer C, the convolution layer D, the pooling layer D, the convolution layer E, and the fully connected layer, and extract the ECG data characteristics of all intermediate layers.

The activation function of the convolutional layer is as described in formulas (1) and (2).

$$x_j^l = f\left(u_j^l\right) \tag{1}$$

$$u_j^l = \sum_{i \in M} x_j^{l-1} * k_{ij}^l + b_j^l \tag{2}$$

Among them, u_j^l is called the net activation of the jth channel of the convolution layer l, it is obtained by convolution summation and offsetting the previous layer output feature map x_j^{l-1}, x_j^l is the output of the jth channel of convolution layer l. $f(\bullet)$ is called an activation function, and functions such as sigmoid and tanh can usually be used. M_j represents the input feature map subset used to calculate u_j^l, k_{ij}^l is the convolution kernel matrix, and b_j^l is the offset to the convolved feature map. For an output feature map x_j^l, The convolution k_{ij}^l core corresponding to each input feature map x_j^{l-1} may be different. "*" is a convolution symbol.

The pooling layer function is described in formulas (3) and (4).

$$x_j^l = f\left(u_j^l\right) \tag{3}$$

$$u_j^l = \beta_j^l down\left(x_j^{l-1}\right) + b_j^l \tag{4}$$

Among them, u_j^l is called the net activation of the jth channel of the pooling layer 1, which is obtained by downsampling weighting and offsetting the previous layer output characteristic map x_j^{l-1}, β is the weighting factor of the pooling layer, b_j^l is the offset term of the pooling layer. Symbol down ($\bullet$) represents a downsampling function,It is divided into a plurality of non-overlapping $n \times n$ image blocks by sliding the window method on the input feature map x_j^{l-1}, The pixels within each image block are then summed, averaged, or maximized, and the output image is then reduced by n times in both dimensions.

The activation function of the fully connected layer classifier is as described in formulas (5) and (6).

$$x_j^l = f\left(u_j^l\right) \tag{5}$$

$$u^l = w^l x^{l-1} + b^l \tag{6}$$

Among them, u^l is called the net activation of the fully connected layer I, which is obtained by weighting and offsetting the previous layer output feature map x^{l-1}. w^l is the weighting factor of the fully connected network, b^l is the offset term of the fully connected layer I.

The second step is the back propagation of the error; The convolutional neural network calculation process is a step-by-step learning process. Therefore, the calculation process will produce errors, and the chain rule of back propagation can be adopted to calculate the gradient of each convolution layer.

The third step is to update the weight value of the convolutional neural network parameters, and use the gradient descent method to update the weight of the network. The calculation formula is as shown in (7).

$$w_l = w_l - \eta \partial J / \partial w_l \tag{7}$$

Among them, η is a balancing factor that controls the rate at which the gradient falls.

The fourth step is to loop through the first to third steps until the algorithm converges or reaches the set number of cycles. The conditions for experimental convergence in this paper are set as follows: Extract 100 running results and set the average accuracy. If the accuracy is greater than or equal to this, the algorithm converges and the operation ends.

(2) Test and verification stage.

After the convolutional neural network training and learning is completed, the actual data can be used for verification testing to see if the algorithm is accurate and reliable.

The first step is to load the trained and learned convolutional neural network model and remove the loss layer.

The second step is to perform classification, first input the test data into the convolutional neural network, then, perform the steps of the training learning stage; thus, a result of classifying the test data can be obtained, then, with the known clinical actual classification, to compare the analysis and calculate the accuracy of the algorithm.

4 Application Effect

In order to verify the effectiveness of the proposed algorithm, the experimental data in this paper uses the INCART data in the PhysioNet standard database. The data set includes 175,728 heart beats. The classification of heart beats adopts the international standard AAMI standard, which can divide the heart beat into F (Incorporating heart beat), N (normal heart beat), S (supraventricular ectopic beat), V (ventricular ectopic beat), Q (unclassified heart beat), totally five types, where F and Q are N, S, V Collection. The characteristic diagram of heart beat is shown in Fig. 2.

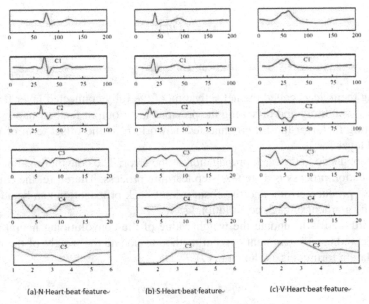

(a) N Heart beat feature   (b) S Heart beat feature   (c) V Heart beat feature

Fig. 2. Characteristic diagram of heart beat.

The specific data is shown in Table 2.

Table 2. Types and quantities of heartbeat data in the INCART database

Database name	Fusion heart beat	Normal heart beat	Ventricular ectopic beat	Supraventricular ectopic heart beat	Unclassified heart beat
INCART	219	153545	20000	1958	6

Because the number of fusion heart beats and unclassified heart beats in the database is very small, the heart beat data taken in the final experiment of this paper is normal heart beat, ventricular ectopic heart beat and supraventricular ectopic heart beat.

The experimental evaluation criteria are accuracy rate A, sensitivity S, and positive predictive value P. The accuracy formula A is calculated as the quotient of the correct classification number and the total number of samples. The sensitivity S is calculated as the average of the sensitivity of each category; The positive predictive values are the average of positive values for each category.

In order to be able to compare with the algorithm of this paper, this paper compares with the experimental results of support vector machine algorithm [9] and K-means algorithm [10] we found that each category data and average value of this paper are very high, detailed experimental results are shown in the Table 3.

Table 3. Comparative analysis of algorithm experiment results

Algorithm	N sensitivity	N positive predictive value	S sensitivity	S positive predictive value	V sensitivity	V positive predictive value	Overall sensitivity	Overall positive predictive value	Accuracy
K-means	95.4%	96.7%	76.2%	40.3%	79.6%	86.2%	83.4%	74.2%	89.5%
Support vector	98.1%	97.8%	87.3%	30.4%	89.6%	95.2%	88.7%	75.1%	92.3%
Our algorithm	99.3%	99.2%	76.8%	69.2%	95.4%	94.2%	91.4%	88.3%	98.1%

The experimental trend of support vector machine algorithm, K-means algorithm and the algorithm of this paper is shown in Fig. 3.

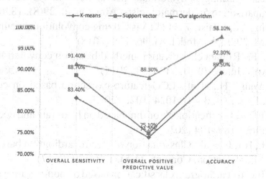

Fig. 3. Comparison of the experimental results of the algorithm.

5 Conclusion

Electrocardiogram classification is an important application field of artificial intelligence in the medical field, so it is very important to improve the accuracy of ECG classification. At present, the classification of team ECG has introduced some data algorithms: support vector machine, K-means algorithm, etc. However, due to the low accuracy of these algorithms, in this paper, we propose to introduce convolutional neural networks in ECG classification, which is more accurate than K-means algorithm and support vector machine; our principle conceivement is that the convolutional neural network uses a multi-level training model, including a 5-layer convolutional layer, which belongs to a deep convolutional neural network; and the scale of the convolution kernel is diversified, and it is better to obtain an accurate network structure through learning to improve the classification accuracy of the electrocardiogram; The experimental results show that the experimental accuracy of the algorithm reaches 98.1%. While, the convolutional neural network is the most advanced classification algorithm at present, which can utilize the structure of multi-level training and learning to greatly improve the classification accuracy of ECG.

Acknowledgements. This work has been partially supported by "The National Key Research and Development Program of China (2018 YFC0810500)" and "2020 scientific research project of basic scientific research expenses of provincial colleges and universities in Heilongjiang Province (2020-KYYWF-0680) ".

References

1. Zhou, F., Jin, L., Dong, J.: A review of convolutional neural networks. J. Comput. Sci. (6), 142–147 (2017)
2. Wang, W., Wang, L., Zhao, M., et al.: Image aesthetic classification based on parallel deep convolutional neural network. Acta Autom. Sin. **42**(6), 904–914 (2016)
3. Haenssle, H.A., Fink, C., Schneiderbauer, R., et al.: Man against machine: diagnostic performance of a deep learning convolutional neural network for dermoscopic melanoma recognition in comparison to 58 dermatologists. Ann. Oncol. **29**(8), 1836–1839 (2018)
4. Hochuli, J., Helbling, A., Skaist, T., et al.: Visualizing convolutional neural network protein-ligand scoring. J. Mol. Graph. Model. **84**, 96–108 (2018)
5. Zhang, Z., Yan, J.: FMRI data classification method based on convolutional neural network. Pattern Recogn. Artif. Intell. **30**(6), 549–558 (2017)
6. Yan, H., An, Y., Wang, H., et al.: ECG feature extraction based on convolutional neural network. Comput. Eng. Des. **38**(4), 1024–1028 (2017)
7. Li, H., Jin, L.: An ECG classification algorithm based on heart rate and deep learning. Aerosp. Med. Med. Eng. **29**(3), 189–194 (2016)
8. Zhou, W., Peng, H., Hu, J., et al.: Classification of electrocardiogram based on wavelet neural network method. Microelectron. Comput. **24**(5), 127–129 (2017)
9. Zhao, C., Ma, X.: Electrocardiogram classification based on non-negative matrix factorization and support vector machine. Comput. Eng. **38**(9), 174–176 (2012)
10. He, Y., Zhang, X., Wan, J., et al.: Classification of ECG waveforms based on improved genetically simulated annealing K-means. Comput. Appl. Res. (11), 3328–3332 (2014)

A Survey on Meta-learning Based Few-Shot Classification

Weizhi Huang[1] , Ming He[2](✉) , and Yongle Wang[2]

[1] School of Computer and Information Engineering, Heilongjiang University of Science and Technology, Harbin 150022, China
[2] College of Computer Science and Technology, Harbin Engineering University, Harbin 150001, China
heming@hrbeu.edu.cn

Abstract. Data-intensive applications have achieved great success in the field of machine learning. How to ensure that the machine can still learn correctly in the absence of labeled samples is the next challenging problem to be solved. This paper first introduces the problem definition of few-shot learning. Secondly, the existing small few-shot learning methods based on meta-learning are comprehensively summarized. Specifically, they are divided into three categories: metric-based learning methods, optimization-based learning methods and model-based learning methods. We conducted a series of comparisons among various methods in each category to show the advantages and disadvantages of each method. Finally, the limitations of existing methods are analyzed, and the future development direction of few-shot learning research is prospected.

Keywords: Few-shot learning · Deep learning · Meta-learning

1 Introduction

Inspired by the human process of learning new things, we hope that machines can also learn new knowledge from a few samples. In recent years, few-shot learning has attracted more and more attention. At the same time, meta-learning methods [23] are also developing rapidly. The purpose of meta-learning is to let the machine learn to learn. In practice, it is found that the meta-learning method fits well with the few-shot learning problem. The main purpose of this paper is to conduct a comprehensive study of meta-learning methods based on solving few-shot problems, focusing on the analysis of typical strategies. In this paper, the existing few-shot learning methods are divided into three categories, namely, metric-based learning methods, optimization-based learning methods and model-based learning methods. The latest research on these three categories will be discussed separately. It must be noted that there is no clear boundaries between these three categories. This paper will analyze various methods of each category in detail.

© ICST Institute for Computer Sciences, Social Informatics and Telecommunications Engineering 2022
Published by Springer Nature Switzerland AG 2022. All Rights Reserved
X. Jiang (Ed.): MLICOM 2021, LNICST 438, pp. 243–253, 2022.
https://doi.org/10.1007/978-3-031-04409-0_23

The rest of the article is structured as follows. Section 2 is an overview of few-shot learning, including definition, problem description and common data sets. Section 3 introduces the past learning problems related to few-shot learning and makes comparisons to clarify the application scenarios of small sample learning. Section 4 introduces metric-based learning methods for few-shot learning. Section 5 introduces the few-shot learning methods based on optimal learning strategies. Section 6 introduces the few-shot learning approach based on optimal model architecture. Finally, Sect. 7 makes a conclusion about the limitations of existing methods and future research.

2 Overview

2.1 Definition and Problem Description

Few-shot learning is a kind of machine learning problem that how to learn the model in the case of insufficient effective samples. The dataset contains three categories: Training set, Support set, and Query set. There are large-scale labeled data in the training set, containing numerous different classes, and many samples in each class, which is used to train the model. The support set usually contains N classes. Generally, there are no classes intersection between the support set and the training set. Each class of the support set has K samples. According to the size of the support set, we call the few-shot learning problem based on the support set as the N-way K-shot problem. The query set is used for the final model test. The goal of few-shot learning is to use the model trained by the training set to identify the labels of the samples in the query set. The class of the query set is not included in the training set but included in the support set, that is, the class of the query set is new for the model.

2.2 Major Application

Most of the existing few-shot learning is applied in the field of computer vision, such as handwritten character recognition [17] and image classification [15], because it's easy to obtain the visual information. And this method has been well-tested on previous machine learning problems. At present, there are two benchmark datasets miniImageNet [29] and Omniglot [16] in image classification and character recognition, and they have achieved high accuracy on two datasets. Therefore, more computer vision applications can be explored, such as image segmentation, neural style transfer, image reconstruction and image generation. In addition to computer vision applications, other fields have been gradually using the idea of few-shot learning such as few-shot translation and few-shot language modeling in natural language processing.

3   Relevant Learning Problems

In the field of machine learning, there are many cross-domain learning problems with few-shot learning, including Weakly Supervised Learning [31], Transfer Learning [20] and Multitask Learning [3]. This section will clarify the relevance and differences between these problems and few-shot learning, so as to determining its applicable scenarios.

Weakly supervised learning: including Semi-supervised learning [32] and Active learning [25]. Semi-supervised learning refers to learning optimal assumptions in mixed data with and without labels. Active learning refers to reducing the cost of labeling by some technical means or mathematical methods. Few-shot learning is different from this, it can be supervised learning, semi-supervised learning and reinforcement learning, which depends on what data are available in addition to limited supervised information.

Transfer Learning: Use the experience of the source task to improve the learning of the target task. The knowledge learned from the source domain and source task of a large amount of training data is transferred to the target domain and target task with limited training data. The inner thinking is based on human inferences, whiles improve the utilization of data. Transfer learning method is widely used in few-shot learning. When the given supervision information is limited to direct learning, few-shot learning needs to transfer prior knowledge from the source task to the current few-shot learning task.

Multi-task Learning: Multi-task learning is a derivation transfer learning method. The main task uses the domain-specific information possessed by the training signal of the related task as an inductive bias to improve the generalization effect of the main task. Multi-task learning involves parallel learning of multiple related tasks at the same time, the gradient is backpropagated at the same time, and multiple tasks help each other learn through the underlying shared representation to improve the generalization effect. To put it simply, multi-task learning puts multiple related tasks together to learn. In the learning process, a shallow shared representation is used to share and complement each other with information related to the learned field, promote each other's learning, and enhance generalization effect.

4   Metric-Based Learning Approach

In the metric-based learning method, we often use the metric criteria we designed to judge the distance of the sample in the feature space. Such learning methods generally include a feature encoder E and a metric function M. The feature encoder E is used to extract the input feature and convert it into a feature vector on the new feature space. The distance between the vectors is judged by the metric function M. Commonly used measurement criteria are Euclidean Distance, Minkowski Distance, Cosine Similarity and so on. In the problem of few-shot learning, the model trained on the training set by this method has the ability to judge the similarity between samples.

4.1   Fixed Distance Metric

Vinyals et al. used the model architecture of Matching Networks [29] to deal with the problem of few-shot learning. It is mainly embedding [12] the support set and the query set, and then uses the query set sample to calculate the attention of each support set sample, and the label of each category is linearly weighted according to the attention score to determine the category of the sample. Snell et al. also proposed a Prototypical Networks [26] model similar to Matching Networks, whose main idea is to take the average obtained by embedding the samples of each category as the characterization of the category, and determine its category by the distance between the query sample and the average characteristics of each category in the feature space.

Siamese Network [14] is a two-way neural network. Koch et al. used Siamese Network to solve few-shot image classification. The core idea of the method is to use the training set to train a neural network, so that the neural network has the ability to identify whether the characteristics of two samples are similar, and to classify the test samples in this way. There are two main methods for constructing training samples. One is by constructing positive and negative samples, sampling two pictures at a time, and if the same type is set as a positive sample, otherwise it is a negative sample. Use positive and negative samples to train a neural network to measure the similarity between two pictures. The second method is the idea of using Triplet Loss [24] proposed by Schroff et al., which is to construct triples. With the anchor as the center, the same kind is denoted as positive, and different types are denoted as negative. Use the metric function to calculate the distance between the anchor and the positive and negative in the feature space, denoted as d^+ and d^-. The model should make d^+ as small as possible, and d^- as large as possible, and d^- must be much larger than d^+, otherwise the model cannot distinguish between the two categories.

Similar to Siamese Network, Relation Network [27] first uses an embedding module to map the supported images and query images into feature vectors. But unlike Siamese Network, Relation Network does not directly calculate their distance after obtaining these vectors, but first connects their feature maps, and then passes through a relation module e to get their relation score, and finally according to This relationship score is classified.

In the case of a small number of samples, the models trained by conventional neural networks often have limited accuracy, and the pre-training method can solve this problem well. Pre-training refers to training a neural network on other large-scale labeled similar data sets to obtain a set of model parameters, initialize the model with the learned model parameters, and then perform fine-tune on the model in a small-sample task. The training method has been proven to have good results in few-shot learning.

Chen et al. first proposed the concept of Classifier-Baseline [4], which is to pre-train a classifier on the base class to learn visual representations, then delete the last fully connected layer that depends on the class, and use the cosine distance in the feature space, Use the nearest centroid to classify the query sample. This process can also be seen as estimating the weight of the fully connected layer of the new class, but there is no need to train parameters for the new class. The article verifies that the Classifier-Baseline method is superior to many more advanced algorithms. Then the author proposed to use meta-learning to improve Classifier-Baseline, and proposed Meta-Baseline [4]. In Meta-Baseline, use the pre-trained Classifier-Baseline to initialize the model, and use the cosine similarity measure to perform meta-learning, that is, use the support set to fine-tunning the initialized model. The model is shown in Fig. 1.

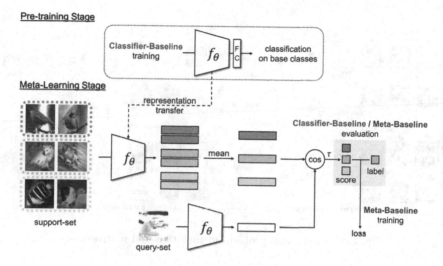

Fig. 1. Classifier-baseline & meta-baseline.

Dhillon et al. made improvements in the fine-tune stage of the pre-training method, and mainly proposed transductive fine-tuning [5], which is to fine-tune the deep network trained with standard cross-entropy loss. The performance of this method in the standard data set is better than the latest technology with the same hyperparameters.

Table 1 summarizes the performance of the metric-based approach on mini-Imagenet.

Table 1. Few-shot classification results trained with the mini-ImageNet dataset.

Model	Backbone	5-way 1-shot	5-way 5-shot
Matching networks	ConvNet-4	46.60 ± 0.84%	60.00 ± 0.73%
Prototypical networks	ConvNet-4	49.42 ± 0.78%	68.20± 0.66%
Relation networks	ConvNet-4	50.44 ± 0.82%	65.32 ± 0.70%
Classifier-baseline	ResNet-12	58.91 ± 0.23%	77.76 ± 0.17%
Meta-baseline	ResNet-12	63.17 ± 0.23%	79.26 ± 0.17%

4.2   Metric-Based Cross-domain Learning

From the perspective of the generalization performance of small-sample classification, many existing metric-based methods have problems. That is, there are significant differences in the distribution of image features extracted from tasks in different domains. Therefore, as shown in Fig. 2, in the training phase, the metric function may overfit the feature distribution encoded only from the known domain, resulting in the inability to generalize to other domains.

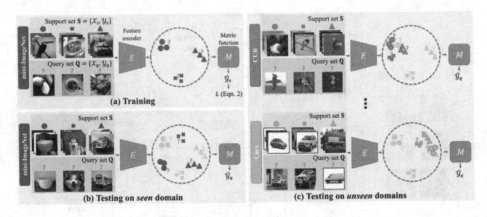

Fig. 2. Cross-domain problem formulation and motivation.

To solve the cross-domain problem, Tseng et al. proposed Feature-wise Transformation Layer [28], which was inserted after the BN layer [10] of Feature Encoder. The core idea is to use a feature-based transformation layer to enhance image features through affine transformation in the training phase to simulate various feature distributions in different domains, thereby improving the generalization ability of the measurement function in the test phase. In addition, there are two hyper-parameters in Feature-wise Transformation Layer that require careful manual adjustment, because it is difficult to model complex changes in image feature distribution in different fields. Based on this, the article developed a learning-to-learn algorithm to optimize the proposed feature conversion layer, that is, let the model learn hyperparameters by itself.

5   Optimization-Based Learning Approach

In traditional learning methods, many of the entire training steps need to be designed by humans, including the network architecture, the initialization parameters, and the way to update the parameters, etc. When we choose a different design, we get a different learning method. When the training steps are adjusted artificially, it is difficult to achieve the desired efficiency and accuracy. The optimization-based learning method considers whether the machine can learn to part of the training steps by itself.

5.1   Parameter Optimization Method

Finn et al. proposed the model-independent meta-learning method MAML [7], which pioneered optimization-based methods. MAML optimizes by letting the machine learn the initialization parameters itself, and the method expects the learned initialization parameters to achieve optimal results with a few updates. MAML can be applied not only to few-shot classification problems, but also to reinforcement learning and regression problems with better results. Nichol et al. proposed Reptile [19] with some improvements on MAML, firstly, by simplifying the parameter update operation and ignoring the second-order differentiation operation to improve the speed of the operation while maintaining its performance. Secondly, the rules of parameter update are relaxed and the constraints of parameter update are reduced.

In addition, Ravi et al. summarize the reasons why deep learning-based optimization algorithms are not applicable in less sample learning. Ones are that gradient-based optimization algorithms such as Adam [13], AdaDelta [30], and Adagrad [6] are not suitable for few-sample situations with a limit on the number of parameter updates. Secondly, for multiple separated tasks, random initialization parameters will affect the task's ability to complete optimization after a few updates. The article found a great similarity between the LSTM [9] internal update and the gradient descent process, based on which the LSTM-based gradient descent method [21] was proposed to allow the network to learn the LSTM network parameters as well as the initialization parameters by itself, enabling it to learn different tasks quickly. Unlike Ravi et al. Andrychowicz et al. proposed that most of the standard optimization procedures consider only first-order differentiation without considering second-order differentiation, which obviously results in a loss of performance. To solve such problems, an LSTM-based optimizer [1] was designed to overcome the drawback of considering only first-order derivatives by using the memory function possessed by recurrent neural networks.

Table 2 shows the performance of the parameter optimization method on mini-Imagenet

Table 2. Results of the parameter optimization method on mini-ImageNet.

Model	Backbone	5-way 1-shot	5-way 5-shot
Meta-learn LSTM	ConvNet-4	$43.44 \pm 0.77\%$	$60.60 \pm 0.71\%$
MAML	ConvNet-4	$48.70 \pm 1.84\%$	$63.11 \pm 0.92\%$
Reptile	ConvNet-4	$49.97 \pm 0.32\%$	$65.99 \pm 0.58\%$

5.2   Cross-task Learning Approach Based on Parameter Optimization

Although meta-learning has achieved good results on many deep learning problems, including image classification and augmentation learning tasks, classical meta-learning approaches ignore an important issue of learning the optimal initial model on multiple tasks, i.e., how to ensure that the initial model obtained from learning is unbiased for all tasks.

Jamal et al. proposed a task-agnostic meta-learning method TAML [11] (Task Agnostic Meta-Learning), which enables the initial model to be treated equally for different tasks by adding a regularization term to it. The article designs two types of regularization, TAML based on entropy reduction maximization and TAML based on inequality minimization, to meta-train the initial model so that the model is less different when facing different tasks.

6   Model-Based Learning Approach

The model-based learning approach aims at finding the optimal architecture, where the model can update parameters quickly mainly thanks to the internal structure of the model or controlled by other meta-learning models. The major difference between this approach and the metric-based approach is that it does not make assumptions about the form of conditional probabilities, but relies on a model that can learn quickly.

In few-shot learning, where the goal of learning is to combine information learned in the past and learn new knowledge quickly, it is not surprising to use models with memory functions. Santoro et al. proposed a MANN [22] (Memory-Augmented Neural Networks) model based on a neural Turing machine [8] (Fig. 3). Although recurrent neural networks such as LSTM also have memory functions, they are mostly internal, whereas MANN uses memory to assist memory. MANN modifies the internal retrieval mechanism as well as the training settings and proposes a new addressing mechanism for assigning attention weights to memory vectors. The model has two major advantages of storing stable information and the size of the storage space is not limited by the size of the model parameters.

Furthermore, Munkhdalai et al. proposed the Meta-Networks [18] model, which consists of two main learners, namely the base learner and the meta-learner, in addition to also being equipped with external memory. The base learner is used to generate parameters Slow Weights based on common optimization methods (e.g., SGD), and the meta-learner is used to generate parameters Fast Weights for another neural network, which are mainly used for cross-task generalization. The combination of Slow Weights and Fast Weights is used throughout the neural network for prediction.

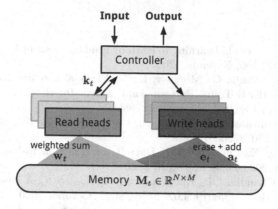

Fig. 3. Neural turing machine.

7 Conclusion

In this paper, we summarize and analyze the classical methods of few-shot learning from different perspectives by comparing the latest research. The metric-based learning method is limited because it is prone to overfitting when the number of samples is too small, and the method is relatively picky about the dataset, which can appear to perform well on some tasks but poorly on others. And this method has low robustness. Optimization-based learning methods or parametric methods usually require multiple update steps to reach a better point when updating weights using gradient descent because of the limitations in optimizer selection and learning rate settings. It makes the learning process so slowly when the model process on a new task. Model-based approaches are very good at handling learning with few samples. But they are usually poor at generalization because it is ambiguous whether the model can successfully embed a large training set into a base model.

Research on few-shot learning with deep learning has grown rapidly over the past few years, and as a result, applying few-shot learning models to practical applications will receive more attention. In this case, how to ensure the accuracy and computation efficiency of the model at the same time is one of the most challenging problems. Existing few-shot learning methods usually use previous knowledge from a single modality, while prior knowledge from multiple modalities [2] can provide prior knowledge for complementary views, but different modalities may contain different structures and need to be handled carefully. The use of multi-modal information in the design of few-shot learning methods is a direction for future research.

References

1. Andrychowicz, M., et al.: Learning to learn by gradient descent by gradient descent. arXiv:1606.04474 [cs], November 2016
2. Baltrušaitis, T., Ahuja, C., Morency, L.: Multimodal machine learning: a survey and taxonomy. IEEE Trans. Pattern Anal. Mach. Intell. **41**(2), 423–443 (2019). https://doi.org/10.1109/TPAMI.2018.2798607
3. Caruana, R.: Multitask Learning. Mach. Learn. **28**(1), 41–75 (1997). https://doi.org/10.1023/A:1007379606734
4. Chen, Y., Wang, X., Liu, Z., Xu, H., Darrell, T.: A new meta-baseline for few-shot learning. arXiv:2003.04390 [cs], April 2020
5. Dhillon, G.S., Chaudhari, P., Ravichandran, A., Soatto, S.: A baseline for few-shot image classification. arXiv:1909.02729 [cs, stat], October 2020
6. Duchi, J., Hazan, E., Singer, Y.: Adaptive subgradient methods for online learning and stochastic optimization. J. Mach. Learn. Res. **12**, 2121–2159 (2011)
7. Finn, C., Abbeel, P., Levine, S.: Model-agnostic meta-learning for fast adaptation of deep networks. In: International Conference on Machine Learning, pp. 1126–1135. PMLR, July 2017
8. Graves, A., Wayne, G., Danihelka, I.: Neural turing machines. arXiv:1410.5401 [cs], December 2014
9. Hochreiter, S., Schmidhuber, J.: Long short-term memory. Neural Comput. **9**(8), 1735–1780 (1997). https://doi.org/10.1162/neco.1997.9.8.1735
10. Ioffe, S., Szegedy, C.: Batch normalization: accelerating deep network training by reducing internal covariate shift. In: International Conference on Machine Learning, pp. 448–456. PMLR, June 2015
11. Jamal, M.A., Qi, G.J.: Task agnostic meta-learning for few-shot learning. In: Proceedings of the IEEE/CVF Conference on Computer Vision and Pattern Recognition, pp. 11719–11727 (2019)
12. Jia, Y., et al.: Caffe: convolutional architecture for fast feature embedding. In: Proceedings of the 22nd ACM International Conference on Multimedia, MM 2014, pp. 675–678. Association for Computing Machinery, New York, November 2014. https://doi.org/10.1145/2647868.2654889
13. Kingma, D.P., Ba, J.: Adam: a method for stochastic optimization. arXiv:1412.6980 [cs], January 2017
14. Koch, G.: Siamese neural networks for one-shot image recognition, p. 30
15. Krizhevsky, A., Sutskever, I., Hinton, G.E.: ImageNet classification with deep convolutional neural networks. Commun. ACM **60**(6), 84–90 (2017). https://doi.org/10.1145/3065386
16. Lake, B.M., Salakhutdinov, R., Gross, J., Tenenbaum, J.B.: One shot learning of simple visual concepts, p. 7
17. Lake, B.M., Salakhutdinov, R., Tenenbaum, J.B.: Human-level concept learning through probabilistic program induction. Science **350**(6266), 1332–1338 (2015). https://doi.org/10.1126/science.aab3050
18. Munkhdalai, T., Yu, H.: Meta networks. In: International Conference on Machine Learning, pp. 2554–2563. PMLR, July 2017
19. Nichol, A., Achiam, J., Schulman, J.: On first-order meta-learning algorithms. arXiv:1803.02999 [cs], October 2018
20. Pan, S.J., Yang, Q.: A survey on transfer learning. IEEE Trans. Knowl. Data Eng. **22**(10), 1345–1359 (2010). https://doi.org/10.1109/TKDE.2009.191
21. Ravi, S., Larochelle, H.: Optimization as a model for few-shot learning, p. 11 (2017)

22. Santoro, A., Bartunov, S., Botvinick, M., Wierstra, D., Lillicrap, T.: Meta-learning with memory-augmented neural networks. In: International Conference on Machine Learning, pp. 1842–1850. PMLR, June 2016
23. Schaul, T., Schmidhuber, J.: Metalearning. Scholarpedia 5(6), 4650 (2010). https://doi.org/10.4249/scholarpedia.4650
24. Schroff, F., Kalenichenko, D., Philbin, J.: FaceNet: a unified embedding for face recognition and clustering. In: Proceedings of the IEEE Conference on Computer Vision and Pattern Recognition, pp. 815–823 (2015)
25. Settles, B.: Active learning. In: Synthesis Lectures on Artificial Intelligence and Machine Learning, vol. 6, no. 1, pp. 1–114, June 2012. https://doi.org/10.2200/S00429ED1V01Y201207AIM018
26. Snell, J., Swersky, K., Zemel, R.S.: Prototypical networks for few-shot learning. arXiv:1703.05175 [cs, stat], June 2017
27. Sung, F., Yang, Y., Zhang, L., Xiang, T., Torr, P.H.S., Hospedales, T.M.: Learning to compare: relation network for few-shot learning. In: Proceedings of the IEEE Conference on Computer Vision and Pattern Recognition, pp. 1199–1208 (2018)
28. Tseng, H.Y., Lee, H.Y., Huang, J.B., Yang, M.H.: Cross-domain few-shot classification via learned feature-wise transformation. arXiv:2001.08735 [cs], March 2020
29. Vinyals, O., Blundell, C., Lillicrap, T., Kavukcuoglu, K., Wierstra, D.: Matching networks for one shot learning. In: Advances in Neural Information Processing Systems, vol. 29, pp. 3630–3638 (2016)
30. Zeiler, M.D.: ADADELTA: an adaptive learning rate method. arXiv:1212.5701 [cs], December 2012
31. Zhou, Z.H.: A brief introduction to weakly supervised learning. Natl. Sci. Rev. 5(1), 44–53 (2018). https://doi.org/10.1093/nsr/nwx106
32. Zhu, X., Goldberg, A.B.: Introduction to semi-supervised learning. In: Synthesis Lectures on Artificial Intelligence and Machine Learning, vol. 3, no. 1, pp. 1–130, January 2009. https://doi.org/10.2200/S00196ED1V01Y200906AIM006

Image Retrieval Algorithm Based on Fractal Coding

Hui Guo⬥, Jie He⁽⊠⁾ ⬥, Caixu Xu⬥, and Dongling Li⬥

Guangxi Key Laboratory of Machine Vision and Intelligent Control, Wuzhou University, Wuzhou, China
64875130@qq.com

Abstract. A traditional fractal image retrieval system needs to code all the images before the retrieval, and thus real-time retrieval cannot be realized. Focusing on this problem, this study puts forward an image retrieval algorithm based on image entropy and fractal blocks. In the algorithm, images are screened at first according to comparison of image entropies. Therefore, the screened images in an image library are similar to a query image to some extent. In this way, the number of images requiring to be matched with the query image in the image library can be reduced. In the meanwhile, the time for image retrieval can be greatly shortened. Then, the retrieval function is realized based on the characteristic computation structure similarity of fractal blocks of images. As shown by the experimental results, the algorithm does not need to extract fractal code documents at first when images are put into the library. Thus, defects in offline retrieval of the traditional fractal image retrieval can be overcome. In addition, a precision ratio and a recall ratio of checking results can be ensured.

Keywords: Image retrieval · Fractal coding · Image entropy · Online retrieval

1 Introduction

Image retrieval has always drawn the joint attention from numerous researchers. In the field of Content Based Image Retrieval (CBIR), people have tried a semantic-based retrieval model and proposed a retrieval model based on image feature sets (e.g. color and layout of images). However, complicated contents of a whole image could not be completely described by the above image features. With the occurrence of the fractal theory and its application in the image retrieval field, solutions have been proposed for solving the above problems. In this technology, a fractal encoding algorithm is used for extracting fractal features of images, namely image fractal codes. Fractal codes are employed for describing trans-scale similarity redundancy information in an image and can uniquely denote the original image. Therefore, by recording image features by fractal codes and applying them to similarity judgment and retrieval of images, the recall ratio and accuracy of image retrieval technology can be increased effectively.

In the end of 1990s, A.D. Sloan [1] took the initiative to apply the fractal technology in image retrieval, since various fractal-based image retrieval algorithms have come up

© ICST Institute for Computer Sciences, Social Informatics and Telecommunications Engineering 2022
Published by Springer Nature Switzerland AG 2022. All Rights Reserved
X. Jiang (Ed.): MLICOM 2021, LNICST 438, pp. 254–269, 2022.
https://doi.org/10.1007/978-3-031-04409-0_24

with one after another. However, the complicated course of fractal image encoding led to excessive time spent on encoding and the failure to realize the rapid retrieval in image retrieval. Therefore, a lot of method have been proposed to increase the encoding speed. Literature [2] proposed a wavelet-fractal based image encoding algorithm and made full use of correlations of sub-bands to improve the quality of reconstructed images, turning global search to neighbor search and thus reducing the encoding time. As proposed in Literature [3], a quad tree partition method was applied iteratively during encoding and a median filter was used after encoding to removal noise in images, aiming to increase encoding efficiency. Literature [4] proposed a method for presenting image blocks by orthogonal sparse encoding and texture feature extraction, by which image reconstruction quality is better and encoding becomes quicker. Till the present, a lot of methods have been proposed for increasing retrieval efficiency. In Literature [5], an improved Hu invariant moment characteristic quantity was extracted from fractal codes as the retrieval index, which can thus obtain good retrieval effects. Literature [6] proposed a fractal image retrieval algorithm based on adjacent matching and proposed a new distance formula capable of quickly judging similar blocks between images, which manage to shorten the encoding time and enhance the accuracy of image similarity judgment. Literature [7] came up with an improved rapid fractal image retrieval algorithm based on HV partition to accelerate encoding. In order to increase the accuracy of image retrieval, a new weighting parameter based on partitioning block sizes was proposed, which could significantly improve the precision ratio of algorithm.

By the above-mentioned methods, the encoding time is reduced through various improvements during fractal encoding, for the purpose of speeding up the retrieval. However, these methods need to conduct fractal encoding of a to-be-retrieved image and images in an image library at first before image retrieval, while fractal codes are adopted for retrieval after obtaining their encoding files. As a result, online real-time retrieval cannot be realized. Aiming at above problems, the paper proposes a rapid image retrieval algorithm based on image entropies and fractal blocks. At first, an image 2D entropy is used to screen an image library so as to decrease the retrieval scope. Then, the to-be-retrieved image is rapidly matched with fractal block parameters of the images in the library. The method does not request pre-encoding of the image, and directly takes the image fractal block, namely R block, as the basis to judge the similarity between images. Therefore, an online real-time retrieval function based on fractal encoding is realized.

2 Basic Fractal Coding Algorithm

At the very beginning, fractal image coding was proposed by Barnsley [8] and Jacquin [9], and then developed. Fractal image compression essentially indicates that real images have high affine redundancy, namely, the images contain a lot of self-reference substances and a lot of parts are self-similar. Besides, each area of the image can be used to express each other through proper conversion. Theoretically, fractal coding means that fractal codes are constructed by self-similarity of images, and image features are extracted by fractal codes. In terms of extraction of fractal codes, the images need to be segmented at first. The image I is divided into n non-intersected sub-blocks Ri (i $= 1, 2 \ldots$n). The set

R_i constitutes an R pol, and the union set of R_i is the image to be coded. According to the specific algorithm rules, the image I is further divided into D_i (i = 1, 2...n) blocks which constitute the D pool. Based on the overall and local similarity of the image, the D_i similar to Ri is searched. The through affine transformation, contrast control and brightness control, a mapping relation ωi, is established, of which the general form is expressed as follows:

$$\omega_i : D_i \to R_i, \mathrm{i} \neq \mathrm{j}, I, j = 1, 2 \ldots, n \tag{1}$$

$$\omega_i(D_i) = \lambda_i(\gamma_i D_i) = s_i t_k(\gamma_i D_i) + o_i \tag{2}$$

where Mapping γi translates D_i to R_i and shrinks to a size consistent with R_i. t_k is an equidistant affine transformation parameter, which can be used for pixel re-arrangement and thus strengthen matching quality. s_i and o_i respectively stand for adjustment of brightness and contrast ratio. In order to find the D block best matched with the R block in the D pool (codebook), it is of necessity to calculate the fractal parameters s_i and o_i. Therefore, according to the collage theory, it is necessary to minimize the following errors:

$$\min \|R_i - (s \cdot D_i + o \cdot 1)\|^2 \tag{3}$$

The first-order partial derivatives of s and o in Eq. (3) are calculated based on differential geometry. The obtained equations are respectively equal to 0, and thus the linear system of equations of parameters s and o can be obtained. Then, s and o can be obtained through solution of the equation system, namely:

$$\begin{cases} s = \frac{\langle R - \overline{R} \cdot 1, D - \overline{D} \cdot 1 \rangle}{\|D - \overline{D} \cdot 1\|^2} \\ o = \overline{R} - s \cdot \overline{D} \end{cases} \tag{4}$$

The s and o of each D block in the codebook, corresponding to the R block, are quantified by a consistent quantification device. The error $E(R, D)$ is calculated:

$$E(R_i, D) = \|R - (s \cdot D + o \cdot 1)\|^2 \tag{5}$$

Equation (4) is substituted into Eq. (5), and thus the following results are obtained in the end:

$$E(R_i, D) = \|R - \overline{R} \cdot 1\|^2 - s^2 \|D - \overline{D} \cdot 1\|^2 \tag{6}$$

D_i is treated by 8 types of isometric transformation and t_k satisfying Eq. (6) is calculated:

$$E(R_i, t_k(D_{M(i)})) = \min_{0 \leq k \leq 7} E(R_i, t_k(D_{M(i)})) \tag{7}$$

At this moment, the optimum similar approach of a R_i can be obtained:

$$R_i = s_i \cdot t_k(D_{M(i)}) + o_i \cdot 1 \tag{8}$$

After following the above steps, the fractal coding parameters of the current R_i block can be obtained, including the quantified brightness control parameter s_i, the contrast control parameter o_i, the subscript M(i) of De block best matching the R_i block as well as the sequence number t_k of isometric transformation. The above steps are repeated for the rest R blocks till all the R blocks obtain fractal coding parameters of their iterative functions.

It can be found from the above introduction to the fractal coding algorithm that the to-be-coded initial image can be selected randomly during coding of the fractal coding algorithm. Meanwhile, the same reconstructed attractor image can be obtained after different times of iterations. Actually, the significance of the fractal coding algorithm is to seek for a more compact piece of digital information to uniquely characterize the original image. In this way, redundancy in the image can be reduced or eliminated.

In view of the feature that a fractal coding document can uniquely characterize the original image, and the document also contains position information of image sub-blocks, it is deemed that the fractal coding documents can be applied to an image retrieval system, which is characterized in following aspects;

1. More similar images will have similar fractal coding documents.
2. It can be considered that the closer the fractal coding documents between images are, the more similar the images will be.

A.D. Sloan [1] took the initiative to employ the fractal coding algorithm in image retrieval. Fractal coding should be conducted when images are put into a library. The obtained fractal coding documents are stored in a feature database, and thus only offline retrieval can be realized. The so-called offline retrieval suggests that, before image matching, the image retrieval system has completed feature extraction of all the images in the database. This retrieval algorithm is poor in feasibility. Therefore, this paper puts forward an online real-time retrieval algorithm which does not need to perform feature extraction of all the images of a database in advance.

3   Improvement of Rapid Image Retrieval Algorithm Based on Fractal Coding

3.1   Image Retrieval Algorithm Based on Fractal Blocks

In the fractal coding algorithm, we are required to divide the image into $B * B$ non-overlapping value domain R blocks and overlapping $2B * 2B$ definition domain D blocks, and find the best matching block $D_{M(i)}$ of the value domain block R_i, as well as calculate the collage error of the best matching block $D_{M(i)}$ of R_i:

$$E\left(R_i, t_i\left(D_{M(i)}\right)\right) = \sqrt{\sum_{a=1}^{n} \sum_{b=1}^{n} (r_{ab} - S(R_i)d_{ab} - o(R_i))^2 / n} \qquad (9)$$

where the pixel value at the position (a, b) of the R block is r_{ab}, and the pixel value at the (a, b) position of the $D_{M(i)}$ block (a, b) is d_{ab}.

The size of the matrix composed of the collage errors of all R blocks is $1/(n * n)$ of the original image size. The use of collage error histogram as the basis for fractal coded image retrieval has been verified in the Literature [10]. Although a collage error is affected by the parameters of the fractal coding document, it cannot completely represent the original image. Besides, the algorithm also needs to generate a fractal coding document index when the image is input into the library, and it is not online retrieval. Therefore, this study proposes a rapid fractal retrieval algorithm based on fractal block R blocks.

For an R block of size $N \times N$, the standard variance:

$$\sigma_R = \frac{1}{N} \| R - \overline{R} \cdot 1 \| = \left(\frac{1}{N \cdot N} \sum_{i=1}^{N \cdot N} (r_i - \overline{R})^2 \right)^{1/2} \tag{10}$$

By combining the standard variance with the J.M. Beaumont fractal coding scheme [11], the R block and the matching D block conform to:

$$R_i = \frac{\sigma_r}{\sigma_d} (t_k(r_i(D_{M(i)}))) + \overline{R_i} - \frac{\sigma_r}{\sigma_d} \overline{M}(t_k(S_i(D_{M(i)}))) \tag{11}$$

where: σ_r represents the standard variance of R_i, σ_d is the $D_{M(i)}$ standard variance of the transformed best matching block, $\overline{M}$ means taking the mean. Formulas (2) and (11) are combined, then:

$$s_i t_k \left(\gamma_i \left(D_{m(i)} \right) \right) + o_{i=} \frac{\sigma_r}{\sigma_d} \left(t_k \left(\gamma_i \left(D_{m(i)} \right) \right) \right) + \overline{R_i} - \frac{\sigma_r}{\sigma_d} \overline{M} \left[t_k \left(\gamma_i \left(D_{m(i)} \right) \right) \right] \tag{12}$$

If the value domain block R_i and the best matching $D_{M(i)}$ block satisfy the equation $s = \frac{\sigma_r}{\sigma_d}$, it is substituted into Eq. (12):

$$o(R_i) = \overline{R_i} - s_i \overline{M} \left[t_k \left(\gamma_i \left(D_{m(i)} \right) \right) \right] \tag{13}$$

From Eq. (13), it can be seen that the grey scale adjustment is not performed on the $D_{M(i)}$ block, then:

$$\overline{M} \left[t_k \left(\gamma_i \left(D_{m(i)} \right) \right) \right] = \overline{M} \left[D_{m(i)} \right] \tag{14}$$

Equation (14) is substituted into Eq. (13), then:

$$o(R_i) = \overline{R_i} - s_i \cdot \overline{M} \left[(D_{M(i)}) \right] \tag{15}$$

It can be found that the pixel average value $\overline{R_i}$ of the value domain block R_i, the pixel average value of the best matching block $D_{M(i)}$, and the brightness adjustment factor s_i determine the offset o_i. All the o_i are combined into an offset image in the form of a matrix, and it is similar with the collage error matrix in Literature [10]. Compared with the use of the collage error as the similarity measurement, eight equidistant transformations t_k need to be calculated. Using the offset o_i as the similarity measurement significantly reduces the amount of calculation.

In fact, fractal coding is a lossy compression algorithm. The main reason is that in the process of fractal coding, a block D adjusts the image brightness through affine transformation, changes the frequency domain information of the original image, and is distorted to the original image. The D block overlapping and segmented in the same image is composed of R blocks that do not overlap each other. Therefore, it can be concluded that the D block is composed of R blocks that are collaged into the block. Then, the image R block can be used as the basis for judging the similarity between the images.

At present, the indicators for calculating graphic similarity include mean square error, Euclidean distance and peak signal-to-noise ratio. However, due to the different sensitivity of the human eyes to color, this calculation method often fails to meet the visual quality standard of the human eye. Therefore, the concept of structural similarity (SSIM) is proposed. This similarity calculation can obtain image structure information from the visual area, which is more in line with the human visual system (HSV). The calculation method is as follows:

$$SSIM = \frac{4\sigma_{xy}\overline{X}\,\overline{Y}}{(\sigma_X^2 + \sigma_Y^2)(\overline{X}^2 + \overline{Y}^2)} \tag{16}$$

The value range of SSIM is $[-1, 1]$, where the gray-scale mean values of images X and Y are expressed as $\overline{X}, \overline{Y}$ and the standard variances are σ_X, σ_Y; σ_{XY} represents the covariance of images X and Y. It indicates the larger the SSIM value is, the more similar the images X and Y are. When the SSIM value is 1, it suggests that the brightness, contrast, and structure of the two images exactly remain the same.

From the above analysis, we can obtain an image retrieval algorithm based on fractal blocks for image X and images in the image library.

(1) According to the fractal coding method, the query image X is divided into value domains of size $B \times B$, which are not intersected with each other. The pixel mean $\overline{R}(i)$ and variance $\sigma_R(i)$ of each R_i block are calculated;

(2) An image Y is extracted in turn from the image library, and then segmented according to step 1. The pixel mean $\overline{R'}(i)$ and variance $\sigma_{R'}(i)$ of each R_i block are calculated;

(3) The gray-level covariance $\sigma_{RR'}$ (i) of R_i of all query images and image-library images R_i' is calculated and all the SSIM (R_i, R_i') is calculated. Finally, the similarity S of two images is obtained:

$$S = \sum SSIM\left(R_i, R_i'\right)/N \tag{17}$$

N is the total number of R blocks;

(4) The similarity S between the images in the image library and the query image X are calculated in sequence according to steps (2) and (3), and sorted in a large-to-small sequence. Meanwhile, the image with a high ranking and large structural similarity is selected as the search result.

Most image retrieval methods cover each image in the entire image database. Although this can ensure the accuracy of the retrieval results, it still consumes a certain amount of time for matching. In order to further improve the time-consuming retrieval of the retrieval system, this paper considers introducing the image entropy for simple and rapid screening of the image library in order to ensure that the re-screened database image and the image to be retrieved are similar to a certain extent as much as possible.

3.2 Image Entropy

In 1865, the German physicist Clausius first proposed the concept of entropy. Zachary J M applied entropy to image retrieval in 2000. Shannon's information theory defines the probability of a certain kind of information as entropy, that is, entropy can be expressed as the degree of disorder of the measured information. The digital image studied in this article is composed of pixels, and each pixel corresponds to a gray value. The data of the image has a non-negative value. The aggregation of pixels with different brightness makes the image display different shapes. Therefore, the concept of image entropy is introduced in line with the definition of information entropy.

The probability and statistics theory is used for calculation. The value of the random variable X is x_i $(1 \leq i \leq n)$, suggesting the amount of signal generated by the signal source, and the corresponding prior probability p_i, $\sum_{i=1}^{n} p_i = 1$. Due to the uncertainty of the information source, information entropy is defined as follows:

$$H(p_1, \ldots, p_n) = -k \sum_{i=1}^{n} p_i \log p_i \tag{18}$$

where: k is 1, and the base of the logarithm is generally e. According to the above Eq. (18) that introduces information entropy, the concept of one-dimensional entropy of an image [12] can be defined. For an image with the size of $M \times N$, the one-dimension entropy $H(f)$ is defined as:

$$H(f) = -\sum_{i=0}^{255} p_i \log p_i \tag{19}$$

where: $p_i = \frac{f(i)}{M \times N}$, f(i) is the statistical number of occurrences of the gray value pixel $i (0 \leq i \leq 255)$ in the image, and p_i is the frequency of occurrence of the pixel value i in the entire image.

Based on the image one-dimensional entropy Eq. (19), the image entropy of the four images in Fig. 1 is calculated, finding that the more similar the images are, the corresponding image entropy is also more similar. Therefore, the image entropy can be considered as the basis for dividing the image database.

Although the one-dimensional entropy of an image reflects the distribution of pixel values in the entire image, as for images with completely different gray-scale histograms, in case of the same probability distribution, they have the same information entropy but fail to reflect the spatial position distribution of the image pixel value in the whole image. Therefore, the spatial position distribution information is introduced, and the gray average value of the pixel neighborhood is added on the basis of the one-dimensional entropy. Both of them constitute the two-dimensional entropy of the image.

H(A₁)=9.613   H(A₂)=9.895

H(B₁)=8.663   H(B₂)=8.783

Fig. 1. One-dimensional entropy of 4 images

For an image of $X \times Y$ size, the 4-neighbor pixel average value of the image pixel and the corresponding pixel gray value are combined into a binary feature group (i, j), $i(i \in [0, 255])$ represents the pixel gray value of the image space position (a, b) and $j(j \in [0, 255])$ is the average gray value of 4-neighborhood pixels. Then:

$$H = -\sum_{i=0}^{255}\sum_{j=0}^{255} p_{ij} \log p_{ij} \tag{20}$$

where: $p_{ij} = \frac{f(i,j)}{X \times Y}$, $f(i,j)$ is the number of occurrences of the pixel gray value feature group (i, j).

H'(A₁)=4.516   H'(A₂)=4.697

H'(B₁)=2.683   H'(B₂)=2.708

Fig. 2. Two-dimensional entropy of 4 images

Formula (20) was used to calculate image 2D entropies of four images in Fig. 1 with the application of Matlab as well, as shown in Fig. 2. It is found through the comparison of experimental data in Fig. 1 and Fig. 2 that the 2D entropy difference between similar images was smaller than that of 1D entropies. However, the 2D entropy difference between dissimilar images was more obvious. For example, the difference between H(A1) and H(A2) was 0.282, and the difference between H(A1) and H(B1) was 0.95. Nevertheless, the difference between H'(A1) and H'(A2) was 0.181, and the difference between H'(A1) and H'(B1) was 1.833. Therefore, compared with 1D entropies of images, 2D entropies can more accurately classify and screen out similar images accurately, significantly promoting the acceleration of image retrieval.

3.3 Rapid Image Retrieval Method Based on Two-Dimensional Image Entropy and Fractal Blocks

By comparing the image entropy, each image in the image library in the image library is screened, and thus the number of images in the image database that need to be matched with the query image can be reduced. Consequently, the total image retrieval time is reduced, and the precision ratio and recall ratio of the retrieval results are taken into account. It is of note that the following two situations will occur when image entropy is combined with image matching strategies based on fractal blocks for image retrieval.

(1) There are images that are exactly the same as the query image in the image library. When the image library is sorted and sequenced, the image entropy of the two can be obtained and must be completely equal. Then, it is feasible to use Eqs. (16) and (17) to calculate the structural similarity between the two, which is equal to 1. If the above two conditions are satisfied, the same image can be deemed to have been retrieved.
(2) When there are only similar images in the image library, the image entropy of the two is definitely different. Besides, the obtained structural similarity is also different. Therefore, it is feasible to use the two-dimensional entropy of the image to screen the images in the image library, and subsequently calculate the structural similarity of the two according to Eqs. (16) and (17) as well as sequence them in descending order, wherein those ranking first can be used as retrieval images.

Briefly, the two-dimensional entropy of the image and the similarity of the image structure based on the fractal block jointly determine the retrieval result. In order to balance the weight between the two, the research considers introducing a linear weighted sum, which can also be called an evaluation function. It is believed in statistics that the average or other values need to be calculated in the statistical process of a group of data and the weight of one piece of data is equivalent to judging its importance in this group of data. In addition, it is believed that the smaller the two-dimensional entropy difference between the two images and the greater the structural similarity between the two images are, the higher the similarity between the two images will be. Therefore, an evaluation function of the retrieval system is constructed. This function is a measurable output concerning the similarity between images:

$$score = \lceil s_x - s_y \rceil \cdot P_s + (1 - S_{xy}) \cdot Q_S \tag{21}$$

wherein, P_s is $\lceil s_x - s_y \rceil$ the ranking after sequencing of the two-dimensional entropy difference between the image X to be retrieved and the image library Y, and Q_S denotes the ranking of the structural similarity S_{xy} between the image X to be retrieved and the image Y in the image library.

Then, the paper will introduce the implementation process of the rapid image retrieval algorithm based on two-dimensional image entropy and fractal blocks proposed in this study:

1. Input the image X to be retrieved, and process the image from color to grayscale.
2. Perform a spatial filtering operation on the image X to create a mask window average_kernel of the average value of the four-neighborhood pixels.
3. Use the mask to perform the linear filtering calculation of the two-dimensional convolution of the image.
4. Use Eq. (20) of the two-dimensional entropy of the image to calculate the entropy value of the query image X and all images in the image library.
5. Calculate the absolute value of the difference between the two-dimensional entropy of the query image X and the image-library image and sequence them in a small-to-large sequence, and select the top N/2 images as the next round of image retrieval library, wherein N is the number of original image-library images.
6. According to the fractal coding method, the query image X and the screened image-library image are divided into 8 × 8-size R blocks. A matching algorithm based on fractal blocks is used to calculate the pixel mean $\overline{R}(i)$ and variance $\sigma_R(i)$ of each R_i block of the query image and the image-library image.
7. Use Eqs. (16) and (17) to calculate the structural similarity S. between the query image and all the screened images in the image library and sequence them from large to small.
8. Calculate the ranking of the query image and the filtered image-library image by the difference of the two-dimensional entropy and the structural similarity ranking.
9. Calculate all the scores according to the evaluation function Eq. (21) of linear weighted sum and sequence from small to large; select the top ten as the search result.

4   Experimental Results and Analysis

The experimental running environment is: processor Intel(R) Core(TM) i5-7200U, memory RAM) is 4.00 GB, and the simulation software Matlab 2016a.

In order to test the effectiveness of the retrieval algorithm based on image two-dimensional entropy and fractal block, 30 texture images are used here. The size of the images is 256 × 256, and each image is divided into 4 blocks according to the "ten" character. Four of the texture images are taken as an example, as illustrated in Fig. 3. If the uncut original image is used as the image to be detected, and if the four sub-block images that have been cut can be detected and all of them rank first, the effectiveness of the algorithm can thus be verified.

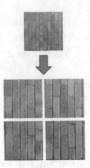

Fig. 3. Segmented texture image

The results retrieved by simulation are shown in Fig. 4 below. Obviously, when any uncut texture image is used as the retrieval image, the image retrieval algorithm based on the two-dimensional entropy fractal block can not only retrieve 4 images completely. The sub-images are segmented, which are placed at the top of the similar images. The same experiment is continued on 30 texture images, and 4 sub-images with the similarity ranking top can be retrieved. The current experiment fully demonstrates the effectiveness and feasibility of the image retrieval algorithm based on two-dimensional entropy and fractal technology.

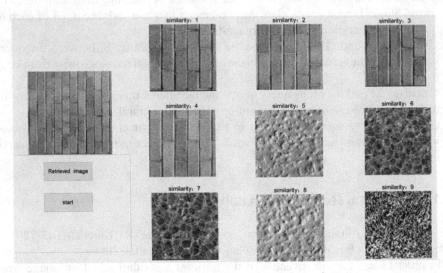

Fig. 4. Retrieval results of segmented texture images

Subsequently, the research tests 300 standard ORL face libraries. There are 30 people in the library, with different facial expressions. There are 10 face images for each, and there are totally 300 face images. This article uses color histogram-based image retrieval algorithms and performs experiments on image retrieval algorithms based on two-dimensional entropy and fractal technology, retrieves the top 20 images with output similarity, and compares and analyzes the experimental results in accordance with the precision ratio and recall ratio performance indicators. For the fairness of the experiment, the two algorithms are tested by the same retrieved image and the detected image is shown in Fig. 5. Test results are displayed in Fig. 6 and Fig. 7.

Fig. 5. Image to be detected

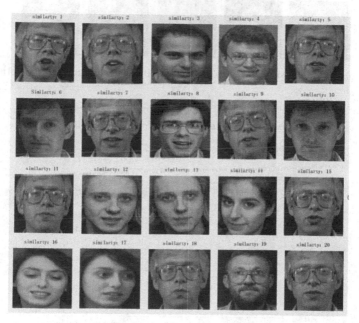

Fig. 6. Detection results of image retrieval algorithm based on color histogram

The precision ratio and recall ratio curves of the two image retrieval algorithms in the ORL face image library are shown in Fig. 8. It can be observed from the diagram that under the same recall rate, the precision ratio of the algorithm in this paper is obviously higher compared with that of the color histogram retrieval algorithm.

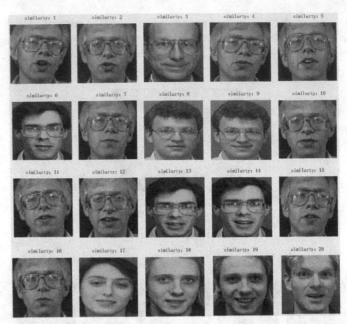

Fig. 7. Test results of retrieval algorithm based on two-dimensional entropy and fractal technology

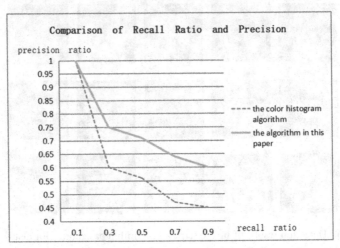

Fig. 8. Comparison of recall ratio and precision ratio between proposed algorithm and histogram algorithm

Finally, the comprehensive image library is tested. The current experiment uses five types of images libraries containing landscape architectural drawings, potted plant drawings, human activity drawings, fruit drawings, and animal drawings. There are 100 images for each category with 500 images in total. Color histogram retrieval method and the retrieval method based on the two-dimensional entropy and fractal technology are used for testing respectively. The following presents a list of the test results of the figure activity diagram of Fig. 9. As shown in Fig. 10 and Fig. 11, among the 9 retrieved approximate images, the color histogram algorithm only retrieves 5 similar images, and the proposed algorithm can retrieve 8 images of the same type. It can be found that the accuracy of the algorithm in this paper is much higher than that of the color histogram algorithm.

Fig. 9. Image to be detected

Fig. 10. Color histogram retrieval results

Fig. 11. Retrieval results of algorithm in this paper

According to the above test results, Table 1 shows the retrieval performance of the two image retrieval methods such as precision rate and recall rate:

According to the test results, the image retrieval algorithm based on two-dimensional entropy and fractal blocks proposed in this paper has higher precision ratio and recall ratio than the color histogram retrieval algorithm in the comprehensive image library retrieval testing. Besides, the retrieval time of the algorithm in this paper is less, further verifying the advantages of the retrieval algorithm proposed in this chapter.

Table 1. Comparison of comprehensive image library test of two retrieval algorithms

Detected image	Color histogram retrieval			Two-dimensional entropy and fractal technology retrieval		
	Recall ratio	Precision ratio	Time(s)	Recall ratio	Precisionratio	Time(s)
Castle	15.4%	44.4%	9.86	30.76%	88.9%	8.72
Pot plant	30.0%	66.7%	10.42	40.0%	88.9%	8.87
Figure	25.0%	55.6%	8.53	40.0%	88.9%	7.23
Fruits	25.0%	33.3%	11.04	41.7%	55.5%	9.51
Rabbit	33.3%	55.6%	10.63	60.0%	100%	10.03

5   Conclusion

To conclude, image retrieval is a hot issue commonly concerned by numerous researchers. The application of fractal technology in image retrieval has been further developed through the research in recent years. However, the extraction speed of fractal codes still needs to be improved continuously. Fractal codes pay more attention to the spatial structure of images, and are not sensitive to the occurrence frequency of the color gray value of an image. It indicates the fractal coding algorithm examines the image from another angle (structure) and is then applied to image retrieval. However, the traditional fractal image retrieval technology must code and store the images in the gallery before retrieval, and cannot be retrieved online in real time. As a result, the fractal image retrieval method proposed in this paper combines the image two-dimensional entropy for screening an image library, and adopts the improved fractal technology to quickly match and find similar images. Experiments show that this improved fractal technology introduces the principle of structural similarity, and calculates the similarity value by calculating the pixel mean and variance of each R block, which can be conducive to realizing rapid matching and effectively reducing the retrieval time.

Acknowledgements. Supported by a project grant from National Natural Science Foundation (Grand No. 61961036&62162054), the University Young Teachers Basic Ability Improvement Project of Guangxi (Grand No. 2018KY0537&2017KY0629), Wuzhou Scientific Research and Technology Development Project (Grand No. 201501014), Guangxi Natural Science Foundation (Grand No. 2020GXNSFAA297259&2018GXNSFBA281173), Wuzhou High-tech Zone, Wuzhou University Industry-Education-Research Project (Grand No. 2020G001), the Guangxi Innovation-Driven Development Special Driven Develop Special Fund Project (Guike AA18118036), the Guangxi Science and Technology Base and Talent Special Project (Guike AD20297148).

References

1. Sloan, A.D.: Retrieving database contents by image recognition: new fractal power. Adv. Imaging **9**(5), 5–15 (1994)

2. Zhang, J.-J., Zhang, A.-H., Ji, H.-F.: Image compression encoding based on wavelet transform and fractal. Comput. Sci. **46**(8), 310–314 (2019)
3. Prashanth, N., Arun, V.S.: Fractal image compression for HD image with noise using wavelet transforms. In: 2015 International Conference on Advances in Computing, Communications and Informatics (ICACCI), New York, pp. 1194–1198. IEEE Press (2015)
4. Pang, H., Zhang, A.: Sparse coding algorithm for fractal image compression based on coefficient of variation. Appl. Res. Comput. **38**(7) (2020)
5. Zhang, Q., Lin, Q.-H., Kang, X.: Research on image retrieval based on kernel density estimation and fractal coding algorithm. Acta Metrologica Sin. **38**(3), 284–287 (2017)
6. Zhang, S.-S., Liu, Y., Zhao, Z.-B.: Fractal image retrieval algorithm based on contiguous-matches. Comput. Sci. **42**(12), 292–296 (2015)
7. Yuan, H., Li, M., Niu, W., Zhang, L., Cui, K.: Fast fractal image retrieval algorithm based on HV partition. Int. J. Simul. Process Model. **15**(2), 111–118 (2020)
8. Barnsley, M.F., Sloan, A.D.: A better way to compress images. Byte **13**(1), 215–223 (1988)
9. Jacquin, A.E.: Image coding based on a fractal theory of iterated contractive image transformations. IEEE Trans. Image Process. **1**(1), 18–30 (1992)
10. Xu, Y., Wang, J.-J.: Fractal coding based image retrieval using histogram of collage errors. J. Electron. Inf. Technol. **28**(4), 603–605 (2006)

Research on Fractal Image Coding Method Based on SNAM Segmentation Scheme

Jie He [ID], Hui Guo[⊠] [ID], Caixu Xu [ID], and Jingjing Li [ID]

Guangxi Key Laboratory of Machine Vision and Intelligent Control, Wuzhou University,
Wuzhou, China
13066724@qq.com

Abstract. Adaptability of the partition method of fractal image compression to gray level textures directly influences the total number of partition blocks and image decoding effects. Hence, it is of critical significance to find a partition method which can accurately reflect image gray level distribution and visual threshold linkage relations in order to speed up encoding and enhance decoding quality. Therefore, in this paper, the SNAM (Square of Non-symmetry and Anti-packing Model) partition method is optimized by thresholds. The optimized method is employed to improve fractal encoding. On the basis of the organic relations between local image textures, human vision threads and encoding efficiency as well as decoding quality, a self-adaption sub-blocks partition method based on a square non-symmetry, anti-packing model and human vision system is proposed. With such method, partitioned image sub-blocks can accurately reflect gray level distribution of images, while the number of partitioned image sub-blocks is reduced. In this way, the calculation and matching times are reduced in encoding. Encoding time is reduced in addition to improvement of restored image quality. Compared with the basic fractal encoding method, the speed is increased by over 30 times.

Keywords: Fractal image coding · SNAM segmentation · Threshold optimization · Human visual system

1 Introduction

Fractal image coding technology was first proposed by Barnsley [1]. It is mainly employed in research fields due to its complex operations. Fractal image compression coding technology can be studied and applied by researchers due to proposition of the image coding algorithm based on fractal block search [2]. The basic fractal image coding algorithm is proposed based on the fractal block algorithm. An image is divided into non-overlapping R blocks and overlapping D blocks. Each block has a certain fractal structure. Using the similarity between image blocks and combined with the iterative function system theory and collage theorem, the D block that is most similar to each R block is found, and relevant parameters are recorded to complete the fractal image coding process.

© ICST Institute for Computer Sciences, Social Informatics and Telecommunications Engineering 2022
Published by Springer Nature Switzerland AG 2022. All Rights Reserved
X. Jiang (Ed.): MLICOM 2021, LNICST 438, pp. 270–283, 2022.
https://doi.org/10.1007/978-3-031-04409-0_25

The basic fractal image coding algorithm has the outstanding characteristics such as ultra-high compression ratio, simple restoration and good restoration effect while it is also disadvantaged in long coding time and complex coding process. In response to the above-mentioned problems, researchers at home and abroad have made considerable efforts [3–6]. They mainly carry out research from the perspectives of image segmentation, combination of transform domain, codebook reduction, matching method and decoding method. The research aims to lower the impact of long fractal coding time on coding efficiency and ensure the quality of reconstructed images. The fractal image coding method based on transform domains processes the image before fractal coding, and adopts fractal coding to the processed image. Both the hybrid coding method combining fractal and wavelet transform proposed in Literatures [7–9] and that integrating fractal and DCT (Discrete Cosine Transform) proposed in Literature [10] have achieved good image restoration results. Literature [11] proposes a search strategy based on iterative control. With this strategy, the search process is controlled through the iterative update times of fractal codes, and the search termination time is set. Besides, the inefficient and invalid searches in the search process are removed, and the coding speed is greatly improved. Literature [12] classified D blocks by fuzzy clustering according to the complex exponential moment invariants of D blocks, further finding the best matching D blocks according to the complex exponential moment invariants of R blocks, thus improving the coding speed while maintaining better decoded image quality. Literature [13, 14] propose a rapid fractal image coding algorithm based on square weighted centroid features, which converts global search into local search and limits the search range in order to reduce the number of codebook.

The paper starts with the block segmentation method, and uses the adaptability of asymmetric segmentation to image gray vein to affect the total amount of blocks and decoding effect. SNAM (Square of Non-symmetry and Anti-packing Model) [15] can segment adaptive image veins through asymmetric inverse layout. The total amount of image blocks and the number of basic representation units generated are smaller than those of extensively used representation methods such as quad tree. Therefore, the paper considers optimizing SNAM segmentation by threshold and applying it to improve fractal coding, aiming to provide a new research idea and find out the accurate linkage relationship among image gray distribution, visual threshold, coding speed and decoding quality.

2 Fractal Coding Algorithm Based on SNAM Segmentation Scheme

2.1 Basic Fractal Coding Algorithm

In fractal coding, an image is first divided into n × n non-overlapping range blocks (R blocks for short) and domain blocks (D blocks for short) with an allowable overlapping size of 2n × 2n. Then, each D block is contracted into n × n sub-blocks by averaging 4-neighborhood pixel values so as to match the size of R blocks. Meanwhile, all the contracted D blocks undergo 8 equidistant transformations to form a codebook Ω.

In the coding stage, for each R block, the best matching D block and self-affine transformation ω are found in the codebook Ω by the global search method. Therefore, the mean square error of ω(D) and R is minimized. In order to find the best matching block of R block, the following minimization problem needs to be solved.

$$\|R - (s \cdot D_m + o \cdot I)\| = \min_{j} \left\{ \min_{s, o \in R, |s| < 1} \|R_i - (s \cdot D_j + o \cdot I)\| \right\} \tag{1}$$

where: m represents the best matching block sequence number of the R block, $I \in R^{n \times n}$ is a constant block with all elements being 1, and $R = (r_1, \cdots, r_k, \cdots, r_N)$ and $D = (d_1, \cdots, d_k, \cdots, d_N)$ ($N = n \times n$) respectively represent vectors obtained after the pixel gray values of the R block and the D block are vectored in a way.

The solution of Eq. (1) is extremely difficult. Hence, in order to reduce the computational complexity, the constraints $|s| < 1$ in Eq. (1) are ignored first, and the minimization of the inner constraints of Eq. (1) is transformed into the minimum problem of Eq. (2) for solution. Then, the contrast factor that does not meet the constraints is truncated for compensation.

$$E(R, D) = \min_{s, o \in R} \|R - (s \cdot D + o \cdot I)\| \tag{2}$$

Then the outer layer minimization problem of Eq. (1) is solved:

$$E(R, D) = \min_{D \in \Omega} E(R, D) \tag{3}$$

Finally, after the solution of formula (1) is transformed into suboptimal solutions (2) and (3), the R-block fractal code obtained is a quaternary $(m, \hat{s}_i, \hat{o}_i, t)$, wherein $\hat{s}_i, \hat{o}_i$ is the quantized value of s_i, o_i, and t denotes the isometric transformation sequence number. The fractal code of the original image is composed of fractal codes of all R blocks, describing a compression transformation that makes the image approximately invariant. Decoding is generated by iterating the compression transform described by fractal codes on any initial image.

2.2 Gray Image Representation of SNAM

The new image representation method should be able to effectively save storage space and have an efficient operation mode, which is suitable for various processing processes such as image compression, feature extraction and restoration. At present, the more mature quad-tree image representation method has achieved good results of application to the segmentation method in image compression. For example, Literature [16] uses the quad-tree segmentation method combined with the characteristics of human visual system to improve the fractal coding method, which can speed up the coding speed besides controlling the decoding distortion within the range imperceptible to human eyes. Literature [17] proposes a rapid fractal image coding algorithm based on HV segmentation to improve image adaptive performance and accelerate fractal code extraction. The above studies show that the adaptability of fractal coding segmentation method to gray vein is directly associated with the total number of blocks and decoding effect. At the same time, the application of appropriate image representation methods to fractal coding can effectively improve the speed of fractal coding. The SNAM representation method proposed in Literature [15] adapts image vein through asymmetric inverse layout segmentation. The total amount of data and the number of basic representation units generated are less than those of widely used representation methods such as quaternary tree. Therefore, the present study applies SNAM representation method to the segmentation scheme of fractal coding, which can effectively shorten the coding time of fractal image compression.

The framework of square sub-patterns is defined in advance. For a given pattern that has been laid out, the pattern is transformed into a combination of a series of square sub-patterns with different scales based on the inverse layout algorithm. The abstract description of SNAM representation in this paper is presented as follows:

If the original mode is Γ and the reconstructed undistorted mode is Γ', SNAM will be undistorted mapping from Γ to Γ':

$$\Gamma' = W(\Gamma) \tag{4}$$

where: W () is a forward mapping function, that is, a coding function.

The forward encoding process is

$$\Gamma' = \bigcup_{j=1}^{n} P_{s_j}(v, A | A = \{a_1, a_2, ..., a_m\}) \tag{5}$$

where Γ' represents the synthesized mode after inverse layout coding; a square sub-pattern set $P = \{Ps\}$ is predefined, n is the total number of square sub-patterns contained in the Γ, and Ps_j is the j-th square sub-pattern in Γ; V is the value of Ps_j, A is the parameter set of square sub-patterns; a_i ($1 \leq i \leq m$) denotes the i-th shape parameter of the square sub-pattern, and m is the total number of parameters of the square sub-pattern.

Figure 1 shows the results of inverse layout encoding and storage of a gray image by employing SNAM method. Figure 1(a) shows the original gray image G of a given size of $2^n \times 2^n$ ($n = 3$). Figure 1(b) is a result of SNAM inverse layout with the application of raster scanning. Six square sub-patterns ($s_1, s_2, s_3, s_4, s_5, s_6$), nine line segments ($l_1, l_2, l_3, l_4, l_5, l_6, l_7, l_8, l_9$) and two isolated points (p_1, p_2) are extracted from the original image. Figure 1(c) is the image matrix of G. Figure 1(d) shows results of representing T using the above sub-pattern.

By combining SNAM image representation (a predefined image laid out), and using the inverse layout algorithm (essentially a flexible asymmetric segmentation method aimed to find the sub-pattern in the largest area within the threshold range), square sub-patterns with different scales are extracted from an image, which is represented by their combinations. It is applied in the classification coding algorithm to segment the image into sub-blocks. During the segmentation, in view of the characteristics of HVS (Human Visual System), a threshold is set, the image is divided into blocks, and the gray value in the block is within a given threshold range, namely, the similarity of the image blocks in the rectangle will be the furthest. Therefore, it can realize the differential processing of different detail parts of the image, and effectively keep the vein features of the image, namely, the flat part in the image is segmented by relatively large image blocks, thus improving the compression ratio. Regarding the detailed part in the image, relatively small image blocks are used for segmentation, thus ensuring higher reconstructed image

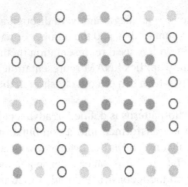

(a) Results of the gray image G with size of 8 × 8 and 8 gray scales

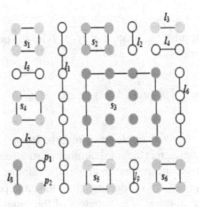

(b) Results of SNAMG inverse layout of G

y/x	000	001	010	011	100	101	110	111
000	100	100	111	010	010	111	101	101
001	100	100	111	010	010	111	111	111
010	111	111	111	000	000	000	000	111
011	100	100	111	000	000	000	000	111
100	100	100	111	000	000	000	000	111
101	111	111	111	000	000	000	000	111
110	001	111	111	101	101	111	011	011
111	001	101	111	101	101	111	011	011

$s_1=\{((000,000),010,100\},s_2=\{(011,000),010,010\}$
$s_3=\{(011,010),100,000\},s_4=\{(000,011),010,100\}$
$s_5=\{(011,110),010,101\},s_6=\{(110,110),010,011\}$
$l_1=\{(010,000),(010,111),111\},l_2=\{(101,000),(101,001),111\}$
$l_3=\{(110,000),(111,000),101\},l_4=\{(110,001),(111,001),111\}$
$l_5=\{(000,010),(001,010),111\},l_6=\{(111,010),(111,101),111\}$
$l_7=\{(000,101),(001,101),111\},l_8=\{(000,110),(000,111),001\}$
$l_9=\{(101,110),(101,111),111\}$
$p_1=\{(001,110),111\},p_2=\{(001,111),101\}$

(c) Image matrix of G   (d) Storage results of G

Fig. 1. Result of inverse layout segmentation and storage of a gray scale image

quality. The SNAM image representation method is applied to image segmentation, and the number of segmented blocks is much fewer than that of classical algorithm. In addition, the vein features of images can be well preserved.

2.3   Fractal Coding Algorithm Based on SNAM Segmentation Scheme

The basic principle of SNAM-based segmentation scheme is to use a segmentation threshold with the starting point gray value of each square as the matching reference value. As long as the gray value of each pixel is within the range of starting point gray value ± segmentation threshold, it can be considered as a gray square. This threshold is based on HVS characteristics. The segmentation threshold is set to distinguish different detail parts of the image. As a result, relatively good vein features of the image can be kept and the similarity of image blocks is likely to fall within the rectangle. In this way, sub-blocks of maximum size can be obtained, which thereby reduces the total number of blocks, and help achieve the purpose of shortening the coding time. On the premise of guaranteeing better decoding quality than that of the basic fractal algorithm, the method can speed up by approximately 30 times.

One typical feature of Human Vision System (HVS) refers to the nonuniform and nonlinear cognitive image. In other words, human eyes cannot completely recognize all the details and changes in images. The subjective sensing intensity of humans is associated with changes in the stimulus intensity. As shown in Fechner's law, with increasing stimulus intensity in geometrical progression, the sensing intensity caused thereby only increases by arithmetical progression, namely a logarithmic relation. Such sense can be vividly expressed by a visual threshold which means the value of a stimulus (interference or distortion) which can just be felt. Edges with varying brightness will "conceal" the signal feelings of nearby pixels, thereby reducing the visual sensitivity of human eyes, which is called the "concealment effect". Due to such feature of vision, human eyes can tolerate great quantization errors in edge areas of images. Therefore, influential factors on visual thresholds are contrast sensitivity and a concealment effect of a brightness threshold at a pixel point. In view of the uniqueness of HVS, human eyes' resolution ratios to gray levels are briefly tested to observe the changing scope of threads, within which image changes cannot be sensed. On this basis, the best threshold scope of the algorithm can be then predicted. The sensitive scope of human eyes to gray levels is generally within dozens of gray levels, wherein the gray level value is selected from 20–40. The SNAM partition solution is employed to test 5 images. Testing data is shown in Fig. 2, In order to ensure decoded image quality and encoding time, the encoding time and PSNR value are optimal when the thresholds of the 5 images are about 30. Therefore, the optimum threshold scope is set around 30.

SNAM segmentation scheme is the key to realize the algorithm in this paper. It is mainly used to adapt the image vein to divide the range blocks. The following displays a schematic diagram 3 of the fixed block segmentation method and SNAM segmentation method:

Fixed block segmentation is the segmentation method of the basic fractal image coding scheme, which is disadvantaged in that the gray vein features between the pixel values of the image are not considered. As shown in Fig. 3(a), even if there is little difference between the adjacent pixel values, they will be divided according to the

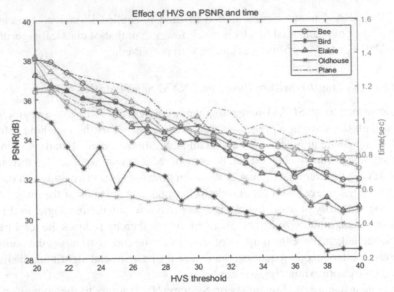

Fig. 2. Test effects of different thresholds

y/x	1	2	3	4	5	6	7	8
1	119	104	130	124	124	162	141	87
2	126	104	120	107	101	155	149	64
3	103	97	95	112	117	33	38	156
4	125	100	120	89	106	46	54	161
5	137	115	130	97	136	52	155	180
6	151	140	132	77	113	117	145	139
7	112	142	135	75	145	126	132	102
8	98	163	128	101	137	203	157	159

y/x	1	2	3	4	5	6	7	8
1	119	104	130	124	124	162	141	87
2	126	104	120	107	101	155	149	64
3	103	97	95	112	117	33	38	156
4	125	100	120	89	106	46	54	161
5	137	115	130	97	136	52	155	180
6	151	140	132	77	113	117	145	139
7	122	142	135	75	145	126	132	102
8	178	163	128	101	137	203	157	159

(a) 8 × 8 fixed block segmentation representation results

(b) 8 × 8 SNAM segmentation method representation results (threshold value is 30)

Fig. 3. Schematic diagram of block segmentation method and SNAM segmentation method

size. Different detail parts of the image cannot be treated differently, which can easily cause poor quality of the restored image. The key point of SNAM segmentation scheme refers to the segmentation threshold. The segmentation threshold is determined by the basis of human visual system (HVS). Therefore, the gray vein features between pixel values of the image are fully considered. The advantages of SNAM segmentation method can be observed from the above Fig. 3(b). Besides being able to better adapt to the vein features of the image, it can also effectively reduce the number of segmentation blocks, which can help subsequent algorithms decrease the amount of computation during matching calculation and thus effectively shorten the coding time. Although the SNAM segmentation method not only has a square sub-mode, but also has the line sub-mode and isolated point sub-mode, combining the advantages of all the aspects, this segmentation method can still improve the coding speed and decoded image quality of the algorithm on the premise of keeping the same compression ratio.

The specific steps of the coding algorithm:

Step 1. Set counting variables *square_num*, *l_num* and *p_num*, record the number of square sub-modes, the number of line segments and the number of isolated points generated in the inverse layout process, and assign an initial value of 0.

Step 2. Use the inverse layout algorithm based on SNAM as the basic idea, and aim at forming a square with the largest area. Set a threshold w, if the gray value of the pixel points is at $(z \pm w)$, continue to reverse the layout to form the square, and mark the pixel points involved in the square in G.

Step 3. Make *square_num* = *square_num* + *1*, record the left upper vertex coordinates (x, y) of the square sub-mode, and perform dimension reduction transformation, namely $sp\_x, sp\_y \leftarrow K(x, y)$, to obtain one-dimensional (K code) coordinates sp_x, sp_y; record the side length and the gray value z, and then store sp_x, sp_y, length and z in the queue square, that is, square *square {square_num}* ← *{sp_x, sp_y, length, z}*. Count and store line segments and isolated points in this way. Regarding line segments, store coordinates and pixel values of starting points and ending points as well as isolated points store point coordinates and pixel values.

Step 4. Repeat Step 2 to Step 3 and stop when there is no new sub-mode. Some square image sub-blocks with different sizes that do not overlap each other are obtained, which are called range blocks (R).

Step 5. Subsample the whole G once, wherein the size of the subsampled image G' is $(M/2) \times (M/2)$.

Step 6. Based on the total number of segmented R blocks *square_num*, transform it from 1 to *square_num*, wherein each count corresponds to an R block, and the square information stored in it is used to determine the sp_x, sp_y, length corresponding to the R block, and find out a best matching sub-block D with the same size as the R block in the sub-sampled image G'. Ensure that the square error between D' and R obtained after gray affine transformation and equidistant transformation of D is minimum, and just store line segments and isolated points.

For each range block R, record the following 5 parameters:

(1) The coordinates *(domain_x, domain_y)* of the upper left corner of the best matching sub-block D searched.
(2) The sequence number t of the isometric transformation that makes R and D become the best match.
(3) Gray contrast factor s and gray translation factor p.

Specific steps of decoding algorithm:

Step 1. Assign any initial value to the size of $M \times M$.

Step 2. Set a counting variable *square_num* to correspond to the number of square sub-patterns generated in the inverse layout process, and assign an initial value of 0.

Step 3. Read fractal codes *{domain_x, domain_y, t, s, p}* according to fractal coding file, count by coding queue square *{square_num} {sp_x, sp_y, length, z}*, namely *square_num* = *square_num* + *1*, obtain one-dimensional (K-code) coordinates *sp_x, sp_y* and side length of the upper left vertex of each square sub-mode in sequence, apply collage formula to carry out operation, and make all R blocks form an iterative image.

Step 4. Output the reconstructed image *bumper* after 9 iterations.

In terms of isolated point sub-mode, only the coordinate point position and pixel value are stored during coding, while for line segment sub-mode, the coordinate value and average pixel value of the first and last pixels of line segment need to be stored. In decoding, only the corresponding positions of point mode and line segment sub-mode need to be filled.

3   Experimental Analysis

In order to verify the feasibility and efficiency of fractal image compression coding algorithm based on threshold optimization segmentation scheme, the author conducts an experimental comparison between this algorithm and the basic fractal compression algorithm. To ensure the unity of evaluation criteria, the basic fractal compression algorithm and the algorithm proposed in the present study adopt 1/2 subsampling method during matching D blocks. The experimental environment configuration includes, processor Intel(R)Core(TM)i7 9700, operating system Microsoft Windows 10 and development software Matlab 2021a. The experimental test images are shown in Fig. 4, involving figures, animals, scenery and other fields. The pictures are different in complexity, with strong representativeness and universality.

(a)bee   (b) Elaine   (c) old house   (d) plane   (e) bird

Fig. 4.   Five 256×256 gray scale images used in the experiment

To make the algorithm proposed by paper comparable with the basic fractal coding algorithm, the proposed algorithm is improved on the basis of Jacquin's basic fractal algorithm. In Jacquin's basic fractal coding algorithm, the size of R block is 4×4, the size of D block is 8×8, and the step size of the sliding window of D pool is 8. Therefore, the number of range blocks after fixed block segmentation is: $(256/4) \times (256/4) = 4096$. In the algorithm proposed by the paper, SNAM segmentation is optimized by threshold, and the size of range block is determined by the set threshold. There are usually many sizes. Because the complexity of each image is different, and the algorithm in the current work is based on the square asymmetric inverse layout model and the adaptive sub-block segmentation of the human visual system. The selection of the threshold Q affects the number of blocks in the range, the peak signal-to-noise ratio PSNR (unit dB), the coding time T (unit of s), and the compression ratio of C. Therefore, different images may have different thresholds to achieve the best segmentation effect. Meanwhile, the final determination of the best threshold needs to be tested many times.

With $256 \times 256 \times 8$ standard gray images bee, elainel, old house, plane and bird as test objects, after performing many tests, this experiment obtains the segmentation data of the algorithm in the case that Q is the best threshold, as shown in Table 1. The fixed block segmentation data of Jacquin's basic fractal algorithm are shown in Table 2.

Table 1. Total number of range blocks under best threshold

Image	Bee	Elaine	Old house	Plane	Bird
Optimal threshold	29	30	30	38	29
Number of range blocks	3489	3634	2436	2908	3894
Line segment	17	11	63	77	12
Point	2962	2821	2601	4361	2702

Table 2. Number of Jacquin fixed block segmentation range blocks

Image	Bee	Elaine	Old house	Plane	Bird
Number of range blocks	4096	4096	4096	4096	4096

The algorithm in this paper improves the original SNAM gray segmentation method and optimizes SNAM segmentation by threshold. Therefore, under the optimal threshold Q segmentation, the number of range blocks segmented in this paper is compared with the total number of range blocks obtained by employing Jacquin's basic fractal algorithm, and the number of range blocks segmented in this paper is reduced. Through conducting the experiments, the coding time of the two methods is obtained, and the acceleration ratio is calculated, as illustrated in Table 3. At the same time, the PSNR values of the restored images by using the two methods are compared, as shown in Table 4.

As displayed in the data in Table 1, Table 2, Table 3 and Table 4, the old house picture has the highest speedup ratio and the highest PSNR restored, that is, the best quality. The reason refers to that the gray distribution of the image is relatively uniform. Therefore, after the optimal threshold Q segmentation, different details of the image will be differentiated. It can retain the vein features of a relatively good image, that is, the sub-blocks divided into uniform vein parts in the image are relatively large, thus

Table 3. Encoding time (s) and speedup ratio (%) using two methods

Image	Bee	Elaine	Old house	Plane	Bird
Jacquin's basic fractal algorithm	27.85	27.93	27.75	27.67	32.77
Algorithm proposed by the paper	0.93	1.03	0.5	0.94	0.76
Acceleration ratio	29.94	27.11	55.5	29.43	43.11

Table 4. PSNR (dB) values of restored images using two methods

Image	Vein	Elaine	Old house	Plane	Bird
Jacquin's basic fractal algorithm	30.99	28.79	27.51	24.15	28.89
Algorithm proposed by the paper	33.94	33.93	35.63	34.69	31.42

minimizing the number of range blocks. As a result, the coding time is less than other images in matching calculation, and the acceleration ratio is naturally the highest. The reason for the best quality of the image is not only that the gray distribution is relatively uniform, but also that the details are relatively simple. The details in the image can be processed better after setting threshold segmentation. In other words, the divided blocks will be relatively small. Thus, the transition between blocks is very good, and PSNR will be improved after the details of the restored image are processed. In a similar way, due to the complex gray distribution and many details of bird, the image has the lower acceleration ratio and the worst restored image quality.

Figure 5 shows the original images of bee, elaine, old house, plane and bird and the images reconstructed by two algorithms respectively. The reconstructed images of bee, elainel, old house, plane and bird using Jacquin's basic fractal algorithm are presented in Fig. 5(b), (e), (h), (k) and (m), respectively. Figure 5(c), (f), (i), (l) and (o) are the decoded images of bee, elainel, old house, plane and bird reconstructed by the algorithm in this paper when the optimal threshold Q is used. The PSNR value at this time is 33.94, 33.93, 35.63, 34.69 and 31.42, respectively. At this time, we can't find the difference between it and the original image subjectively. Objectively, the decoded PSNR also exceeds 30. Figure 5(k) shows a decoded image after plane reconstruction obtained by Jacquin's basic fractal algorithm. At this time, the PSNR is 24.15. At this moment, we can still observe the difference between it and the original image subjectively. The decoded PSNR does not reach 30, while the PSNR value of the image restored by this algorithm is 34.69, which is higher than Jacquin's basic fractal algorithm. Hence, the difference with the original image is basically invisible to naked eyes.

It can be easily found from Tables 3 and 4 that when the optimal threshold Q is used, the decoded image quality of the algorithm in this paper is better than that of the basic algorithm. The coding speed of the algorithm in this paper is about 30 times that of the basic algorithm, demonstrating that it is an effective image compression method.

(a) Original Bee image

(b) Bee image re-constructed by the basic algorithm

(c) Bee image reconstructed by the algorithm proposed in the paper

(d) Original elaine image

(e) Elaine image reconstructed by the basic algorithm

(f) Elaine image reconstructed by the algorithm proposed in the paper

(g) Original old house image

(h) Old house image reconstructed by the basic algorithm

(i) Old house reconstructed by the algorithm proposed in the paper

Fig. 5. Original image and image reconstructed by two algorithms

(j) Original plane image

(k) Plane image reconstructed by THE basic algorithm

(l) Plane image reconstructed by the algorithm proposed in the paper

(m) Original bird image

(n) Bird image reconstructed by basic algorithm

(o) Bird image reconstructed by the algorithm proposed in the paper

Fig. 5. continued

4   Conclusions

To conclude, a good block segmentation scheme can not only accelerate the fractal coding speed, but can also improve the restored image quality. Therefore, this paper proposes a threshold optimization SNAM segmentation scheme to improve fractal coding. In addition, the effectiveness of the proposed algorithm is confirmed by theoretical analysis and experimental simulation. However, there still remains room for improvement. For example, the isolated points and line segments in the image region that cannot form the SNAM square sub-pattern are simply filled back to the original position, which may retard the reduction of the compression ratio. In the future, the research ordination is to propose a better inpainting method for these isolated point patterns and line segment patterns, aiming to improve the compression ratio without lowering the quality of restored images.

Acknowledgements. Supported by a project grant from National Natural Science Foundation (Grand No. 61961036&62162054), the University Young Teachers Basic Ability Improvement Project of Guangxi (Grand No. 2018KY0537&2017KY0629), Wuzhou Scientific Research and Technology Development Project (Grand No. 201501014), Guangxi Natural Science Foundation (Grand No. 2020GXNSFAA297259&2018GXNSFBA281173), Wuzhou High-tech Zone, Wuzhou University Industry-Education-Research Project (Grand No. 2020G001), the

Guangxi Innovation-Driven Development Special Driven Develop Special Fund Project (Guike AA18118036), the Guangxi Science and Technology Base and Talent Special Project (Guike AD20297148).

References

1. Barnsley, M.F., Demko, S.G.: Iterated function systems and the global construction of fractals. Proc. Roy. Soc. Lond. A **399**, 243–275 (1985)
2. Jacquin, A.E.: Image coding based on a fractal theory of iterated contractive image transformations. IEEE Trans. Image Process. **1**(1), 18–30 (1992)
3. Gupta, R., Mehrotra, D., Tyagi, R.K.: Comparative analysis of edge-base fractal image compression using nearest neighbor technique in various frequency domains. Alex. Eng. J. **57**(3), 1525–1533 (2018)
4. Roy, S.K., Kumar, S., Chanda, B., et al.: Fractal image compression using upper bound on scaling parameter. Chaos Solutions Fractals **106**, 16–22 (2018)
5. Polvere, M., Nappi, M.: Speed-up in fractal image coding: comparison of methods. IEEE Trans. Image Process. **9**(6), 1002–1009 (2000)
6. Ismail, B.M., Reddy, B.E., Reddy, T.B.: Cuchoo inspired fast search algorithm for fractal image encoding. J. King Saud Univ. (Comput. Inform. Sci.) **30**(4), 462–469 (2018)
7. Zhang, J.-J., Zhang, A.-H., Ji, H.-F.: Image compression encoding based on wavelet transform and fractal. Comput. Sci. **46**(8), 310–314 (2019)
8. Pang, H., Zhang, A.: Sparse coding algorithm for fractal image compression based on coefficient of variation. Appl. Res. Comput. **38**(7) (2020)
9. Rong, Z., Hui, W., Aihua, Z.: Fractal image coding and compression algorithm based on wavelet transform. Comput. Appl. Softw. **36**(11), 262–266 (2019)
10. Xie, M., et al.: Research on a fast image compression algorithm based on DCT Appl. Res. Comput. (02), 150–152 (2002)
11. Zheng, Y., Li, X.: Fast fractal image compression algorithm based on iterative control search strategy. J. Huazhong Univ. Sci. Tech. (Nat. Sci. Ed.) **48**(7), 1–6 (2020)
12. Zhu, Z.-L., Wang, Y.-Y., Ping, Z.-L.: A fast-fractal image coding based on complex exponent moment and fuzzy clustering. Microelectron. Comput. **35**(12), 129–132 (2018)
13. Wang, L., Liu, Z.: Fast fractal image compression coding based on square weighted centroid feature. Telecommun. Eng. **60**(8), 871–875 (2020)
14. Wang, L., Liu, Z.: A fractal image compression algorithm based on centroid features and important sensitive area classification. Comput. Eng. Sci. **42**(5), 869–876 (2020)
15. He, J., Zhang, X.-Q., Guo, H.: Square NAM-based representation method for binary images. Manuf. Autom. **33**(3), 213–214 (2010)
16. Guo, H., Zheng, Y., He, J.: A fast fractal image compression algorithm using improved quadtree partitioning scheme. In: Wang, X., Wang, F., Zhong, S. (eds.) Electrical, Information Engineering and Mechatronics 2011. LNEE, vol. 138, pp. 745–751. Springer, London (2012). https://doi.org/10.1007/978-1-4471-2467-2_88
17. Zhang, L.-N., Yuan, H.-J.: Fast fractal image coding algorithm based on HV segmentation. Softw. Guide **16**(11), 33–35 (2017)

Aircraft Detection in Aerial Remote Sensing Images Based on Contrast Self-supervised Learning

Yuanyuan Liu[(⊠)] [iD]

School of Computer and Information Engineering, Heilongjiang University of Science and Technology, Harbin 150022, China
YuanyuanLiuch@gmail.com

Abstract. UAV aerial remote sensing images, which have the advantages of high resolution, convenient acquisition, high amount of information, and simple pre-processing process, are widely used in classification and detection tasks. The difficulty in the study of aircraft target detection in remote sensing images is that it relies on a large amount of labeled data and the target is relatively small. Therefore, this paper firstly studies the existing comparative learning methods in the self-supervised field, and then proposes the ZL (a comparative learning method in the remote sensing field) method for the small sample remote sensing data set to realize the extraction of the representation of the aircraft target. The ZL method mainly modifies the data enhancement combination form in data augmentation pipeline of the training process and the fine-tuning process and modifies the activation function in the projection head. Finally, the ZL trained model is combined with Faster R-CNN to improve the accuracy of aircraft target detection in aerially remote sensing images.

Keywords: Aerial remote sensing images · Small sample data set · ZL method · Target detection

1 Introduction

The emergence of remote sensing expands human's knowledge of their living environment by using non-contact, long-range detection technology to achieve large-range, multi spectral imaging for object detection. Aerial remote sensing has the advantages of mature technology, large imaging scale, high ground resolution, suitable for large-area terrain mapping and small-area detailed investigation, etc. It provides a new way for grounding target detection. Therefore, the research on target detection in aerially remote sensing images is of great significance. At the same time, an aircraft plays an important role in transportation, and play an important role in civil and military. In this context, aircraft small target detection is one of the hot research directions in the field of remote sensing environment detection.

X. Jiang (Ed.): MLICOM 2021, LNICST 438, pp. 284–296, 2022.
https://doi.org/10.1007/978-3-031-04409-0_26

Target detection using convolutional neural networks is one of the most challenging projects in the field of computer vision, which contains two main sub-tasks, target localization and target classification. Convolutional neural network based target detection algorithms can be divided into two categories, one is region based target detection algorithms, represented by R-CNN as a two-stage algorithm. One category is regression-based target detection algorithms, forming a single-stage algorithm represented by You Only Look Once (YOLO) [9–11] and SSD (Single Shot multibox Detector). Gong et al. [2] put forward a context-aware convolutional neural network (CA-CNN) method to improve the performance of object detection. Liu et al. [3] proposed a multi-layer abstraction salience model for airport detection in synthetic aperture radar (SAR) images. Wei et al. [13] came up with an HR ship detection network (HR-SDNet) to perform precise and robust ship detection in SAR images. Those methods are more suitable for large-scale targets with high contrast in natural scenes, but the accuracy of detection results is lowed in the case of complex background and small target detection. Meanwhile, in order to achieve the fit of neural network models for application problems, large-scale data sets are required to be trained upfront, and the degree of models fit are affected by the accuracy of the labels in training set. The production of labels for large-scale data sets is time-consuming and expensive, and problems such as model generalization errors, false associations and adversarial attacks are encountered.

Based on the above problems, the main contributions of this article are show below: Firstly, this paper proposes a small target detection framework for aerially remote sensing images following the process of "ZL (A comparative learning method in remote sensing) self-supervised representation learning+Faster R-CNN target detection". Secondly, we design a comparative learning method of ZL in the field of remote sensing. It is a more suitable for small-sample aerial remote sensing images, and it is applicable to the characterization learning method of target detection with complex background, diverse targets and small size. Most importantly, the ZL contrast learning method is first to train model based on OPT Aircraft v1.0 data set to achieve higher accuracy in classifying aircraft types. We extract some of these weight parameters in this model, further base on RSOD data set and Faster R-CNN to achieve aircraft small target detection for aerial images.

2   Related Work

2.1   Analysis of Existing Comparative Learning

Self-supervised learning is a special type of unsupervised learning method with a supervised form, where the supervision sources self-supervised tasks instead of prior knowledge. The general idea consists of two main parts: a self-supervised training part and a downstream task part specific to a certain application. In the self-supervised training phase, the learning of the neural network model for the target representation is trained using a pretext task, rather than artificial labeling, to generate pseudo-labeled information. In the downstream task, the corresponding computer vision related tasks, such as classification, detection, segmentation, future prediction, etc., are done with the help of pseudo-labeled and the trained convolutional neural network model.

Contrast learning is a differentiated approach, a self-supervised task in the self-supervised training phase, for generating pseudo-labels of images. In principle some measure of similarity is used to bring similar samples closer together and different samples away from each other. Most of the early research in this area combined some form of instance-level classification methods [1, 7, 15] with contrast learning, and in recent years, many contrast learning approaches have been proposed, such as AMDIM [5], MoCo [14], SimCLR [8], BYOL [4], and SwAV [6]. The classification accuracy trained using these contrast learning approaches on the ImageNet [11] data set is comparable to that of supervised learning methods.

William Falcon et al. proposed a conceptual framework for CSL methods [12], which describes CSL methods in terms of five aspects: data augmentation pipeline, encoder selection, representation extraction, similarity metric, and loss function. Based on this framework, we analyze the existing comparative learning methods of AMDIM, MoCo, SimCLR, BYOL and SwAV (Table 1 Comparison of AMDIM, MOCO, SimCLR, BYOL, and SWAV methods).

Table 1. Comparison of AMDIM, MoCo, SimCLR, BYOL, and SWAV methods.

Author	Method	Data Augmentation Pipeline	Encoder	Representation extraction	Loss Function
Philip Bachman et al. (2019.7.8)	AMDIM	Random resizing of cropping Random color jitter Random grayscale	Self Encoders for ResNet	maximizing mutual information between arbitrary features extracted from multiple views of a shared context	Negative Contrast Estimation (NCE) loss
Kaiming He et al. (2020.3.23)	MoCo	Random resizing cropping Random color jitter Random horizontal flipping Random grayscale	Standard encoders for ResNet	Discrete dictionaries Momentum update	InfoNCE
Ting Chen et al. (2020.7.1)	SimCLR	Random crop Resizing to original size Random color jitter Random Gaussian blur	Standard encoders for ResNet	Final feature map Projection head	Negative Contrast Estimation (NCE) loss
Jean-Bastien Grill et al. (2020.9.10)	BYOL	Random crop Resizing to original size Random color jitter Random Gaussian blur	ResNet with deeper (50,101,152 200 layers) and wider (from 1× 4×)	The online network The target network	Positive sample loss estimation L_θ^{BYOL}
Mathilde Caron et al. (2021.1.8)	SWAV	Multi-crop strategy to increase the number of samples	Standard encoders for ResNet	Online clustering approach Projected head A "swap" prediction mechanism	$l(z_t, q_s)$

AMDIM method is mainly proposed by increasing multi-scale DIM information (between global and local features), maximizing negative samples of each image independently augmenting each image, maximizing mutual information between multiple feature scales, and a powerful encoder architecture designs to achieve technical innovation. The use of self-encoder design increases the complexity and poor practical results, while the use of feature map cross-validation increases the computational effort. The MOCO method is a mechanism for building dynamic dictionaries for comparison learning, maintaining dictionaries as queues of data samples: the coded representation of the current small batch enters the queue and the oldest leaves the queue. The queue decouples the dictionary size from the small batch size, making it larger. However, it uses dynamic refreshing of the coding area, which leads to inconsistency between old and new candidate codes, while occupying larger memory. SimCLR greatly improves the quality of the learned representation mainly by introducing a learnable nonlinear transformation between representation and contrast loss, and representation learning to use contrast cross-entropy loss benefits from normalized embedding and properly tuned temperature parameters. The nonlinear projection approach exacerbates the opacity of feature extraction and compresses the feature map to the implicit space, reducing the impact of the data augmentation pipeline. However, interpret ability of the data is reduced and the impact of unknown dimensions is unknown. BYOL relies on two neural networks, called the online network and the target network, which interact with and learn from each other. Starting from the enhanced view of an image, we train the online network to predict the target network representation of the same image under different augmentation pipeline. Meanwhile, we update the target network with a slow moving average of the online network. The BYOL method creatively combines GAN network ideas in MOCO and SimCLR, using only positive samples for training, for negative samples are not involved in training, and the small variability between samples is not considered. SWAV increases the number of views of an image without computation or memory overhead by introducing a multi-cropping strategy. Utilizes a scalable online clustering loss those works in both large and small batch settings without large memory banks or momentum encoders.

2.2 ZL Comparative Learning Method

The purpose of the data augmentation pipeline is to generate anchors, positive and negative features for comparative learning. It is experimentally demonstrated that the extraction strategy of the representations depends on the different data augmentation methods in the early stage. Different data augmentation pipeline affects not only the computational complexity, but also the effectiveness of representation extraction in the later stage. For example, the random flipping and random color grayscale processing strategies used by AMDIM have negligible effects on the results, but increase the computational complexity.

The resolution of aerially remote sensing images is higher than that of satellite remote sensing images, which has the advantages of high clarity, large scale and small area. The accuracy of aerial images depends on the aerial altitude under the same resolution of camera lens; and aerial photography can freely choose the weather and time. Aerially images mainly contain the top view information of ground objects, and the same type of targets are prone to rotational variability. Scale variability between the same target in the information collected by sensors of different heights and impulse noise and gaussian noise are common in aerially remote sensing images. Those issues need attention in processing aerial remote sensing images.

Based on the characteristics of the remote sensing aerial images and the technology of existing data augmentation pipeline, the ZL method data enhancement methods (Fig. 1 ZL's positive sample data augmentation pipeline, Fig. 2 ZL's negative sample data augmentation pipeline) are mainly median filter processing, random rotation, random cropping resizing to original size, random flip, random color distortion, random grayscale transformation, and random Gaussian blur. The random rotation processing of positive and negative samples are necessary to improve the accuracy of top-1 linear evaluation by 1% in the image classification task of a 100 epoch trained ResNet-50 model with small batch processing. Secondly, this method combines the same image enhancement set of SimCLR for positive samples with random cropping followed by fifty percent probability level (left-to-right) flip, random color dithering, Gaussian blur, etc.

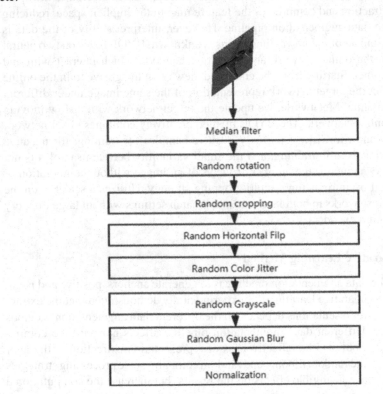

Fig. 1. Positive sample data augmentation pipeline of ZL.

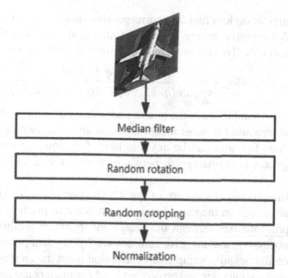

Fig. 2. Negative sample data augmentation pipeline of ZL.

Encoders play an essential role in any self-supervised learning pipeline, as they are responsible for mapping input samples into a latent space, enabling the transformation of an input sequence of indefinite length into a variable of fixed length. ZL method uses a dual channel encoder based on the Resnet network and end-to-end updates via backpropagation in training. At the same time, non-linear changes are added after the encoder to remove the information related to the enhancement channel of the image, and the number of negative samples is increased using a batch operation. This method is based on the nonlinear projection and implicit layer of SimCLR, and modifies the activation function in the projection header to a Sigmoid function. Based on a small sample size data set, the train and val training sets use the same augmentation pipeline, combine with normalization processing, and fine-tuning of label information using 10% of the data. The result achieves about 9% improvement in accuracy relative to the SimCLR method top-1.

A representation is a collection of unique characteristics that allows a system as well as humans to understand how something differs from other objects. This method uses the final feature map for comparison and reduces the corresponding computational effort. The excuse tasks used is a simple target classification task to extract images representation.

The measure of similarity is to measure the closeness between two sample embedding, and this method uses the cosine similarity, which the cosine similarity of two variables (vectors) is the cosine of the angle between them, which is defined as follows formula 1:

$$\cos\_\mathrm{sim}(A, B) = \frac{A \cdot B}{\backslash A \backslash \backslash B \backslash} \tag{1}$$

The loss function uses contrasting positive-negative samples to represent learning ability and is defined as a combination of positive and negative scores reflecting learning progress. The minimization loss function corresponds to maximizing the positive scores and minimizing the negative scores. The loss functioned used in ZL method is the negative contrast estimate (NCE) loss, which is defined as follows formula 2.

$$L_{NCE} = -\log \frac{\exp(\mathrm{sim}(q, k_+)/\tau)}{\exp\big(\mathrm{sim}(q, k)_+/\tau\big) + \exp(\mathrm{sim}(q, k)/\tau)_-} \tag{2}$$

where q is the original sample, k_+ is the positive sample, and k_- is the negative sample. τ is the hyperparameter used in most recent methods and is known as the temperature coefficient. The $sim()$ function can be any similarity function, but generally uses the cosine logistic regression to distinguish between observed data and some artificially generated noise.

In summary, the process at the core of the ZL comparison methodology is as follows: Where N samples from the same batch are extracted to produce $2N$ sample data representation representations through the image enhancement method, encoder, and projection head processing, and negative samples are $2(N\ 1)$ data points from the same batch. The positive and negative sample representation point data are normalized using cosine similarity, and the encoder and projection head parameters are updated in reverse by minimizing the NCE loss function.

3 Experiment

3.1 Processing of the Data Set

In order to verify the effectiveness of the proposed ZL method based on remote sensing data, and to validate the accuracy of target detection based on aerial aircraft, extensive experiments are conducted in the paper with the existing data sets OPT Aircraft v1.0 and aircraft data in RSOD. OPT Aircraft v1.0 data set from Chinese Academy of Sciences based on public data set DIOR, UCAS AOD, NWPU VHR-10, DOTA and Google Earth images extracted from some valid images, total 3594 images, size 96 96 pix. RSOD aircraft data is labeled by Wuhan University team, total 446 images, size 1044 915, spatial resolution 0.3–3 m. Based on the above data, we eliminate some unreasonable data and rationalize the images to make them uniform in specification.

3.2 Learning of Aircraft Features Based on ZL Method

The types of aircraft at airports can be divided into swept-back aircraft, swept-back aircraft, swept-forward aircraft with trailing edge, deltawing aircraft, flat-wing aircraft, propeller aircraft, helicopters and so on mainly based on the color of the aircraft and the color of the engine. The similarity between different types is high, and it is difficult to learn sample features without classification labels, while the contrast learning method can better explore the differences between similar samples, so as learning features with more sample differentiation, which is more conducive to downstream task such as detection and classification of aircraft targets within the scene.

To verify the effectiveness of this method for aircraft feature learning, a linear evaluation protocol is used to train a linear classifier frozen on top of the underlying network for the aircraft classification task to test the accuracy validity of the characterization extraction on the OPT Aircraft v1.0 data set.

3.3 Faster R-CNN Based Aircraft Target Detection

In the aircraft target detection phase, the Faster R-CNN model, which has performed well on target detection tasks for generic scenarios, is used. The model consists of a backbone (base network) for feature extraction, an RPN for generating regions of interest (ROI), and the ROI-Head for generating the final detection results, where the ROI-Head includes two branches of classification and localization.

Backbone consists of a deep convolutional neural network that maps the input image into a deep feature map. The backbone parts of the model in the paper is initialized with the feature extraction network parameters obtained from the self-supervised aircraft feature learning to train in phase 1 to provide the target detection model with as much a prior knowledge of the airfield environment and aircraft-related knowledge as possible, and then the backbone parameters are finetuned while the rest of the model is trained. Figure 3 shows the part of the ZL learning method based on the ResNet50 network structure combined with the Faster R-CNN network structure, replacing part of the structure in the BackBone in Faster R-CNN.

The RPN network uses the feature map to generate a series of candidate boxes by outputting the offset of the predicted boxes relative to the anchor points, using the predefined anchor points as a reference. By integrating the feature map with the candidate frame information, the features of each region of interest can be obtained. In the paper, ROI-Align (ROI alignment) method is used instead of ROI-Pooling (ROI pooling) method to implement the process. In addition, the cross-first loss function and the Smooth L1 loss function are used for the classification task and the localization task, respectively, during the model training process.

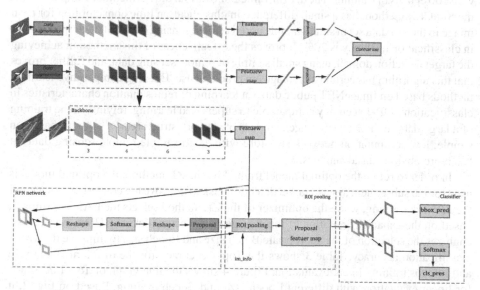

Fig. 3. ZL learning method combined with Faster R-CNN network structure.

At the same time, to better verify the effectiveness of the self-supervised pre-training method proposed in the paper, a type-independent aircraft target detection is performed, which all targets in the images are classified as "targets".

4 Experimental Verification and Result Analysis

In the self-supervised aircraft feature learning phase, the coding in the model are used in the ResNet-50 network, and the model is trained using image data from the OPT Aircraft v1.0 data set (without using its corresponding labels), and the learned features are directly used for aircraft classification, which a linear classification layer is trained in a self-supervised manner with a fixed feature extraction network.

In the aircraft target detection phase, the backbone part of the model uses the -50 trained in the previous phase for model initialization, which ResNet-50+FPN is used to form the network structure of Faster R-CNN, and the training and testing of target detection are performed in the RSOD data set, which is divided into train and val as the training set, while the post test data set for the testing of the model. In the testing phase, average accuracy (AP) and average recall (AR) are selected as the scoring criteria, and the tests are conducted under the conditions of intersection over union (IOU) threshold of 0.3 and 0.5, respectively. The ZL comparative learning method is used to learn aircraft features on the OPT Aircraft v1.0 data set, and a linear classifier is trained on this basis to complete the classification task for 7 classes of aircraft. Table 2 shows the Top-1 for classification on the OPT Aircraft v1.0 data set. The experimental process is compared by training both the SimCLR method for self-supervised feature learning and the ZL method with 100 epochs of training. The data in Table 2 shows that the ZL method, compared with the SimCLR method, has a small difference in classification time consumption for each image in the test data set in small-sample aerial remote sensing data, but the improvement in classification accuracy is 20%. It proves the effectiveness of this method in achieving the target detection domain using small sample of remote sensing data, and further proves that this algorithm has certain advantages in practical use. Existing comparative learning methods based on ImageNET public data set learning of representation characteristics in classification TOP-1 accuracy comparable to supervised learning, relying on the training of a large data set in the early stage and deeper network structure as a support, based on simple, low computation network structure with small sample remote sensing data set has more obvious disadvantages.

In order to refine the optimal model trained by the ZL method, the optimal model is used for the subsequent aircraft target detection task to improve the convergence speed of the network training, while the optimizer of the ZL method selects the LARS optimizer, based on the capacity limitation of the storage of the actual device CUDA, and further analyzes the selection of the appropriate Batch size and Epoch size to improve the Top-1 classification accuracy. Table 3 shows the Top-1 accuracy for the different Batch size and Epochs training linear evaluation. Figure 4 shows the line graph of Top-1 accuracy for linear evaluation with different Epoch size and Epoch training. Based on Fig. 2, it can be intuitively seen that the optimization efficiency is better and the rate is faster under the same epoch of high batch size compared to the setting of low batch size data, but the improvement of the later data is relatively less. To sum up, in the process of characterization learning, we should avoid raising Batch size, which causes unnecessary experimental settings, and determine the respective stable growth range through rough Batch size and Epoch settings, and reduce unnecessary iterations and excessive Batch size settings while adjusting the experimental accuracy to efficiently realize the learning rate in the training process. Rationalization of the parameter adjustment.

Table 2. Aircraft Top-1 on the OPT aircraft v1.0 dataset.

Method	Top-1	Training time	FPS
SimCLR	0.222841	70 min	22.27
ZL	0.423398	60 min	22.72

Table 3. Accuracy of Top-1 for linear evaluation with different batch size and epoch training.

Epoch Batch_size	100	200	300	400
64	0.3272980	0.3372987	0.3782993	0.4442896
128	0.3272980	0.4916435	0.5172930	0.5181001

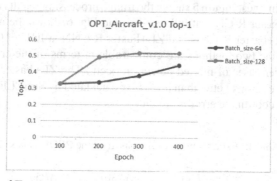

Fig. 4. Line graph of Top-1 accuracy for linear evaluation with different Batch size and Epoch training.

Based on the above data, In the small-sample unlabeled data, the ZL contrast learning method is used for training, in terms of time, is significantly lower than the time to make a large number of labels and train them, while the better classification level for small-sample unlabeled remote sensing data can be improved by reasonable planning of epoch and batch size sizes. Thus the method proves to be effective as a feature for learning unmarked remote sensing data, thus better serves for downstream aircraft classification and aircraft target detection.

To further validate the adaptability of the ZL contrast learning method, class-neutral target detection was performed on the RSOD data set using the Faster R-CNN framework, and ResNet-50 was used for BackBone, but a different pre-training approach was adopted for them, both using a structure based on 80% of the data set as training data and 20% as test data. Table 4 shows the experimental results based on the RSOD data set. Among them, Faster R-CNN indicates the result of training in a supervised way without modifying the internal hierarchy of the model based on OPT Aircraft v1.0 data set with batch size of 128; SimCLR+Faster R-CNN indicates SimCLR based on OPT Aircraft v1.0 data set ResNet50 with batch size of 128 and epoch of 200 as the BackBone of the Faster R-CNN network structure, trained on the RSOD data set; ZL+Faster R-CNN denotes ZL trained on the OPT Aircraft v1.0 data set with batch size of 128 and epoch of 200., epoch of 200 trained ResNet50 as BackBone of Faster R-CNN network structure, training results in RSOD data set. Through the analysis in Table 4, the ZL method and Faster R-CNN have significant advantages over Faster R-CNN and SimCLR+Faster R-CNN methods in all metrics for the target detection task. When IOU = 0.5, the AR value of ZL contrast learning method does not have a significant advantage, but there is a slight advantage relative to the current SimCLR method, thus proving that it is feasible based on the use of label-free contrast learning method for the analysis aspect of remote sensing images. Figure 5 shows the image processing results in SimCLR+Fast R-CNN and ZL+Faster R-CNN at IOU = 0.3, and Fig. 6 shows the image processing results in SimCLR+Faster R-CNN and ZL+Faster R-CNN at IOU = 0.5. Analyzed by Fig. 5 and Fig. 6, the two methods are comparable in terms of the error rate of target detection, and fewer cases of missed detection occur. The ZL+Faster R-CNN method fits the actual aircraft target better than the BBox calculated by SimCLR+Faster R-CNN, and the four-point coordinate error is smaller.

Table 4. Experimental results based on the RSOD data set.

Method	$AP30$	$AR30$	$AP50$	$AR50$
Faster R-CNN	0.6378	0.7194	0.4432	0.4989
SimCLR+Faster R-CNN	0.6384	0.7013	0.4801	0.5216
ZL+Faster R-CNN	0.6908	0.7404	0.5327	0.5528

Fig. 5. Image processing results in SimCLR+Faster R-CNN and ZL+Faster R-CNN at IOU = 0.3 ((a) the result in SimCLR+Faster R-CNN (b) the result in SimCLR+Faster R-CNN).

Fig. 6. Image processing results in SimCLR+Faster R-CNN and ZL+Faster R-CNN at IOU = 0.5((a) the result in SimCLR+Faster R-CNN (b) the result in SimCLR+Faster R-CNN).

5 Conclusion

In this paper, self-supervised representation learning is introduced into the field of remote sensing small target detection, based on a new ZL method for aircraft

target feature learning on smaller-scale unlabeled aerial remote sensing data, and the learned features are later used for aircraft target detection tasks. The experimental results show that the method is feasible for aircraft target detection, breaking through the dilemma of training on large-scale labeled remote sensing target data set. Remote sensing images are widely researched and used for their large range and multi-channel information collection, but in practice there is fewer images information available for a certain area, and the labeling of images requires a lot of wasted manpower and material resources, so the research application for small sample unlabeled remote sensing data is an important research direction to deal with emergencies in the future. Furthermore, remote sensing data provides relatively little information about the side of the object, and the data is affected by deformation, so its efficient accuracy in terms of network design and feature extraction in target detection is an issue of concern specific to the field of remote sensing.

References

1. Bachman, P., Hjelm, R.D., Buchwalter, W.: Learning representations by maximizing mutual information across views. arXiv:1906.00910 (2019)
2. Bojanowski, P., Joulin, A.: Unsupervised learning by predicting noise. In: International Conference on Machine Learning, pp. 517–526. PMLR (2017)
3. Dosovitskiy, A., Fischer, P., Springenberg, J.T., Riedmiller, M., Brox, T.: Discriminative unsupervised feature learning with exemplar convolutional neural networks. IEEE Trans. Pattern Anal. Mach. Intell. **38**(9), 1734–1747 (2016). https://doi.org/10.1109/TPAMI.2015. 24961411
4. Falcon, W., Cho, K.: A framework for contrastive self-supervised learning and designing a new approach. arXiv:2009.00104 (2020)
5. Grill, J.B., et al.: Bootstrap your own latent: a new approach to self-supervised learning. arXiv:2006.07733 (2020)
6. Henaff, O.: Data-efficient image recognition with contrastive predictive coding. In: International Conference on Machine Learning, pp. 4182–4192. PMLR (2020)
7. Karras, T., Laine, S., Aila, T.: A Style-based generator architecture for generative adversarial networks. In: Proceedings of the IEEE/CVF Conference on Computer Vision and Pattern Recognition, pp. 4401–4410 (2019)
8. Oord, A.V., Kalchbrenner, N., Kavukcuoglu, K.: Pixel recurrent neural networks. In: International Conference on Machine Learning, pp. 1747–1756. PMLR (2016)
9. Redmon, J., Divvala, S., Girshick, R., Farhadi, A.: You only look once: unified, real-time object detection. In: Proceedings of the IEEE Conference on Computer Vision and Pattern Recognition, pp. 779–788 (2016) 1
10. Redmon, J., Farhadi, A.: YOLO9000: better, faster, stronger. In: Proceedings of the IEEE Conference on Computer Vision and Pattern Recognition, pp. 7263–7271 (2017)
11. Redmon, J., Farhadi, A.: YOLOv3: An Incremental Improvement. arXiv:1804.02767 (2018)
12. Schroff, F., Kalenichenko, D., Philbin, J.: FaceNet: a unified embedding for face recognition and clustering. In: Proceedings of the IEEE Conference on Computer Vision and Pattern Recognition, pp. 815–823 (2015)
13. Wu, Z., Xiong, Y., Yu, S., Lin, D.: Unsupervised feature learning via non- parametric instance-level discrimination arXiv:1805.01978 (2018)
14. Xiao, X., Zhou, Z., Wang, B., Li, L., Miao, L.: Ship Detection under complex backgrounds based on accurate rotated anchor boxes from paired semantic segmentation. Remote Sens. **11**(21), 2506 (2019). https://doi.org/10.3390/rs112125062.1
15. Zhu, J.Y., Park, T., Isola, P., Efros, A.A.: Unpaired image-to-image translation using cycle-consistent adversarial networks. In: Proceedings of the IEEE Inter- national Conference on Computer Vision. pp. 2223–2232 (2017) 2.1

Fast Fractal Image Compression Algorithm Based on Compression Perception

Lixian Zhang[1] , Caixu Xu[2](✉) , and Jie He[2]

[1] School of Electronic and Information Engineering, Wuzhou University, Wuzhou 543002, China
[2] Guangxi Key Laboratory of Machine Vision and Intelligent Control, Wuzhou University, Wuzhou 543002, China
xucaixu0815@163.com

Abstract. To address the problem of long coding time of fractal image compression algorithm, this paper proposes a fractal image compression algorithm based on compression perception. Firstly, the algorithm is coded in the wavelet domain by separating the high and low frequency signals of the image, then, the low frequency information is fractally coded, while the sparse high frequency signals are sampled and coded in a compression-aware manner, and finally, a better image reconstruction compensation effect is achieved with the premise of reducing the number of coding searches and coding time. The experimental results show that this algorithm has a slight decrease in coding quality and compression ratio compared to fractal coding image compression, but has a superior improvement in coding speed.

Keywords: Image compression · Fractal coding · Compression perception · Wavelet transform

1 Introduction

Fractal images coding is an image coding strategy that takes advantage of the self-similarity of images of different scales and replaces the overall value domain block iterative search process of a series of radiometric transformations such as scaling, rotation and scale transformation of locally defined domain blocks, thus achieving a high compression ratio. However, there is a serious imbalance between the coding time and decoding time of fractal compression, and the improvement to decoding reconstruction quality is positively correlated with the coding time, making it difficult for fractal coding to meet the needs of practical applications. Therefore, how to achieve a better breakthrough in coding time and coding quality has become a key hot issue in the research of fractal image compression algorithms. Most of the current mainstream fractal image compression and coding optimisation algorithms are based on Jacquin coding scheme [1], and are mainly reflected on two aspects: firstly, in terms of coding speed improvement, there are mainly block classification strategies, fast search and other strategies, and

X. Jiang (Ed.): MLICOM 2021, LNICST 438, pp. 297–306, 2022.
https://doi.org/10.1007/978-3-031-04409-0_27

secondly, in terms of image reconstruction quality improvement, there are mainly image block segmentation method improvements. The above methods can only improve the performance unilaterally, and there are few balanced performance optimisation solutions that combine both coding time and image reconstruction quality.

Fractal image compression coding can directly improve the coding speed. Guo Hui et al. used the value domain block variance as a classification index to improve the fractal coding process, and used the nearest neighbour search method to reduce the number of value domain blocks and definition domain blocks to be coded during the search process in order to shorten the coding time [2]. Zheng Yunping et al. proposed a fast fractal imaged compression algorithm based on an iteration-controlled search strategy [3], which controls the search process by using the number of fractal code iterations to remove invalid searches and inefficient searches, and ultimately achieves a significant increase in coding speed. Wang Li et al. proposed a fractal image compression algorithm based on center-of-mass features and important sensitive region classification [4]. The algorithm transforms the global search problem of R blocks in the codebook into a local fast search problem by constructing prime features, thus simplifying the block search process and achieving a reduction in coding time. Zhang Aihua et al. implemented a fractal image compression method based on sparse decomposition by processing the original image and combining it with relevant hardware execution structures [5].

Fractal image compression coding can also be combined with other algorithmic terms to improve the coding speed and quality. Lou Li et al. [6] proposed a hybrid coding algorithm based on the combination of wavelet and fractal. The algorithm performs wavelet decomposition of the image, encodes the low-frequency signal separately, and carries out fractal prediction based on the texture features of subgraphs in different directions, thus greatly reduced the fractal coding time. Zhang Aihua et al. [7] proposed a fractal image compression coding algorithm based on DCT compensation, which combines a fractal image compression coding method with a discrete cosine transforms approximation to find the best defined domain block and its mapping by adjusting the grey scale transform to achieve reconstruction image quality increment and reduce the coding time. Li-Xiu Wu et al. [8] proposed a generic reference-free stereo image quality evaluation algorithm using the quadratic tree wavelet transformed in order to effectively evaluate the quality of various types of distorted stereo images. He J et al. [9] used the characteristics of the human visual system to optimize the SNAMG segmentation method for images using visual thresholding on those and used it for adaptive sub-block segmentation of fractal image compression, which greatly improved the efficiency of the coding process.

This paper proposes a fast fractal image coding algorithm based on compression-awareness. The algorithm makes full use of the characteristics of wavelet variations, firstly fractal coding the low frequency part of the wavelet transform as a way to reduce the coding time, and then sampling and coding the sparse data of the high frequency part using the compression-aware method, finally forming a hybrid image coding framework. Finally, the theoretical analysis and experimental results verify the superiority, robustness and efficiency of the method described in this paper.

2   Compression-Aware Fractal Image Compression Algorithm

Fractal image coding mainly uses the self-similarity of images at different scales in different regions to achieve compression, and when coding, the image is firstly segmented into fixed blocks to obtain the value domain R blocks and the definition domain D blocks, then the D blocks are shrunk in the spatial domain to obtain the codebook, and then the best matching D blocks are found for each R block and their fractal codes are recorded to obtain the iterative function system, and finally the decoding is based on the iterative function system and the fractal code iteration The decoded reconstructed image is obtained by iterative decoding based on the iterative function system and the sub-codes. Since each R-block searches for matching a large number of times, a long coding time usually occurs, so this subsection will first analyse the characteristics of the branching coding process, then introduce the wavelet transform into the branching coding strategy, and finally develop a hybrid coding and decoding scheme combining compression-awareness and fractal coding for the high and low frequency signal data obtained by the wavelet transform.

2.1   Optimisation of Fractal Coding Algorithms Based on Classification Methods

Fractal images coding uses the similarity in images of different scales in different regions to achieve compression. The coding process performs a fixed block segmentation of the image into a number of mutually non-stacked values domain blocks R blocks, then the image is segmented from left to right and from top to bottom by step B to obtain the corresponding definition domain D blocks, and the set of definition domain blocks is fractally coded between groups of codebooks Ω, as shown in the following Fig. 1.

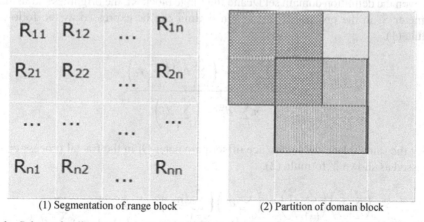

(1) Segmentation of range block   (2) Partition of domain block

Fig. 1. Schematic diagram of value domain block partitioning and definition domain block partitioning

The best matching block is selected as the ∆D block of the smallest mean square error in the codebook, and the one with the smallest error in the eight equidistant transformations Tq is selected as the equidistant transformation parameter, thus obtaining the best approximate solution to Ri. The overall transformation process is as shown in Fig. 2.

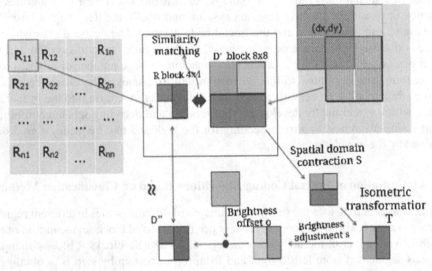

Fig. 2. Value domain block matching process for fractal image coding

Given the definition domain set Di and the range block RI, the brightness adjustment parameter Si in the process of distraction coding can be expressed as the following formula (1).

$$s_i = \frac{n \sum\limits_{i=1}^{n} d_i r_i - \left(\sum\limits_{i=1}^{n} d_i\right)\left(\sum\limits_{i=1}^{n} r_i\right)}{n \sum\limits_{i=1}^{n} d_i^2 - \left(\sum\limits_{i=1}^{n} d_i\right)^2} \tag{1}$$

By the same token, the luminance offset parameter Oi in the fractal process can be expressed as shown in formula (2).

$$o_i = \frac{\left(\sum\limits_{i=1}^{n} r_i\right)\left(\sum\limits_{i=1}^{n} d_i^2\right) - \left(\sum\limits_{i=1}^{n} d_i\right)\left(\sum\limits_{i=1}^{n} d_i r_i\right)}{n \sum\limits_{i=1}^{n} d_i^2 - \left(\sum\limits_{i=1}^{n} d_i\right)^2} = \frac{1}{n}\left(\sum\limits_{i=1}^{n} r_i - s \sum\limits_{i=1}^{n} d_i\right) \tag{2}$$

The mean squared error of Ri and Dj in the coding process can be expressed as shown in formula (3).

$$\min_{s_i,o_i \in R} f(s_i, o_i) = \frac{1}{n} \left[\sum_{i=1}^{n} r_i^2 + s \left(s \sum_{i=1}^{n} d_i^2 - 2 \sum_{i=1}^{n} d_i r_i + 2 \cdot o_i \sum_{i=1}^{n} d_i \right) \right.$$
$$\left. + o_i \cdot \left(o_i \cdot n - 2 \sum_{i=1}^{n} r_i \right) \right] \tag{3}$$

Fractal coding algorithms need to spend a lot of time for global search, however, the texture distribution of a large number of images shows a strong regional nature, as shown in Fig. 2 and 3, the pixels at point O in the image are relatively uniformly distributed and the pixels at point G have a large variation in texture. Therefore, the segmented value domain blocks R blocks can be classified according to their texture characteristics during fractal coding, i.e. blocks of uniform pixel distribution are classified as simple classes and blocks with large pixel variation are classified as complex blocks. By classifying the value domain blocks according to whether their mean squared deviation is less than a set threshold, and less than the threshold then the mean value is directly substituted for the best matching block search strategy. In addition, for most blocks similarly defined domain blocks D blocks usually exist in the vicinity of the value domain blocks R. By limiting the interval of the best search to the region near the value domain blocks R blocks, both can reduce the coding time.

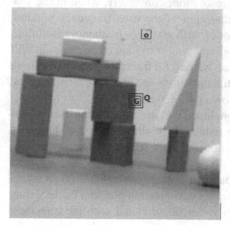

a Classification of value field blocks

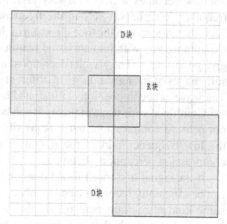

b Search range for value field blocks

Fig. 3. Fractal coding strategy for classification methods

This thesis adopts a priori strategy to define the classification threshold R = 6.0, and then calculates the mean square error of the value domain blocks R_{var} and constructs a classification basis to determine the classification match with the following formula (4).

$$R_{var} = \sqrt{\frac{1}{R \times R}(\sum_{x}^{R}\sum_{y}^{R}R_{xy}^2) - (\frac{1}{R \times R}\sum_{x}^{R}\sum_{y}^{R}R_{xy})^2} < 6.0 \qquad (4)$$

The R blocks that satisfy the above conditions are simple blocks and their averages R_{ave} are saved and the averages are calculated as shown in formula (5).

$$R_{ave} = \frac{1}{R \times R}\left(\sum_{x}^{R}\sum_{y}^{R}R_{xy}\right) \qquad (5)$$

Otherwise, a search for the best matching block in the restricted range is processed and the corresponding sub-code is saved.

2.2 Fractal Image Compression Algorithm Combining Compression-Awareness and Wavelet Transform

Wavelets has different scales of time-frequency resolution refinement characteristics, when in the centre of the higher frequency, wavelets in the time direction of the time frequency window becomes narrower, in the frequency direction of the time frequency window becomes wider, with very high time resolution; conversely, when in the low frequency centre, wavelets in the frequency direction of the time frequency window becomes narrower, in the time direction of the wider, with very high frequency resolution. Combining this with human visual features and applying it to image compression will give good results. The wavelet decomposition can be used for fractal coding by obtaining sub images of strong similarity in different spatial directions and at different resolutions. The wavelet decomposition is illustrated as shown in Fig. 4 and Fig. 5.

Combined with wavelet theory it can be concluded that the wavelet transforms does not achieve compression, but it is possible to reduce the coding time by coding only the low frequency part of the fractal image, and the high frequency parts will take compression perception of coding.

If the signal in a transformed domain is sparse or compressible, the original signal can be efficiently reconstructed by solving a convex optimisation problem by designing some kind of measurement matrix that is somewhat uncorrelated with the transform base, and this method is highly cost-effective in terms of compression because the length of the measurement matrix is much smaller than the length of the original signal. The high-frequency part of the image after wavelet transform is sparse, and the coding and decoding of the high-frequency signal by means of compression-awareness can effectively improve the efficiency of coding compensation.

The theory of compressed sensing to consists of three main components: the sparse representation of the signal, the selection of the measurement matrix and the design of the reconstruction algorithm. Firstly, the sparse representation capability of the transform base is measured by the sharp decay of the transform sparse, and a suitable transform

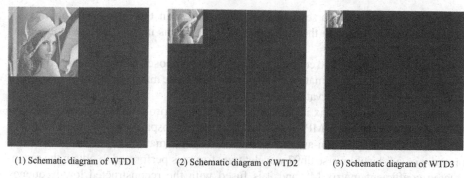

(1) Schematic diagram of WTD1   (2) Schematic diagram of WTD2   (3) Schematic diagram of WTD3

Fig. 4. Schematic diagram of wavelet transform decomposition

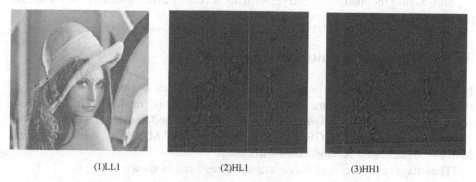

(1)LL1   (2)HL1   (3)HH1

Fig. 5. Subplots in different directions

base is selected to represent the signal, maintain efficient sparsity and achieve high accuracy decoding and reconstruction capability. Then, by projecting the sparse signal onto an observation matrix that is disjoint from the transform base, the Gauss matrix with finite isometric Rip is selected as the measurement matrix to achieve the effect of data acquisition and compression by satisfying $(1 - \delta_K)||x||_2^2 \leq ||\phi x||_2^2 \leq (1 + \delta_K)||x||_2^2$ when solving parameter $\delta_K < 1$. Finally, the signal is reconstructed by solving for the optimal solution $\alpha' = \min ||\alpha||_{l_0}$ $s.t.$ $y = \phi \psi \alpha$ to the L0 parametrization.

The steps of the fractal image compression algorithm based on the combination of compression perception and wavelet transform are as follows.

Input: image to be encoded orig, measurement matrix φ.

Output: decoded reconstructed image res.

Step 1. Perform db97 wavelet transforms into the input image to be encoded and save the low-frequency submap LL and the high-frequency submaps in three different directions of horizontal and vertical details.

Step 2. Perform fractal encoding of the low-frequency submap LL, record and save the fractal code, and use the fractal code to iterate to obtain the reconstructed low-frequency submap LL$'$.

Step 3. Calculate the low frequency difference subgraph LL0 = LL − LL$'$.

Step 4. Construct a sparse sparse subgraph based on the difference subgraph of the low-frequency part with the high-frequency subgraphs in three different directions matrix.

Step 5. The reconstructed coefficient matrix is decomposed at 5 levels using the db97 wavelet to obtain the sparse matrix x, and project the sparse matrix onto the measurement matrix φ to obtain the observation matrix $y = \varphi x$.

Step 6. The sparse matrix is reconstructed with high probability of a small number of measurements y using OMP's improved arithmetic subspace tracking algorithm SP.

Step 7. The compression-aware reconstructed sparse matrix is inverse sparse transformed, i.e., a 5-level inverse db97 wavelet transforms is performed to obtain the reconstructed coefficient matrix M', and it is fused with the reconstructed low-frequency subgraph LL' of the fractal encoding wait to obtain the matrix $M1 = M' + LL'$.

Step 8. fuse the matrix M1 and perform the inverse wavelet transform to obtain the reconstructed image res.

3   Experimental Results and Analysis

In this thesis, representative images of different scenes such as animal (Figure a), plant (Figure b), landscape (Figure c), geometric (Figure d) and medical (Figure e) were selected. The computer configuration was Win7 flagship and above, Intel (R) core CPU @2.60 GHz i5-3230M 2.60 GHz, 4.00 GB of memory (RAM), 64-bit operating system, Matlab 7.0 integrated development environment.

The images and results of the experimental tests are as shown in Fig. 6.

(a)Animal drawings   (b)Botanical drawings   (c)Landscape drawings   (d)Geometric drawings   (e)Medical diagrams

Fig. 6. Test image data

Aiming at the above images, this paper systematically verifies the relevant performance of basic fractal algorithm, fractal combined wavelet and compression aware fractal image compression from three aspects: compression ratio (C), running time (time) and peak signal-to-noise ratio (PSNR) [as shown in formulas (6) and (7)].

Compression ratio (C) is the ratio of compressed data size (CDS) to pre compressed image size (SIC). The calculation formula is shown in formula (6):

$$C = \frac{CDS}{SIC} \tag{6}$$

Subjective fidelity is to judge the reconstruction quality of the image by human eye judgment, while objective fidelity usually takes the peak signal-to-noise ratio (PSNR) as the evaluation criterion. The formula of signal-to-noise ratio is shown in formula (7):

$$PSNR = 10\log\frac{255^2}{MSE}(db) \qquad (7)$$

In formula (7), MSE is the pixel error between the original image f (x, y) and the reconstructed image f (x, y)′, and the calculation is shown in formula (8):

$$MSE = \frac{1}{MN}\sum_{x=0}^{M}\sum_{y=0}^{N}\left(f(x, y) - f(x, y)'\right)^2 \qquad (8)$$

The experimental comparison parameters are shown in the table below (Table 1):

Table 1. Algorithm comparison experimental parameters table

Image	Experimental parameters	Basic fractal algorithm	Fractal combined with wavelet algorithm	Compression-aware fractal image algorithm	Acceleration ratio compared to basic algorithm
Bird	Time/s	2967.76	1.05	1.31	2256.67
	Psnr/db	39.10	29.82	32.56	
	C	4.74	17.65	2.87	
Rose	Time/s	3500.17	0.99	1.06	3301.88
	Psnr/db	35.58	27.76	31.38	
	C	4.74	17.65	2.92	
Visible	Time/s	2964.85	1.81	2.04	1453.35
	Psnr/db	35.77	26.30	30.71	
	C	4.74	17.65	2.811	
Shape	Time/s	2969.82	1.04	1.24	2395.01
	Psnr/db	38.33	34.27	39.25	
	C	4.74	17.65	2.90	
Heci	Time/s	3933.01	0.88	1.10	3543.57
	Psnr/db	31.98	30.12	35.18	
	C	4.74	17.65	2.91	

The above experimental results show that in terms of coding time, as this algorithm combines the advantages of fractal, wavelet coding and compression-aware coding, although there is a slight increase in coding time compared to the fractal combined with wavelet algorithm, the fractal combined with wavelet is inferior to the algorithm described in this paper in terms of image restoration quality, and the time efficiency is about 1000 times faster compared to the basic fractal coding. In terms of image quality restoration, the algorithm in this paper is based on fractal combined wavelet coding of high-frequency subgraphs and low-frequency difference maps, and its decoding and reconstruction quality is much better.

4 Conclusion

Compared with the basic fractal coding algorithm, the coding speed is greatly improved with a slight decrease in decoding quality; compared with the fractal combined with wavelet coding method and the compression-aware coding method, the coding time is slightly longer but the restored image quality is higher. Therefore, the algorithm in this paper can guarantee the decoding image quality while shortening the fractal coding time, which is of practical significance to the popularization of fractal image coding methods.

Acknowledgments. Supported by a project grant from National Natural Science Foundation (Grand No. 61961036 & 62162054), the University Young Teachers Basic Ability Improvement Project of Guangxi (Grand No. 2018KY0537 & 2017KY0629), Wuzhou Scientific Research and Technology Development Project (Grand No. 201501014), Guangxi Natural Science Foundation (Grand No. 2020GXNSFAA297259 & 2018GXNSFBA281173), Wuzhou High-tech Zone, Wuzhou University Industry-Education-Research Project (Grand No. 2020G001), the Guangxi Innovation-Driven Development Special Driven Develop Special Fund Project (Guike AA18118036), the Guangxi Science and Technology Base and Talent Special Project (Guike AD20297148).

References

1. Jcquin, A.E.: Fractal image coding: a review. Proc. IEEE **8**, 1451–1465 (1993)
2. Guo, H., He, J.: Research on fast fractal image compression algorithm based on classification method. J. Wuzhou Univ. **06**, 1–8 (2015)
3. Zheng, Y., Li, X.: Fractal image compression algorithm based on iterative control search strategy. J. Huazhong Univ. Sci. Technol. (Nat. Sci. Ed.) (07), 1–6 (2020)
4. Wang, L., Liu, Z.: A fractal image compression algorithm based on center-of-mass features and important sensitive region classification. Comput. Eng. Sci. (05), 869–876 (2020)
5. Zhang, A.H., Tang, X.L., Han, J.: Design of fractal image compression system based on sparse decomposition in real time. Mod. Electron. Technol. (17), 29–33 (2020)
6. Lou, L., Liu, T.: Image compression optimization algorithm based on the combination of wavelet and fractal. Microelectron. Comput. **06**, 145–148 (2010)
7. Zhang, A., Chang, K.: Fractal image coding combined with DCT compensation. Comput. Technol. Dev. **01**, 61–64+68 (2014)
8. Wu, L., Yao, X., Wang, S., Gao, S.: Reference-free image quality evaluation based on multi-core learning and quaternion wavelet transform. Wirel. Interconnect. Technol. (11), 119–121 (2020)
9. He, J., Guo, H., Li, L.: A fractal image compression method based on SNAMG segmentation. J. Nat. Sci. Xiangtan Univ. **03**, 93–100 (2015)

Color Image Fast Encryption Algorithm Based on JPEG Encoding

Ma Rong[1] (ID), Yao Gaohua[2(✉)] (ID), and Guo Hui[2] (ID)

[1] School of Electronics and Information Engineering, Wuzhou University, Wuzhou 543002, China

[2] Guangxi Key Laboratory of Machine Vision and Intelligent Control, Wuzhou University, Wuzhou 543002, China

12348906@qq.com

Abstract. In order to strengthen the security of standard JPEG format color images in network transmission, this paper proposes a kind of JPEG color image encryption algorithm which combines the efficient and stable compression encoding with encrypting selectively. First, it selects out mapping better chaotic characteristics as a pseudo-random number generator, and uses the generated chaotic sequence for the encryption algorithm. Then, it uses the edge detection algorithm to find the blocks with rich image contour information, which provides a basis for selection and encryption of later images. It Encrypts the quantized image coefficients and embeds in the important block information. The experimental results shows that the algorithm in this paper can hide the color information and contour information of the plaintext image effectively. At the same time, the key is more sensitive. Compared with the classic encryption algorithm AES, it has better performance in terms of time complexity and encryption quality.

Keywords: JPEG · Chaotic system · DC hiding · Encrypting selectively

1 Introduction

Image encryption algorithm is an important research issue in the fields of digital image processing, computer vision, and reliable video transmission [1]. With the increasing demand for image privacy in the context of the Internet, image encryption algorithms have been widely used in key areas such as politics, economy, military, and medical care [2]. Most mainstream image encryption algorithms are to hide data in the frequency domain and spatial domain. So, the mainstream image encryption can be divided into two categories: one is to select the larger part of the information in the image for the encryption algorithm, so as to reduce the amount of encrypted data; the other one is to use the encryption algorithm throughout the entire image compression coding process to reduce the generation of compressed data redundancy.

With the help of the idea of selective encryption, Xiao Ning et al. proposed an infrared image selection algorithm based on multi-feature difference detection and joint control

© ICST Institute for Computer Sciences, Social Informatics and Telecommunications Engineering 2022
Published by Springer Nature Switzerland AG 2022. All Rights Reserved
X. Jiang (Ed.): MLICOM 2021, LNICST 438, pp. 307–314, 2022.
https://doi.org/10.1007/978-3-031-04409-0_28

mapping [3]. Yu Ping et al. solved the problem of insufficient secure transmission on encryption algorithms, and proposed an infrared target selection encryption algorithm basing on geometric active contour mode and coupled mapping [4]. On the basis of selective encryption, Khan Naqash Azeem et al. proposed a new chaotic-based S-box to encrypt JPEG graphics selectively [5]. Yang Wei et al. proposed a three-dimensional image joint encryption and compression algorithm by optimizing the decryption accuracy and compression ratio [6]. Li Peiya et al. proposed JPEG joint graphic compression and encryption algorithm on JPEG graphics compression [7]. Liu Zhuo et al. proposed an image compression encryption algorithm based on the two-dimensional coupled image lattice model [8]. By encrypting images selectively, the amount of calculation can be greatly reduced, but the security cannot be guaranteed. The compression encryption algorithm is superior in encryption performance and security but time-consuming. Therefore, Considering the contradiction between efficiency and security, there are few reports on the combination of selective encryption and compression algorithms so far.

This paper analyzes the characteristics of two mainstream encryption algorithms systematically, and optimizes the whole image encryption process by the combination of image compression process encryption and selective encryption. First, it blocks scrambling and encrypting the original image, and then encrypts DCT coefficients and their rich symbols during JPEG encoding to realize hiding the image DCT coefficients. Simultaneously, it Chooses a map with better chaotic effects as a pseudo-random number generator to generate a chaotic sequence for the encryption algorithm, encrypting the edge detection image blocks with rich texture by the approach of edge detection, and then embeds the encrypted relevant information into the DCT coefficients. The final theoretical analysis and experimental results show that compared with the traditional encryption algorithms, the algorithm described in this paper is more advantageous, stable and robust in terms of timeliness, security, encryption quality, etc.

2   Color Image Encryption Algorithm Based on JPEG Encoding

Encryption algorithm of JPEG color image in this paper uses edge detection strategies to select regions with rich textures for image encryption and adopts chaotic coding strategy to realize spatial scrambling encryption of image. Then it completes the encryption operation in the frequency domain when the image data undergo DCT transformation, and at the same time it embeds the selected encrypted information into the image data. The overall flow chart of the algorithm is as follows (as shown in Fig. 1).

2.1 Image Edge Detection

If all DC coefficients and AC coefficients are encrypted, it is not only computationally expensive but also time-consuming. The selective encryption can effectively reduce various expenses in the encryption process and ensures the encryption effect. So, this paper focuses on selective encryption for areas with richer edge information.

First, the encrypted image is divided into 8×8 area, then it selects the Canny operator to detect the edge of the encrypted image, choosing a reasonable threshold T based on

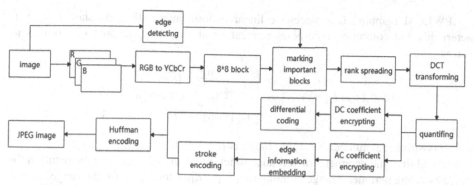

Fig. 1. Flow chart of color image encryption algorithm based on JPEG encoding

the amount of information at the edge of each block to complete the screening of whether there are key encrypted blocks in each block.

The images obtained after edge detection is shown below (as shown in Fig. 2).

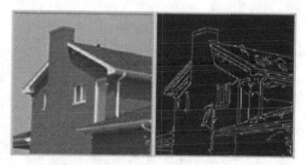

Fig. 2. The result of House edge detection by canny operator

2.2 Key and Chaotic Sequence Generation

The characteristics of concealment, unpredictability, complexity and easy implementation of chaotic signals can completely match the relevant requirements of encryption algorithms for keys. Encryption algorithm in this paper uses the keys such as K1, K2, K3, K4, K5, etc., and adopts the Henon mapping and PWLCM mapping in the discrete chaotic sequence system to generate three sets of mixed sequences (H1, H2), P1 and P2. The Henon map is a two-dimensional discrete chaotic system.

The mapping equation is as follows:

$$\begin{cases} x_{n+1} = 1 - 1.4x_n^2 + y_n \\ y_{n+1} = 0.3x_n \end{cases} x \in (-1.5, 1.5), y \in (-0.4, 0.4) \tag{1}$$

PWLCM mapping is a piecewise linear chaotic map with good statistical characteristics and computer fixed-point realization ability. The mapping equation is as follows:

$$x(k+1) = C[x(k); \mu] = \begin{cases} \frac{x(k)}{\mu}, x(k) \in [0, \mu) \\ \frac{x(k)-\mu}{0.5-\mu}, x(k) \in [\mu, 0.5) \\ C[1 - x(k); \mu], x(k) \in [0.5, 1) \end{cases} \qquad (2)$$

μ is a positive real number, the value range is $\mu \in (0, 0.5), x \in (0, 1)$.

In addition, the parameter disturbance function is defined to control the result in the corresponding parameter range. Among them, γ Adjust the factor for the range.

$$F(a, b, c) = \gamma \times \frac{a+b+c}{3} \qquad (3)$$

The specific implementation steps are shown in the following figure (as shown in Fig. 3):

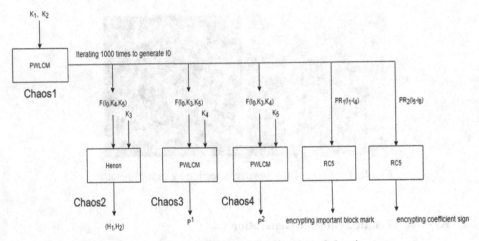

Fig. 3. The application of keys and the generation of chaotic sequences

2.3 Process of Image Spatial Space Block Scrambling Encryption

When the digital image is JPEG encoded, it is usually necessary to encrypt the image in the airspace first. Scrambling images is one of the commonly used airspace encryption methods. The parameters used in the scrambling process are inherently random, and the sequence generated by the discrete chaotic mapping system can be used as the image scrambling process.

The image scrambling method based on chaotic mapping can be summarized as follows:

1. Using Henon chaotic mapping to generate chaotic sequence (H_1, H_2).
2. Scrambling the lines of the image block map. Each row is cyclically shifted to the right, and the number of shifts is determined by the Henon chaotic mapping sequence H_1. In the same way, each column is shifted in blocks, and the number of shifts is determined by the *Henon* chaotic mapping sequence H_2.
3. Multiple rounds of block row and column cyclic shift operations can achieve encryption effects. The scrambling operation is realized by "modulo operation", and the result of the operation is controlled within the value range of the number of blocks. The formula is as follows:

$$\begin{cases} x_i = (x_i \times 1000000) \bmod L(x_i \in H_1) \\ y_i = (y_i \times 1000000) \bmod C(y_i \in H_2) \end{cases} \tag{4}$$

As shown in formula 3, L is the number of rows and C is columns in the block. Corresponding to the i-th row, the number of shifts in the i-th row is a x_i block, and the same is for columns.

2.4 Selective Encryption of Image DCT Domain Coefficients

After the image is transformed by DCT, the DC coefficient holds most of the information of the image, while the AC coefficient holds relatively little information. Therefore, the same strategy is adopted to realize the selective encryption of DC coefficients. Using the P^1 chaotic sequence generated by PWLCM mapping as the key stream of the sequence cipher to encrypt each coefficient, the process is shown in the following formula:

$$d_i = d_i xor((P_i^1 \times 1000000) \bmod (1023/Q_1)) \tag{5}$$

In formula (4), P_i^1 represents the i-th value in the chaotic sequence, and Q_1 is the same value in the quantization table as the coefficient position of each block. Since the DCT coefficient value range is -1024 to 1023, dividing 1023 by Q_1 and taking the remainder is to ensure that the DC coefficient is within the value range after XOR encryption.

The encryption of AC coefficients depends on the marking of image blocks, using Zig-zag method to select the first 16 AC coefficients from all marked blocks to encrypt. The calculation method is as follows:

$$a_i = a_i xor((P_i^1 \times 1000000) \bmod Q_i) \tag{6}$$

As shown in formula (5), it encrypts all 16 coefficients. P_i^1 is the i-th value in the chaotic sequence, and Q_i represents the same value in the quantization table as the position of the AC coefficient of each block.

In the algorithm for encrypting DCT coefficients, encrypting the absolute values of the DCT coefficients to be encrypted with serial ciphers, then it takes out the symbols of these coefficients to form a symbol bit sequence and encrypts them to achieve the effect of hiding the DCT coefficient information completely.

3   Analysis of the Results

3.1   Experimental Platform and Standard Test Library

The relevant configuration of the machine in this experiment is: Intel(R) Core (TM) i5-4210U processor, 8G running memory, Win10 system, MatlabR2014a integrated development environment.

The experimental test image and the encryption result obtained by the algorithm in this paper are as follows (as shown in Fig. 4 and Fig. 5):

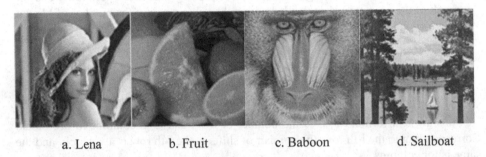

a. Lena   b. Fruit   c. Baboon   d. Sailboat

Fig. 4. Experimental test image

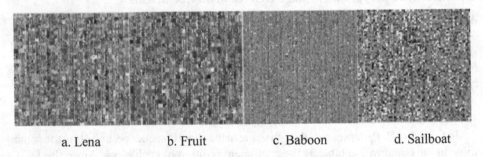

a. Lena   b. Fruit   c. Baboon   d. Sailboat

Fig. 5. Algorithm encryption effect

The experiment selects four representative color images in the USC-SIPI image library, and verifies and compares the classic AES encryption algorithm with the encryption algorithm described in this article. The experimental results show that the algorithm in this paper has better results in both the encryption effect and the encryption efficiency compared with the AES encryption algorithm. At the same time, it is verified that the algorithm described in this article is more superior, stable and robust in terms of timeliness, security, encryption quality, etc.

The algorithm encryption result evaluation table is as follows (as shown in Table 1).

PSNR and MSSIM and LSS in Table 1 respectively represent important parameters such as peak signal-to-noise ratio, average structure similarity index, and brightness similarity of the image. The algorithm in this paper has achieved better results in various

Table 1. Encryption algorithm and AES algorithm encryption results evaluation index data

Image	The algorithm in this paper			AES algorithm encryption		
	PSNR/dB	MSSIM	LSS	PSNR/dB	MSSIM	LSS
Lena	6.071	0.004	−20.348	7.906	0.008	−18.755
Fruit	6.170	0.002	−18.262	7.759	0.008	−18.010
Baboon	6.194	0.004	−15.369	8.776	0.008	−15.155
Sailboat	5.965	0.004	−21.013	8.114	0.010	−19.678

indicators. For images with rich textures, the peak signal-to-noise ratio and average structure similarity index are more convenient and effective.

The experimental situation of the algorithm when it is used in encryption is as follows (as shown in Table 2).

Table 2. Comparison of time-consuming algorithm encryption and AES algorithm encryption

Image	Size/px	Time consuming encryption algorithm/s	AES algorithm encryption time consuming/s
Lena	256 × 256	2.21	93.59
Fruit	256 × 256	2.31	91.00
Baboon	512 × 512	11.04	483.80
Sailboat	512 × 512	10.51	487.61

According to the data in Table 2, the algorithm in this paper has obvious advantages in terms of time over the AES algorithm, and the execution time of the encryption algorithm is more than tens of times faster than the AES algorithm.

4 Conclusion

This paper mainly studies image encryption technology, and designs the encryption algorithm fully according to the characteristics of the image data structure. Therefore, using color image compression encoding encryption and selective encryption, this paper proposes an encryption algorithm based on JPEG image compression coding. A certain amount of experimental results verify that the algorithm in this paper is more superior, stable and robust than traditional encryption algorithms in terms of timeliness, security, encryption quality, etc.

Acknowledgments. Supported by a project grant from National Natural Science Foundation (Grand No. 61961036 & 62162054), the University Young Teachers Basic Ability Improvement Project of Guangxi (Grand No. 2018KY0537 & 2017KY0629), Wuzhou Scientific Research and Technology Development Project (Grand No. 201501014), Guangxi Natural Science Foundation (Grand No. 2020GXNSFAA297259 & 2018GXNSFBA281173), Wuzhou Hightech Zone, Wuzhou University Industry-Education-Research Project (Grand No. 2020G001), the Guangxi Innovation-Driven Development Special Driven Develop Special Fund Project (Guike AA18118036), the Guangxi Science and Technology Base and Talent Special Project (Guike AD20297148).

References

1. Wade, M.I.: Distributed image encryption based on a homomorphic cryptographic approach. In: 2019 IEEE 10-th Annual Ubiquitous Computing, Electronics & Mobile Communication Conference (UE-MCON), New York, USA, 2019, pp. 0686–0696, (2019). https://doi.org/10.1109/UEMCON47517.2019.8993025

2. Abdmouleh, M.K., Khalfallah, A., Bouhlel, M.S.: "A novel selective encryption dwt-based algorithm for medical images. In: 2017 14th International Conference on Computer Graphics, Imaging and Visualization, Marrakesh, Morocco, pp.79–84 (2017). https://doi.org/10.1109/C-GiV.2017.10

3. Ning, X., Aijun, L.: Infrared image selection encryption algorithm based on multi-feature difference detection and joint control mapping. Appl. Opt. **38**(03), 406–414 (2017)

4. Ping, Y., Qiang, Y., Lijun, Z.: Infrared target selection encryption algorithm based on geometric active contour. Comput. Eng. Des. **39**(04), 1148–1154 (2018)

5. Khan, N.A., Altaf, M., Khan, F.A.: Selective encryption of JPEG images with chaotic based novel S-box. Multimedia Tools Appl. **80**(6), 9639–9656 (2020)

6. Wei, Y., Qingzhu, W., Renjie, S., Yuandong, Z.: Joint encryption and compression algorithm for three-dimensional images. Microelectron. Comput. **37**(07), 78–81 (2020)

7. Li, P., Lo, K.T.: Survey on JPEG compatible joint image compression and encryption algorithms. IET Signal Process. **14**(8), 475–488 (2020)

8. Zhuo, L., Yong, W.: Image compression and encryption scheme based on two-dimensional coupled image lattice model. J. Chongqing Univ. Posts Telecommun. (Nat. Sci. Edition) **32**(06), 1048–1057 (2020)

Review of Research on Speech Emotion Recognition

Yali Yang[✉] [ID] and Fangyuan Xu [ID]

School of Computer and Information Engineering, Heilongjiang University of Science and
Technology, Harbin 150022, China
17803428680@163.com

Abstract. Language is an effective way to express human emotions, but emotions
are difficult to describe and judge with computers, so it is an important task to
analyze their emotions through speech. We summarized the current situation of
speech emotion recognition from five aspects: the development of speech emotion
recognition, emotion description model, emotion speech database, feature extraction, and emotion recognition algorithm. By summarizing and analyzing these five
aspects, we can predict the future development trend of speech emotion recognition and improve recognition accuracy combined with other information for joint
analysis. In this paper, we summarized the commonly used emotion database,
compared the popular attention mechanism in speech emotion recognition, and
finally, proposed the prospect of speech emotion recognition.

Keywords: Speech emotion recognition · Recognition algorithm · Attention
mechanism

1 Introduction

The expression of human emotions is carried out in various ways. The speaker's emotional state can be effectively understood based on the speaker's reaction, behavior, body
posture, and physiological signals. However, it is very difficult to interpret the speaker's
emotional state from the speech in a non-contact way [1]. Speech emotion recognition,
one of an important direction in the speech research, is to judge the emotional state that
the speaker wants to express based on the person's speech. As an important branch of
artificial intelligence, speech emotion recognition has been widely used in the diagnosis
and evaluation of depression or some mental diseases, and in analyzing the emotions
of students so as to make course contents adjustment in distance learning and online
learning [2]. The task of speech emotion recognition is to find the features related to
emotion from the speaker's speech, and then judge the speaker's emotion through these
features [3].

There are currently two models describing speech emotions: discrete and dimensional emotion models. The former describes emotions as discrete emotions, such as
happiness and anger, which are widely used in the research of speech emotion recognition. The latter describes the emotional state as points in a multi-dimensional emotional

© ICST Institute for Computer Sciences, Social Informatics and Telecommunications Engineering 2022
Published by Springer Nature Switzerland AG 2022. All Rights Reserved
X. Jiang (Ed.): MLICOM 2021, LNICST 438, pp. 315–326, 2022.
https://doi.org/10.1007/978-3-031-04409-0_29

space, which is actually a Cartesian space with each dimension. Each dimension represent an emotional feature. The dimensional emotional database is relatively less than the discrete database. The current ones are mainly VAM, Semaine, etc. [4]. With the research on speech emotion recognition, it has made significant progress in two aspects: one is the combination of speech emotion recognition and deep learning algorithms for feature extraction, emotion classification and regression that make the recognition efficiency higher. The other is a variety of methods are integrated and the more and more complex networks are used in the process of emotion recognition.

This paper will describe the current technology and progress from five aspects: the development of speech emotion recognition, emotion description models, emotion speech databases, feature extraction, and emotion recognition algorithms. In this paper we mainly discussed the research progress of feature extraction, recognition and classification algorithms in the process of speech emotion recognition, summarized the limitations of speech emotion recognition in the context of deep learning algorithms, and finally proposed the future prospects of speech emotion recognition.

2   The Development of Speech Emotion Recognition

The earliest speech emotion recognition originated in the mid-1980s. Acoustic statistical features was used for the first time in emotion analysis and obvious speech differences was found under different emotions. In 1987, Professor Minsky proposed the idea of "making computers have emotional capabilities" [5], and consequently more researchers are engaged in the research of speech emotion recognition. In the early 1990s, the MIT laboratory constructed an "emotion editor" [6] that used the collection and analysis of various emotional signals from the outside world to identify various emotions, and then proposed the viewpoint of affective computing in 1995. At the end of the ninth decade in the twentieth century, Moriyama applied the voice interface of a graphics acquisition system to an e-commerce system [7], making speech emotion recognition commercially available. In this period, speech emotion recognition is still in its infancy stage, mainly analyze acoustic features. At this time, emotion recognition infrastructure was incomplete, the sample data was relatively simple, and no generalized method was established [8].

Speech emotion recognition has been developed at a high speed in the 21st century under the background of the rapid development of computers and deep learning algorithms. In 2000, the "Speech and Emotion" symposium was held in Ireland. For the first time, scholars of speech emotion recognition research were gathered together to summarize the previous problems of speech emotion recognition, and proposed the future development direction and goals of speech emotion recognition. And subsequently some important speech emotion recognition special issues were opened so that it attracted worldwide attention and entered a golden period of development. At the same time, many research institutions and universities started this research, such as the multimedia laboratory led by Professor Pricard of Massachusetts Institute of Technology, and the Institute of Human-Computer Communication at the Technical University of Munich in Germany. Speech emotion recognition in China started at the beginning of this century. In 2001, Professor Zhao Li of Southeast University was the first person to study on speech emotion information. Chinese Academy of Sciences host the first Chinese Affective Computing and Intelligent Interaction Academic Conference in 2003, and the first International Affective Computing and Intelligent Interaction Academic Conference was held in 2005. Southeast University, Tsinghua University, Zhejiang University laboratories have made more contributions to speech emotion recognition in the past ten years. The Institute of Automation, Chinese Academy of Sciences completed the recording of the CASIA Chinese emotion database. In the development of speech emotion recognition, Support Vector Machine (SVM) in traditional machine learning methods is relatively basic for emotion recognition. For example, Zhang [9] compared several SVMs' recognition efficiency based on different kernel functions, used genetic algorithm and particle swarm algorithm to optimize the parameters and achieved better results. With the development of deep learning algorithms and the rise of attention mechanisms, Wang improved the efficiency and accuracy of recognition through speech emotion recognition models based on CNN, BLSTM, attention mechanisms and the Adam optimizer. Bao [10] combined CNN with BLSTM to extract the spatiotemporal features of speech emotion, and then improved the recognition performance by using the attention mechanism. At this stage, speech emotion recognition has been largely developed, the efficiency of recognition significantly improved, and the accuracy of discrete speech emotion recognition obviously increased, and the speech database greatly enriched. However, there are some emotions such as irony and sarcasm still do not have a standard emotional set method and publicly recognized data, and some complex emotions cannot be identified.

3 Emotional Description

3.1 Model

Emotion recognition description models are divided into two types: discrete and dimensional. Discrete emotion recognition models, which is widely used, include basic and relatively independent emotions from all human emotions, such as anger, fear, happiness, etc. Table 1 list the division of basic emotions by different scholars.

Table 1. Basic emotions by different scholars [11].

Scholars	Sentiment classification
Ekman, Friesen [12]	Joy, sadness, anger, fear, sorrow, disgust
Arnold	Anger, aversion, courage, dejection, despair, dear, hate, hope, love, sadness
Gray	Desire, happiness, interest, surprise, wonder, sorrow
Tomkins	Anger, interest, contempt, disgust, distress, fear, joy, shame, surprise
Carroll Izard	Interest, Joy, Surprise, Sadness, Anger, Disgust, Contempt, Self-Hostility, Fear, Shame, Shyness, Guilt

The dimensional emotion recognition model believes that emotions are depend of each other. There is a smooth transition from one emotion to another. Each emotion corresponds to a point in the dimensional space. An emotional state can be expressed in multiple dimensions [4]. Compared with discrete emotions, the dimensional emotion recognition model is more detail, and can more precisely represent people's emotions in real life. Evaluation and activation are the two main dimensions that describe the main aspects of emotions. For some dimensional emotions [13], we even can't recognize what emotions they are. Nowadays, common dimensional models include two-dimensional, three-dimensional [14] and four-dimensional emotional models. The figure below is a two-dimensional dimension emotion recognition model (Fig. 1).

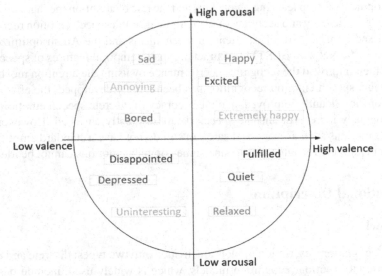

Fig. 1. Two-dimensional emotion recognition model.

3.2 Emotional Speech Database

As the performance of emotion recognition is also closely related to the quality of the database, emotional speech database is the key to speech emotion recognition. Emotional speech database is divided into discrete and dimensional, and then divided into natural type, performance type and guide type according to the classification of emotion generation. Speech recording is generally carried out in the laboratory in order to ensure the quality of speech. Due to differences in language and expression of emotions, there is no standard database that has been accepted by all researchers. However, speech emotion databases have become more and more perfect.

(1) Belfast data set [15]

This emotion database is an English database [16] which was recorded by 40 recorders, consist of are 20 men and 20 women, interpreted 35–40 sentences. This database contains 5 basic discrete emotions, including anger, sadness, happiness, fear and neutrality.

(2)　EMO-DB data set [17]

The EMO-DB data set was recorded by the Technical University of Berlin. This data set is interpreted in German. It consists of 5 long and 5 short sentences expressed by five men and five women with 7 different emotions, a total of 800 sentences. The database contains 7 emotions: neutral, angry, scared, happy, sad, disgusted and bored. This data set was recorded in a recording studio, with a high degree of emotional freedom, a strong sense of reality, and no specific emotional preference.

(3)　IEMOCAP data set

The IEMOCAP data set is collected by the Sail Lab of the University of Southern California. It is an interactive emotional binary motion capture data set. It contains data of ten actors and actresses in improvisation or scripted scenes. There are videos, voice, facial motion capture and text transcription. The dialogue of this data set is divided into two parts, one is scripted dialogue, and the other is free to play in specific situations. There are 7433 sentences in total and six emotions are labeled, including neutrality, happiness, sadness, anger, surprise and excitement as well as dimension labels, such as activation, dominance and so on. This data set is often used for multi-modal emotional research due to its high quality and multi-modal information.

(4)　CASIA data set

The CASIA data set is a Chinese data set recorded by the Institute of Automation, Chinese Academy of Sciences. It contains six different emotions: angry, happy, scared, sad, surprised and neutral. A database of 9600 sentences was recorded by four professional speakers. It contains 300 sentences with the same text and different sentiment, and 100 sentences with different text that can better express the sentiment features.

(5)　VAM data set [18]

The VAM data set is a typical open dimensional data set. This data set is a purely natural and unrestricted voice communication database. It is obtained from a German interview program and contains three parts: a speech warehouse, a video warehouse and an expression warehouse. There are a total of 1018 sentences, expressing the emotions Valence, Activation and Dominance in three dimensions, and the label value is between -1 and 1. This data set expresses more negative emotions.

(6)　SEMAINE data set [19]

The SEMAINE data set is a multi-modal dialogue material. It is a typical dimensional data set that consists of a dialogue between four robots with fixed emotions and 20 users. This data set is recorded in a professional recording studio and consists of four emotional dimensions, namely Valence, Arousal, Expectancy, and Power. The first three dimensions are continuous values between -1 and 1, and Power is a continuous value greater than or equal to 0. Part of the data in this dataset is used in AVEC2012 competition.

4 Feature Extraction

4.1 Prosodic Features

In the traditional way of prosody expression [20], it is generally defined by linguists. It has stress [21], pitch, rhythm, etc., which can help listeners to better understand speech. Among the most commonly used prosodic features [22] are duration, baseband [23], energy, etc. Fundamental frequency features include a large number of features that characterize speech emotions, which are very important for speech emotion recognition. The pitch period is the reciprocal of the vocal cord vibration frequency, and the period of vocal cord vibration is actually the pitch period. The fundamental frequency has a large range of changes, so it is difficult for researchers to detect. The commonly used methods for extracting fundamental frequency features include autocorrelation function method [24], average amplitude difference method and wavelet method [25]. The first two methods are aimed at the time domain part of speech, and the wavelet method is mainly frequency domain part of speech. The amplitude energy of sound signals of different emotions is different. The emotional amplitude energy of surprise and happiness are increased, while the emotional energy of sadness is decreased. Prosody does not affect the content of the speech [26], but it affects the true meaning of the content. The same sentence has different meanings for different prosodic structures. Nowadays, the research of speech emotion recognition uses more prosodic features as an auxiliary reference.

4.2 Based on Spectral Correlation Features

With the popularity and application of deep learning, spectrum widely used in speech emotion recognition include spectrograms and other variants [27]. Spectrograms can reflect different emotions that usually the abscissa represents time and the ordinate represents frequency. The coordinate point value represents the energy of the speech data, and the size of the energy value is generally expressed by color. The darker the color, the stronger the speech energy of the point. Commonly used features are the Mel frequency cepstral coefficient, which is displayed in the Mel label [28]. For the cepstrum parameters extracted from the frequency domain, the Mel scale describes the non-linear characteristics [29] of the human ear frequency. Some people used Gabor wavelet to combine gray-level co-occurrence matrix, Tamura method with LBP method to extract features of spectrogram to improve the accuracy of feature extraction. With the development of deep learning algorithms, traditional feature extraction methods sometimes have no superiority. Other built a feature extraction method for the context of the spectrum sequence. After the cepstral coefficients were obtained by the discrete cosine transform, the context processing was carried out. And the cepstrum coefficients [30] are combined with the feature coefficients obtained from the context processing to obtain the spectral series context features. This extraction method significantly improves the performance of feature extraction and reduces the influence of many external factors in feature extraction.

5 Recognition Algorithm

5.1 Classic Machine Learning Algorithms

The Hidden Markov Model (HMM) [31] algorithm was proposed in the 1970s and has become a common method in signal processing. It is a statistical analysis signal model in speech emotion recognition, mainly regarding the cumulative probability of speech. In the course of training and recognition using the HMM algorithm, each emotion corresponds to an HMM model [32] whose parameter is obtained from the emotion samples. Although the algorithm has good system scalability, its shortcomings involved in unqualified classification and decision-making ability, inaccurate recognition in similar emotions, and poor robustness. In view of the above-mentioned shortcomings of the HMM algorithm, the researchers combined the HMM with strong time modeling ability and the ANN algorithm with strong classification learning ability to improve the robustness. Some Combine RBF and HMM algorithms to form an emotion recognition model to improve recognition efficiency.

Gaussian Mixed Model (GMM) [33] is one of the common speech emotion recognition models, which is used to represent the acoustic characteristics of sound units. It describes the emotional feature parameters through the linear weighted superposition of Gaussian probability density functions. The calculation [34] amount of the GMM algorithm is much smaller than that of the HMM, so the robustness of the GMM algorithm is better than that of the HMM [35]. In the improved GMM speech emotion recognition model, an optimal parameter set was found and then a final GMM model was obtained by iteration, which verifies that the improved GMM recognition model has better performance and higher recognition rate than the traditional GMM model.

Support vector machine (SVM) [36] is a classifier developed from the generalized portrait algorithm for pattern recognition in 1964. The traditional SVM is mainly used to solve binary classification problems. SVM seeks an optimal classification hyperplane as much as possible in solving linear classification problems [37]. In order to convert nonlinear problems into linear problems, a kernel function was introduced in solving nonlinear classification problems. For the nonlinear SVM, it is very important to select the kernel function, due to the choice of kernel function will affect the classification effect in dealing with nonlinear problems. On the speech emotion recognition technology based on feature selection and decision tree combined with SVM, recognition efficiency of genetic algorithm and particle swarm are compared in parameters selection. It is concluded that the performance of the genetic algorithm is better than particle swarm algorithm, and the recognition efficiency of the decision tree combined with SVM in feature selection strategy is higher than that of the traditional SVM algorithm.

5.2 Deep Learning Algorithm

Convolutional Neural Network (CNN) [38] is a type of feedforward neural network that includes convolutional calculations. The algorithm, began in the 1980s and 1990s, includes an input layer, a hidden layer, and an output layer [39]. The hidden layer includes a convolutional layer, a pool Convolution layer and fully connected layer. The convolution layer, the core of CNN, is mainly used to perform convolution operations on data through convolution kernels. The other improved CNN by using multi-level residual convolution. The neural network model, which contains multiple convolutional pooling layers and a multi-level residual structure, further reduces the amount of calculation, thereby improving the efficiency of recognition.

The long and short-term memory network is the most commonly used network for speech emotion recognition. The LSTM [40] network is a special network structure with three gate mechanisms: forget gate, input gate and output gate. This network can effectively determine information that should be forgotten or retained, which solves the learning of long-distance information. The structure in the hidden layer in the recurrent neural network is replaced with a long and short-term memory module. The idea of self-loop is introduced in LSTM. The weight value of self-loop is determined according to the context. And the gates control the weight of self-loop that change dynamically in accumulated time. Since LSTM can only achieve one-way transmission, when the sentence sequence is changed, the key part sentence appears in the back of network and thus make LSTM inapplicable. So a bidirectional long-short term memory network (BiLSTM) [40] was proposed, which can be regarded as an acyclic graph composed of two unidirectional LSTM networks [41], and output results are obtained under consideration of the relevant influencing factors in the front and back parts of network. The recognition rate of BiLSTM is much higher than the LSTM, whereas the latency of BiLSTM is relatively longer [42]. For example, researchers compared the unidirectional to the bidirectional long-short term, and drew a conclusion the BiLSTM can learn the front and back information of the current speech frame.

5.3   Attention Mechanism

The attention mechanism [43] is originated from human vision. When processing information, humans focus on a part of all information while ignoring other unimportant visible parts. It was originally used for machine translation and has become an important concept in neural network. The common attention mechanisms [44] are Soft Attention, Local Attention and Hard Attention according to the calculation area of attention.

Soft Attention is widely used in natural language processing and speech recognition. This mechanism calculates the weight probability of all keys, and then input them into the next layer. Soft attention covers the whole range of the network because each key has its own weight. This mechanism can be embedded in a network for training and is so rational that can be used as a comparison standard for other attention mechanisms to measure the recognition efficiency.

Hard Attention is a mechanism relative to Soft Attention. It attaches importance to part of the information, while the Soft Attention calculates all keys. The mechanism sample is a random process that calculate part of hidden layers of the encoder according to the weight probability of keys and accurately locate a certain key, which means the probability of the selected part is 1 and all other parts are 0. This method has high requirements for precise positioning, and thus rarely used in research.

Local Attention is a compromise and combined mechanism of the first two mechanisms. The mechanism focuses on a part of the decoder hidden states and selectively calculates a small window area, which can avoid the same computational overhead as Soft Attention and train easier than Hard Attention. The accuracy of the mechanism depends mainly on the accuracy of the position area. Overall, the Soft Attention mechanism has a wider range of applications than other two attentions.

The attention mechanism can be divided into General Attention and Self Attention according to the category of the information used. The mechanism of General Attention uses external information, which is suitable for the construction of two-paragraph text relationship, while Self Attention only uses internal information, key equals value and value equals query. Self Attention, proposed by Google in the transformer model, occurred between the internal elements of the input or the output. Self Attention mechanism can be better applied to long-distance dependent learning, because it easily capture the long-distance interdependence features in sentences. Researchers combined the local attention advantages of CNN, RNN and Self Attention mechanism in the ACRNN recognition model, and enabled the model to learn the most emotional features. As a result, the efficiency of ACRNN is about 0.5% higher than CRNN and then the effectiveness of the attention mechanism was proved in speech emotion recognition.

According to hierarchical relationships in the structure, the attention mechanism can also be defined single-layer attention mechanism, multi-layer attention and multi-head attention. Multi-head-attention performs linear transformations on query, key and value, and then performs and splices many times of scaling dot product attention, and finally perform a linear transformation. At this time the value obtained is the result of the multi-head attention mechanism. Some people used the multi-head attention mechanism to construct a module to combine the audio module with the video module. And finally the emotional prediction value was obtained through linear transformation.

With the wide application of attention mechanism, more and more types of attention mechanism emerged. Researchers proposed Component Attention and Monotonic Attention in speech emotion recognition research, compared the recognition efficiency of different attention mechanism, showed that Monotonic Attention is better than other attention mechanisms on the IEMOCAP data set, and thus furtherly proved that the attention mechanism play an indispensable role in the current speech emotion recognition.

6 Conclusion

From the application of classic machine learning algorithms to the improved various deep learning speech emotion recognition models, the current research on speech emotion recognition has made great achievements through decades of development. Furthermore, the addition of attention mechanism into speech emotion recognition made its the efficiency furtherly improved. This article describes five aspects of speech emotion recognition: the development of speech emotion recognition, emotion description models, emotion speech databases, feature extraction, and emotion recognition algorithms. Due to the high complexity of human emotion, the research of speech emotion still faces many problems. Firstly, speech emotion recognition lacks a widely recognized database. It is difficult to collect the data and organize the database as the result of complexity of emotions. Besides, most of the existing databases are recorded in the laboratory, so it is very difficult to label emotions in dimensional databases. However, the speech database is the basis of research and an inevitable requirement; Secondly, the development of emotion recognition tend to the combination of multimodality, such as speech, expression and text are combined to recognize the emotion, which makes the recognition efficiency higher than each one of them; Finally, different languages and cultures lead to different ways of emotional expression. Therefore, different models were built due to different speakers and language differences in the training data set in the training process of the speech emotion recognition model. In addition, there is untargeted research on some complex human emotions. Above all, there are broad prospects in speech emotion recognition.

References

1. Swain, M., Routray, A., Kabisatpathy, P.: Databases, features and classifiers for speech emotion recognition: a review. Int. J. Speech Technol. **21**(1), 93–120 (2018). https://doi.org/10.1007/s10772-018-9491-z
2. Weninger, F., Wöllmer, M., Schuller, B.: Emotion Recognition in Naturalistic Speech and Language—a Survey. In Emotion Recognition, pp. 237–267. Wiley (2015). https://doi.org/10.1002/9781118910566.ch10
3. El Ayadi, M., Kamel, M.S., Karray, F.: Survey on speech emotion recognition: features, classification schemes, and databases. Pattern Recogn. **44**(3), 572–587 (2011). https://doi.org/10.1016/j.patcog.2010.09.020
4. Lugger, M., Yang, B..: Psychological Motivated Multi-Stage Emotion Classification Exploiting Voice Quality Features. In tech Open (2008). https://doi.org/10.5772/6383
5. Minsky, M.: The society of mind. Person. Forum **3**(1), 19–32 (1987)
6. Cahn, J.: Generation of affect in synthesized speech. J. Am. Voice I/O Soc. **8** (2000)
7. Moriyama, T., Ozawa, S.: Emotion recognition and synthesis system on speech. In: Proceedings IEEE International Conference on Multimedia Computing and Systems, vol. 1, pp. 840–844 (1999). https://doi.org/10.1109/MMCS.1999.779310
8. Williams, C.E., Stevens, K.N.: Emotions and speech: some acoustical correlates. J. Acoust. Soc. Am. **52**(4B), 1238–1250 (1972). https://doi.org/10.1121/1.1913238
9. Zhang, L.: Speech emotion recognition algorithm based on modified SVM–Journal of Computer Applications. Accessed 03 Sept 2021. https://en.cnki.com.cn/Article_en/CJFDTotal-JSJY201307039.htm
10. Zhao, Z., Bao, Z., Zhang, Z., Cummins, N., Wang, H., Schuller, B.: Attention-Enhanced Connectionist Temporal Classification for Discrete Speech Emotion Recognition, pp. 206–210 (2019). https://doi.org/10.21437/Interspeech.2019-1649
11. Ortony, A., Turner, T.J.: What's basic about basic emotions?. Psychol. Rev. **97**(3), 315–331 (1990). https://doi.org/10.1037/0033-295X.97.3.315
12. Varghese, A.A., Cherian, J.P., Kizhakkethottam, J.J.: Overview on emotion recognition system. In: 2015 International Conference on Soft-Computing and Networks Security (ICSNS), pp. 1–5 (2015). https://doi.org/10.1109/ICSNS.2015.7292443
13. Borchert, M., Dusterhoft, A.: Emotions in speech - experiments with prosody and quality features in speech for use in categorical and dimensional emotion recognition environments. In: 2005 International Conference on Natural Language Processing and Knowledge Engineering, pp. 147–151 (2005)
14. Cowie, R., et al.: Emotion recognition in human-computer interaction. IEEE Signal Process. Mag. **18**(1), 32–80 (2001)
15. Cowie, R., Douglas-Cowie, E., Savvidou, S., McMahon, E.: FEELTRACE: an instrument for recording perceived emotion in real time, undefined (2000). Accessed 05 Sept 2021. https://www.semanticscholar.org/paper/FEELTRACE%3A-an-instrument-for-recording-perceived-in-Cowie-Douglas-Cowie/5b35fe6950db00ad32f6af8ad0162028e15c2f27

16. McGilloway, S., Cowie, R., ED, C., Gielen, S., Westerdijk, M., Stroeve, S.: Approaching automatic recognition of emotion from voice: a rough benchmark (2000)
17. Burkhardt, F., Paeschke, A., Rolfes, M., Sendlmeier, W., Weiss, B.: A Database of German Emotional Speech, p. 4 (2005)
18. Grimm, M., Kroschel, K., Narayanan, S.: The Vera am Mittag German audio-visual emotional speech database, pp. 865–868 (2008)
19. Mckeown, G., Valstar, M., Cowie, R., Pantic, M.: The SEMAINE corpus of emotionally coloured character interactions, pp. 1079–1084 (2010)
20. Ang, J., Dhillon, R., Krupski, A., Shriberg, E., Stolcke, A.: Prosody-based automatic detection of annoyance and frustration in human-computer dialog (2002)
21. Batliner, A., Fischer, K., Huber, R., Spilker, J., Noth, E.: desperately seeking emotions: actors, wizards, and human beings. In: Proceedings of the ISCA Workshop on Speech and Emotion, pp. 195–200 (2000)
22. Beeke, S., Wilkinson, R., Maxim, J.: Prosody as a compensatory strategy in the conversations of people with agrammatism. Clin. Linguist Phon. **23**(2), 133–155 (2009). https://doi.org/10.1080/02699200802602985
23. Busso, C., Lee, S., Narayanan, S.S.: Analysis of emotionally salient aspects of fundamental frequency for emotion detection. IEEE Trans. Audio Speech Lang. Process. **17**, 582–596 (2009). https://doi.org/10.1109/TASL.2008.2009578
24. Lee, C.M., Narayanan, S.S., Pieraccini, R.: Combining acoustic and language information for emotion recognition (2002)
25. Lee, C., et al.: Emotion Recognition based on Phoneme Classes, presented at the Proceedings of ICSLP (2004). https://doi.org/10.21437/Interspeech.2004-322
26. Leinonen, L., Hiltunen, T., Linnankoski, I., Laakso, M.-L.: Expression of emotional–motivational connotations with a one-word utterance. J. Acoust. Soc. Am. **102**(3), 1853–1863 (1997). https://doi.org/10.1121/1.420109
27. Ramdinmawii, E., Mohanta, A., Mittal, V.K.: Emotion recognition from speech signal. In: TENCON 2017 - 2017 IEEE Region 10 Conference, pp. 1562–1567 (2017). https://doi.org/10.1109/TENCON.2017.8228105
28. Bou-Ghazale, S.E., Hansen, J.H.L.: A comparative study of traditional and newly proposed features for recognition of speech under stress. IEEE Trans. Speech Audio Process. **8**(4), 429–442 (2000)
29. Bitouk, D., Verma, R., Nenkova, A.: Class-level spectral features for emotion recognition. Speech Commun. **52**(7–8), 613–625 (2010). https://doi.org/10.1016/j.specom.2010.02.010
30. Chauhan, R., Yadav, J., Koolagudi, S.G., Rao, K.S.: Text independent emotion recognition using spectral features. In: Aluru, S., et al. (eds.) IC3 2011. CCIS, vol. 168, pp. 359–370. Springer, Heidelberg (2011). https://doi.org/10.1007/978-3-642-22606-9_37
31. Cairns, D.A., Hansen, J.H.L.: Nonlinear analysis and classification of speech under stressed conditions. J. Acoust. Soc. Am. **96**(6), 3392–3400 (1994). https://doi.org/10.1121/1.410601
32. Athanaselis, T., Bakamidis, S., Dologlou, I., Cowie, R., Douglas-Cowie, E., Cox, C.: ASR for emotional speech: clarifying the issues and enhancing performance. Neural Networks **18**(4), 437–444 (2005). https://doi.org/10.1016/j.neunet.2005.03.008
33. Akaike, H.: A new look at the statistical model identification. IEEE Trans. Autom. Control **19**(6), 716–723 (1974). https://doi.org/10.1109/TAC.1974.1100705
34. Yuan, G., Lim, T.S., Juan, W.K., Ringo, H.M.-H., Li, Q.: A GMM based 2-stage architecture for multi-subject emotion recognition using physiological responses. In: Proceedings of the 1st Augmented Human International Conference, pp. 1–6. New York, NY, USA (2010). https://doi.org/10.1145/1785455.1785458
35. Tang, H., Chu, S.M., Hasegawa-Johnson, M., Huang, T.S.: Emotion recognition from speech VIA boosted Gaussian mixture models. In: 2009 IEEE International Conference on Multimedia and Expo, pp. 294–297 (2009). https://doi.org/10.1109/ICME.2009.5202493

36. Banse, R., Scherer, K.R.: Acoustic profiles in vocal emotion expression. J. Pers. Soc. Psychol. **70**(3), 614–636 (1996). https://doi.org/10.1037/0022-3514.70.3.614
37. Burges, C.J.C.: a tutorial on support vector machines for pattern recognition. Data Min. Knowl. Discov. **2**(2), 121–167 (1998). https://doi.org/10.1023/A:1009715923555
38. Aldeneh, Z., Provost, E.M.: Using regional saliency for speech emotion recognition. In: 2017 IEEE International Conference on Acoustics, Speech and Signal Processing (ICASSP), pp. 2741–2745 (2017)
39. Fayek, H.M., Lech, M., Cavedon, L.: Evaluating deep learning architectures for Speech Emotion Recognition. Neural Networks **92**, 60–68 (2017). https://doi.org/10.1016/j.neunet.2017.02.013
40. Tzirakis, P., Zhang, J., Schuller, B.W.: End-to-End speech emotion recognition using deep neural networks. In: 2018 IEEE International Conference on Acoustics, Speech and Signal Processing (ICASSP), pp. 5089–5093 (2018)
41. Tzinis, E., Potamianos, A.: Segment-based speech emotion recognition using recurrent neural networks. In: 2017 Seventh International Conference on Affective Computing and Intelligent Interaction (ACII), pp. 190–195 (2017)
42. Mirsamadi, S., Barsoum, E., Zhang, C.: Automatic speech emotion recognition using recurrent neural networks with local attention. In: 2017 IEEE International Conference on Acoustics, Speech and Signal Processing (ICASSP), pp. 2227–2231 (2017)
43. Bahdanau, D., Cho, K., Bengio, Y.: eural Machine Translation by Jointly Learning to Align and Translate. arXiv:1409.0473 [cs, stat] (2016). Accessed 02 Sept 2021. http://arxiv.org/abs/1409.0473
44. Luong, T., Pham, H., Manning, C.D.: Fective approaches to attention-based neural machine translation. In: Proceedings of the 2015 Conference on Empirical Methods in Natural Language Processing, pp. 1412–1421. Lisbon, Portugal (2015)

PM2.5 Concentration Prediction Based on mRMR-XGBoost Model

Weijian Zhong[1,2], Xiaoqin Lian[2], Chao Gao[2], Xiang Chen[1,2(✉)], and Hongzhou Tan[1,2]

[1] School of Electronics and Information Technology, Sun Yat-sen University, Guangzhou 510006, China
chenxiang@mail.sysu.edu.cn

[2] Key Laboratory of Industrial Internet and Big Data, China National Light Industry, Beijing Technology and Business University, Beijing 100048, China

Abstract. Air pollution is one of the main environmental pollution, in which air pollution component prediction is an important problem. At present, there have been many studies using machine learning methods to predict air pollution components. However, due to its numerous influencing factors and incomplete determination, there are still problems in accurate prediction. In this paper, the gas factors and meteorological factors collected by the self-developed integrated system are firstly used to construct the original feature set. Then, the mRMR algorithm is used to select data features from the perspective of maximum correlation and minimum redundancy. Finally, a prediction method of PM2.5 concentration in the next hour based on feature selection and XGBoost is designed by combining the data after dimension reduction with the XGBoost model. The experimental results show that mRMR algorithm can effectively select the features of air, and the prediction accuracy is improved even when only half of the features of the original data are used.

Keywords: PM2.5 · Feature selection · mRMR · XGBoost · Concentration prediction

1 Introduction

With the development of society, China's economic development has been accelerated, but behind it is often accompanied by environmental pollution. Air pollution is one of the main environmental pollution. Pollution gas can lead to a

The work is supported in part by the State's Key Project of Research and Development Plan under Grants (2019YFE0196400), Industry-University-Research Cooperation Project in Zhuhai (ZH22017001200072PWC), Guangdong Provincial Special Fund For Modern Agriculture Industry Technology Innovation Teams (No. 2021KJ122), and the Open Research Fund Program of Key Laboratory of Industrial Internet and Big Data, China National Light Industry, Beijing Technology and Business University.

X. Jiang (Ed.): MLICOM 2021, LNICST 438, pp. 327–336, 2022.
https://doi.org/10.1007/978-3-031-04409-0_30

variety of diseases, among which PM2.5 has a greater threat to human health due to its small particle size and can cause haze weather. More efficient and accurate forecasting of air pollution components can provide some reference and guiding significance for people's safe travel and related environmental protection departments' work on air pollution prevention and control.

Numerical model prediction is one of the methods for predicting atmospheric pollution components. This method needs a wide range of data and its system is complex, which is relatively immature. The other method is statistical model prediction, which is more convenient and efficient, and its prediction effect is better. Therefore, people generally use statistical models to learn the relationships between numerous relevant features and air pollution components, so as to realize the prediction of air pollution components.

A large number of researches predict air pollution components based on machine learning model. The optimization of the model is mainly in data processing, model selection and combination, and model parameter optimization [1]. In order to get the optimal combination, different combination methods should be analyzed according to the specific data set.

The quality of data features determines the upper limit of machine learning predictive performance [2]. There is a strong correlation between a number of air related features selected in this paper. In order to further improve the performance of air pollution component prediction, this paper introduces the mRMR algorithm to dimension the data features from the perspective of maximum correlation and minimum redundancy, select important features, and reduce the influence of redundancy features. Finally, XGBoost model is used to mine the information between air features and PM2.5 concentration labels, and a high-performance PM2.5 concentration prediction model for the next hour is constructed based on feature selection and XGBoost.

2   Data Set Analysis

The data used for PM2.5 concentration prediction in this paper are collected by the self-research integrated system in Foshan. The data are hourly data for four contaminated gases and four weather factors from 1 March 2020 to 2 September 2020, specifically SO_2, NO_2, PM10, PM2.5 and temperature, relative humidity, wind speed, and wind direction. Finally, combined with the hourly information on the day of the observation data, the complete data set with 9 features used in this paper is formed. The unit of gas, temperature, relative humidity, wind speed and wind direction are $\mu g/m^3$, $°C$, $\%R.H.$, m/s and degree respectively. The characteristics of the data set are analyzed in the following part.

2.1   Data Description Statistics

The following is a descriptive statistical analysis of the data set with the help of SPSS statistical software. The statistical results are shown in Table 1. According to the average value of polluted gases, the local air quality during this period

Table 1. Data description statistics.

Feature	Sample number	Minimum	Maximum	Mean	Standard deviation
HoD	4390	0.00	23.00	11.50	6.9210
SO_2	4390	0.10	9.54	6.32	1.5750
NO_2	4390	0.18	34.98	19.19	6.5518
PM10	4390	0.48	190.98	30.73	28.4012
PM2.5	4390	0.13	118.65	18.87	17.1331
Temperature	4390	13.9	40.2	28.31	5.5065
Humid	4390	24.74	100.00	76.40	14.0128
Speed	4390	0.00	37.25	7.47	4.1491
Direct	4390	43.60	322.13	156.27	58.6787

is good; according to the maximum value, serious air pollution exists; according to the standard value, the concentration of PM10 and PM2.5 changes relatively large.

2.2 PM2.5 Time Series

By looking at time series, we can get a general idea of the data. Time series of PM2.5 concentration values are given here, as shown in Fig. 1. As can be seen

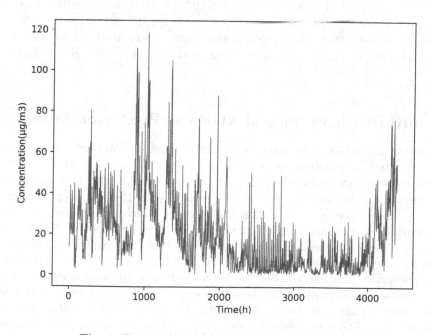

Fig. 1. Time series of PM2.5 concentration values

from the figure, the concentration of PM2.5 varies greatly, which basically stays at a low level in summer.

2.3 Normalized Mutual Information Between Features

Mutual information theory describes how much information a random variable contains another random variable, in which the value range of normalized mutual information is [0,1], and the larger the value is, the larger the amount of information is. The normalized mutual information among the features in the data set is shown in Table 2, where PM2.5n represents the concentration of PM2.5 in the next hour. As can be seen from the table, there is a strong correlation between PM2.5 concentration value in the next hour and several features, and at the same time, there is a certain mutual information among other features, which will lead to a certain degree of redundancy among features.

Table 2. Normalized mutual information between features

	PM2.5n	HoD	SO$_2$	NO$_2$	PM10	PM2.5	Temp	Humid	Speed	Direct
PM2.5n	1.000	0.472	0.781	0.892	0.932	0.918	0.703	0.923	0.870	0.949
HoD	0.472	1.000	0.274	0.429	0.497	0.472	0.196	0.483	0.388	0.528
SO$_2$	0.781	0.274	1.000	0.750	0.798	0.781	0.522	0.788	0.721	0.820
NO$_2$	0.892	0.429	0.750	1.000	0.906	0.892	0.670	0.898	0.842	0.925
PM10	0.932	0.497	0.798	0.906	1.000	0.932	0.721	0.937	0.884	0.962
PM2.5	0.918	0.472	0.781	0.892	0.932	1.000	0.702	0.923	0.870	0.949
Temp	0.703	0.196	0.522	0.670	0.721	0.702	1.000	0.711	0.634	0.745
Humid	0.923	0.483	0.788	0.898	0.937	0.923	0.711	1.000	0.876	0.954
Speed	0.870	0.388	0.721	0.842	0.884	0.870	0.634	0.876	1.000	0.903
Direct	0.949	0.528	0.820	0.925	0.962	0.949	0.745	0.954	0.903	1.000

3 mRMR Algorithm and XGBoost Prediction Model

A reliable feature set is an important part of machine learning, so we analyse air data sets from different perspectives in the previous section. All the features in the data set are collected by the actual system. However, it is not certain whether all the features are strongly correlated with PM2.5 concentration, or some redundancy may occur among the features, which reduces the prediction performance of the model. Therefore, in order to ensure the reliability of the prediction model, we need to properly process all the features before feeding the data set into the machine learning model. In addition, we also need to choose the appropriate machine learning model, according to the characteristics of the actual data set, fully mining the data relations in it, so as to achieve better prediction effect. Therefore, the following will introduce the mRMR feature selection algorithm and XGBoost prediction model used in the prediction method in this paper.

3.1   mRMR Feature Selection Algorithm

mRMR is based on mutual information, which is derived from the concept of entropy [3]. Entropy gives abstract information a certain metric, which can be used to describe the uncertainty between random things. Mutual information partly represents a common part between two random variables, and the more common information, the greater the mutual information between them, and thus the greater the interaction between them. The mutual information between random variables x and y can be calculated as follows:

$$I(x,y) = \iint p(x,y) \log \frac{p(x,y)}{p(x)p(y)} dxdy. \tag{1}$$

The $p(x)$ and $p(y)$ are the respective edge probability densities of the two variables, and $p(x,y)$ is their binary probability distribution. It can be seen that mutual information is the statistical mean of random variables x and y under the probability distribution of $p(x,y)$.

mRMR is a feature selection algorithm which on the one hand measures the correlation between two sets based on mutual information to identify the subset of features with the greatest correlation with the target set. On the other hand, it measures the redundancy among the features in the set on the basis of maximum correlation, so as to exclude the redundancy in the features on the basis of maximum correlation. Therefore, mRMR eliminates redundant information on the basis of retaining key features to achieve the purpose of reducing the complexity of the model and effectively preventing the over-fitting problem of machine learning models [4]. The maximum correlation in mRMR can be expressed as:

$$\max D(S,c), \quad D = \frac{1}{|S|} \sum_{x_i \in S} I(x_i, c). \tag{2}$$

The $I(x_i, c)$ is the mutual information described above, here specifically represents the mutual information between the variables x_i and c, and S is the feature matrix containing all x_i. $|S|$ is the characteristic matrix dimension used to represent the number of elements in S, and c is the target variable. It can be seen that the maximum correlation is expressed as the average value of mutual information. The minimum redundancy can be expressed as:

$$\min R(S), \quad R = \frac{1}{|S|^2} \sum_{x_i, x_j \in S} I(x_i, x_j). \tag{3}$$

The $I(x_i, x_j)$ represents the mutual information between the variables x_i and x_j. Finally, the criterion for selecting the optimal feature subset is given:

$$\begin{cases} \max \psi(D, R) \\ \psi = D - R \end{cases} \tag{4}$$

3.2   XGBoost Prediction Model

Both XGBoost and GBDT algorithms belong to Boosting algorithm. Based on GBDT, XGBoost is proposed and mainly optimizes its objective function and improves the basic learning machine [5]. The XGBoost model works by providing a number of weak learners and adding up their base predictions and residuals to get the final prediction. Its expression is as follows:

$$\dot{y}_i = \sum_{i=1}^{k} f_i(x_i). \tag{5}$$

The k represents k weak learners, f_i represents the ith weak learner, x_i represents the i-th data set, and $\dot{y}_i$ represents the final predicted value after accumulation.

XGBoost model is an ensemble learning framework, which contains many decision trees. Different from other ensemble learning tree models, the training process of XGBoost model is more complex. Compared with GBDT, which is also Boosting algorithm, it adds regular term to the objective function and optimizes the feature splitting process. Its objective function is expressed as follows:

$$obj = \sum_{i=1}^{n} L(y_i, \dot{y}_i) + \sum_{i=1}^{k} \Omega(f_i). \tag{6}$$

The $L(y_i, \dot{y}_i)$ represents the loss function, $\Omega(f_i)$ represents the regular term of the i-th tree, and n represents the sample size. Unlike GBDT, the loss function can be defined case by case, training a tree to make the target function as small as possible. When training the t-th tree, its objective function can be approximately expressed as follows after second-order Taylor expansion:

$$obj^t \approx \sum_{i=1}^{n} \left[g_i f_t(x_i) + 0.5 h_i f_t(x_i)^2 \right] + \Omega(f_t). \tag{7}$$

The g_i represents the first derivative of the loss function, h_i represents the second derivative of the loss function, and the regular term is:

$$\Omega(f_t) = \gamma T + 0.5\lambda \sum_{j=1}^{T} w_j^2. \tag{8}$$

At this point, the minimum point of the objective function can be easily obtained [6], so as to finally calculate the minimum value of the objective function. The smaller the minimum of the objective function is, the better the performance of the tree is. In order to obtain the minimum of the objective function, the greedy algorithm can be used to find the tree that can get the minimum of the objective function from a series of tree structures. Then, by calculating and comparing the information before and after splitting, when a certain information gain can be obtained, the characteristic splitting is adopted. And so on, all the tree structures can be obtained eventually, until all the learning of the weak learner is finished and the training of the whole model is completed.

4   Experimental Studies

4.1   Evaluation Index of the Experimental Results

In order to objectively and reasonably judge and compare the prediction performance of the model, certain evaluation indexes need to be selected. In this paper, three evaluation indexes, $RMSE$, MAE and R^2, are adopted, and their expressions are shown as follows:

$$RMSE = \sqrt{\frac{1}{m} \sum_{i=1}^{m} (y_i - \widehat{y_i})^2}, \tag{9}$$

$$MAE = \frac{1}{m} \sum_{i=1}^{m} |(y_i - \widehat{y_i})|, \tag{10}$$

$$R^2 = \frac{TSS - RSS}{TSS} = 1 - \frac{RSS}{TSS}. \tag{11}$$

The y_i represents the actual observed value, $\widehat{y_i}$ represents the predicted value, and m represents the number of samples.

$RMSE$ is the root mean square error, which can describe the degree of difference between the predicted value and the measured value. When the value is large, it generally means that most of the samples have large differences. MAE is the mean absolute error, which gives an average of the difference between the actual observed value and the predicted value. R^2, the coefficient of determination, describes how much of a change in the real value is due to the predicted value.

4.2   Comparative Experiment of Prediction Model

In the selection of prediction models, SVM, KNN and RF prediction models are used to compare with XGBoost. In the experimental process, all nine features of the data set are adopted to divide the first 3900 samples in the data set into training sets, and the last 490 samples into verification sets, the same with the subsequent experiments. The experimental results are shown in Table 3. The unit of time is second.

Table 3. Evaluation indexes of prediction performance of different models

Model	Training time	RMSE	MAE	R^2	Forecast time
SVM	1.033249	5.04196	3.54826	0.90921	0.140781
KNN	0.006981	5.06853	3.55584	0.90825	0.005984
XGBoost	0.228560	4.49273	3.08974	0.92791	0.000998
RF	0.966385	4.86782	3.44089	0.91537	0.007978

It can be found from the experimental results that the training time of XGBoost prediction model is short, and compared with other models, its prediction error is the smallest, the degree of fit is the highest, and the prediction time is the shortest. Since the XGBoost model has the best prediction effect of PM2.5 concentration in the next hour, the following experiments will be conducted on the mRMR feature selection algorithm based on this model.

4.3   Comparative Experiment of Feature Selection Algorithm

Finding out important features in the data set can reduce the feature dimension and obtain a more efficient dataset, so as to improve the performance of the prediction model. In this paper, mRMR algorithm is used for feature selection. Meanwhile, three feature selection algorithms, Pearson [7], PCA [8] and ReliefF [9], are used to compare with it. XGBoost is used as the prediction Model to study their performance in PM2.5 concentration prediction. The experimental results are shown in Table 4, which lists the evaluation indexes that each feature selection algorithm can make the prediction effect optimal and the number of features used.

Table 4. The optimal performance and the number of features of each feature selection algorithm

	$RMSE$	MAE	R^2
Pearson	$4.49273[n=9]$	$3.01377[n=8]$	$0.92791[n=9]$
PCA	$4.53118[n=9]$	$3.19081[n=9]$	$0.92667[n=9]$
ReliefF	$4.49273[n=9]$	$3.08974[n=9]$	$0.92791[n=9]$
mRMR	$4.43299[n=5]$	$2.99519[n=6]$	$0.92982[n=5]$

The process of feature selection is to continuously exclude features with low scores, and finally select the situation that can achieve the best prediction effect. Figure 2 and Fig. 3 are the trend graphs of predicting R^2 and $RMSE$ in the process of feature selection using each algorithm, which is helpful for us to further understand the process of feature selection method. To facilitate the understanding of the important details, the longitudinal axis in the figure is limited to a certain range, where the value of the $RMSE$ curve corresponding to the PCA feature selection algorithm is 16.59454 at the characteristic number of 1 and the corresponding R^2 curve is 0.01650 at the characteristic number of 1.

As can be seen from the figures, the overall trend of model prediction evaluation increases with the increase of features, because the more features there are, the more information they can provide to the model. It can also be found that the mRMR feature selection algorithm can make the model get better performance in the case of learning fewer features, while the other three algorithms can hardly get better prediction effect than using the original data set in the process

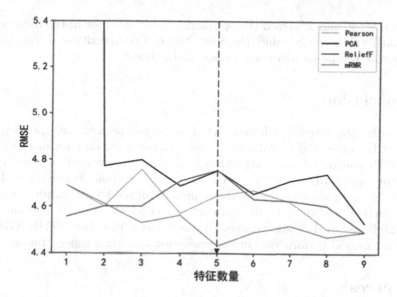

Fig. 2. $RMSE$ curve of each feature selection method

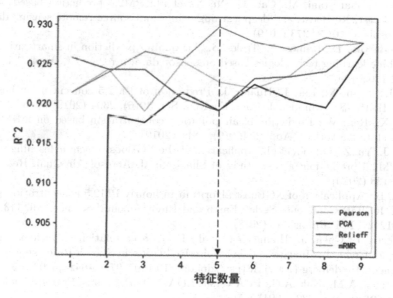

Fig. 3. R^2 curve of each feature selection method

of feature selection. This is because there is indeed redundancy between features, and some features help the model less than their own redundancy does. However, only when the features that contribute less to the prediction are accurately eliminated can better results be obtained. In the process of feature selection using mRMR algorithm, when the corresponding prediction performance evaluation indexes $RMSE$ and R^2 reach the optimum, only 5 features in the data set are used, which can not only reduce the computational complexity of the model, but also improve the prediction performance of the model.

5   Conclusion

In this paper, the air related data collected by the self-research integrated system is used to form the original data set. In order to make the data set more reliable, the mRMR feature selection algorithm is used to reduce its dimension to get the feature set that can make the prediction effect optimal. Finally, the selected data set is combined with the XGBoost prediction model for learning, training and prediction, and the mRMR-XGBoost model for the next 1 h concentration of PM2.5 is designed. The experimental results show that the mRMR-XGBoost model has a good performance in the prediction of PM2.5 concentration.

References

1. Zamani Joharestani, M., Cao, C., Ni, X., et al.: PM2.5 prediction based on random forest, XGBoost, and deep learning using multisource remote sensing data. J. Atmosphere **10**(7), 373 (2019)
2. Iskandaryan, D., Ramos, F., Trilles, S.: Air quality prediction in smart cities using machine learning technologies based on sensor data: a review. J. Appl. Sci. **10**(7), 2401 (2020)
3. Li, J.X., Liu, X., Liu, J., Huang, J.: Prediction of PM2.5 concentration based on MRMR-HK-SVM model. J. Chin. Environ. Sci. **39**(6), 2304 (2019)
4. Xu, X., Ren, W.: Prediction of air pollution concentration based on mRMR and echo state network. J. Appl. Sci. **9**(9), 1811 (2019)
5. Ma, J., Yu, Z., Qu, Y., et al.: Application of the XGBoost machine learning method in PM2.5 prediction: a case study of Shanghai. J. Aerosol Air Qual. Res. **20**(1), 128–138 (2020)
6. Pan, B.: Application of XGBoost algorithm in hourly PM2.5 concentration prediction. In: IOP Conference Series: Earth and Environmental Science, vol. 113, no. 1, p. 012127. IOP Publishing (2018)
7. Benesty, J., Chen, J., Huang, Y., et al.: Pearson correlation coefficient. In: Benesty, J., Chen, J., Huang, Y. (eds.) Noise Reduction in Speech Processing, pp. 1–4. Springer, Heidelberg (2009). https://doi.org/10.1007/978-3-642-00296-0_5
8. Martinez, A.M., Kak, A.C.: PCA versus LDA. J. IEEE Trans. Pattern Anal. Mach. Intell. **23**(2), 228–233 (2001)
9. Zhang, Y., Ding, C., Li, T.: Gene selection algorithm by combining reliefF and mRMR. J. BMC Genom. **9**(2), 1–10 (2008)

An Improved Crowd Counting Method Based on YOLOv3

Shuang Zheng, Junfeng Wu, Fugang Liu(✉), Yunhao Liang, and Lingfei Zhao

Heilongjiang University of Science and Technology, Harbin 150022, China
liufugang_36@163.com

Abstract. This paper proposes a method of crowd counting. We use ResNeSt-50 as the backbone network of YOLOv3. After the backbone network, we add SPP (Spatial Pyramid Potential) and PANet (Path Aggregation Network) to enhance the receptive field of convolutional neural network and improve the accuracy of stream of people or crowd counting in real application scenarios. In the application scenario of high-density crowd counting, an improved VGG network is used to design a deep network to capture high-level semantic information. At the same time, a shallow network is constructed to detect the head blob of people far away from the camera. The deep network and the shallow network are combined to detect high-density crowd. Finally, through the effective fusion of the above two network models, the accuracy and applicability of the algorithm are further improved. It can improve the detection accuracy in the case of small number of people and occlusion, and effectively reduce the estimation error in the scene with high density crowd.

Keywords: Crowd density · Target detection · Convolutional neural network · YOLOv3

1 Introduction

Computer vision, including human detection, human posture recognition, crowd counting and other technologies, is one of the research hotspots in recent years, and has become an important branch of artificial intelligence industry. Among them, the crowd density estimation technology has a broad prospect in the field of security, new retail and other applications because of its far higher accuracy and speed than the naked eye count. According to different application scenarios, the technology is mainly divided into low-density crowd estimation and high-density crowd estimation. In the aspect of low density crowd estimation, the detection algorithms mainly include the target detection algorithm based on Region Proposal represented by RCNN (including RCNN, SPP-NET, FAST RCNN, FAST RCNN, etc.) and the target detection algorithm based on regression represented by YOLO (including YOLO series, SSD, etc.). In the aspect of high-density flow estimation, the method of Density Map is mainly used at present. Zhang et al. [1] used multi-column convolutional neural network to extract head features of different scales. The disadvantage of this multi network model is that it has many parameters

X. Jiang (Ed.): MLICOM 2021, LNICST 438, pp. 337–350, 2022.
https://doi.org/10.1007/978-3-031-04409-0_31

and large amount of calculation, so it can't carry out real-time crowd count detection. Vishwanath et al. [2] proposed four modules: Global Context Estimator (GCE), Local Context Estimator(LCE), Density Map Estimator(DME) and Fusion-CNN (F-CNN), which can generate high-quality crowd density and count estimation by explicitly incorporating global and local contextual information of crowd images. The authors in [3] used a dilated CNN as the back-end and uses the dilated kernel to provide larger reception fields and to replace pooling operations. It made CSRNet easy to train. CSRNet is used in four data sets (ShanghaiTech dataset, UCF_CC_50, WorldEXPO'10 and UCSD dataset),and high accuracy is obtained.

According to the research of current scholars, the current research in this field mainly tends to the high-density crowd estimation, but this kind of high-density crowd estimation network is difficult to accurately estimate the low-density crowd. To solve this problem, we propose an improved algorithm based on YOLOv3. In this paper, we modify the backbone network, add feature enhancement module, design deep network and shallow network to improve the detection accuracy and applicability of the algorithm. It can improve the detection accuracy in the case of small number of people and occlusion, and effectively reduce the estimation error in the scene with high density crowd.

2   YOLOv3

2.1   The Structure of YOLOv3

The schematic diagram of YOLOv3 structure module is shown in Fig. 1. Inside the red dotted line is the backbone network Darknet-53.The modules in the three dotted boxes below are the core structure of YOLOv3. DBL contains the corresponding convolution layer, batch normalization layer (BN)and leaky relu, which is the basic unit of YOLOv3. In order to reduce the over fitting problem caused by too many layers, YOLOv3 adds a new residual module ('n' in 'resn' is the number, which means n residual units). In Fig. 1, y1, y2 and y3 are characteristic maps of YOLOv3 with three different scales. Taking the experiment of coco data set [4] as an example, because there are 80 categories in this data set, each box outputs a probability for each category, and each grid cell detects 3 boxes, and each box needs five basic parameters, so the depth of the three characteristic graphs is $(3 \times (5 + 80))$.

2.2   Backbone Network Darknet-53

YOLOv3 uses Darknet-53 network for feature extraction. Table 1 shows the network structure of Darknet-53. Darknet-53 is to deepen the convolution layer on the original network structure of YOLOv2 [5] and use the residual structure module. The network uses continuous 3×3 and 1×1 convolution kernels. 1×1 convolution kernel is used to reduce the dimension and 3×3 convolution kernel is used to extract features. Multiple convolution kernels are used alternately to reduce the dimension and extract features.In the process of forward propagation, the step size of convolution kernel is changed to realize the tensor size transformation. For example, the step size of convolution kernel in the red box in Table 1 is 2, which is equivalent to the image side length is reduced to

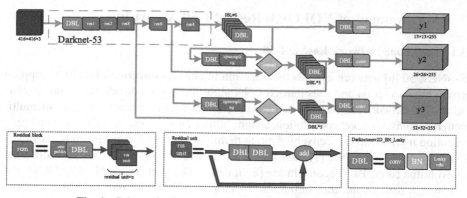

Fig. 1. Schematic diagram of the structure module of YOLOv3.

half of the original, and the area is reduced to one fourth of the original. In Table 1, a total of 5 times of reduction, the area became 1/32 of the original. When the size of the input feature map is 416 × 416, the output is 13 × 13.

Table 1. Darknet-53 network structure.

Type	Output channel	Convolution kernel	Output size	
Conv	32	3×3	256×256	
Conv	64	3×3/2	128×128	
Conv	32	1×1		
Conv	64	3×3		×1
Residual			128×128	
Conv	128	3×3/2	64×64	
Conv	64	1×1		
Conv	128	3×3		×2
Residual			64×64	
Conv	256	3×3/2	32×32	
Conv	128	1×1		
Conv	256	3×3		×8
Residual			32×32	
Conv	512	3×3/2	16×16	
Conv	256	1×1		
Conv	512	3×3		×8
Residual			16×16	
Conv	1024	3×3/2	8×8	
Conv	512	1×1		
Conv	1024	3×3		×4
Residual			8×8	
Average pooling	1024	Global pooling	1×1	
FC			1000	
Softmax			1000	

3   Improvement of YOLOv3+ResNeSt-50 Algorithm

3.1   Backbone Network ResNeSt-50

ResNeSt-50 [6] network extends the attention in channel direction to feature mapping group representation and uses unified CNN algorithm for modularization and acceleration. The network structure of its core module (Fig. 2) combines the ideas of multi-path mechanism, packet convolution, channel attention mechanism and feature mapping attention mechanism respectively. Among them, the multipath mechanism has a significant effect in GoogleNet [7], in which each network block is composed of different convolution cores. Packet convolution [8] appears in ResNet "bottle block" of ResNeXt [9], which realizes the transformation of multi-path structure into unified operation. Channel attention mechanism is introduced in SE-Net [10] to realize adaptive recalibration of channel feature response. The attention mechanism of feature mapping is proposed in SK-Net [11] and applied in two branches of network.

In order to compare with ResNet variant series [12], Hang Zhang et al. cut all network input images to 224 × 224 for training. In order to train better inference speed and reduce the amount of model, they moved the average pooling operation to the 3 × 3 convolution layer, and built ResNeSt fast model on the feature map sampled under convolution layer. Table 2 uses the mean average precision (mAP) of each category to quantify the network performance. It shows the experimental comparison results, which show that the accuracy of ResNeSt is the best in the ResNet variant series when only the backbone network is replaced, and the ResNeSt structure is better than the ResNet structure with the same network parameters.

The performance of split attention module in ResNeSt has been improved in classification, detection, instance segmentation and semantic segmentation. Based on the above characteristics, we modified Darknet-53, the backbone network of YOLOv3 in Fig. 1, to ResNeSt-50. The experiment in the fifth part of this paper shows that, compared with the original network, this scheme can improve the detection accuracy by about 3 percentage points.

3.2   Feature Enhancement

In order to strengthen the receptive field [13] of the network, SPP (spatial pyramid potential) [13] and PANet (Path Aggregation Network) [14] are added after the backbone network. Figure 3 is the structure diagram of ResNeSt-50 adding SPP and PANet. By adding SPP, multiple windows are used for any size feature map to get fixed size feature vector, so as to achieve the effect of enhancing network receptive field. The information flow is enhanced by PANet, and the path enhancement method from bottom to top is adopted to improve the accuracy of feature location in the lower level structure and shorten the information path of the lower and upper level features. In this paper, the adaptive feature pool is used to connect the feature grid and all feature layers, so that

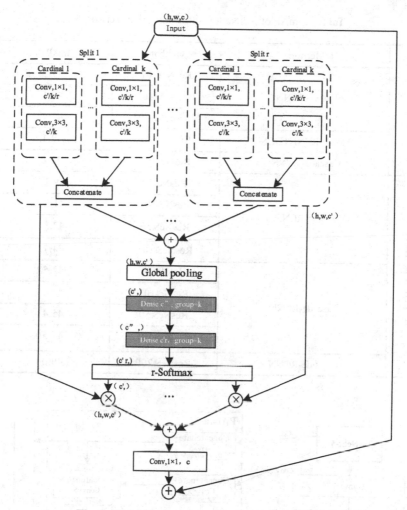

Fig. 2. Network structure of ResNeSt core module.

the useful information in each feature layer can be directly propagated to the following sub network. The network can extract feature information more quickly and improve the processing speed of the network. As far as CNN network is concerned, the addition of SPP and PANet has no effect on the network structure, which is equivalent to replacing the original pooling layer.

Table 2. mAP of ResNeSt vs. ResNet variant network.

	Method	Backbone	mAP%
Prior Work	Faster-RCNN	ResNet101	37.3
		ResNeXt101	40.1
		SE-ResNet101	41.9
	Faster-RCNN+DCN	ResNet101	42.1
	Cascade-RCNN	ResNet101	42.8
Experiment results	Faster-RCNN	ResNet50	39.25
		ResNet101	41.37
		ResNeSt50	42.33
		ResNeSt101	44.72
	Cascade-RCNN	ResNet50	42.52
		ResNet101	44.03
		ResNeSt50	45.41
		ResNeSt101	47.50
	Cascade-RCNN	ResNeSt200	49.03

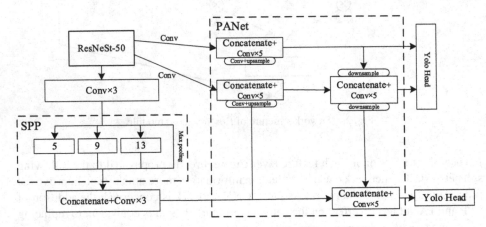

Fig. 3. Feature enhancement module SPP and PANet.

4   Density Map Network

In this paper, deep and shallow networks are designed to detect high density traffic. The density map is generated by combining the deep layer and the shallow layer network, and the Gauss density algorithm is used to detect the traffic of the generated density map. The overall convolution network structure is shown in Fig. 4.

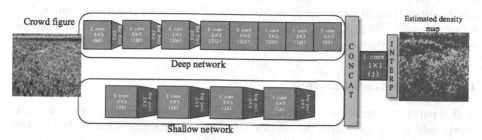

Fig. 4.   Network structure of density graph.

4.1   Deep Network Structure

Deep network is a model based on VGG-16 [15]. Because crowd density estimation requires super-pixel detection, which is different from image classification. The latter is to assign a single discrete label to the whole image, so it is necessary to remove the full connection layer in VGG-16 network to obtain pixels for detection, so that the network is completely convoluted in structure. VGG-16 network has five maximum pooling layers. In this paper, the fourth maximum pooling layer and the fifth pooling layer are deleted, and the dilated convolution with dilated rate of 2 is added to the last six convolution layers. In dilated convolution, if the convolution core with $k \times k$ size is amplified to the size of $k + (k - 1)(k + 1)$ with the expansion step of r, the receiving field can be expanded without increasing the number of parameters and the amount of calculation (as shown in Fig. 5). At the same time, dilated convolution can aggregate multi-scale context information and keep the same resolution, so that sparse kernel can replace pooling layer and convolution layer.

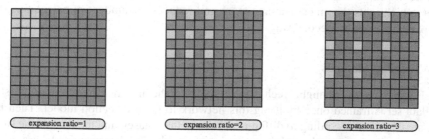

Fig. 5. 3×3 Convolution kernels with dilations of 1, 2 and 3

The formula of dilated convolution is as follows:

$$y(m, n) = \sum_{i=1}^{M} \sum_{j=1}^{N} x(m + r \times i, n + r \times j) w(i, j) \tag{1}$$

$y(m, n)$ is the output of the dilated convolution of the input $x(m, n)$ and the convolution kernel $w(i, j)$, whose length and width are M and N respectively. The parameter r is the dilated rate. If $r = 1$, the dilated convolution becomes normal convolution. It is found that when $r = 2$, the effect is the best. This enables the network to detect when the input is 1/8 times the original resolution, and increases the receptive field of the network.

4.2 Shallow Network Structure

In this paper, we construct a shallow convolutional network to identify people in the photos who are far away from the camera. The depth of the network has six layers. The number of channels in the first four floors is 24, and that in the fifth and sixth floors is 12. The convolution kernel size of the first four layers is 5×5, and that of the fifth and sixth layers is 3×3. The shallow network is mainly used to detect small head blob, and the average pooling is used in the shallow network to prevent the loss of high-dimensional information caused by the maximum pooling.

5 Experimental Analysis

5.1 Data Preprocessing

The data set of this paper uses the data of Baidu's crowd density. Some training data refer to public data sets (such as ShanghaiTech, UCF-CC-50, WorldExpo'10, Mall, etc.), and the data annotation of data sets is in the corresponding json file. Because there are ignored areas in the data, and the annotation is not uniform, so this paper unifies the annotation of the data, and then fills the ignored areas in the image. In this paper, the size of all images is normalized to keep the same size of all input images. For the dimension of image output, we can have three choices: Directly output a density map without compression, or directly output a compressed density map, or directly output an actual value of the number of people detected. Through the comparison of the three schemes, the second scheme highlights the image features more and reduces the amount of calculation. So this paper chooses the second way.

5.2 Training Methods

In this paper, we use ShanghaiTech data set to detect the high-density of crowd. Firstly, the data set is trained once by using this network to get a detection model. Then the data are classified according to different scenes of the dataset, and the data of the same scene are trained separately, and the trained scene model and detection model are fused. Because of the complexity of the network in this paper, the transfer learning method is used in the training, and the weight of ResNeSt-50 model is used for pretraining, so that the training can get a fast convergence effect. We finds that the loss rate is very low in the process of training by directly using density map as the result output, but it is quite different from the actual number of people. Therefore, this paper changes the loss function into the result of adding the mean square error of density map and the number of people.

Through the network structure designed in this paper, using a single Tesla V100 GPU to train, the "person part" iterates 20000 times, the "head part" iterates 30000 times, and the images classified for different scenes iterate 5000 times. The average training time of "person part" is about 23 h, the average training time of "head part" is about 16 h, and the training time of different scene images is about 3 h. In this paper, momentum is used to optimize the training, and the momentum is 0.9. The initial learning rate is 0.001. After every 1000 iterations, the learning rate is reduced to 0.1 times of that before, and the batch_size is 8. The single Tesla V100 GPU is used to train the density map network for 400 rounds. Using Adam to optimize training, the learning rate is 0.001, and the batch_size is 26.

5.3 Experimental Results

There are 11 different scenarios in Baidu's data set of crowd density. There is only one person with the least people flow, and there are hundreds of people with more people flow. There are thousands of people with more people flow in Shanghai's data set. To ensure the accuracy of the test results, this paper selects 25 images from the test set of Baidu traffic density data firstly. Among them, two images are randomly selected from each of the 11 scenes, and the remaining three images are randomly selected. Finally, 25 images are randomly selected from the test set of Shanghai data. The accuracy of the model is verified by 50 selected images. Figure 6 shows the comparison between the detection count and the actual count of each image in the selected 50 data sets. It is observed from Fig. 6 that the number of most people detection is close to the actual number. When the number of people in the image exceeds 2000, the error between the number of model detection and the actual number is large. The reason for this error may be that the density of crowd is too large, the number of heads in the picture is too dense, and the small objects are mistakenly considered as human in the detection and recognition of the model, thus causing interference to the experimental results.

Table 3 shows the comparison between the proposed algorithm and the original algorithm, as well as the comparison of the improved model of the original algorithm.

It can be concluded from Table 3 that the detection accuracy of the original YOLO3 model is 79.32. After the replacement of the network backbone, the accuracy of the model is improved by about 3 percentage points. On this basis, the accuracy of the final model is 86.76, which is 7.5 percentage points higher than that of the original model.

5.4 Result Analysis

1. Analysis of SPP and PANet.
Adding SPP module and PANet to ResNeSt-50 structure, the results of contrast enhancement are shown in Table 4. It is found that the accuracy of the improved YOLOv3 algorithm is improved, but the effect is not ideal.

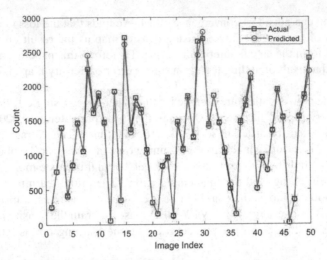

Fig. 6. Comparison between actual count and detection count.

Table 3. Comparison of recognition performance with different networks.

Method	mAP	FPS
YOLOv3	79.32	43.468
YOLOv3+ResNeSt-50+SPP+PANet (head)	82.15	54.605
YOLOv3+ResNeSt-50+SPP+PANet (person)	82.52	46.572
Fusion density map (head)	83.22	54.785
Fusion density map (person)	84.86	46.683
In this paper	86.76	53.861

The reason is that the original algorithm of YOLOv3 contains the fusion of high and low-level feature information, while PANet only improves the feature information fusion. In this paper, the data analysis is carried out in the data processing, and the compression algorithm is adopted for the image, and SPP module only ensures that the input image does not distortion when zooming. So the overall effect of SPP module and PANet only plays a supplementary role.

2. Analysis of density map fusion.

The performance comparison after enhancement is shown in Table 5. In this Table, "Fusion density map" means the density map fusion is added to the improved YOLOv3 algorithm. As can be seen from the figure, after fusing the density map, the accuracy of detecting some high-density pedestrian flow images will be improved by about 2 points, and the recognition speed will also be improved a little.

Table 4. Comparison of recognition performance after adding SPP and PANet.

Method	mAP	FPS
YOLOv3	79.32	43.468
YOLOv3+ResNeSt-50 (head)	81.56	54.401
YOLOv3+ResNeSt-50 (person)	81.79	45.214
YOLOv3+ResNeSt-50+SPP+PANet (head)	82.15	54.605
YOLOv3+ResNeSt-50+SPP+PANet (person)	82.52	46.572

Table 5. Comparison of recognition performance after merging density map.

Method	mAP	FPS
YOLOv3	79.32	43.468
YOLOv3+ResNeSt-50+SPP+PANet (head)	82.15	54.605
YOLOv3+ResNeSt-50+SPP+PANet (person)	82.52	46.572
Fusion density map (head)	83.22	54.785
Fusion density map (person)	84.86	46.683

3. Analysis of dilated convolution.

Compared with the effect of adding dilated convolution in the density map, it is found that the accuracy of this method is about 1% higher than that of the previous simple density map fusion method (Table 6). (as shown in Table 6). This shows that dilated convolution is better than simple pooling.

Table 6. Comparison of recognition performance with adding dilated convolution in density map.

Method	mAP	FPS
YOLOv3	79.32	43.468
Fusion density map (head)	83.22	54.785
Fusion density map (person)	84.86	46.683
Fusion density map (head)+Dilated convolution	84.65	53.954
Fusion density map (person)+Dilated convolution	85.64	46.124

4. Analysis of data enhancement.

In this paper, the Autoaugment technology is used to automatically select the optimal data enhancement operation. The data is improved by automatic search, and the optimal transformation strategy is found from the data itself, so that the neural network can produce the highest verification accuracy on the target data set.

The specific operation process is as follows: first, prepare 16 basic data enhancement operations, such as cropping, deformation, scaling, erasing, filling and a series of simple operations; Then five operations are randomly selected from them, and each operation is called a sub-policy; Finally, five operations are used to train each batch of images. After a certain epoch, the network begins to learn the effective transformation strategy. Through the feedback of the generalization ability of the training model in the verification set, the five sub-policies are concatenated, and then the final training is carried out to obtain the optimal enhancement algorithm. After data enhancement with Autoaugment, the comparison of accuracy and real-time performance of each algorithm is shown in Table 7.

Table 7. Comparison of recognition performance after data enhancement.

Method	mAP	FPS
YOLOv3	79.32	43.468
YOLOv3+ResNeSt-50+SPP+PANet (head)	82.15	54.605
YOLOv3+ResNeSt-50+SPP+PANet (person)	82.52	46.572
Fusion density map (head)	83.22	54.785
Fusion density map (person)	84.86	46.683
YOLOv3+Data enhancement	81.86	41.961
YOLOv3+ResNeSt-50+SPP+PANet (head)+Data enhancement	83.95	52.564
YOLOv3+ResNeSt-50+SPP+PANet (person)+Data enhancement	84.05	45.512
Fusion density map (head)+Data enhancement	85.55	52.684
Fusion density map (person)+Data enhancement	85.94	44.531

6 Conclusion

Aiming at the problem of detection density of crowd, this paper designs two algorithm models. In order to improve the YOLOv3 algorithm, ResNeSt-50 is used as the backbone network of YOLOv3, and the feature enhancement module SPP and PANet are added after the backbone network to enhance the receptive field of convolutional neural network and improve the detection accuracy of human flow density in real application scenarios; The other is density map network, which uses the improved VGG network to design a deep network for capturing high-level semantic information, and constructs a shallow network for detecting distant head spots in pictures, which combines the deep network with the shallow network to detect high-density people flow. Through the combination of the two models, we can improve the accuracy of the flow density detection. In this paper, the error rate of verification is only 0.1006 in the test set of Baidu, which achieves a relatively high accuracy, proving the feasibility and accuracy of the algorithm.

The main problems of further research are as follows: (1) There is no in-depth research in the complex situation of high-density pedestrian flow occlusion, the detection of this situation is insufficient, and the number of heads is difficult to estimate in high-density. In the future, we need to further study the situation of severe occlusion and too dense number of heads. (2) The way of image processing will greatly affect the detection of network traffic. How to strengthen the characteristics of people in the image and improve the learning efficiency of the algorithm is worth studying. (3) The model of this paper is large, for the problem of hardware device embedding, it increases the cost, and the model will be lightweight later, so that the model of this paper can be better applied in practice.

Acknowledgements. This work has been partially supported by "Heilongjiang Science Foundation Project (LH2021F052)" .

References

1. Zhang, Y., Zhou, D., Chen, S., et al.: Single-image crowd counting via multi-column convolutional neural network. In: 2016 IEEE Conference on Computer Vision and Pattern Recognition (CVPR), pp. 3290–3298. IEEE, Las Vegas, NV, USA (2016)
2. Sindagi, V.A., Patel, V.: Generating high-quality crowd density maps using contextual pyramid CNNs. In: 2017 IEEE International Conference on Computer Vision (ICCV), pp. 1879–1888. IEEE, Venice, Italy (2017)
3. Li, Y., Zhang, X., Chen, D.: CSRNet: dilated convolutional neural networks for understanding the highly congested scenes. In: 2018 IEEE/CVF Conference on Computer Vision and Pattern Recognition, pp. 1091–1100, IEEE, Salt Lake City, UT (2018)
4. Redmon, J., Farhadi, A.: YOLOv3: An Incremental Improvement. arXiv:1804.02767 (2018)
5. Redmon, J., Farhadi, A.: YOLO9000: better, faster, stronger, In: IEEE Conference on Computer Vision and Pattern Recognition, pp. 6517–6525. IEEE, Honolulu HI (2017)
6. Zhang, H., Wu, C., Zhang, Z.: ResNeSt: Split-Attention Networks. arXiv:2004.08955 (2020)
7. Szegedy, C., Liu, W., Jia, Y.Q., et al.: Going deeper with convolutions. In: 2015 IEEE Conference on Computer Vision and Pattern Recognition. pp. 1–9. IEEE, Boston, USA (2015)
8. Krizhevsky, A., Sutskever, I., Hinton, G.E.: Imagenet classification with deep convolutional neural networks. Adv. Neural. Inf. Process. Syst. **25**, 1097–1105 (2012)
9. Xie, S., Girshick, R., Dollár, P., Tu, Z., He, K.: Aggregated residual transformations for deep neural networks. In: 2017 Proceedings of the IEEE Conference on Computer Vision and Pattern Recognition, pp. 1492–1500. IEEE, Honolulu, Hawaii (2017)
10. Hu, J., Shen, L., Sun, G.: Squeeze-and-excitation networks. In: 2018 In Proceedings of the IEEE Conference on Computer Vision and Pattern Recognition, pp. 7132–7141. IEEE, Salt Lake City, UT, USA (2018)
11. Li, X., Wang, W., Hu, X., Yang, J.: Selective kernel networks. In: 2019 Proceedings of the IEEE Conference on Computer Vision and Pattern Recognition, pp. 510–519. IEEE, Long Beach, CA, USA (2019)
12. He, K., Zhang, X., Ren, S., Sun, J.: Deep residual learning for image recognition. In: 2016 IEEE Conference on Computer Vision and Pattern Recognition (CVPR), pp. 770–778. IEEE, Las Vegas, NV (2016)
13. He, K., Zhang, X., Ren, S., et al.: Spatial pyramid pooling in deep convolutional networks for visual recognition. IEEE Trans. Pattern Anal. Mach. Intell. **37**(9), 1904–1916 (2014)

14. Liu, S., Qi, L., Qin, H., et al.: Path aggregation network for instance segmentation. In: 2018 IEEE/CVF Conference on Computer Vision and Pattern Recognition (CVPR), pp. 8759–8768. IEEE, Salt Lake City, UT, USA (2018)
15. Simonyan, K., Zisserman, A.: Very deep convolutional networks for large-scale image recognition. In: The 3rd International Conference on Learning Representations, pp. 7749–8758. IEEE, Banff, Canada (2014)

Correction to: Deep Learning Technique for Desert Plant Classification and Recognition

Najla Alsaedi, Hanan Alahmadi, and Liyakathunisa Syed

Correction to:
Chapter "Deep Learning Technique for Desert Plant
Classification and Recognition" in: X. Jiang (Ed.): *Machine*
Learning and Intelligent Communications, **LNICST 438,**
https://doi.org/10.1007/978-3-031-04409-0_17

In an older version of this paper, there was an orthographical error in the title. This has been corrected.

The updated version of this chapter can be found at
https://doi.org/10.1007/978-3-031-04409-0_17

Correction to: Automatic Detection and Classification of Anti-islamic Web Text-Contents

Rawan Abdullah Alraddadi and
Moulay Ibrahim El-Khalil Ghembaza

Correction to:
Chapter "Automatic Detection and Classification
of Anti-islamic Web Text-Contents" in: X. Jiang (Ed.):
Machine Learning and Intelligent Communications,
LNICST 438, https://doi.org/10.1007/978-3-031-04409-0_16

In the originally published chapter 16 the first- and last name order of one of the authors was incorrect. The author's name has been corrected as "Ghembaza, Moulay Ibrahim El-Khalil".

The updated original version of this chapter can be found at
https://doi.org/10.1007/978-3-031-04409-0_16

Author Index

Printed in the United States
by Baker & Taylor Publisher Services

Printed in the United States
by Baker & Taylor Publisher Services